AF361502

The Civil War on the Mississippi

THE
CIVIL WAR
ON THE
MISSISSIPPI

UNION SAILORS,
GUNBOAT CAPTAINS,
AND THE CAMPAIGN
TO CONTROL THE RIVER

BARBARA BROOKS TOMBLIN

Scholarly publisher for the Commonwealth,
serving Bellarmine University, Berea College, Centre College of Kentucky, Eastern
Kentucky University, The Filson Historical Society, Georgetown College, Kentucky
Historical Society, Kentucky State University, Morehead State University, Murray State
University, Northern Kentucky University, Transylvania University, University of
Kentucky, University of Louisville, and Western Kentucky University.
All rights reserved.

Editorial and Sales Offices: The University Press of Kentucky
663 South Limestone Street, Lexington, Kentucky 40508-4008
www.kentuckypress.com

Photographs are courtesy of the Library of Congress.

Library of Congress Cataloging-in-Publication Data

Names: Tomblin, Barbara, author.
Title: The Civil War on the Mississippi : Union sailors, gunboat captains,
  and the campaign to control the river / Barbara Brooks Tomblin.
Description: Lexington, Kentucky : University Press of Kentucky, 2016. |
  Includes bibliographical references and index.
Identifiers: LCCN 2016011181| ISBN 9780813167039 (hardcover : alk. paper) |
  ISBN 9780813167053 (pdf) | ISBN 9780813167046 (epub)
Subjects: LCSH: Mississippi River Valley—History—Civil War, 1861–1865– |
  United States—History—Civil War, 1861–1865—Campaigns. | United
  States—History—Civil War, 1861–1865—Riverine operations. | United
  States—History—Civil War, 1861–1865—Naval operations.
Classification: LCC E470.8 .T66 2016 | DDC 973.7/462—dc23
LC record available at http://lccn.loc.gov/2016011181

This book is printed on acid-free paper meeting the requirements of the American
National Standard for Permanence in Paper for Printed Library Materials.

Manufactured in the United States of America.

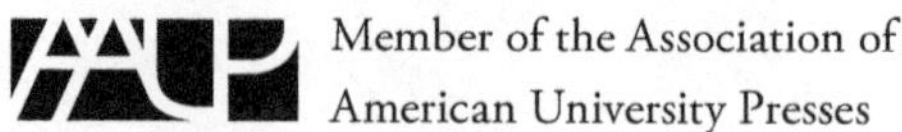 Member of the Association of
American University Presses

Contents

Photographs follow page 178

The Mississippi River, 1861–1863 (Richard A. Gilbreath, University of Kentucky Cartography Lab)

Introduction

When the citizens of St. Louis, Missouri, picked up copies of the *Daily Missouri Republican* on Sunday, April 14, 1861, a headline announced: "Probable Commencement of the Civil War at Last." The following day, the paper printed news of Fort Sumter's unconditional surrender and Major Robert Anderson's refusal to strike the flag. When the bombardment of Fort Sumter ended on April 14, former army officer William Tecumseh Sherman recalled, "We then knew that war was actually begun."[1]

In Washington, President Abraham Lincoln learned of Fort Sumter's surrender on Saturday, April 13. The following morning after church services, he called a meeting of his cabinet, which had been grappling for several months with the thorny issue of whether to reinforce and supply Fort Sumter or evacuate it. Now that Anderson had capitulated, Lincoln and his cabinet were faced with critical decisions regarding what attorney general Edward Bates called "an open war."[2]

Bates, a longtime resident of the Mississippi Valley, may have considered it "open war," but without the consent of Congress, which was not in session, President Lincoln could not declare war. He could, however, issue a proclamation calling for the states to raise a total of 75,000 militiamen for ninety days' service. Lincoln informed the cabinet of his decision, and the following day a call-up was issued to all but the seven rebellious states of Louisiana, Texas, Mississippi, Alabama, Georgia, Florida, and South Carolina.[3]

Newspapers in the Northeast predicted the war would be over in a matter of months. Most greeted the president's April 15 proclamation positively. The fall of Fort Sumter had stirred strong patriotic feelings among those in the Northeast and parts of the Midwest. Small towns from New England to Wisconsin held "war meetings" to recruit troops and secure pledges of loyalty to the Union, but St. Louis was a city divided. Missouri's secessionist governor Clairborne Fox Jackson minced few words, denouncing Lincoln's call for troops as "illegal, unconstitutional, and revolutionary in its object, inhuman, and diabolical," and he ordered the state militia to muster in St. Louis.[4]

Not everyone in St. Louis agreed with Jackson, however. A little over a week after the fall of Fort Sumter, Sherman wrote to his brother John from his office at the Fifth Street Railroad Company and expressed his approval of the president's decision. Sherman had definite opinions about how the war should progress: "I take it for granted that Virginia will be attacked with great force this summer, and that the great problem of the . . . Mississippi will be reserved for the next winter." As Sherman and many other loyal citizens in the upper Midwest knew, keeping the Mississippi River open to navigation and commerce would be critical to a Union victory over the new Confederate States of America. Sherman conveyed this view to Thomas Ewing, predicting that this would be "the hardest and most important tasks of the war."[5]

The US Army's general in chief, Lieutenant General Winfield Scott, shared Sherman's appreciation of the importance of the mighty Mississippi River. On March 3, in anticipation that Lincoln would be safely inaugurated and that Secretary of State William Seward would be the head of his cabinet, Scott had sent Seward a memorandum outlining four plans to meet what he termed "the extraordinary exigencies of the times." Scott predicted that in less than sixty days the remaining slaveholding states would join the Confederacy. He then listed several possible courses of action: to close the ports over which the government had lost command and blockade them, to "conquer the seceded States by invading armies," or to "say to the seceded States, 'Wayward sisters, depart in peace.'" The general advised that an invasion of the South might succeed in two or three years, given "a young and able general," but it would require a force of 300,000 disciplined men. Furthermore, Scott argued, "The destruction of life and property on the other side would be frightful" and would be "completed at the enormous waste of human life to the North and Northwest and incur a large national debt." Although Scott did not specifically endorse any one of these plans, he favored a blockade of Southern ports as a less expensive, more indirect means of bringing the seceded states back into the Union.[6]

Within days of the fall of Fort Sumter, Lincoln's cabinet debated the merits of an earlier proposal from Seward (undoubtedly influenced by Scott's memorandum) that Southern ports be blockaded immediately. Secretary of the Navy Gideon Welles argued that according to international law, taking this step would acknowledge that the United States had recognized the Confederacy, which might encourage foreign powers to extend belligerent rights to the South. A contentious discussion followed, but after due consideration, Lincoln chose to implement the blockade, and on April 19, 1861, he issued a formal proclamation to that effect.[7]

Though once a formidable warrior, Scott was now seventy-four years old and physically worn out, but he had not lost his keenness of mind or determination to serve his country. Scott's overall strategy, which became known as the Anaconda Plan, was to prosecute the war in a two-step process. First, the Union navy would establish a blockade of the Southern coast, closing all the ports the Confederacy could use to export cotton and other commodities or to import goods and war materials. Second, joint army-navy forces would use the Mississippi and Ohio Rivers as a natural highway into the Southern states, seizing and fortifying supply bases from which to advance farther down the river into the Mississippi Valley. A larger army would then follow as the advance force seized even more bases at Memphis, Vicksburg, and finally New Orleans. Critics considered the plan too slow, and they ridiculed such an indirect approach to crushing the rebellion, but as historians have noted, Scott's proposed thrust down the Mississippi River was the only direct combat envisioned by the Anaconda Plan.[8]

On May 3, 1861, Scott sent Major General George B. McClellan, commanding the Ohio Volunteers in Cincinnati, his plan for the campaign. Scott wrote that in connection with a blockade, "we propose a powerful movement down the Mississippi to the ocean, with a cordon of posts at proper points, and the capture of Forts Jackson and Saint Philip, . . . so as to envelop the insurgent States and to bring them to terms with less bloodshed than by any other plan." He specifically called for "from twelve to twenty steam gun-boats, and a sufficient number of steam transports (say forty) to carry all the personnel (say 60,000 men) and material of the expedition, most of the gun-boats to be in advance to open the way, and the remainder to follow and protect the rear of the expedition & c." Scott advised that the best regulars be employed for the advance, as well as three-year volunteers, well officered, with four months' prior instruction.[9]

On the same day Scott sent his proposal, the governors or representatives of several western and border states gathered in Cleveland. Addressing the convention, Wisconsin governor Alexander W. Randall said, "There is but one course for us to pursue, and that should be followed. We should transport an army down the Mississippi, and blaze a broad track through the whole South, from Montgomery to Charleston." Randall sent Lincoln a memorandum expressing some of the convention's suggestions. He urged Lincoln to defend the area between the free and slave states. "From Pittsburg to Cincinnati to the mouth of the Ohio, on the northern side of the river, the country is almost entirely defenseless against an armed enemy," Randall argued. Taking Cairo, Illinois, and holding it seemed paramount, and controlling the business and commerce of the Ohio River and the upper Mississippi was a matter of absolute necessity. Clearly, the governors put a premium on free navigation of the Mississippi and its tributaries and called for the government to take immediate action.[10]

"The war feeling is not abating here much, although hostilities appear more remote than they did a few days ago," Ulysses S. Grant told his father Jesse in a letter written on May 6, 1861. A West Point graduate, Grant was now assisting in the adjutant general's office at Springfield, Missouri. He told his father that three of the six regiments mustered from Missouri were now at Cairo, with two more expected. Following Lincoln's call for volunteers, Grant had assisted with recruitment efforts in Galena, Illinois, and nearby towns. "The Northern feeling is so fully aroused that they will stop at no expense of money and men to insure the success of their cause," he assured Jesse.[11]

As Grant so cogently predicted, the war would consume vast sums of federal dollars and thousands of lives. To implement Scott's strategy for winning the war, the US government would have to raise hundreds of thousands of troops. To enforce a blockade of the South, the navy would need to construct or lease dozens of steam-propelled warships and transports. Numbering just ninety vessels in April 1861, less than half of them steam powered, the Union navy was incapable of enforcing a strict blockade of 3,500 miles of Confederate coastline. Many of these warships were on foreign stations. As historian Robert Browning noted, "Lincoln's call for blockade, which created the need for a large navy, may have been his wisest wartime decision."[12]

Welles grasped the pressing need to acquire more vessels. He sent his brother-in-law, George D. Morgan, off to purchase or lease dozens of steamers to be converted into blockaders, and he found close to a hundred more vessels from other sources. To construct a modern naval force, Welles contracted with shipyards to build twenty-three 500-ton gunboats, fourteen screw sloops, and twelve side-wheelers. Fortunately, the North had ample shipyards and shipbuilders, and before the war the Navy Department had acquired knowledge of manufacturers capable of producing the steam machinery required for a modern steam-powered fleet.[13]

Anticipating a conflict, Southern congressmen had authorized the construction of only deep-draft naval vessels in the late 1850s. Now, to fully implement Scott's plan to send troops and gunboats down the Mississippi River, the Union needed vessels suitable for operations on western rivers. The War Department claimed inland waters as its jurisdiction and argued that river forces should be administered by the army; however, it did allot the Navy Department the task of constructing, outfitting, manning, and commanding a "brown water" navy.[14]

Hundreds of steamers or riverboats had plied western rivers in the years before the Civil War, but few if any were armed or protected against shot and shell. The navy quickly had to develop a new kind of warship and place orders for its construction at inland shipyards in river towns such as Cincinnati, Ohio; Madison and New Albany, Indiana; Cairo, Illinois; and St. Louis, Missouri. Anticipating the need to lease, purchase, or build suitable vessels, in May 1861 Scott asked the army's chief engineer, Brigadier General Joseph G. Totten, to send him information on potential facilities and shipyards and on the availability of steamers in the upper Mississippi Valley. Confederate or secessionist sentiments precluded the use of sites in the lower Mississippi Valley such as Memphis, but the river port of St. Louis offered one of the Union navy's best options.[15]

Unfortunately for the Union cause, Missouri's pro-Southern Governor Jackson called up the state's volunteer militia in May. Reinforced by Confederate artillery from Baton Rouge, the militiamen set up camp in St. Louis, but before they could seize the Illinois arsenal, federal troops removed some 60,000 stands of arms. Federal militia and regular troops were called in to wrest control of the Missouri militiamen's camp and place the city firmly under federal control. Securing St. Louis proved advantageous to the Northern war effort for many reasons, not the least of which was its utility as a base for the construction of Union gunboats.[16]

To explain the strategic and economic significance of St. Louis and the western rivers to Welles at the Navy Department, attorney general Bates enlisted the support of James B. Eads. A civil engineer and businessman with "a most thorough knowledge of our Western rivers," Eads was experienced in building and salvaging river craft. At Bates's request, Eads traveled at least twice to Washington to present his ideas on river warfare to the Navy Department.[17] Eads suggested that the government establish a base at Cairo to control the passage of vessels up and down the Mississippi and Ohio Rivers. He wrote to Welles: "The effect of this blockade would be most disastrous to the South, as it would close the main artery through which flows her food. It would establish a tollgate through which alone her dutiable goods could enter, or through which her products could find their way to market." Closing the Mississippi to the South would leave the Confederacy with only the Tennessee and Cumberland Rivers and railroads from Louisville to Nashville and Chattanooga. "Close them and the great Mississippi, and starvation is inevitable in less than six months," Eads optimistically predicted.[18]

After listening to Eads's proposal, Welles invited him to present it to a board of naval officers. They approved the recommendations and sent them along to Samuel Pook, a naval constructor at the Washington Navy Yard. Secretary of War Simon Cameron accepted Eads's proposition and on May 14 sent it to McClellan for his approval. Two days later, Welles ordered Commander John Rodgers to go to McClellan's headquarters in Cincinnati and advise the general on the establishment of naval armament on the Mississippi and Ohio Rivers, "with a view of blockading or interdicting communication and interchanges with the States that are in insurrection."[19]

Forty-nine-year-old Rodgers, son of the famous Commodore John Rodgers, had been appointed a midshipman in 1821, served in the Mediterranean, led an expedition of naval infantry and marines during the Seminole Wars, and commanded the North Pacific Exploring and Surveying Expedition in the 1850s. McClellan welcomed Rodgers's expertise and sent him to Cairo, Mound City, and St. Louis to locate boats suitable for river warfare and construction sites for gunboats and floating batteries. Though he was a blue-water sailor and unfamiliar with riverboats, Rodgers hustled off to St. Louis to inspect Submarine No. 7, a snag boat that Eads had recommended be converted into a gunboat. One look convinced Rodgers that even if its vulnerable parts were protected by cotton bales, the snag boat was not a practical answer. He returned to Cincinnati and, with assistance from Pook, chose three side-wheel, high-pressure steamboats to be converted to armed gunboats. For the sum of $62,000, Rodgers bought the *A. O. Tyler, Lexington,* and *Conestoga.* To protect the crew from enemy riflemen along the riverbanks, Rodgers proposed to have bulwarks of five-inch-thick oak plank applied to these vessels, but he noted that the boilers and engines "can not be defended against cannon shot." A contract was drawn up with the Marine Railway and Dry Dock Company of Cincinnati to make the alterations.[20]

In mid-June 1861 Rodgers traveled to Washington to choose armament for the new gunboats, selecting ten 8-inch and seven 32-pounder smoothbores. Rodgers also recommended that the seven gunboats designed by Samuel Pook, the so-called Pook turtles, be armed with 9-inch Dahlgren smoothbores and rifled army 42-pounders. With Secretary Cameron's approval, he arranged for the army's Ordnance Department to rifle and prepare 42-pounders for each of the sixteen projected gunboats. He then returned to Cincinnati. When the water level of the Ohio River began to fall, Rodgers ordered Seth Ledyard Phelps to take the three unfinished timberclad gunboats to Cairo. An Ohioan, Phelps was an experienced career naval officer who had entered the navy in 1841 as a midshipman and served under sail off West Africa and in the Mexican War. The boats hurriedly left Cincinnati with workmen still aboard and steamed as far as Louisville, where low water prevented them from getting over the Portland Bar.[21]

In letters written from Cincinnati, Rodgers poured out his concerns to his wife, Ann Hodge Rodgers. On July 6, 1861, he wrote: "Oh Ann, Ann, I fear the gunboats are caught by the low water and cannot get below Louisville. I am really very much distressed a bit—disheartened, distressed—annoyed and out of sorts." Three days later Rodgers lamented, "I am still here and see no immediate chance of getting away—I trust however in a rise in the river—which will enable the boats to proceed to Cairo where they are much wanted." Rodgers confided, "Some of the secessionist criticism of these boats is anything but flattering—but they are not so bad altogether as thus painted neither are they wonders of comfort—but men I hope may stand them—and in them. I do not propose to engage batteries with them. Yet with 8 inch guns they will not be altogether despicable adversaries." In this same letter, Rodgers confessed to his wife that he was "disappointed in the navy . . . which delays me, since men must be shipped." Manning the new boats indeed proved a challenge. In late June three naval officers, Phelps, Roger N. Stembel, and Joshua Bishop, arrived in Cincinnati to assist Rodgers in fitting out the gunboats and recruiting crews. "I am shipping men here not but fast—most of the river men have joined the army," Rodgers explained to his wife. "I have sent L. Phelps to Louisville to open a shipping office there—I hope he will have success—I have an idea of sending to the Lakes, but have no convenient means—I may yet do so, however."[22]

When Phelps reached Louisville and found the *Lexington, Tyler,* and *Conestoga,* he despaired. The new timberclads were, he wrote, "sorry looking craft, their huge wheel houses disproportioned to the squatty hull and the tall chimneys rather looking as if they would capsize the whole concern." Phelps set about finding a way to free the gunboats that had been grounded by low water in the river, but he was unable to do so. Instead, he spent the summer rounding up arms and ammunition and recruiting men for the crews. He managed to enlist coal heavers and firemen but found most river men unsuitable. "The army is not fit for shipboard duty and won't do at all," he reported to Rogers. "We ought to have few old men-of-war men."[23]

In early August, Rodgers sent Bishop to St. Louis to rent a recruiting office, enlist 100 men for the gunboat service, and hire a small steamboat as a rendezvous for the men. By then, Rodgers had appointed officers to the gunboats, selected engineers, and managed to convince river pilots to accept the wages he offered, which were less than the Pilot Association had fixed before the war.[24]

Fortunately, the Ohio River rose during the first week of August, allowing the *Tyler* and *Lexington* to get over the Portland Bar and dragging the *Conestoga* over as well. They proceeded downriver to New Albany, where they received their batteries. The three boats arrived at Cairo on the afternoon of August 12. Early on, Bates, Governor Randall, and others had understood that Cairo enjoyed a strategic location at the confluence of the Ohio and Mississippi Rivers. The river town was also the terminus of the Illinois Central Railroad and could serve as a staging area for army operations in the upper Mississippi Valley and as a base to defend St. Louis. On April 19 the secretary of war had ordered Illinois governor Richard Yates to secure Cairo, and within days Yates had seven companies of state militia entrained at Chicago, headed for the strategic river town. Cairo proved a fine choice for the timberclads' home port. Nearby shipyards and docks at Mound City, on the Ohio River, provided repair facilities and construction sites for the Western Gunboat Flotilla.

By the time the *Conestoga, Tyler,* and *Lexington* managed to reach Cairo, earthworks had been erected and soldiers had encamped at Bird's Point. Sending a garrison to Cairo was one of the Union's crucial early decisions.

As one historian wrote, "Cairo, the most southern point in northern territory, was a dagger pointing at the heart of the confederacy."[25]

The three timberclads were welcome additions to the defense of Cairo and St. Louis. Two days before their arrival, the Confederates had scored a victory at Wilson's Creek. In the aftermath of this defeat, General John C. Fremont, who had replaced McClellan at the end of July, ordered Ulysses S. Grant to command Union forces in central Missouri. Recently promoted to brigadier general, Grant went to Jefferson City to train recruits, but at the end of August he was reassigned to Cape Girardeau, near Cairo, with orders to take the offensive against rebel leader Jeff Thompson.[26]

In the meantime, Phelps reported that the commanding officer at Cairo was "very anxious that the gunboats should make a demonstration down the river toward New Madrid, and also be prepared to assist in the defense of Cairo." Accordingly, Phelps quickly manned two of the boats, procured ammunition from the fort, and got under way to examine the Mississippi above and below Bird's Point. On August 15 he steamed down to New Madrid, "meeting with no enemy or batteries and without demonstration against us from any of the towns," he reported to Rodgers.

On the following day, however, Lieutenant Roger Stembel took Colonel Waagner of the artillery corps on board the *Lexington* and made a reconnaissance down to Cape Girardeau. Near Commerce, Missouri, they were hailed by a number of families on shore who informed Stembel "that the citizens were all deserting their homes on account of about 800 rebel forces then on their way to sack, pillage, and burn their town, a very pretty village, containing about 600 inhabitants." Stembel landed at the town, took on board a large number of alarmed citizens, and transported them to Cape Girardeau. When the gunboat went back to Commerce on August 17, Stembel found the town almost entirely deserted.[27]

The new gunboat had certainly made an impression. Several days later, Rodgers took the *Tyler* down to Commerce, where he discovered the population in a state of fearful excitement owing to reports of a rebel force of 800 to 1,000 men armed with shotguns, rifles, and muskets. The rebels had erected a battery there, Rodgers reported to Welles, and he was determined to dislodge it. "We arrived here and found that upon our coming in sight they had left the town with a train of about 50 wagons, principally laden with corn." When a number of rebels opened fire on the *Tyler* from a hilltop the next evening, Rodgers ordered the gunboat to lob a couple of shells at them. Pleased that the new timberclad had proved its worth, and noting that Commerce commanded the river, Rodgers decided to dispatch a gunboat to lie off the place.[28]

The Western Gunboat Flotilla's first three gunboats had officially entered service and engaged the enemy. These ungainly looking, flat-bottomed, wooden-sided timberclads formed the nucleus of the Union army's brownwater navy. Armed with heavy guns and more suitable for the shallow, twisting western rivers than the Union navy's tall-masted, deep-draft wooden frigates, they proved surprisingly serviceable.

For the next two years, the *Tyler, Lexington,* and *Conestoga* participated in a series of naval engagements and campaigns on western rivers. This trio of timberclads was merely the vanguard of the Union's building program in the West. In May, General Totten had consulted the chief of the navy's Bureau of Construction and Repair, John Lenthall, about the feasibility of building armed steam vessels from the keel up for service on western rivers. On June 10 Scott forwarded his study to the secretary of war, urging the War Department to construct sixteen gunboats based on Lenthall's design. Cameron passed the recommendation on to Welles, who suggested the gunboats be built by western men familiar with such river craft, but he did offer the assistance of naval constructor Samuel Pook. In early July, Pook sent models, plans, and specifications for two ironclad gunboats. The second design met with the navy's approval, and chief engineer Benjamin Isherwood advised on the type of engines and boilers needed. Within a month, Scott had ordered the Quartermaster Department to draw up plans for the construction of seven ironclad gunboats for the flotilla. Named for western cities, they became known as city-class gunboats or, more often, "Pook's turtles." Quartermaster Meigs let the contract for the ironclads to St. Louis entrepreneur Eads, with the expectation that they would be completed in three months under Rodgers's supervision. Within weeks, the Carondelet Marine Railway and Dry Dock Company in Carondelet, Missouri, and the Hambleton, Collier, and Company dry docks in Mound City had begun construction.[29]

The city-class ironclads *St. Louis, Carondelet, Cairo, Pittsburg, Louisville, Cincinnati,* and *Mound City* were all launched and in commission by January 1862. The new gunboats put teeth into the Western Gunboat Flotilla and enabled Union forces to pursue Scott's plan to secure the Ohio River and advance down the Mississippi and up the Tennessee and Cumberland Rivers into the South, securing strongpoints and bases.

In addition to acquiring and constructing vessels for western rivers, the

Union navy had to fit the vessels out, recruit and train crews to man them, and secure reliable, experienced river pilots. The commanders of both the Western Gunboat Flotilla and the Gulf Blockading Squadron struggled to recruit seamen and resorted to enlisting African Americans; they also asked that soldiers be detailed to serve in the navy. Finding sufficient personnel to man newly constructed gunboats and replace crewmen who had been injured or fallen ill continued to be one of the Union navy's most pressing issues. Likewise, keeping these men healthy in the debilitating, fever-prone Southern climate proved to be a problem, as did caring for ill and wounded soldiers and sailors and transporting them to hospitals or hospital boats.

Operating in the South brought Union navy vessels into contact with sizable populations of African American slaves, many of whom sought sanctuary on federal vessels or came into Union lines or camps seeking protection. The Lincoln government therefore had to establish policies with regard to fugitive slaves: should they be returned to their owners; employed to dig canals, stevedore vessels, cook or do laundry for Union troops and seamen, or work in hospitals or on hospital ships; or enlisted (the able-bodied males) to serve in the Union navy or Union army? Although the Fugitive Slave Law of 1850, requiring that fugitive slaves be returned to their owners, was in effect when the war began, it was not strictly enforced. Many naval officers, in fact, refused to return African Americans seeking sanctuary on their vessels. Major General Benjamin F. Butler went even further, refusing to return runaway slaves because, he argued, the Union and the Confederacy were at war, and the slaves could be considered contraband of war. Setting them free would deprive the rebels of valuable labor. As a result of Butler's policy, these fugitives became known as "contrabands."

To carry out Scott's strategy of pushing down the Mississippi River and securing bases, the Union army and navy had to work together at the command level. They had to develop tactics and weapons to conduct amphibious operations in the West, and they had to deal with new weapons designed by the Confederacy to counter federal naval forces, the most deadly of which was the "torpedo" or mine. Union navy operations to "open the Mississippi River" have been the subject of various studies by historians, including John Milligan, Gary Joiner, Benton R. Patterson, H. Allen Gosnell, Jack Coombe, and James McPherson. Combined operations on western rivers leading up to the surrender of Vicksburg in July 1863 have been chronicled and analyzed by Rowena Reed and others, as has the contribution of senior Union navy commanders such as Charles Davis, Andrew Hull Foote,

David Glasgow Farragut, and David Dixon Porter. Less attention has been paid to the experiences of junior officers, midshipmen, and ordinary sailors. Although there are fewer surviving diaries and letters written by sailors compared with their army counterparts, their accounts of service on western gunboats provide fresh insight into the navy's engagement with Confederate forces and the obstacles faced by the "brown-water navy." The authors of these diaries, memoirs, and letters range in rank from fleet captain to first-class boy and include Fleet Captain Henry Bell; Captain Henry Walke; Lieutenants Francis Roe, George Dewey, A. J. Sypher, and George Blodgett; navy surgeons Nimian Pinckney and Aaron Oberly; Ensign Elias Smith; Second Master D. P. Rosenmiller; surgeon's assistant Preston Bishop; and sailors Daniel Kemp, Elliot Callendar, Anthony O'Neil, George Yost, and John G. Morison and marine private Oscar Smith. Their letters and journal entries often echo the official reports, but they also write about going ashore on foraging parties, shoveling snow from an ironclad's deck, assisting the surgeon in amputating a fellow crewman's arm, and liberating supplies of whiskey from a captured enemy vessel. They also offer candid assessments of their commanding officers, observations about the people living along the river, relationships with African Americans, and personal views of a war that lasted far longer than many expected or hoped and became increasingly cruel.

News correspondent Franc Wilkie and civilian observer Thomas Bacon also wrote accounts of the war on the western rivers. Many of these news articles, letters, and diary entries add to our knowledge of lesser-known incidents from the autumn of 1861 to the fall of Vicksburg in July 1863. They recount brushes with rebel guerrillas, the combined operation to take Arkansas Post and Fort Hindman, an expedition up the White River, and the federal engagements at Simmesport and Gordon's Landing. The following narrative incorporates many of these vivid and candid accounts and personal observations.

1

The Western Gunboat Flotilla

"A Mongrel Service"

This rebellion must soon cease, the West is clamoring for her rivers
to be open, she must have her commerce, the Mississippi is what she
depends up on and if we do not open it soon, she will go with the
South and then open it by compromise.

—Frederic Davis

Walking through the muddy streets of Cairo, Illinois, Commander Henry
Walke must have wondered what turn of fate had brought him to that
ragged town to take command not of a proper warship but of some new-
fangled gunboat called a timberclad. Walke had come west from Williams-
burg, New York, to Cairo, which was little more than a miserable collection
of shacks sunk in a basin and either mired in mud or knee-deep in dust.
Miserable or not, the Western Gunboat Flotilla called Cairo home port,
and Walke must have been grateful for any command.

Assistant Navy Secretary Gustavus Fox's orders, dated September 6,
1861, were a welcome surprise to Walke and a reprieve from the indignity
of the "retired list." Fox directed him to proceed from his assignment as
lighthouse inspector of the Eleventh Lighthouse District to St. Louis, Missouri, and report to none other than Captain Andrew Hull Foote, newly
named to command naval forces on the western rivers. "He had been my
fellow-midshipman in 1827, on board the United States ship *Natchez* in
1827, of the West India squadron, and was then a promising young officer,"
Walke later wrote.[1] Walke had seen Foote only once since their midship-

13

man days, but he was aware of Foote's successful career in the US Navy. Foote had served in the Mediterranean, circumnavigated the globe in the USS *John Adams,* and cruised the African coast in the USS *Perry* suppressing the slave trade. He was well known for his opposition to flogging and had a reputation as an avowed abolitionist. After promotion to commander in 1856, he assumed command of the USS *Portsmouth* in the East India Squadron, and just prior to the Civil War he had been commandant of the Brooklyn Navy Yard. In June 1861 Foote attained the rank of captain.[2]

Despite his service afloat during the Mexican War, Walke's career, in contrast, had foundered on the shoals of the Gulf of Mexico. He had been the executive officer of the bomb brig *Vesuvius,* assigned to blockade duty with Commodore Matthew Calbraith Perry's Gulf Squadron. The mission of clearing the Tabasco River fell to the Mosquito Flotilla, commanded by Lieutenant David Dixon Porter. When the *Spitfire, Scourge, Vixen,* and several bomb vessels went up the river, Mexican sharpshooters opened fire on the *Vesuvius* from the banks, shooting a sailor on its forecastle. The gunboat returned fire with its mortar, dispersing the snipers, and the squadron continued upriver and anchored. Landing parties went ashore, scaled the steep cliffs, and rushed the Mexican works. Porter then led the American gunboats upriver to seize Fort Iturbide.

His Mexican War service stood Walke in good stead with the US Navy until January 1861, at which time Walke commanded the USS *Supply* based at Pensacola, Florida. When Confederate forces demanded the surrender of the US Navy Yard at Pensacola, Captain James Armstrong dutifully capitulated, but Walke chose to support the defenders of Fort Pickens who refused to surrender. Four days later, contrary to his orders to report to the US naval squadron at Vera Cruz, Walke got the *Supply* under way and headed for Brooklyn, New York, determined to evacuate loyal navy yard employees, Union soldiers, and sailors. For following his conscience but disobeying his orders, Walke endured the wrenching indignity of a court-martial. Although he ultimately received only an admonition, he spent the summer of 1861 in limbo, wondering whether he would ever be given another command.[3]

Now, with orders in hand, Walke reported to the newly appointed Commodore Foote in St. Louis. Though he looked older, his face was fuller, and his scraggly beard was graying, Foote was still the same amiable gentleman Walke remembered. The Western Gunboat Flotilla was commissioning several new ironclad gunboats designed by Samuel Pook for operations on the

Mississippi River, and Foote needed every experienced officer he could find. So, without any allusion to the Pensacola affair, Foote ordered Walke to proceed immediately to Cairo, where the navy had established a headquarters.

Arriving in Cairo in early September 1861, Walke went to the city's only first-class hotel, the St. Charles, which was home to many of the journalists covering the war. At the time, word of Foote's appointment to replace Rodgers as flotilla commander had enlivened the reporters' discussions and spurred speculation. Many claimed it was "all General Fremont's doing." The reporters, for the most part, disliked Fremont, who had been given command of the western armies but had done little. As commander of the Department of Missouri, Fremont had asked Lincoln to remove Rodgers, who had alienated many influential local businessmen by shifting lucrative contracts away from them. His defenders pointed out that Rodgers had stood up to Fremont and claimed jurisdiction over all western shipping.[4]

Having labored for three months to put together a brown-water navy to serve on the western rivers, Rodgers was surprised by Foote's unexpected arrival in St. Louis to assume command of the flotilla. Although Foote reported to Fox that the veteran naval officer "behaved well, officer-like and gentlemanly," Rodgers wrote privately to Secretary Welles, defending his work. Recounting that he had "labored silently" to procure gun carriages, anchors, rowboats, chains, and cooking apparatus; had appointed superintendents; and had ensured properly constructed iron plating for the gunboats, Rodgers complained about his replacement, using this analogy: "when the plant that thus watered and cultivated gives its first prematurely ripe fruit, the crop is turned over to another with cold words."[5]

The seven ironclads Rodgers had under construction would be launched in a month, forming the backbone of the new western flotilla that he would no longer command. That privilege would go to Foote, a contemporary and colleague but senior in rank to Rodgers. Welles's choice of Foote puzzled some naval officers, for he had "neither the wealth, showy name, or scholastic attainments of a man like Samuel Francis Du Pont." In the small officer corps of the antebellum US Navy, the reputations of most officers were well known. Furthermore, Foote and Welles had known each other during their youth, attending the same prep school in Connecticut. Walke described Foote as a man of "firm and tenacious purpose," noting, "He was not a man of striking physical appearance, but there was a sailor-like heartiness and frankness about him which made his company very desirable." Foote, Walke said, "has been called 'the Stonewall Jackson of the Navy.'"[6]

When Foote arrived in St. Louis on September 6, 1861, he went directly by train to the shipyards of James B. Eads at Carondelet. Eads, a semiretired partner in a salvage and construction company and the inventor of a diving bell, was considered an expert in navigating the Mississippi River. President Lincoln had chosen Eads to build gunboats designed by Pook for service on the western rivers.[7]

As directed by Foote, Walke reported to Commander Alex M. Pennock at the navy's unusual headquarters. "In consequence of the overflow of the Mississippi and Ohio rivers, Captain Pennock's command was at first almost entirely and necessarily afloat," Walke recalled. "It was built upon large wharf boats, steamboats, barges and lighters—everything available being pressed into the service, the whole representing a somewhat novel appearance, not unlike to a floating village." Pennock commanded the naval depot at Cairo assisted by Lieutenant J. P. Sanford, Lieutenant O. H. Perry, Chief Engineer Merrit, Quartermaster Wise, and Master Mechanic and Acting Constructor R. Friganza.[8]

At Cairo, Walke learned he was to command the *Tyler*, one of the converted side-wheel steamers, or timberclads, stationed at Paducah, Kentucky. Under the command of Rodgers, the *Tyler* and the *Conestoga* had just accompanied a little-known army general named Ulysses S. Grant on an expedition to seize the strategic town of Paducah on the Ohio River. The expedition had encountered no opposition from the rebels, and Foote had arrived in time to see the town surrender. Taking Paducah secured Union control of the exits of the Ohio, Tennessee, and Cumberland Rivers.[9]

The flotilla's three new gunboats, *Conestoga, Lexington,* and *Tyler,* had come down the Ohio River in August, arriving in Cairo on the twelfth. The *Conestoga* and *Lexington* had gone down the Mississippi ahead of Grant's troops and had encountered some Confederate batteries on the Kentucky shore at Lucas Bend. The *Conestoga,* commanded by Seth Ledyard Phelps, had engaged the rebel batteries, which alerted the Confederate gunboat *Yankee.* Phelps and the *Lexington*'s captain, Roger Stembel, ordered their gunners to open fire. Hit twice, the *Yankee* withdrew.

Accompanied by Foote, Walke went to Paducah on September 12, 1861, to relieve Rodgers of command of the *Tyler*. Located at the junction of the Tennessee and Ohio Rivers and just ten miles from the mouth of the Cumberland River, Paducah was a strategic acquisition for the Union. Both the Tennessee and the Ohio flow north from the heart of the Confederacy, and the town had the air of a Southern city, with good buildings, curb stones, and several macadamized streets. Standing on the landing at Paducah, Walke caught sight of the *Tyler* and must have thought it a sorry-looking craft. The gunboat's large side wheels, awkwardly covered in wooden planks, dwarfed its squatty hull and two tall, thin smokestacks that rose above the timberclad's sloping decks. The *Tyler*, which had been built in 1857 at Cincinnati, had been bought by the Union navy and converted into a gunboat. At 429 tons and 180 feet overall, the *Tyler* seemed ungainly, but Walke knew the odd-looking craft packed a wallop with its six 8-inch guns and one 32-pounder. When the three gunboats had traveled downriver from Cincinnati to Cairo, onlookers had gawked at the strange-looking craft and predicted the guns' recoil would shake them to pieces. Or, as one wag claimed, rebel shore batteries would surely send them quickly to the bottom of the Ohio River. The timberclads' early successes against the Confederates came as a surprise to many.[10]

When Walke assumed command of the *Tyler*, the gunboat's second in command was Lieutenant Joshua Bishop, a Missouri native who had entered the navy in 1854 and had recently joined the new river flotilla. Bishop knew the *Tyler*'s new commanding officer had been on the retired list, and he was aware of Walke's daring actions at Pensacola. Bishop may have wondered at the time whether his new commander had mixed feelings about the present hostilities. The son of a distinguished American family, Walke had been born on a plantation on the Lynnhaven River in Virginia in 1809, making him a Southerner in some eyes. His father, Anthony Walke, had attended Yale College and served in the Virginia legislature before moving the family to Ohio when Henry was just two years old. Henry's older brother Anthony had inherited the name and whatever family fortune there was, so in 1827 young Henry went to sea as a midshipman, assigned to the frigate *Alert* under Commander (and future admiral) David Glasgow Farragut.[11]

After touring the *Tyler* and meeting the crew, Walke and Bishop probably retired to the wardroom for a drink. In the days before the navy abolished the grog ration, officers were allowed to have as much liquor on board as they could afford. Here, perhaps over a glass of whiskey, Bishop undoubtedly brought the *Tyler*'s new captain up to date on affairs in the West. He had been involved in recruiting men for the river flotilla and might have explained that the three timberclads had been ready for service since mid-

August, manned by naval personnel but under army control. The men of the *Tyler* took great pride in being the first Union navy vessel to fire a shot in anger on the Mississippi. Although some of the flotilla's officers may have thought they were serving in a mongrel service on the Ohio or Mississippi River, Bishop hoped they were going to give the rebels a run for their money.[12]

On September 14 the river began to fall, and Foote ordered the lighter-draft *Conestoga* to Paducah to trade places with the deeper-draft *Tyler*. Walke took the *Tyler* to Cairo, as ordered, to confer with Brigadier General Ulysses S. Grant. On July 31, 1861, Lincoln had promoted the relatively unknown Illinois militia colonel to brigadier, and General Fremont had put Grant in charge of Union forces in central Missouri. Walke had never met Grant, but the rowdy reporters who hung around the St. Charles Hotel knew that Grant was a West Pointer who had fought in the Mexican War and been commended for bravery. After the war, Grant had gone out to California and resigned his commission, but unable to make a go of civilian life, he had returned to the army. Franc Wilkie and many others in Cairo had heard that Major General Henry W. "Old Brains" Halleck feared that Grant might be rash, or worse. But they thought Grant was a fighter.[13]

Fremont had ordered Grant to assume command of federal forces from General Benjamin M. Prentiss at the small garrison at Cape Girardeau. Fremont wanted Grant to counter the Missouri state guard forces led by Jeff Thompson, organize several ongoing federal movements designed to chase the Confederates out of southeastern Missouri, and then move into Kentucky and occupy Columbus. By mid-September, the new commander of the Confederate Western Department, General Albert Sidney Johnston, had secured a defensive line across southern Kentucky, with flanks at Columbus on the Mississippi River and in the mountains at the Cumberland Gap. The recent Confederate occupation of Columbus by Generals Leonidas Polk and Gideon Pillow had convinced the Kentucky legislature to side with the Union, adding to the difficulty of defending the vast territory under Johnston's command, which was spread across Kentucky, Tennessee, Arkansas, and Missouri. With just 40,000 troops, one-quarter of them in Missouri under Sterling Price, Johnston resorted to raids and tactics designed to convince the Union that he had a much larger force.[14]

On September 14 the *Tyler*'s new captain met Grant at his Cairo headquarters. Grant detailed members of his staff to accompany Walke on a reconnaissance down the Mississippi River "to within gunshot of Columbus, in search of rebel batteries reported to be in course of construction," Walke recalled. The gunboat would be cooperating with the movement of advance troops camped at Norfolk, six miles below Cairo. Grant wanted to advance but admitted he did not have a sufficient force. He had asked Fremont for more troops and equipment, as well as for permission to move on Columbus, but none had been forthcoming. Grant had not given up the idea of advancing on that strategic river town, so he needed Walke to find out what the rebels were up to. "Columbus, situated twenty miles below Cairo, on the Mississippi, was appropriately styled the 'Gibraltar of the West,' as it was perfectly fortified," Walke explained in his memoirs, "and was garrisoned with an army much larger than our own force at Cairo."[15]

At Norfolk, the *Tyler* took on 100 men of the 9th Illinois Regiment and then proceeded downriver with the *Lexington* in search of enemy batteries. As the *Tyler* neared Columbus, Walke observed rebel fortifications on Iron Banks, several batteries on the spurs of a bluff, and a ten-gun battery about fifty feet above the river. The rebels had also moored a large floating battery of sixteen guns at the Columbus landing. "Off these works, the Taylor [Tyler] rounded to, fired eight or ten 64 pound shell into them, killing (as reported) three, and wounding several of the enemy," Walke reported. The timberclad then returned to Norfolk, unloaded the troops, and went on to Cairo to put the army officers ashore.[16]

This brief reconnaissance had given Walke a chance to operate with the *Lexington* and get better acquainted with its commanding officer, Roger N. Stembel. A fellow Ohioan, the fifty-one-year-old Stembel had received an appointment as a midshipman in the antebellum US Navy after graduating from Miami College. The two men had never served together, but Walke knew that Stembel had cruised in the West Indies in 1836 on the sloop *Vandalia* and had also taken part in the Seminole War and served with the Coast Survey. In 1843 Stembel had married Laura McBride, the daughter of a prominent family in Hamilton, Ohio, just north of Cincinnati. When the war began, the navy assigned Stembel to St. Louis, where he oversaw the construction of gunboats for the Mississippi. When he assumed command of the *Lexington,* his fifteen-year-old son, James McBride Stembel, went to serve as an aide to Commodore Foote.[17]

After returning to Cairo, the *Tyler* went into dock at Mound City for alterations to adapt the timberclad for river service. Workers installed a gun in the *Tyler*'s stern and made arrangements for officers' cabins, changes suggested by Rodgers before he departed.[18]

For Walke and his fellow commanders, gunboat service on these inland waters was fraught with frustration. Filling out the *Tyler*'s crew topped the list of Walke's numerous headaches. Foote sent him frequent messages, one of which read, "You will ship all men that you can at Cairo for the gunboat service." Where Foote expected Walke to find these men remained a mystery. They were certainly not just hanging around the bars of Cairo waiting to be asked. Foote promised to send some men in a few days and told Walke to go ahead and make arrangements to heat his vessel, "with a due regard to comfort and economy."[19]

The *Tyler* spent the rest of September and most of October cruising up and down the river on picket duty, "reconnoitering the enemy often within gunshot of their batteries," until it was relieved by the *Lexington*. Then, on October 6, Grant summoned the *Tyler* to Cairo for another reconnaissance. Setting off with the *Lexington* again, the *Tyler* approached Iron Bluffs, where Walke spotted the *Jeff Davis*, but he could not get near enough to engage the rebel steamer. Two miles above Columbus, the two gunboats opened fire on half a dozen Confederate batteries armed with rifled cannon. "Fortunately," Walke later recalled, "the range from the batteries was too high, and their first volley of screaming shells flew over and far behind the frail gunboats; and by a timely and necessary retreat they escaped harm." Both Stembel and Walke wisely decided to turn back for Cairo, throwing a few shells into the rebel batteries at Lucas Bend for good measure.[20]

The *Tyler* made repeated surveys of the Mississippi. One morning near Lucas Bend, while standing on deck, Walke looked toward shore and saw a sudden movement: a figure, probably an enemy picket, mounted his horse and raced off at full speed. A fence running along the bank kept the horse and rider from fleeing inland to safety, so the *Tyler* chugged along, keeping as near to shore as possible. "The chase being short but exciting," Walke recalled. "The faithful horse, with his rider soon left the tardy gunboat behind; but a 64 pounder shell overtook them, and burst so near that nothing was seen of them after the smoke and dust had cleared off, and the roar of the explosion had subsided."[21]

Back at Cairo, a visiting senator pronounced that Grant was "doing wonders and is bringing order out of chaos." Grant had indeed taken charge, incessantly drilling his men, organizing his command into brigades, and bringing in supplies. When the soldiers complained about firing blank rounds during practice, Grant issued them live ammunition. The boys cheered as they took aim at the weeds and a target they had named "Jeff Davis."

Fremont had been dismissed by now, and McClellan divided the Western Department into two commands, appointing Don Carlos Buell to command in eastern Kentucky and Tennessee and putting Halleck in charge of the rest. An Ohioan, Buell was a West Point graduate and had been brevetted for bravery in the Mexican War. After commanding a division in the Army of the Potomac, he was promoted to brigadier general in November 1861 and succeeded Sherman in command of the Department of the Ohio. Scott had recommended that forty-six-year-old Halleck, a scholar, lawyer, and career army officer, be given the rank of major general, and in November he replaced Fremont in the Department of the Missouri.

When headquarters in St. Louis learned that Confederate general Polk was moving reinforcements from Columbus to support the Missouri militia's General Sterling Price in western Missouri, Grant was ordered to make demonstrations against the rebel stronghold at Columbus. Grant, itching to take the offensive, put two brigades of troops on six transports. "On the evening of the 6th of November, 1861, I received instructions from General Grant to proceed down the Mississippi with the wooden gun-boats *Tyler* and *Lexington,* on a reconnoissance, and as convoy to some half dozen transport steamers," Walke remembered. "But I did not know the character of the service expected of me until I anchored for the night, seven or eight miles below Cairo."[22] The transports steamed downriver some nine miles and anchored on the Kentucky bank for the night. Grant and his staff spent the evening in the ladies' cabin on the transport *Belle Memphis.* Seated at a table, Grant puffed on his pipe and went over plans for the coming demonstration against Columbus.

In the wee hours of November 7, a messenger arrived. By the dim light of the transport's chandeliers, Grant read the correspondence and shared it with his staff. Colonel H. L. Wallace had learned from what he deemed to be a reliable informant that the enemy had been crossing troops from Columbus to Belmont. He surmised that the goal was to cut off Colonel Oglesby's forces, and Grant agreed. This new information gave Grant the opportunity to turn a demonstration into a battle, and as biographer Brooks Simpson has noted, "a clash would season his men (and himself) under fire, and prick Confederate overconfidence." Grant was exceeding his orders, but as the general explained to his staff, if they were repulsed at Belmont, the troops could easily reembark on the transports.[23]

Grant ordered his chief of staff, John A. Rawlins, and his adjutants to write the orders and send them immediately to Walke and to his brigade commanders, Brigadier General John A. McClernand and Colonel Henry Dougherty. A loyal southern Illinois Democrat, McClernand had been a congressman before the war. By November 1861 he had resigned from Congress, raised a brigade of troops in Illinois, and been commissioned a brigadier general of volunteers.[24]

Early on November 7, Grant's orders arrived on board the *Tyler*. They called for the gunboats to take the advance, followed by McClernand's brigade and then a second brigade under Dougherty. The order read: "The entire force will debark at the lowest point on the Missouri shore, where a landing can be effected in security from the rebel batteries. The point of debarkation will [be] designated by Captain Walke, commanding naval forces." Stembel's *Lexington* was to accompany the *Tyler*.[25]

Word that the *Tyler* would soon be going on a mission with Grant's troops spread quickly—as rumors often did aboard ship. No one knew the expedition's destination, but there were the usual guesses. The officers surmised that the objective was Columbus, a rebel stronghold. Previous federal expeditions to both Columbus and Belmont had led to skirmishes with the rebels, and the *Tyler*'s officers had heard that Grant thought the Confederates were concentrating in the area. Later, when the gunboat turned down the Mississippi, the crew knew they were headed for Columbus. "We're going to attack the rebs at Columbus," they whooped and cheered. To his officers and men, Walke seemed pleased with the prospect of an engagement with the Confederates, but he had to be feeling the burden of command. The entire crew, with the exception of Walke and the acting gunner, consisted of volunteers, most of whom had never been in combat.[26]

On the eve of the expedition, Walke undoubtedly recalled events from the Mexican War, especially sharpshooters taking aim at his crew from the riverbank. Confederate sharpshooters might do to the Union gunboats on the Mississippi what the Mexicans had done to Porter's gunboats. But, Walke may have reminded himself, the navy had learned valuable lessons during the Mexican War about using steam-propelled warships and conducting amphibious warfare along coastal towns and rivers—lessons that, Walke hoped, would come in handy now.

In his memoirs, Walke explained that the enemy batteries consisted of about twenty heavy guns. "Some were planted on the 'Iron Banks,' a short distance above Columbus, at an elevation of about two hundred feet, and another of about fifty feet in elevation, overlooking a long bend in the river." He and Stembel would have to "observe great caution to prevent the gunboats from being disabled, as they were needed to guard the troops on their return."[27]

On board the transport *James Montgomery,* the young men of Colonel Napoleon Bonaparte Buford's 27th Illinois Infantry tried to sleep. Many had bedded down on the vessel's deck, their weapons beside them, but thoughts of the upcoming battle with the rebels made most of them too nervous to fall asleep. The men had confidence in Buford, the regiment's fifty-four-year-old colonel, who had attended West Point and served as a company-grade artillery officer before resigning his commission in 1835. After studying law at Harvard, Buford became a civil engineer and was one of the organizers of the Rock Island Railroad. By 1861, however, the once energetic and forceful Buford had aged. Surgeon John H. Brinton called him a "fussy old gentleman, an old granny, but kind and amiable." He may have been kindly, but he had drilled the newly organized 27th Illinois mercilessly. The regiment's green recruits grumbled, and some of the officers became resentful; a few threatened to resign. But now, as the regiment glided down the Mississippi to its baptism of fire, many of Buford's soldiers had reason to thank the "old granny" for preparing them so well.[28]

On the *Belle Memphis,* Brinton, the district medical director, had no difficulty falling into a deep sleep. The previous day, from his sickbed at Union headquarters in Cairo, Brinton had learned of Grant's planned attack on the enemy. He managed to don his uniform and then went downstairs and reported to Grant. The general shook his hand. "I thought you were too ill to go," he said. "I ordered them not to disturb you, but here you are! You deserve the best mount we can provide." Later, Brinton strapped his blankets to the saddle, gave his instruments to a clerk who would act as his orderly, and embarked on an army transport. Too ill to stand, Brinton lay down on a berth and dropped off to sleep.[29]

The *Tyler* and *Lexington* got under way at 3:00 that morning with orders to proceed downriver and engage the Confederate batteries at Columbus. When darkness gave way to a dense fog, however, a disappointed Walke reluctantly turned the gunboats back to their anchorage opposite Norfolk. If Walke was worried that Grant's upcoming "demonstration" against Belmont would turn into a real engagement that might bring disaster and the Navy Department's wrath down on him, he gave no hint in his memoirs. As an experienced naval officer, he knew that one cannot always predict a battle's outcome. The *Tyler* had been downriver on reconnaissance, and its gun crews had even dropped shells onto the shore, but the gunboat had never fully engaged heavy Confederate batteries or endured concentrated enemy fire. Although the *Tyler* was a maneuverable little gunboat and capable of speed, its five-inch oak planks provided only so much protection. During the side-wheeler's conversion to a gunboat, the boilers and engines had been dropped into the hold and the steam pipes had been lowered, but as the boat's first skipper had admitted, "the boilers and engines can not be defended against cannon shot. We must take our chances."[30]

Historian Rowena Reed aptly termed Grant's expedition to Belmont "a shoestring operation involving raw troops 'covered' by two undermanned wooden gunboats." It would be the first real test of the Union navy's "mongrel" service and of the Lincoln government's strategy to push down the Mississippi River.[31]

As first light appeared, the *Tyler*'s watch keepers could see that the fog had given way to a calm, clear day. Aboard the transports, sergeants roused the sleepy soldiers, nudging some awake and occasionally casting a fatherly look at the younger, more anxious ones. The men rubbed their eyes, looked around for their haversacks, and dug into whatever cooked rations they had brought with them. Most of them hadn't had a real breakfast in months. But that day, as they munched on their cornbread and whatever food they had, many wondered whether this breakfast might be their last.

As the sun rose, the transports and gunboats got under way and steamed down the placid Mississippi with the *Tyler* in the lead. When the convoy reached the end of Lucas Bend, outside the range of rebel guns at Iron Banks, the transports *Memphis, James Montgomery, Chancellor, Rob Roy, Aleck Scott,* and *Keystone State* stopped. At about 7:00 Grant's troops began disembarking at a small landing called Hunter's Farm, on the west bank of the Mississippi a short distance above Belmont.[32]

Glad to be off the *Montgomery,* the men of Buford's 27th Illinois Infantry splashed ashore. All around them were marshes and thick woods, but in the distance they could see a clearing. Once Buford's regiment was ashore, the colonel rode up on his horse and addressed his men, telling them in a strong, clear voice: "We are sufficient in number, are well armed, General Grant is our commander, but the Lord of Hosts is our leader and our guide." Buford's soldiers then doffed their hats and sent up a wild cheer. At about 8:00 Grant rode up on his horse and deployed two brigades. He proceeded for another mile or so and then halted on some marshy ground and deployed skirmishers. The rest of his troops trudged on. When they reached a cornfield, the men formed a line running from north to south. Buford's infantrymen pushed and shoved one another playfully, stomping on the cornstalks as they joked and laughed. A rebel shell screamed overhead, then another. Suddenly an enormous shell crashed down, failing to explode but burying itself in the soft mud.[33]

At around 8:30 the two brigades formed up, with the 27th Illinois leading off. An officer barked, "Battalion, forward march," and the federals set off toward the settlement of Belmont—really, little more than a few log houses and a steamboat landing—about three miles away. Trees cut by the rebels to make abatis impeded their progress, forcing the soldiers to stop and clear them. As the sun warmed the air, the men of the 31st Illinois doffed their heavy overcoats, setting off a chain reaction of soldiers to the rear doing the same. At the edge of the woods, the men halted at a line of timber.[34]

While Grant's soldiers advanced, Walke's gunboats took a position within a mile and a half of the rebel batteries and opened fire at 8:45 a.m. Closing to the shore, the *Lexington* began shelling rebel defenses along the bluff. The *Tyler*'s gunners got off several rounds as well, and the Confederates returned fire. Walke watched the enemy missiles arc over the *Tyler*, fall across the two gunboats' decks, and splash into the river, cutting ricochets through the air. "Their shot mostly passed over us, though in some instances coming very close to us," Walke noted. "At this time, with their long-ranged rifle cannon, they sent a large number of shot half-a-mile above the transports. I requested the captains of the transports to move up and out of range of their cannon," Walke explained in his official report. Anxious moments followed, but the transports slowly lumbered away to a safe distance.[35]

Standing near the bow of his transport, surgeon Brinton saw a puff of smoke a ways off. A few seconds later a huge projectile flew past him, far above his head. "It seemed to me to be making a bee-line for my eye, but fortunately changed its mind, and passing above our heads, and apparently between our smoke pipes, buried itself in the dirt of the Missouri bank of the river." Seized with a desire to possess the rebel shot, Brinton offered two African American deckhands half a dollar apiece if they would dig it out for him. The next day the men presented Brinton with a conical shell about eighteen inches long and filled with lead. "I paid the money and secured the prize, but found, when I had it, that [it] was an elephant in my hands." He left the cumbersome souvenir in Cairo.[36]

At 10:00 Walke heard the sound of musket fire. The battle of Belmont had begun. Both sides were going at each other in what was, for most, a baptism of fire. McClernand had led his regiments forward, and as they approached a clearing, the Confederate troops and their commander, Brigadier General Pillow, were plainly visible. Pillow's one Arkansas and four Tennessee regiments had formed their battle line on a low ridge northwest of Belmont. McClernand's regiments, Buford's 27th on the far right, halted to wait for the men of Colonel John Logan's 31st Illinois to align themselves. No one spoke; only the sound of shuffling feet and the clank of the metal muskets broke the eerie quiet. The suspense was palpable. Suddenly, a colonel sputtered, "I don't care a damn where I am, as long as I get into this fight!"[37]

Skirmishers went ahead, and one of Buford's platoons ran into a Confederate cavalry unit that had been scouring the woods for Yankees. They drove the cavalrymen off, and Buford extended his line and brought up the rest of the regiment. Getting down from his mount, the colonel led the advance. "Double-quick march," he cried, and the men moved toward the enemy. The bluecoats stepped out, but the crackle of musket fire revealed Confederate infantry in the thickets. Buford's men paused, raised their muskets, and fired. Shots echoed, and the rebels retired.

Realizing Buford had encountered rebel infantry, McClernand ordered supporting units brought up. When Grant gave the order to advance into the woods toward Belmont, McClernand, hat in hand, drew his sword and charged. Shots rang out, and Captain Alexander Bielaski of McClernand's staff urged the men forward. Many were killed or wounded, and a musket ball shot Bielaski's horse out from under him. The captain grabbed the colors and continued on foot, only to be cut down by enemy fire. Over the next few hours, the federals pushed the rebels back toward their camp at Belmont.[38]

On the shore, Brinton, with some assistance from two soldiers, mounted his roan horse and rode to a small house on the edge of the wood, which he had requisitioned for a field hospital.[39] Meanwhile, offshore, the gunboats' crews went back to their action stations. On his own initiative, Walke had decided to take the *Tyler* and *Lexington* back to Iron Banks and bombard the rebel emplacements a second time. "The heavy firing with its continuous roar warned us that our troops were having hot work with the enemy," wrote a correspondent on board the *Lexington*. "And having seen that re-enforcements were marching over the distant bluffs, the gunboats dropped down the stream, and shelled the Confederate batteries for three quarters of an hour, with what success we could not tell, but the shell apparently burst immediately over their heads." This time, Walke ordered his gunners to aim for the enemy's upper guns; unfortunately, this allowed their lower guns to fire on Belmont. As Walke learned later, this had the unintended consequence of enabling Confederate transports to ferry fresh troops across the river. After twenty minutes, the two gunboats went back to the transport area, but at noon they returned for a third time to occupy rebel gunners at Iron Banks.[40]

Realizing that the Confederate gunners had been overshooting their mark, Walke "took advantage of the circumstance by running his gunboats far within the range of the batteries, and then with impunity, and for about half an hour fired broadside after broadside, the enemy's shot all passing over them." Walke thought he could see shells hitting the enemy guns, but it proved to be a defective rebel gun exploding. Determined to keep out of the enemy gunners' range, Walke ordered the two gunboats to remain under way, moving in a circle. "The enemy's batteries being in full play, their shot and shell began to have a telling effect," Walke wrote. "A cannon ball came down obliquely through the side deck and scantling of the 'Taylor,' taking off the head of Michael Adams, and wounding several others." The 24-pound shot broke the arm of James Wolfe, injured another sailor, and bounded across the deck, smashing into a stanchion. Quickly, Wolfe's shipmates carried him down to the *Tyler*'s surgeon, Thomas H. Kearney.[41]

The *Tyler*'s gunners fired a few more rounds, but Walke decided "to remove his vessels to a greater distance, so as to stand a better chance of security." As long as the range held, however, the timberclad's stern gunners kept up a steady fire. As the *Tyler* pulled away, one enemy shell fragment struck the stern but caused little damage, and the gunboats returned to the transport area. Walke has been criticized for not taking his gunboats down to Columbus to capture or chase off the enemy's transports. But Walke defended his decision not to close the rebel batteries or attempt to pass below them, writing in his memoir, "After firing a few more broadsides, therefore, and perceiving that the firing had ceased at Belmont, he returned to the landing with the gunboats, which movement was indispensable not only to the safety of the gunboats, but also the ultimate protection of our transports and army." Had the gunboats been destroyed, it might have resulted in the loss of the army and "our most important military depot in the West, at Cairo."[42]

By now, Grant's raw recruits had broken the enemy's line and pushed the rebels back toward Camp Johnston. Grant was everywhere, urging his boys on. Later, he told a reporter that he had kept his men going because "I had not the moral courage to halt and consider what to do."[43]

Pursued by federal artillery shells, the rebels' retreat turned into a panicky flight, with the men abandoning their guns and even their colors as they tried to get back to the river and their two transports. The 31st Illinois formed and fired a mass volley that felled dozens of rebel soldiers, and soon the Illinoisans had reached the Confederate camp.[44] There, they discovered that the rebels had "skedaddled." Some of the men crouched curiously over enemy cannon; others rifled through the rebels' abandoned backpacks or picked up random items as souvenirs. Discipline eroded, and the Union victors began celebrating, dancing, and looting. A regimental band appeared near the flagpole flying the Stars and Stripes and began to play "Yankee Doodle" and "Dixie." This prompted an officer from Illinois to mount a cannon and lead the jubilant young soldiers in a chorus of song. The victory had turned into a wild celebration more fitting for a July Fourth picnic than a military operation. Grant arrived on horseback and, attempting to control the chaos, began shouting out orders to set fire to the rebels' canvas tents.[45]

Walke and the *Tyler*'s crew could see none of this, but in midafternoon federal troops began to arrive on the shore, bent on returning to their transports. By 4:00 Walke could make out Union soldiers lining the transports' decks. A correspondent on board the *Lexington* told readers, "After nearly all had embarked, General Grant ordered the gunboats to drop down below the transports, as the enemy was coming upon our rear in large force, and was so near as to be plainly visible from the decks of the boats." As soon as the rebels saw "that we were dropping down, they went into the woods, but soon re-appeared in a corn-field abreast of our transports, and immediately came up to the river bank six or eight deep; when within one hundred feet of our transports they commenced firing on us. Our men returned the fire." Through his spyglass, Walke could see that rebel troops had rallied under cover of the riverbank and a wooded point of land in the bend of the river. "The Confederates, coming up through a corn-field en masse, opened a desperate fire of musketry and light artillery upon the transports, filled, or being filled, with our retreating soldiers," Walke recalled. Realizing that the rebels were trying to get between Grant's men and the transports to cut them off, Walke ordered the gunboats to open fire. A correspondent for the *New York Herald* wrote, "The gunboats *Tyler* and *Lexington* took a position between us and the enemy, and opened their guns upon them, letting slip a whole broadside at once. This movement was performed so quickly that the rebels did not get time to fire effectively upon us. Their guns were silenced as soon as they opened, or were probably dismounted. The first shot from the gunboats made a perfect lane through the enemy's ranks."[46]

Those on the *Tyler*'s deck could see the rebels plainly, but as the timber-clad moved downriver, the Southerners went into the woods and then reappeared. As the enemy approached the riverbank, they began firing on the transports. A mere hundred feet from shore, the *Tyler* closed to within sixty yards of the enemy, and the gun crews gave them grape and canister. From the deck, Walke and Bishop could watch the rounds land and see the horses and riders somersault into the air. "After playing on them half an hour—the 'Taylor' throwing some seventy rounds, and the 'Lexington' between thirty and forty—the smoke from the battle scene became so thick and black that the sun could not be seen," the reporter on the *Lexington* wrote. "We then steamed up the river, protecting the transports, and throwing shell back among the rebels until all had disappeared."[47]

Meanwhile, Grant's men had charged and defeated the rebels, allowing most of the troops to reembark. The majority of the 27th Illinois Regiment was not among them, however. In the chaos of the battle, they had been cut off from the landing and the safety of the transports.[48] The army commanders on the transports, unaware that the 27th had wandered off, were waiting for Buford's regiment to arrive. This allowed the rebels to cross more fresh troops from Columbus, and they opened fire from the riverbank. Sharp blasts from the gunboats' whistles forced Grant up from his sofa on the *Belle Memphis* to watch. From the deck, he could see the guns on the *Chancellor* throwing grapeshot at a lane full of Confederate troops. Federal soldiers on the *Aleck Scott* propped their rifles on the rails and blasted away at the enemy, but the rebels fired back, hitting the *Memphis*'s cabins and boats. Grant saw that the upper works had been riddled with balls, but he sighed with relief that none of his boys had been injured.[49]

Finally, Grant's half dozen transports cut their lines and got under way, moving toward the Kentucky shore. The two gunboats followed, maneuvering between the enemy and the transports. The *Belle Memphis,* however, became snagged, and the pilot frantically worked the stern wheel to shake the vessel free. As the transport untangled, the *Memphis* drifted downstream toward the enemy, preventing the *Lexington*'s gunners from having a clear shot at the rebels. "Lie down, lie down!" Stembel yelled at the soldiers on deck. The *Tyler* and *Lexington* then opened fire with their bow guns, throwing an occasional shell into the riverbanks. The first shells plunged into the rebel gunners, plowing a lane through their ranks. Then the gunboats let go with broadsides. From the pilothouse, Walke watched as a shell sped toward an enemy gun crew, just as the rebel gunner was about to pull the lanyard. It burst under the gun carriage, killing the gunner and several other soldiers and tossing debris into the air.

Three miles or so upriver the gunboats hove to, waiting for Buford's regiment to come up. The exhausted soldiers, their faces blackened by powder, sat on the decks of the transports. Most had removed their overcoats before the battle and had left their blankets in the fields, so there was little available to cover the wounded. The boys placed their injured comrades gently on deck, where they moaned or cried out for water.

When the transport *Chancellor* came alongside, McClernand boarded the *Tyler*. The general's horse had been shot out from under him three times, but he appeared cool and collected. He informed Walke that they had left some of the boys behind and asked him to go back and find them. The *Tyler* and *Lexington* immediately headed downriver and found the soldiers on the Missouri shore. A correspondent explained to readers what had happened: "Colonel Buford informed me that when he heard the firing at the landing, he took the road which led from the enemy to a point farther up the river, and under the protection of the gunboats. The officers and men of this portion of the army, say that the shot for the gunboats, after passing through the enemy's rank, almost reached our cavalry, but none of our people were hurt, though forcibly apprised of the danger of being intercepted by the Confederate army."[50]

At about 6:00 the *Lexington* began taking some of the men of the 27th Illinois on board. It was joined by the *Tyler*, which loaded more of the soldiers and about forty prisoners. Some were badly wounded, and the *Tyler*'s sailors tried to alleviate their suffering, furnishing them with their own hammocks and bedding. At 7:30 the *Lexington* took off a number of cavalry from the *Chancellor*. Then both gunboats headed upriver, convoying the remaining transports part of the way to Cairo. The *Tyler* landed at the head of Island No. 1, where it remained until morning. By then, the *Lexington* had also returned to Cairo and put the troops ashore.[51]

The federal expedition to Belmont proved to be a less than all-out attempt to take the Confederate stronghold and move decisively down the Mississippi. As one historian aptly wrote, "it turned out to be a big raid." On November 7 Commander Perry wired Foote in St. Louis that the *Lexington* and *Tyler* had accompanied Grant's forces, which had taken rebel batteries at Belmont. "The loss on both sides is great," Perry told Foote. "The gunboats did their duty." In his report to Welles, composed two days after the battle, Foote acknowledged that the gunboats had rendered effective service and had covered the final retreat with "well directed fire of grape and canister, mowing down the enemy, [and] prevent[ing] our troops from being almost, if not entirely, cut to pieces." Foote had every reason to be pleased with the gunboats' contribution, but he was disappointed that neither Grant nor Walke nor Stembel had telegraphed him and informed him of the gunboats' participation in the expedition. Foote explained to Welles that, in his haste to get the expedition off, Grant had forgotten to wire Foote. This incident highlighted Foote's difficulty equipping, manning, and fitting out the "army's navy," or the Western Gunboat Flotilla, at his present rank of captain. He had previously shared these concerns with Fox, but following the battle of Belmont he wrote to Welles and stated that he needed the rank of flag officer to give him "immunity from the orders of brigadier general down to lieutenant colonel who are inexperienced in the naval matters."[52]

In his memoir, Walke insisted that Foote never sent Welles a report of the role played by the gunboats. Not all Walke's fellow officers failed to appreciate the gunboats' contribution to the battle of Belmont. Phelps wrote to his mentor, Whittlesey, "There the gunboats opened a most destructive fire and cut up the enemy in a most terrible manner. Whole regiments were swept away, while our force had [an] opportunity to embark. On the opposite side of the river too, above Columbus, the gunboats had fired with destructive effect on the men in the rebel lines & fortifications."[53]

Although both Confederate and Yankee newspapers hailed the battle of Belmont as a victory for their side, in the final analysis, the credit went to Grant. Northern newspapers criticized him for a costly, meaningless fight, but others conceded that, despite making some tactical mistakes, Grant had certainly proved himself a calm, decisive leader who was able to improvise in adversity. Although a costly battle in terms of killed and wounded, Belmont gave the Union control of Missouri and prompted alarm in the South over future Union amphibious operations. In his study of Grant, Bruce Catton noted that Belmont gave the general "an unbounded confidence in the fighting capacity of Volunteers." For his part, Grant's official report complimented Walke and Stembel and gave credit to the gunboats that had "convoyed the expedition, and rendered most efficient service. Immediately upon our landing they engaged the enemy's batteries on the heights above Columbus, and protected our transports throughout." In the future, Grant would have far greater confidence in the brown-water navy.[54]

2

USS *Carondelet* and Fort Henry

It will, besides, have a moral effect upon our troops to advance toward the rebel states.

—Ulysses S. Grant

The *Tyler* and *Lexington* remained on picket duty, at anchor off Fort Holt, for some time after the battle of Belmont. In November the *Conestoga* made numerous incursions up the Cumberland and Tennessee Rivers, occasionally encountering pesky rebel sharpshooters. However, the weeks following the battle of Belmont brought little action for Walke and the *Tyler*.[1]

The *Tyler*'s officers and men spent the Christmas season anchored in the river. To Walke's annoyance, musket fire from soldiers posted at Fort Holt forced him to change the *Tyler*'s position repeatedly, but that did not prevent a minié ball from striking one of the ship's guns and glancing in the porthole; another hit the upper deck. The normally even-tempered Walke complained to Foote. The following day, however, Walke reported that three balls passed over the deck, barely missing the officer of the deck; one ball struck the water near a seaman who was outside washing his hammock.[2]

New Year's Eve found Walke in Cairo alone. Phelps's wife and daughter had joined him for the holidays, but Walke's wife Jane did not make the long trip west, preferring to stay in Staten Island with her family. The new year would bring Walke a new command—a squat gunboat dubbed a "Pook turtle" for its ungainly shape. Christened the USS *Carondelet* after the St. Louis shipyard where it was built, Walke's ship was one of seven new city-class ironclad gunboats designed to be the backbone of Foote's Western

Gunboat Flotilla. In his memoir, Walke hinted at his reaction to this new assignment: "When the 'Carondelet' was given to Captain Walke, she was considered the least desirable one of the plated boats; but Walke had, however, in this instance, good reason to be thankful and satisfied, as the vessel proved a most successful craft, though not as fast a boat as the other gunboats of her class." On January 1, 1862, Foote's Western Gunboat Flotilla included the flagship *Benton;* the ironclad gunboat *Essex;* the city-class ironclad gunboats *Carondelet, Louisville, Mound City, Cincinnati, Cairo, Pittsburg,* and *St. Louis;* and the timberclads *Conestoga, Lexington,* and *Tyler.* Walke recalled, "They proved, however, invaluable on the Mississippi, as they had already been found to be most serviceable on smaller rivers, such as the Tennessee and Cumberland, where, on account of shoals, the heavier boats could not at all times navigate."[3]

With the commissioning of the new city-class ironclads, Foote would have the force necessary to support Grant's army as it advanced into the Confederate heartland. McClellan, who had replaced Scott as general in chief in November, had been training and preparing his Army of the Potomac to take the offensive in Virginia, but he had also turned his attention to Union operations in the West. He and President Lincoln preferred a major operation in eastern Tennessee, where Unionists had attacked Confederate outposts and burned five railroad bridges in November. Hoping to encourage pro-Union sentiment and sever a vital east-west Confederate rail line between Virginia and Memphis, Lincoln urged McClellan to pressure Buell into attacking east Tennessee. Citing poor roads and winter weather, Buell declined, claiming that a move against Nashville was a better option. In early January 1862 Lincoln wired Halleck and Buell about cooperating on an advance on Nashville, but Halleck insisted that his troops were not ready and claimed to have no knowledge of Buell's plans. In January Buell sent troops under the command of Brigadier General George H. Thomas toward Tennessee, and they clashed with rebel forces in eastern Kentucky and won a victory near Mills Springs. However, Buell argued that he needed better logistical support before attempting to secure east Tennessee.[4]

In the meantime, preparations proceeded to complete the city-class ironclads and put them into service. In his memoirs, Walke described the *Carondelet:* "She was 150 feet long, and drew seven feet of water. The sides and casemate were built to the water line at an angle of about 45 deg with the level of the gun decks, which was about a foot above the water, and covered with casemate to the curve of the bow and stern, enclosing the wheel, with all her machinery; three ports in the bow, four on each broadside, and two in the stern." An article in the *New York Times* pointed out the gunboat's vulnerability to enemy shot and shell: "The boats are not plated on the roof, which consists of 2½ plank. Of course a shot falling upon this deck, even at an acute angle, would go through, and a heavy shell so entering would blow up the boat, but the chances of this occurring are not as one in a thousand."[5]

In the first gun division, *Carondelet* had three guns in the bow—two old 42-pounder rifled guns, and one 64-pounder of the oldest pattern. The gunboat's broadside batteries consisted of two 42-pounders (rifled), two 64-pounders, and four light 32-pounders; its stern battery consisted of two light 32-pounders. Walke noted that at least four of the thirteen guns were of heavy caliber "and threw a shell a great distance with extraordinary precision; but unfortunately they were weak in the 'reinforce,' and exploded too easily to be reliable." According to the *New York Times,* "The gunboats are intended in action, to be kept bows on hence the superior strength of the bow battery. Broadsides can be delivered with terrible effect while shifting position." The ironclad's five coal-fired boilers fed two horizontal high-pressure steam engines that turned two paddle wheels amidship, giving the vessel a speed of between four and nine knots.[6]

Even those among the *Carondelet*'s crew who had spent time on riverboats had never seen such an odd vessel. The Pook turtle had a broad, flat bottom; bulwarks that ran along its upper deck shoulder high; and a pilothouse situated forward near the bow, just in front of the stacks that vented smoke from the fireboxes and hot gases from the boilers. A wheelhouse or unarmored casing surrounded the paddle wheel, and beneath the pilothouse was the galley. The captain's cabin was situated aft on the upper deck, above the engine room and shell rooms. The gunboat's designer had divided a large cabin into two staterooms for the captain, two mess rooms, and four tiny, two-person staterooms for the junior officers. Each stateroom had a berth, a bureau, and a washstand. Master's mates, carpenters, and assistant engineers shared the lower deck with the enlisted men, who slept in hammocks slung on the gun deck or, weather permitting, on the deck under awnings.[7]

For Foote, the *Carondelet*'s commissioning was the culmination of many long, frustrating months of trying to expedite the construction of the new ironclad gunboats. "Weary days are my lot . . . this fitting out vessels where no one knows anything is discouraging," he wrote to his wife.[8] The contracts for the gunboats had been let back in early August, with every intention that they would be completed in sixty-five days—an optimistic schedule if there ever was one. Despite the employment of 4,000 workers from seven midwestern states toiling day and night in the Mound City and St. Louis yards, construction of the seven gunboats met obstacle after obstacle. Shipwrights threatened to strike for more money; the suppliers of the engines, gun carriages, and iron plate proved unreliable. But on October 12, 1861, the first two gunboats, the *St. Louis* and the *Carondelet,* slid down the ways, followed within weeks by the rest.[9]

Finding crews to man the new gunboats proved a daunting task. Just weeks short of their commissioning, Foote lamented the difficulty of filling out his crews. He told Fox that unless 1,000 men were sent from the East immediately, he would have to employ men from various army regiments. Foote had asked Halleck for volunteer soldiers, he told Fox, not for officers. "We want men to fight the guns and work the boats."[10]

The navy might have been short on manpower for the western waters, but as Foote fully realized, the army had plenty of recruits. In January 1862, 10,000 federal soldiers had converged on the city of Cairo. Assigned to Grant's regiments, the soldiers thronged the streets, shopping in the stores for little luxuries and medicines to take back to camp.

With Foote's concurrence and the support of the gunboat flotilla, Grant had decided to take the offensive, press up the Tennessee and Cumberland Rivers, take Forts Henry and Donelson, and then cut the Memphis and Ohio Railway bridge, severing lateral communication between Confederate generals Polk and Hardee. When Grant met with Halleck on January 6, 1862, however, Halleck rejected the plan. Grant wrote, "I was cut short as if my plan was preposterous. I returned to Cairo very much crestfallen."[11]

Once aboard the *Carondelet,* Walke had an opportunity to look over his officers and crew. When the new gunboat had its full complement, it would be home to 17 officers and 175 men. But Foote had been able to send only 60 men to each of the gunboats while he awaited the 1,000 men promised by the War Department. They were a motley group of bluejackets; some were surly steamboat hands from the western rivers, and others were freshwater sailors recruited on the Great Lakes. The *Carondelet*'s crew included many Irish as well as a few Scots and some French, Germans, and Swedes. Looking at the men's faces, Walke realized that the majority of his sailors were very young. Most came from Philadelphia or Boston, and few had any shipboard experience. In civilian life they had been blacksmiths, brewers, machinists, teachers, or farmers. Fortunately, the *Carondelet* had just enough older men to leaven the ship with naval discipline. The *Carondelet*'s first master, forty-six-year-old Richard M. Wade, was an experienced riverboat captain. Before the war he had served on several river steamers and had commanded the wooden stern-wheeler *Mansfield* in 1854, plying the Ohio and Mississippi Rivers for the U.S. Mail Line.[12]

By January 16, 1862, all seven of the new Pook turtles—*St. Louis, Carondelet, Cairo, Cincinnati, Louisville, Mound City,* and *Pittsburg*—had been put into commission. Lacking sufficient power, the larger sixteen-gun *Benton* would be commissioned later. In an effort to get the new ironclads into service, they had received whatever armament was available.[13]

As commander of the Western Gunboat Flotilla, Foote was responsible for selecting commanders for the newly commissioned gunboats. He had promised Phelps command of the *Cairo,* but when a more senior officer, Lieutenant Nathaniel Bryant, showed up, he had to renege. The other commanders were Roger Stembel on the *Cincinnati,* Lieutenant Commander Leonard Paulding on the *St. Louis,* Commander Benjamin M. Dove on the *Louisville,* Commander Augustus H. Kilty on the *Mound City,* and Lieutenant Egbert Thompson on the *Pittsburg.* Thirty-six-year-old Paulding, the son of Rear Admiral Hiram Paulding, had risen from midshipman in 1841 to lieutenant in 1855. Also a career naval officer, Dove had entered the navy as a midshipman in 1826 but had been court-martialed twice and dismissed from the service; he had been reinstated in 1841 by President Tyler. A native of Annapolis, Maryland, Kilty had also been a midshipman, serving in the West India and East India Squadrons; after being promoted to commander he was put on the retired list in 1855, only to return to service four years later as a recruiting officer. Thompson, who had been promoted to lieutenant in 1850, followed a similar career path: he was a veteran of the Mexican War, had been a midshipman on the brig *Somers,* and had served on several steam warships, including the iron-hulled *Michigan,* and just prior to the war on the steam sloop *Powhatan.* All seven officers went on to notable service as ironclad captains. A bitterly disappointed Phelps gained Foote's promise that he would command the newly constructed *Benton.*[14]

The *Conestoga* had spent early January steaming up the Cumberland River looking for Confederate activity. The *Conestoga*'s energetic captain had discovered the industrious rebels perfecting their defenses at both Dover and Fort Henry. They had a large force of African Americans working on these defenses, which included four 32-pounders mounted on a hill. Phelps cautioned Foote that it was too late to move against the work on either the Tennessee or Cumberland River unless he had a "well appointed and powerful naval force." The federal gunboat continued down to Columbus but found neither mines nor obstacles in the river within range of the Confederate works. Two days later, Foote cautioned Phelps not to expose his vessel to enemy fire, explaining that a larger force would be sent up the Tennessee. Although Foote urged secrecy as to the expedition's planned target, the Confederates guessed that federal forces would advance on Fort Henry. When the *Essex* and *St. Louis* went downriver, the rebels sent three gunboats up from Columbus to confront them, and a brisk twenty-minute engagement ensued. The two new Union navy gunboats drove the rebels back, and the *Essex*'s commanding officer, William D. Porter, claimed to have disabled one of the Confederate vessels.[15]

Grant had spent much of the month in Cairo, at Union headquarters in the Safford's Bank building, anxiously awaiting word from Halleck about an operation to take Fort Henry. Sketching out his plan in fuller detail, Grant explained to Halleck that if he took Fort Henry on the Tennessee River, that would make it easier to operate on the Cumberland River or against Memphis or Columbus. "It will, besides, have a moral effect upon our troops to advance toward the rebel states," Grant pointed out. Nudged by Buell to accept Grant's strategic plan, McClellan finally ordered Halleck to perform a reconnaissance up the two rivers. The results only strengthened Grant's conviction that an attack on Fort Henry was a practical move. Foote backed him up and, sensing a potential victory and a possible promotion, the reluctant Halleck finally agreed. On January 30, 1862, he sent Grant a telegram: "Make preparations to take and hold Fort Henry, I will send you written instructions by mail."[16]

Halleck may have been swayed by an alarming wire from McClellan, informing him that Confederate general Beauregard had departed for Kentucky with fifteen infantry regiments. The report proved erroneous—Beauregard was accompanied by only a few officers—but Confederate authorities knew that if Union forces took Forts Henry and Donelson, then their entire defensive line in Kentucky would be outflanked. Additional orders from Halleck told Grant to attack Fort Henry with all his available forces from Smithfield, Paducah, Fort Holt, and Bird's Point. Because of the poor roads in the area, Grant was instructed to move his troops by boat, escorted by Foote's vessels, and land them below the fort. Then, Halleck said, he should send cavalry forward to the railroad and render it impassable, but keep the railroad bridges intact.[17]

That same day, Phelps went to the headquarters of Brigadier General Lewis Wallace, who commanded a brigade slated to make the attack. Phelps informed the general that he was going up the Tennessee in the *Conestoga* to make one last reconnaissance before the assault on Fort Henry, and he invited Wallace to accompany him. Wallace agreed, noting in his memoirs that he thought "the experience would be novel. I could see somewhat of sailor life under unusual conditions." The following morning Wallace was rowed out to the *Conestoga,* anchored in midstream. As the launch pulled alongside the timberclad, Wallace recalled, "I remember not more of her than that she was flat bottomed, very broad, and black all over; that her upper deck was in the style of a sea-goer, with bulwarks up to my shoulder; and there was a great gun on her bow, and that the pilothouse, and commander's quarters were on the upper deck." The general later remarked on "the exceeding whiteness of that deck planking, the stealthy silence of the ships going, and the cheerfulness with which everybody on board went about his duty."[18]

The gunboat got under way the following morning, and Wallace accompanied Phelps as he made his rounds. Two men stationed at either side of the bow did not come to attention when the officers arrived, but kept looking over the bulwark. Wallace inquired, "Why are we going slow?" Phelps explained that they were in a torpedo zone, and the two men were searching the river for signs of what had become known as "those infernal machines." Phelps, Wallace remembered, "whipped out a long binocular hanging strapped to his shoulder, and making it ready, followed the shore slowly." He then announced, "Soldiers, mounted, and going full speed. If the enemy is not already notified of our coming, he will be." As the gunboat moved into the main stream, they could make out the fort, built on low ground. The *Conestoga* slowed, then stopped. "I am satisfied," Phelps said to Wallace. "There is one large gun newly mounted—the third one from the water battery." Turning to the wheelhouse, Phelps waved his hand, and the *Conestoga* dropped behind the screen of Panther Island and headed back.[19]

On the *Carondelet,* Walke waited impatiently for orders to move ahead. For two weeks he had drilled his crew while workmen put the finishing touches on the new ironclad gunboat. However, concealing the departure of thousands of troops from prying eyes proved difficult. Soon the ever-curious journalists and most of the bluejackets knew the expedition's objective. "The grand expedition up the Tennessee and Cumberland rivers is about to start!" a reporter for the *Chicago Tribune* wrote, claiming that a 22,000-man force would attack Forts Henry and Donelson. At long last, on February 1, a message arrived from Foote directing Walke to take the *Carondelet* to Paducah the next morning.[20]

Back in Cairo, Grant and his staff had been pushing ahead with preparations for the operation. On his headquarters boat, the *W. H. Brown*, Grant paced the deck, a cigar clamped tightly in his mouth. Grant had ordered McClernand to have his men ready to move out on February 2 with three days' rations; he had told Brigadier General C. F. Smith to advance with a brigade from Paducah and all the troops at Smithfield, leaving behind one battalion of his choice and the 52nd Illinois to counter any Confederate raids on the town.[21]

Foote issued orders for the attack, which included very detailed instructions to his captains to make sure that the hoods covering the gratings of the hatches at the bow and stern were taken off. "Otherwise," Foote argued, "great injury will result from the concussion of guns firing." Foote's order called for the gunboats to attack the fort in a parallel line; by following the flagship's movements, he explained, "it will be difficult for the enemy to get an accurate range of the gunboats." The flagship would open fire first, and the others would follow. "There must be no firing until correct sights can be obtained, as this would not only be throwing away ammunition, but would encourage the enemy to see us firing wildly and harmlessly at the fort." Random firing, Foote insisted, "encourages the enemy to greater resistance. The great object is to dismount the guns in the fort by the accuracy of our fire." But he cautioned the commanders to avoid hitting their own troops.[22]

Capitalizing on Phelps's experience on the Tennessee and Cumberland Rivers, Foote assigned him to command the unarmored gunboat division (*Conestoga, Tyler,* and *Lexington*), which would take a position astern of his own division of four armored gunboats. As day broke on February 2, the *Cincinnati, Carondelet, Essex, St. Louis,* and *Lexington* slipped out of Cairo and headed for Paducah. Foote followed in the timberclad *Tyler,* arriving that evening. The army transports had not yet arrived from Cairo, which was a cause for concern because, as Foote told Welles on February 3, "the river is falling." He also informed the secretary, "I proceed up the Tennessee early in the morning, and will there make the *Cincinnati* my flagship." In a postscript, Foote noted that several transports had just arrived.[23]

Grant had hoped to go south on February 2 as well, but delays had dogged his departure. He did not set off from Cairo until the next evening, visibly relieved that Halleck had not called off the operation.[24] At Paducah, Grant and his staff conferred with McClernand and Smith. Short on transports, they directed McClernand's division to a position just below Fort Henry that night. The soldiers would land on the right bank, and the transports would return to Paducah for Smith's division.[25]

Foote's gunboats, including the *Carondelet,* had already gone up the swollen Tennessee River, which had not yet overflowed its banks. All along the shore, Walke could see African Americans waving, shouting, and dancing with glee at the sight of the federal gunboats. In the afternoon, however, a steady southwest wind came up; then rain began pelting the gunboat's sloping sides.

Tuesday, February 4, 1862, dawned clear. From the pilothouse, Walke could see all of Foote's vessels anchored seven miles or so below Fort Henry. Later in the day, Walke and Wade watched the other transports delivering McClernand's soldiers. In the meantime, Grant had boarded the *Essex* and steamed upriver with the *St. Louis* and *Cincinnati* to the head of Panther Island to reconnoiter the fort.

On board the *Carondelet,* Walke and his officers and crew could only wait. When Foote's gunboats returned, word of their encounter with the fort's batteries spread quickly. The *Essex, St. Louis,* and *Cincinnati* had opened fire on the Confederate works, which returned the favor. The *New York Daily Tribune* reported, "During a brisk fire between the gunboats and the fort, the enemy used five guns, only one of them, a rifled 24-pounder, reaching the boats." One shell struck the *Essex* and passed "over the spar deck among the officers, through the officers' quarters, visiting in its flight the steerage, commander's pantry and cabin, passing through the stern, doing, however, no damage except breaking some of the captain's dishes, and cutting the feet from a pair of his socks." "Good shooting that," Porter supposedly remarked. "Now we will show them ours." After firing a few more shells, Foote took his gunboats back downriver, and Grant ordered his troops to reboard the transports to be landed at a safer location, Fisher's Landing, opposite the town of Buffalo, Kentucky.[26]

The *Carondelet*'s crew occupied themselves that afternoon with building wooden barricades around the boilers to protect them from enemy shot and shell. According to a *New York Times* reporter, the gunboats also hooked up large hose pipes to spray hot water from the boilers on any unsuspecting rebel boarders.[27]

Crews of the gunboats also had to contend with debris in the river, which had been swollen by heavy rains. The rapid current had sent quantities of driftwood, fences, and lumber downstream and had torn torpedoes, or mines, from their moorings. "They floated down the river in great numbers. The torpedoes were first discovered by the 'lookout' of the 'Carondelet,' then anchored in advance of our fleet," Walke recalled.[28] When Foote inspected the *Carondelet,* Walke reported the presence of the mines, and Foote observed even more of them floating past upon his return to the *Cincinnati.* He promptly sent Phelps upriver with the *Tyler* and *Lexington* to drag for mines. Using special cutters, they brought up six wet, useless mines. The following day, Phelps's boats shelled the fort, sounded the channel, and searched for mines, finding two more.[29]

That night, the distant sound of thunder warned of an approaching storm. When the storm hit, heavy downpours caused the river to rise even higher, and the *Carondelet*'s engine room crew worked frantically to keep pressure up in the boilers so the paddle wheel would prevent the anchors from dragging. Others spent the evening trying to shove heavy timbers away from the *Carondelet*'s bow, fearing they might stove in the hull. From the deck, Walke watched flashes of lightning illuminate the driftwood, lumber, fences, and trees careening past in the swollen, swirling river. Tomorrow they would attack Fort Henry. If, after a long night of fending off timber and flotsam, his weary crew could muster enough energy, Walke was confident they would do their duty.[30]

Morning dawned cloudy, with a light fog. Suddenly, a cry from a lookout roused the *Carondelet*'s crew, exhausted and disheartened by a long, sleepless night spent trying to keep the gunboat from drifting. "This adversity appeared to dampen the ardor of our crew," Walke recalled, "but when the next morning they saw a large number of white objects, which through the fog looked like polar bears, coming down the stream, and ascertained that they were the enemy's torpedoes forced from their mooring by the powerful current, they took heart, regarding the freshlet as providential and a presage of victory." They also heaved a sigh of relief, for "if the torpedoes had not been disturbed, or had broken loose at night while we were shoving the driftwood from our bows, some of them would surely have exploded near or under our vessels."[31]

Later in the morning, just before 10:00, Foote summoned his captains to the flagship *Cincinnati.* Walke took his gig over to the flagship, where he was joined by Stembel, Phelps, Porter, William Gwin, J. W. Shirk, and

Leonard Paulding. The always pious Foote looked tired, having spent the night praying for victory, but he gathered his commanders in the wardroom and delivered a pep talk. As Walke explained it, the plan conceived by Grant and Foote called for federal troops and naval forces to attack Fort Henry simultaneously on February 6, 1862. The ironclads *Essex, Cincinnati, Carondelet,* and *St. Louis,* with the wooden gunboats *Tyler, Lexington,* and *Conestoga* in reserve, would "attack the enemy from the river while the land forces under General Grant marched around to attack it in the rear." When Walke and the other captains left the wardroom to return to their vessels, Foote extended his hand to each man and prayed for God to look after them.[32]

Below the fort, McClernand's division stood poised to advance. Heavy rains had turned the roads to mud, but at about 11:00 he gave the order to march. Noting the muddy roads, Foote turned to Grant and made a bold promise: "General, I shall have the fort in my possession before you get into your position."[33]

At 10:50 a.m. the *Carondelet*'s wheel began to churn, and the ironclad moved ahead in line, abreast with the *St. Louis* and *Essex* on the right and the *Cincinnati* on the left. All but the *Essex* were identical, with a different colored band painted on the smokestacks of each to identify them. Phelps's three timberclad gunboats, also ranged abreast, followed them, steaming upriver toward the west channel. Walke took his place in the *Carondelet*'s pilothouse, where he could observe the river and the other vessels. For a time, Panther Island hid the approaching gunboats from the Confederates' view. It was deathly quiet. "As we slowly passed up this narrow stream, not a sound could be heard nor a living object seen in the dense woods which overhung the dark and swollen river," Walke recalled. "The gun crews of the 'Carondelet' stood silent at their posts, impressed with the serious and important character of the service before them." Walke had ordered the gunboat's four 8-inch Dahlgren smoothbore guns and the two stern guns manned, just in case he needed to deliver a broadside, but the bow guns would fire first.[34]

Foote had issued specific orders for the bombardment of the fort. His battle plan called for the dismounting of the fort's guns "by the accuracy of our fire." He told his commanders they might occasionally throw a shell into the rebel troops but to take care they did not fire on their own men. Remembering Foote's instructions, Walke reminded his gunners not to waste ammunition and then told the *Essex*'s James Laning, in charge of the gun battery, to make every shot count. According to Foote, every charge fired from one of the guns "costs the government about eight dollars."[35]

As Walke remembered it, "About noon, the fort and the Confederate flag came suddenly into view, the barracks, the new earth-works, and the great guns well manned. The captains of our guns were men-of-wars men, good shots, and had their men well drilled." When they came to within 1,700 yards of Fort Henry, Foote told Stembel to give the order to open fire. The *Cincinnati*'s bow guns barked out the first round, followed by those of the other three ironclads. "At once the fort was ablaze with the flame of her eleven heavy guns. The wild whistle of their rifle-shells was heard on every side of us," Walke wrote.[36]

"The battle commenced soon after dinner, and was ended in an hour and twenty minutes," A. J. Sypher, an officer on board the *St. Louis,* wrote to his brother, the editor of the *Lancaster Daily Evening Express:* "The fire was opened at twenty-five hundred yards from the fort; the boats moved steadily forward until within six or eight hundred yards of the enemy's stronghold, and at that distance all the power of the little fleet was brought to bear, and the shot and shell, quick and sharp, rattled down on the heads of the defending rebels." According to Sypher, "On the *Carondelet* not a word was spoken more than at ordinary drill, except when Matthew Arthur, captain of the starboard bow-gun, asked permission to fire at one or two of the enemy's retreating vessels, as she could not at that time bring his gun to bear on the fort." Arthur fired one shot, "which passed through the upper cabin of a hospital-boat, whose flag was not seen but injured no one."[37]

When the *Carondelet*'s bow guns fired, whiffs of acrid smoke drifted back over the pilothouse. Then the roar of the guns from both the gunboats and the fort increased, drowning out any other sounds, and thick smoke from the rebels' 10-inch and rifled 24-pounder gun batteries enveloped the boats. The *Carondelet*'s gunners, their faces blackened by the powder, doffed their coats as they worked the guns and strained to see the target.[38]

Daniel Weaver, the *Carondelet*'s pilot, rang the bell to go ahead, but the gunboat moved astern and, falling back, locked with the *St. Louis.* Realizing that the bell lines had been reversed and he had rung the wrong bell, Weaver corrected his mistake. The *Carondelet* moved forward, and the two boats parted, firing all the while. Shells began to strike the *Carondelet*'s bow plating; one carried away the hammock nettings, and another shell took part of the port awning stanchion. More hits followed as rebel gunners got the range, hitting the *Carondelet* a total of nine or ten times. To Walke's great relief, they suffered not one casualty. The *Carondelet* expended 101 shells and one solid shot during the bombardment of the fort.[39]

Shells splashed all around Foote's gunboats, but the rebel gunners concentrated on the flag officer's pennant flying on the *Cincinnati.* One shell struck the flagship, but as the range decreased, the rebels set their sights on the *Essex,* which then bore the brunt of the attack. Confederate shells struck the vessel more than a dozen times; one came through the side forward port, continued through a heavy bulkhead, and burst in the center boiler. The rush of escaping steam scalded several crewmen and entered the pilot-house, instantly killing pilots Ford and Bride. They were discovered later, when the steam had escaped, scalded to death in position. Ford was still at the wheel, his left hand holding the spoke and his right hand grasping the signal bell rope. Acting master's mate S. B. Brittan Jr. was standing on the gun deck when a shot struck the top of his head, scattering his brains in every direction. Injured by the explosion, Commander Porter flung himself out a porthole and into the water. He was saved by the quick action of a seaman, who held him up until another man could hoist the commander to the guard rail and into the boat. "I'm injured, Mr. Laning," Porter reportedly muttered to the second master. "Find First Mate Riley. If he, too, is disabled, take over the ship, Mr. Laning." Fortunately, Riley was unharmed and took command as the *Essex,* hit repeatedly, drifted downstream.[40]

The *St. Louis* escaped damage, despite taking five hits. As Sypher wrote, the only casualty was "the knocking down of one of the pilots by a splinter torn from the pilot-house; but he got up again in a few minutes without a scratch, and stood at his post." Sypher praised the *St. Louis*'s captain, Leonard Paulding. "During the whole time of the fight he was at the side of the gunners or standing on one of the starboard guns, very much exposed, where he could see the effect of every shot and direct his men accordingly; it is therefore not surprising that the rebels complimented the good shooting of the *St. Louis,* and were appalled at its havoc."[41]

Foote's flagship did not fare as well as the others. Confederate shells rained down on the *Cincinnati,* smashing chimneys, the after cabin, and all the boats. Enemy fire also disabled two guns, and one shot pierced the casemate shield, killing one sailor and wounding eight others, two seriously. "I happened to be looking at the flag-steamer when one of the enemy's heavy shot struck her," Walke recalled. "It had the effect, apparently of a thunder bolt, ripping her side-timbers and scattering splinters over the vessel. She did not slacken her speed, but moved on as though nothing unexpected had happened." Walke credited the Confederate gunners, who "had the advantage of practicing on the ranges the gunboats would probably occupy as they approached the Fort." Foote's gunboats, he explained, were better protected by their casemates from distant firing than was the fort by its fresh earthworks.[42]

The cost to Foote's gunboats proved minor compared with the cost to the rebel gunners. Federal shells slammed into the fort's earthworks, and one of their rifled guns burst, killing the entire crew. Before the federal attack even commenced, the fort's commander, Brigadier General Lloyd Tilghman, had expressed doubts that Fort Henry, poorly situated at the level of the now flooded river, could be successfully defended. So he ordered all but a hundred artillerymen from the garrison and sent them across a neck of land to Fort Donelson. Just after 1:30 p.m., when Tilghman learned that the majority of his command had gotten away, he ordered the white flag hoisted in surrender. Suspicious that the flag was a ruse, Foote held back and waited. Then, as Foote and Stembel watched, a small boat shoved off from below the fort and came alongside the flagship with a request for a conference.[43]

"A soon as the rebel flag was hauled down the boats moved rapidly forward," Sypher related to his brother. "The *St. Louis* was first at the landing; and volunteer-like we all struck for the shore, but Commodore Foote, very properly and promptly, ordered every man aboard, and commanded that no one be allowed to go ashore." The order to recall the boats that were already in midstream and headed for the landing was, Sypher wrote, "highly proper" and according to navy regulations, but the men felt it unjust. They believed that those who had fought so well and won such a brilliant victory should at least be allowed the privilege of viewing the work they had done.[44]

The *Cincinnati* and *Carondelet* steamed up and flanked the batteries, but just as the order came for the engines to be stopped, the *Carondelet* ran aground and the *Cincinnati* began to drift downstream. The incident remained clear in Walke's mind for years, and he wrote: "At first sight the 'Carondelet' appeared to be steaming ahead of the flag-officer, and Foote immediately hailed her commander, with a few sharp technicalities to keep his station, but the 'Carondelet' was immovable: sticking fast to the flats." The gunboat stubbornly remained in position ahead of the other boats, despite Walke's orders, and the engines could not back it off. An agitated Foote "came forward in haste, and trumpet in hand and called out again and again to stop the 'Carondelet' (unaware of the fact that his own vessel was all the time drifting down the river) until at last he gave up the undertaking in favor of a junior officer." The "poor fellow" proved quite inadequate to the task of moving the *Carondelet*. Happily, the gunboat finally slid off the bank into deep water.[45]

Anticipating a formal surrender, Foote sent Phelps and Stembel in a cutter to Fort Henry, where Tilghman met them onshore. "General Tilghman was a soldiery looking man, a little above medium height, with piercing black eyes and a resolute, intelligent expression of countenance," Walke recalled. "He was dignified and courteous, and won the respect and sympathy of all who became acquainted with him." The two naval officers went to the fort and raised the American flag. Leaving Phelps behind to take custody of the fort and the rebel prisoners, Stembel escorted Tilghman and his staff back to the *Cincinnati*.[46]

After greeting Tilghman, Foote sent for Walke and instructed him to take command of Fort Henry and hold it until Grant arrived. Entering the fort, Walke and a party of sailors from his ironclad found that "some of the cabins in the rear of the fort were still on fire," and they extinguished the flames. The men also discovered several of the *Essex*'s 9-inch shells lying unexploded in the rear of the cabins. "The first glance over the fort silenced all jubilant expressions of the victorious," Walke recalled, for the lifeless bodies and shattered implements of war gave the men pause. "Our eyes then met each other's gaze with a sadness, full of meaning, that forbade any attempt to speak, and, in the quietness like to that of a graveyard, we walked slowly over the desolate scene." Walke and his men also found a Confederate surgeon, coatless, tending to the wounded. Blood covered the dirt floor, and pieces of broken gun carriages littered the place. The bodies of two dead soldiers lay on the ground, almost covered by mounds of earth. Soon, federal cavalry arrived to take charge of the prisoners, and within the hour Grant himself entered Fort Henry. "General Grant, with his staff, rode into the fort about 3 o'clock on the same day," Walke wrote, "and relieved me of the command. The general and his staff then accompanied me on board the *Carondelet* (anchored near the fort), where he complimented the officers of the flotilla in the highest terms for the gallant manner in which they had captured Fort Henry." Grant had expected his troops to take part in the land attack, Walke explained, but heavy rains had made the roads to the fort almost impassable.[47]

In a wire to Halleck, Grant wrote: "Fort Henry is ours. The gunboats silenced the batteries before the investment was complete. I think the garrison must have commenced the retreat at night. Our cavalry followed, finding two guns abandoned in the retreat."[48]

When Grant arrived at the fort, Phelps returned to his gunboat and, following Foote's orders, led the three timberclads up the Tennessee River. Their mission was to seek out and destroy the railroad tracks on either side of the Memphis and Louisville Railroad bridge above the fort. Once that was accomplished, Phelps steamed upriver in search of any rebel vessels. As Walke watched them depart, a messenger arrived on the *Carondelet* with a note from Grant. "The party sent last night to destroy the railroad bridge found it guarded by rebel troops and came back," it read. Grant asked Walke to take twenty men and do the job. The *Carondelet* took on board a colonel named Webster, several of his officers, and two companies of sharpshooters. It then steamed up the Tennessee, and Walke landed the troops near the railroad bridge. They found the rebel camp deserted but destroyed the bridge.[49]

Meanwhile, the aggressive Phelps took the timberclads *Conestoga, Tyler,* and *Lexington* past the bridge, all the way to Florence. When they arrived at the railroad crossing, they found the drawbridge closed and the machinery to operate it disabled, so Phelps landed a party, and they managed to open the drawbridge. He then ordered men ashore to destroy a portion of the railroad track while he and Shirk pursued some escaping rebel gunboats. "In five hours this boat succeeded in forcing the rebels to abandon and burn three of their boats, loaded with military stores," Phelps explained. At Cerro Gordo, Tennessee, they found the half-finished steamer *Eastport* being converted by the rebels into a gunboat. Phelps told Gwin to remain with the *Tyler* and guard the *Eastport* while the *Lexington* and *Conestoga* continued up the river. On February 8, 1862, they seized two steamers and then went all the way to Florence, Alabama, at the foot of Muscle Shoals. "Coming in sight of the town, three steamers were discovered, which were immediately set on fire by the rebels," Phelps reported. He landed a party and seized some supplies marked "Fort Henry." Phelps assured the townspeople that since the bridge had no military importance, he would not destroy it. In the end, they took just three of the rebel steamers and one half-finished gunboat and went back downriver to the *Eastport*.[50]

Phelps's timberclads had enjoyed a successful cruise, and Walke longed for some recognition for his own boat. Happily, soon after the attack on Fort Henry, a messenger brought a letter from First Assistant Engineer

Charles Caven and Paymaster J. W. Nexsen regarding information obtained from one of the Confederate gunners. He had said, referring to the *Carondelet:* "The center boat, or the boat with the red stripes around the top of her smokestacks, was the boat which caused the greatest execution. It was one of her guns which threw a ball against the muzzle of one of our guns, disabling it for the remainder of the contest." The gunner claimed that the *Carondelet* "at each shot committed more damage than any other boat. She was the object of our hatred, and many a gun from the fort was leveled at her alone. To her I give more credit than any other boat in capturing one of our strongest places."[51]

Foote's gunboats had, in fact, pounded Fort Henry into surrendering; they had captured the Confederate works single-handedly, without the aid of Grant's troops. The federals had taken ninety-four prisoners of war, but as Grant and Foote soon learned, and as newspaper accounts confirmed, Tilghman had withdrawn most of his troops from the garrison before the battle began. Nonetheless, it was an impressive Union victory, the first of two that would force the Confederates to evacuate their strategic position at Columbus. The gunboats had broken the enemy line separating the Confederate troops at Columbus from those at Bowling Green, opening the Tennessee to further incursions by Foote's flotilla. Letters of congratulations from Lincoln, Halleck, Welles, Fox, and others poured in to Foote's flagship. The most candid came from Lieutenant H. A. Wise at the Bureau of Ordnance and Hydrography, who wrote, "We all went wild over your success, not unmixed with envy, when the news came of the reduction of Fort Henry. Uncle Abe was joyful—in his plain, sensible appreciation of merit and skill."[52]

Sypher wrote, "The battle commenced soon after dinner and was ended in an hour and twenty minutes, being a shorter time than it requires for a Southern nabob to eat his hog and hominy and drink his claret." Sypher concluded his piece with a story about one of the *Essex*'s badly injured sailors, who asked a comrade, "'Have the Stars and Stripes gone up yet over the fort?' When answered in the affirmative, he laid himself down saying, 'That is all I want, now I will die—and immediately expired."[53]

The Northern newspapers touted the victory over Fort Henry, but in the minds of the ironclads' officers and crew, the press did not fully credit the contribution of the *Carondelet* and the ironclads. One New York paper that scarcely mentioned the ironclads puffed up the role of what some dubbed the "western bandboxes"—*Conestoga, Lexington,* and *Tyler.* But as

Walke noted in his report, they had been astern of the *Carondelet* and the ironclads during the whole fight. To Walke's and his men's disappointment, the timberclads' adventure up the Tennessee had captured the Northern public's attention, for the country was starved for any positive news.[54]

3

Fort Donelson

Make your name famous in history by the capture of Fort Donelson and Clarksville. The taking of these places is military necessity.
—General Henry Halleck

Taking Fort Henry was just the first step, as Grant well knew. On February 8 he wired General Halleck that he intended to move on Fort Donelson. Heavy rains made the roads impassable, however, forcing Grant to wait. Furthermore, as Grant admitted in a letter to his wife Julia, he now commanded an army larger than Winfield Scott's in Mexico, and it needed far more logistical support than that required by a regiment or a division. Reinforcements had to be sent to Fort Henry from Paducah, and supplies had to be forwarded. In addition, reconnaissance had to be undertaken, which was made more difficult because Foote had sent his gunboats back to Cairo for repairs, leaving Grant with only one ironclad immediately available—the *Carondelet.*

Townspeople on the waterfront at Cairo had broken into cheers when Foote's returning boats appeared flying the Stars and Bars flag upside down. Word of the Union victory at Fort Henry had reached the town, but the crowds had gathered in suspenseful waiting, as news accounts were never trustworthy. Foote quickly sent the *Essex* and *Cincinnati* into the yards and hounded the workers to repair the damage suffered at Fort Henry.[1]

In St. Louis, Halleck received Grant's message. He too realized that with Fort Henry in Union hands, Fort Donelson had to be their next objective. Thirty miles up the Cumberland River from Donelson lay the town of Clarksville and a key railroad bridge that linked both wings of Johnston's

Confederate army. Fearing that the loss of Fort Donelson would trap his forces at Bowling Green, Johnston had moved his troops to Nashville, and two days before the attack on Fort Henry he had sent General Beauregard to take charge of Polk's force at Columbus. On February 10 Halleck wired Grant: "If possible destroy the bridge at Clarksville. Run any risk to accomplish this." The following day Halleck told Grant to send some gunboats up the river, and he wired Foote, "Make your name famous in history by the capture of Fort Donelson and Clarksville. The taking of these places is military necessity. Delay adds strength to them more than to us. Act quickly, even though only half ready." Foote then dashed off orders to Walke: "Run *Carondelet* and the timberclads up the Cumberland and take possession [of] the river, engage the enemy's attention, and prevent the rebels from reinforcing the fort."[2]

Walke took on coal in Paducah, and the *Carondelet,* towed by the *Alps,* proceeded slowly up the river. The gunboat arrived off the fort two days later. From the pilothouse deck, Walke could see the fort, built on a bluff some 120 feet above the Cumberland River where it bent slightly to the east. From that heavily armed fort, the Confederates could command the river and approaches to Nashville. In mid-January Johnston had ordered Brigadier General Gideon Pillow to take 5,000 men to Fort Donelson, but he had dallied until February 7. Brigadier General John B. Floyd was senior commander of the fort. "Fort Donelson occupied one of the best defensive positions on the river," Walke later wrote. Although a dusting of snow covered the hills and woods on the west side of the river, Walke could clearly see black rows of heavy guns pointing down on the gunboat. As ordered, at 12:50 p.m. the *Carondelet*'s bow guns fired into the fort to announce Walke's arrival to Grant and to unmask the enemy guns. All but one of the ten shells fell into the fort, yet the rebels made no response. An echo broke the silence, and the *Carondelet* went back downriver to anchor for the night.[3]

Grant and his staff had departed the previous day in the *Tigress* for Fort Donelson. When the steamer reached shore, they debarked and took one of the two roads leading from Fort Henry to Fort Donelson.[4] As the daylight dwindled, Grant and the lead columns reached the outskirts of Donelson. Grant intended to have his men encircle the fort, let Foote's boats bombard the rebels, and then move in. His intelligence sources had reported that the rebel defenses were weak, and with Pillow in command, Grant evidently did not anticipate any difficulty taking the fort. Unbeknownst to Grant, following Fort Henry's surrender, Johnston had ordered reinforcements sent to Fort Donelson, and some 10,000 Confederate troops were already on the march. To divert the enemy's attention, Grant ordered Walke to shell the Confederates.[5]

Walke received Grant's message on the morning of Thursday, February 13, a calm, spring-like day. The general explained that he had arrived the day before and had succeeded in positioning his forces to invest the enemy's works. He told Walke, "Most of our batteries are established, and the remainder soon will be. If you advance with your gunboats at 10 o'clock a.m., we will be ready to take advantage of every diversion in our favor."[6]

Immediately, under the cover of a heavily wooded point of land, the *Carondelet* approached Fort Donelson, and Walke gave the order to open fire with the 8-inch smoothbores, which could shoot a 52.7-pound shell a maximum of 2,600 yards at 11 degrees of elevation. The gunboat threw some 139 shells into the fort, which replied with all its batteries. Most of the shells passed over the *Carondelet,* but one 128-pound solid shot struck the gunboat's forward port casemate, glanced over the barricade at the boilers and over the steam drum, and burst in the steam heater before falling into the engine room. "When it burst through the side of the *Carondelet,*" Walke recalled, "it knocked down and wounded a dozen men, seven of them severely. An immense quantity of splinters was blown through the vessel. Some of them as fine as needles." The startled sailors shrieked, and some ran to aid their wounded comrades. "Several of the wounded were so much excited by the suddenness of the event and the suffering of their comrades," Walke wrote, "that they were not aware that they had been struck until they felt the blood running into their shoes."[7]

The *Carondelet* ceased firing and backed down, out of range of the rebel guns. Executive officer Wade had the men stand down to have their midday meal. He had already set the ship's carpenters and crew to repairing the damage to the ironclad, and after the meal Walke ordered the wounded taken to the *Alps.* When Walke heard distant firing, he ordered the *Carondelet* back to bombard the fort again. At dusk, with no more firing from shore, Walke called it a day. He retired to his cabin for the night, confident that when Foote and the other gunboats arrived, they would bombard Fort Donelson into submission, just as they had Fort Henry. Recalling the wrecked gun carriages and mangled bodies at Fort Henry following the federal bombardment, Walke may have concluded that earthen forts could not stand up to a naval attack. Unbeknownst to him, by February 13 the Confederates had reinforced the garrison at Fort Donelson with twenty-eight infantry regiments, one cavalry regiment, and enough soldiers to man six light batteries and seventeen heavy batteries of guns.[8]

That evening, as a heavy snow blanketed the riverbanks and dusted the *Carondelet*'s sloping deck, the *St. Louis, Louisville,* and *Pittsburg* and the timberclads *Tyler* and *Conestoga* arrived off Donelson. Already irritated, Foote became more anxious about the operation when he learned that Grant had not waited for his arrival and that the *Carondelet* had already begun bombarding the fort. Foote named Phelps acting fleet captain and instructed him to inspect both the *Pittsburg* and the *Carondelet* and direct their officers to conduct a short exercise to ensure that the gun crews could aim and fire properly.[9]

In preparation for the attack on Fort Donelson, the *Carondelet*'s crew dragged heavy articles such as chains, lumber, and bags of coal to the gunboat's upper decks and laid them out to protect the vessel from plunging enemy shot. They opened the magazines and piled up hammocks in exposed areas to act as barriers against rebel sniper fire. In the wardroom, "Cook" McBride and his "boys" prepared for the upcoming engagement, grinding enough coffee beans to make large kettles of a strong brew to keep the officers and men going.

The *Carondelet* weighed anchor at 2:00 p.m., and four abreast, the Pook turtles slowly steamed up to about a mile from the fort. Foote's wooden gunboats followed 1,000 yards astern. Seeing that the *Pittsburg* and *Louisville* were lagging behind, Foote hailed them with a megaphone and told them to "steam up." From the *Carondelet,* Walke and Wade watched as two enemy shots came toward the gunboat but fell short.[10]

When the *St. Louis* got within a mile of Fort Donelson, Foote ordered the ironclad to open fire, and the others followed suit. Walke's gunners began a slow, well-directed fire but soon picked up the pace. Striding back and forth on the flagship's deck and observing his boats carefully, Foote hailed the *Carondelet:* "Cease firing so fast." The gunners obediently slowed down, but they kept at it for more than two hours and remained, Walke noted, "cool and composed as old veterans" as the fort's batteries furiously returned fire. "We heard the deafening crack of the bursting shells, the crash of the solid shot, and the whizzing of fragments of shell and wood as they sped through the vessel."[11]

As the federal boats drew closer to the fort, the rebels' light batteries found the range. Shot and shell hit the *Carondelet,* and a 128-pounder landed smack on the anchor, smashing it into flying bolts; it then bounced over the gunboat, cutting the smokestack clean away. Another shot hit the boat davits and cut them away, dropping the boat into the river. Suddenly, one enemy shot struck the pilothouse, jamming the wheel and knocking the plating into pieces. A shower of iron fragments and splinters struck the pilots, and one of them fell mortally wounded. The volume of enemy fire only increased, ripping off the *Carondelet*'s flagstaffs and shearing off pieces of side armor.

The *Carondelet*'s crew fought desperately to keep themselves in the battle. Now just 500 yards from the fort, the gunboat had to elevate its guns to reach the enemy works situated above the level of the river. On the gun deck the crews sweated and strained, but as enemy fire increased, they began loading too hastily. At about 5:00 one of the rifled guns suddenly burst. "I was serving the gun with shell," one sailor recalled. "When it exploded it knocked us all down, killing none, but wounding over a dozen men and spreading dismay and confusion among us." Minutes passed before he realized he was "more scared than hurt, although suffering from the gunpowder which I had inhaled." When a cry rang out that the ship was on fire, he ran to the pumps. "While I was there, two shots entered our bow ports and killed four men and wounded several others. They were borne past me, three with their heads off." The *Carondelet*'s decks ran red with blood. The ship's carpenters dashed about plugging holes in the deck and sides, and the *Carondelet* "continued in line, or a little in advance, firing with her remaining two guns without intermission," Walke noted.[12]

Now within 400 yards of the fort, the ironclad took more pounding from the rebel guns, whose crews realized they were safe from all but a direct hit from the gunboat. "Our pilot house was struck again and another pilot wounded, our wheel was broken, and shell from the rear boats were bursting over us," Walke wrote. "All four of our boats were shot away and dragging in the water." Looking out to bring his broadside guns to bear, Walke saw the other gunboats retiring. The *St. Louis* and *Louisville* had been struck numerous times by enemy fire; their tiller ropes had been shot away when shells from their own rear boats burst over them. Both of them dropped out of the battle. One enemy shot had pierced the flag steamer's pilothouse, killing the pilot and wounding Foote. Unable to steer properly, Foote gave the order for the gunboats to retire at 4:15 p.m.

The *Pittsburg* and *Carondelet,* the latter leaking badly, continued to bombard the fort for another few minutes. Then, in its haste to get out of range of the fort, the *Pittsburg* collided with the *Carondelet,* breaking its starboard rudder. To clear the *Pittsburg* and a point of rocks below, Walke shouted, "Full steam ahead," and the gunboat churned toward the fort. "There was no alternative for the *Carondelet* in that narrow stream but to keep her head to the enemy and fire into the fort with her two bow-guns, to prevent it, if possible from returning her fire effectively." At that moment, the new acting gunner, John Hall, came forward and took charge of the starboard bow rifled gun. "He instructed the men to obey his warnings and follow his motions and he told them that when he saw a shot coming he would call out 'Down' and stoop behind the breech of the gun as he did so; at the same instant the men were to stand way from the bow ports." When the lookouts informed Walke that the flotilla was dropping out of the battle, he ordered the engines stopped and reversed. Walke later insisted that he would have steamed past the batteries had he not "so recently received the admonition not to precede the flag steamer, and as he had not received instructions to pass Fort Donelson, but to follow the motions of the flag-officer." The *Carondelet* then backed down the river, out of range of the fort's batteries, the last of Foote's gunboats to leave.[13]

Standing on the riverbank, Grant watched them withdraw and realized that Foote's boats had been beaten; they would be unable to go upstream and block the road from Dover to Clarksville. He decided to cancel the order for an advance on the right, move McClernand's men to the right to cover the road over the lowlands south of Dover, and bring up the fresh troops of Wallace's division. Grant feared that if the road remained open, then the Confederates might use it to withdraw from Fort Donelson. Accompanied by his aide, Grant returned to the farmhouse that served as his headquarters and sent Halleck's chief of staff a telegram. "Appearances indicate now that we will have a protracted siege here," it read. Grant explained that, given the Confederates' rout of Foote's gunboats and the difficult terrain, a frontal assault stood little chance of success. He would order up more ammunition and invest the works. He assured Halleck, "I feel great confidence . . . in ultimately reducing the place." Then he and his staff spent an anxious night huddled around the farmhouse's fireplace for warmth.[14]

As night fell, Walke retired to his cabin on board the *Carondelet*. The day had been a bitter disappointment and a costly one. The Pook turtles had been shot to pieces, and the flag steamer had suffered many casualties. Walke's losses were four seamen killed and twenty-eight wounded, including the pilot (perhaps mortally); Thomas Burns, the gun captain; John Doherty, the second master; John McBride, the ship's cook; and the quartermaster. Walke must have wondered why Foote had not concentrated on putting the rebels' long-range guns out of commission. Then he could have stood off and battered their 32-pounders at will. Most of their shot and shell had gone over the fort and fallen into their own lines, causing more damage to Union troops than to the Confederates. In his report to Welles, Foote called it a "hotly contested but unequal fight" and explained that the enemy had brought twenty guns to bear, whereas his four boats could return fire with only twelve bow guns. They had, however, driven the rebel gunners from their batteries, and in another fifteen minutes they might have captured the fort if two of his boats had not suffered disabled steering gear.[15]

Very early the next morning, February 15, a messenger arrived at Grant's headquarters with a note from Foote explaining that because of his injured foot, he could not ride a horse, and he asked if Grant would come down to the flag steamer to meet with him. Mounting his horse in the pale light, Grant, accompanied by just one orderly, rode to the landing. They passed the troops of the 20th Ohio, just emerging from a cold night spent in hastily made bivouacs, shaking themselves awake and pounding their arms to get warm. An occasional burst of musketry or a cannon firing could be heard. Trying to calm his orderly, Grant muttered, "Skirmishers, nothing more."[16]

On board the *St. Louis,* Foote offered Grant a cigar and explained the damage done to his vessels. Foote informed Grant that he would have to take his boats back to Cairo for repairs, and he asked whether the general could besiege Fort Donelson and hold on until the flotilla returned in ten or fifteen days. Grant replied that he needed Foote's boats, damaged or not, and asked him to stay until his soldiers could assault the fort. After further discussion, the two men decided that Foote would take his two most heavily damaged vessels back to Cairo and leave the rest. Knowing that he had the Confederates trapped at Donelson and that they would have to break his lines to get out, Grant agreed to entrench his troops partly around the fort and wait for reinforcements.[17]

Around noon, Grant was headed back to his farmhouse headquarters when a rider appeared, galloping toward him on the icy road. As the man neared, Grant recognized him as one of his staff officers. The officer's white face registered concern, even panic. "General Grant, sir," the officer cried, "the Rebs have hit McClernand's division hard, he is withdrawing!" Spurring his horse, Grant rode back to the farmhouse. Along the way, he found less panic among Smith's troops, but McClernand's men down the line looked somewhat the worse for wear; they were disheveled and discouraged, and the fight had gone out of them. No officers were present, and the men were standing in small groups. They had found three days of cooked rations in the rebel prisoners' haversacks. When Grant got wind of this, he realized that the rebels did not intend to remain in camp. "Some of our men are pretty badly demoralized, but the enemy must be more so, for he has attempted to force his way out, but has fallen back; the one who attacks first now will be victorious and the enemy will have to be in a hurry if he gets ahead of me," he remarked to Colonel J. D. Webster. The Confederates had abandoned most of the ridge to support their attack in the south, so Grant rode back to Smith and calmly ordered him to assault the weakened Confederate left flank. He also sent a messenger to Foote, telling him to have the gunboats throw a few shells at long range to support the attack.[18]

When Grant's messenger arrived at the landing, he found that Foote had already departed for Cairo on the *Conestoga*. Commander Benjamin Dove was now the senior officer present, so the messenger handed him Grant's hastily scribbled message: "If all the gunboats that can will immediately make their appearance to the enemy it may secure us a victory. Otherwise all may be defeated." The note explained that, in his absence, the enemy had attacked the federal line, but Grant believed the rebels to be demoralized. "If the gunboats do not show themselves it will reassure the enemy and still further demoralize our troops." He was going to attack, he told Foote. "I do not expect the gunboats to go into action, but to make an appearance and throw a few shells fired at long range."[19]

Responding to Grant's request, Dove immediately consulted Walke on the *Carondelet* and Paulding on the *St. Louis*. He learned that the *Carondelet* could not be moved, but he ordered the *St. Louis* up the river and followed himself in the *Louisville*. The *St. Louis* took a position below the water batteries and fired off several shells; toward dark, both gunboats returned to their anchorage.[20]

Wallace and McClernand's federals then advanced to secure the ground lost that morning, and Grant ordered Smith to counterattack. Sticking his cap on the point of his sword, Smith and his men overran the rebel rifle pits. In the face of this onslaught, the Confederates crumbled. As evening came, General Floyd, surveying the thousands of dead and wounded on the freezing field, chose to surrender. He and Pillow had decided that ordering the men to fight their way out would be suicidal. Floyd and Pillow fled, however, leaving the actual surrender to one of the brigade commanders, Brigadier General Simon B. Buckner, who had agreed to stay behind. Only Nathan Bedford Forrest's cavalry managed to escape to fight another day.[21]

On the morning of February 16, Grant received a message from Buckner asking about surrender terms. "No terms except unconditional and immediate surrender can be accepted," Grant replied. Buckner called it "ungenerous and unchivalrous," but since he had little choice, he told his men to raise two white flags. From a tugboat, Dove saw the tokens of surrender and landed near the fort. When a Confederate army major came out and handed Dove his sword, Dove refused to take it and escorted the major onto the tug. He then went to Buckner's headquarters, where he found Wallace. Grant soon arrived and accepted the surrender. When one Iowa soldier learned that General Smith "desired to give the 2nd Iowa the distinguished honor of moving into the fort first and of planting the flag upon the ramparts of their citadel," he wrote, "I wept like a child. We marched in and such a sight! 25,000 prisoners were there . . . to receive us."[22]

Walke and the officers and men of the *Carondelet* had spent February 15 burying their dead shipmates. Under the ship's flag flying at half-mast, Walke had read the Episcopal service. Then, borne by their solemn comrades, those who had given their lives in the bombardment of Fort Donelson were carried to a field in the shadow of the hills above the river. Suddenly, a Roman Catholic priest arrived and, with Walke's permission, read the prayers for the dead. As the service ended, those present could hear a distant rumbling, like thunder—the sound of battle.

The day after the surrender, the *Carondelet* went back to Cairo. Approaching the city in a dense fog, the pilot blew the gunboat's whistle, which greatly alarmed some of the townspeople. They had been expecting a Confederate attack from the direction of Columbus and mistook the Pook turtle for a rebel gunboat. The *Carondelet*'s pilot found the landing in the fog, and Walke shared the news that Donelson had surrendered to army forces. They had taken 15,000 prisoners, including Bushrod Johnson and Simon Buckner, Walke told the townsfolk, who cheered and celebrated.[23]

Although Walke reported that Floyd had escaped with 5,000 men during the night, the word that Fort Donelson had surrendered buoyed Foote, who had gone back to Cairo nursing his wounded foot and shaken by the sight of so many injured sailors. Feeling that he had been forced into battle before his flotilla was ready, Foote confided in a letter to his wife, "We will keep a good distance for the rebel forts in future engagements. I won't run into fire again, as a burnt child dreads it." He had brought only four half-manned ironclads to the fight for Fort Donelson and had clearly overestimated the gunboats' ability to silence a fort manned by experienced gunners.[24]

When Foote heard that Dove had refused to accept the Confederate major's sword, he was astounded and called him that "old, stupid Dove." Foote, Walke, and many other naval officers and men believed the gunboats had demoralized the enemy, making them "easy prey to the army the next day as they are afraid to see the black boats arriving into their teeth and belching forth shot and shell." Critics argued that the *Carondelet* and *Pittsburg* had not been so badly disabled as to prevent them from supporting the army's attack. David Dixon Porter claimed, "though struck pretty often, [they] were still intact and fit for any service, and their two commanders would have been glad to have availed themselves of the opportunity to run past the batteries and enfilade them on the side where they were least protected." Porter denied that the rebels had been demoralized by the gunboats' fire and pointed out that "all the credit for the capture of Fort Donelson belongs to the Army." In a telegram to Welles, Foote judiciously gave the army credit. "The army has behaved gloriously," he wrote. Then he said he would take two ironclad gunboats and go up the river to Clarksville. "My foot is painful, but not dangerous," Foote explained. "The trophies of war are immense and the particulars will soon be given."[25]

The nation hailed the capture of Fort Donelson, the first real Union victory in months. Businessmen in St. Louis stopped to sing "The Star-Spangled Banner" and gathered in front of Halleck's headquarters, cheering until he came out and spoke to them. "The backbone of the rebellion is broken," wired one newsman from Cairo. Overcome with joy, folks in Cincinnati shook hands and embraced one another. In Washington, General McClellan rode through a rainstorm to personally deliver the news of victory to the War Department. Guns in the capital boomed in salute.

Capturing Forts Henry and Donelson opened the Cumberland and Tennessee Rivers to Union traffic and forced the Confederates to retreat and abandon their defensive line in Kentucky and Tennessee. For his ability to win battles, Lincoln promoted Grant to major general. Soon, word of his "immediate and unconditional surrender" order spread far and wide, prompting many to say that his initials stood for "Unconditional Surrender." For Walke and the crew of the USS *Carondelet,* the captures of both forts were proud moments that confirmed the value and importance of the oddly shaped Pook turtle.[26]

4

Island No. 10

Until the Star Spangled Banner floats over every rebel stronghold
down the Mississippi.

—Francis Kilburn

Foote did not rest on his laurels. With the Tennessee and Cumberland Rivers now open to federal forces and Nashville rumored to be in a state of panic, Grant and Foote agreed to attack the city on February 21. Halleck, however, threw a wrench into their plans, ordering them not to proceed beyond Clarksville without his approval. Acting on reports that General Beauregard had reinforced Columbus, Kentucky, and might be preparing to attack Paducah or retake Fort Henry, Halleck preferred to use Foote's gunboats to occupy Columbus, the so-called Gibraltar of the West. His decision to delay an attack on Nashville gave the Confederates ample time to remove cannon, ammunition, small arms, rations, and valuable foundry equipment from the city.[1]

Taking Columbus would, however, refocus Foote's efforts on the Western Flotilla's main mission: opening the Mississippi River. The fall of Forts Henry and Donelson had forced the Confederacy to move its line of defense farther south, anchoring the line on Island No. 10, Fort Pillow, and Memphis—all points on the Mississippi River—and across to Pittsburg and Chattanooga, Tennessee. Confederate forces still controlled the river south of Cairo, a distance of less than 500 miles as the crow flies but, given the river's winding course, closer to 1,100 miles. Farms, grazing lands, and Gulf ports west of the river provided the rebels with crucial food supplies, and as one historian noted, "controlling the Mississippi River from Cairo to

New Orleans would, therefore, enable federal forces to cut a vital lifeline of support for the Confederate war effort."[2]

Before mounting an attack on Columbus, Foote wished to conduct a reconnaissance of the rebel stronghold. Consequently, on February 23 the *Cincinnati, St. Louis, Mound City, Carondelet,* and *Conestoga* moved downstream, accompanied by two mortar boats and five transports loaded with troops. General Fremont had originally ordered thirty-eight mortar boats, each armed with one 13-inch mortar, but Halleck, skeptical of the boats' ability to inflict serious damage on enemy batteries, had stalled Foote's efforts to have them constructed and fitted out. In December 1861 Foote had admitted to Halleck that he had "some misgivings about the mortar boats," and he blamed construction delays on a "want of money, credit, and hesitation of the Government in accepting the boats." Phelps expressed more confidence in the efficacy of mortar fire against enemy points on the Tennessee and Cumberland Rivers. "Effective mortar boats must prove the most destructive adversaries earth forts can have to contend with," he told Foote. In tests conducted in early February 1862 the first completed mortar boat withstood the recoil of the 13-inch mortar, which fired a 227-pound shell in a high, arching trajectory designed to drop down on the target. President Lincoln favored the use of these mortars, and the Northern public saw these weapons as a means of accomplishing a "stand off bombardment" of river fortifications. Lincoln pressed for completion of the mortar boats, and by the end of February, all thirty-eight boats ordered by Fremont were serviceable.[3]

Foote's flotilla steamed downriver for "a little excursion . . . to Columbus," *Mound City* crewman Symmes Browne wrote, and most of the men were anticipating an attack on the rebel stronghold. The son of a Cincinnati clergyman, twenty-five-year-old Browne had followed his brother Henry into the Union navy in early 1862, and both brothers served on the *Mound City.* Symmes's accounting education at Farmers' College had qualified him to be appointed a paymaster steward. He reported, "At 10 a.m. we were rounding the point eight miles above Columbus and were greeted by the roar of a heavy gun from the fort & saw the ball splash the water a mile ahead of us. We continued on our course with the gunboats, but the transports came to a stop so as not to come in range of their guns." The gunboats formed in line, but when a steamer appeared flying a flag of truce, the flagship and a tug went down to meet it. During this conference with the Confederates, Foote learned that Polk had requested that the wives of

Confederate officers be allowed to visit their husbands who were being detained at Fort Donelson. Foote sent the request to Halleck, but he thought it was just a ruse designed to give the rebels time to evacuate Columbus. At 2:45 p.m. Foote's gunboats returned to Cairo. The following day Halleck relented and allowed Brigadier General Buell to move troops from his Army of the Ohio and advance on Nashville. Two brigades embarked on transports and steamed to the Tennessee capital, which surrendered on February 25, 1862.[4]

Despite Foote's repeated requests for men, most of the Western Flotilla's gunboats remained short on crew. Before departing Cairo, however, the *Carondelet* had received a number of replacements. Among them was John G. Morison, an Irish-born sailor who kept a journal during his Civil War service. He wrote: "Monday Feb 24th—Thirty men were to be sent on board the Carondelet and I was sent amongst the number. This boat suffered severely in the fight at Donelson, having 4 men killed and 30 wounded. She has about 70 shot holes in her. Her captain is great on the fight, I am told." The *Carondelet* then steamed up to Mound City to undergo needed repairs. Morison noted, "Arrived here about 3 P.M. when the carpenters went to work on her immediately to keep on all night. At night the captain had an awning broke out for us to sleep on and the ship's cook to keep a fire on all night for fear that the men would catch cold in the absence of heat from the boilers. Seems a very kind man."[5]

When Foote returned to Cairo on February 24, he learned that Captain Henry Maynadier, an ordnance officer of the Mississippi Mortar Flotilla assigned to command the mortar boats, had arrived with a draft of 350 men. To Foote's disappointment, the officers reported their own men to be, "with few exceptions, the offscourings of the Army." "I am pained and discouraged to have to take such men into action," Foote told Welles. "We want no more from the Army. I prefer to go into action only half manned than to go with such men."[6]

Based on rumors that the rebels may have evacuated Columbus, Foote sent Ledyard Phelps, now the *Benton*'s captain, with a flag of truce down to Columbus on March 1. Phelps had been in Cairo supervising the *Benton*'s conversion from a snag boat to an ironclad gunboat twice as large as the Pook turtles and armed with sixteen heavy guns. The newly converted gunboat would serve as Foote's flagship, with Phelps in command.[7]

Phelps's place as captain of the *Conestoga* went to twenty-five-year-old Lieutenant George M. Blodgett, a Naval Academy graduate, class of 1856.

"The noble craft which I have the honor of commanding is not iron clad," Blodgett told his aunt, "but is the fastest vessel in the fleet. She carries 4 heavy 32 pdrs of 42 cwt each and 1 rifled Dahlgren which has a range of about 2 miles and a half—Our complement of men and officers are one hundred men and fifteen officers."[8]

When Phelps returned to Cairo from Columbus, he reported that the Confederates were removing their heavy guns from the bluffs above the fort, but not the guns from their water battery. They were burning their winter quarters, military stores, and equipment, and based on the large fires observed in Columbus, Phelps thought the rebels were wreaking destruction on the town. Not entirely convinced, Foote wished to see Columbus for himself, so he ventured downstream with the *Conestoga, Cincinnati,* and *Louisville* to reconnoiter. Although rain and fog obscured the bluffs, Foote could see fires burning at Columbus "and in the rear of the bluff upon which heavy guns had been mounted, indicating an evacuation." Assuming the rebels were leaving, he proposed on March 3 that Halleck's chief of staff, Brigadier General George W. Cullum, confer with Halleck and suggest that in a few days they go down with several gunboats and mortar boats to land troops and take possession of Columbus.[9]

March 3 dawned cold and wintry. The officers and men of the *Carondelet* spent that day preparing to depart for another mission. "All hands were station[ed] at their guns, my station being No. 7, first shotman at No. 5 gun," coxswain Morison wrote. "At 8 p.m. the boilers were lit and the carpenters hurried up with their work so that we could get off at the appointed time."[10]

At 4:00 the next morning the *Carondelet*'s crew turned out, had breakfast, and began steaming downriver toward Columbus with Foote's flotilla of six gunboats, four mortar boats, and a number of troop transports loaded with Brigadier General William T. Sherman's new division. The flotilla eased its way into the current and swiftly moved to within a few miles of Columbus. Foote and Phelps strained to see whether the enemy had guns mounted and manned on the bluffs that rose some 150 feet above the river, but they could not see clearly. All reports indicated that the enemy had evacuated their defenses, but knowing the inaccuracy of intelligence reports, Foote ordered the men to prepare for action and the flotilla to come about and face upriver. The *Carondelet* drifted opposite the rebels' water battery in the swift current, but no guns went off "to let us know we were treading on dangerous ground," Morison wrote. Foote sent a tug to reconnoiter, and it "signaled back the joyful news that Columbus was evacuated. Ye gods, what cheering was done. Was enough to wake up all the dead rebels in the vicinity."[11]

Two weeks earlier, Beauregard had received permission to abandon Columbus and had ordered Polk to evacuate his men while it was still safe to do so. Using the Mobile and Ohio Railroad, rebel soldiers took away guns, stores, and as much ammunition as possible; burned thousands of bushels of corn and hay; and dumped the leftover ordnance in the river. "The Rebs destroyed everything of any consequence before they left," Morison wrote, "so that our men found nothing except broken whiskey bottles and numberless packs of cards, which seem to be the rebels decalogue."[12]

With support from Foote's Western Flotilla, Sherman's troops took Columbus, removing a major obstacle to the Union's mission of opening the Mississippi. Now Foote turned his attention to the next objective: Island No. 10 and New Madrid. Citing the need to repair the damage inflicted in the engagements with Forts Henry and Donelson, Foote ruled out an immediate move downriver. Halleck wanted Foote to go ahead and not wait for repairs, but Foote argued, "That can not be done without creating a stampede amongst the pilots and most of the newly made officers, to say nothing of the disaster which must follow if the rebels fight as they have done of late."[13]

By the end of February, Foote had finally received the men needed to man his gunboats and mortar boats—600 volunteers and soldiers detailed from the Army of the Potomac. Some of the new men were trained seamen. "Carter has raised you 100 men at Erie, and 50 seamen will go from New York. We do this with five ships waiting for crews, and these *Narragansett* not yet relieved, though their times are up," Fox wrote. Clearly, the Union navy was experiencing manpower shortages. Finally, on March 7, Foote wired that his new flagship *Benton* was under way and moving slowly down the Ohio River, and on Wednesday he hoped to take seven ironclads and ten mortar boats down to attack Island No. 10.[14]

By then, the *Mound City* had returned to Cairo from the Cumberland River to repair its engines. The crew knew little of the gunboat's next assignment. Browne wrote, "Our latest advices here are to the effect that the rebels are trying to make a defense at Island 'No. 10' in the Miss., but as the movements of our boats will be very rapid down that river, they will have but very little chance to build substantial defenses." Unbeknownst to Browne, the Confederates had been fortifying Island No. 10 since the previous summer as an extension of their new defensive line from Memphis east to Chattanooga. Polk had erected a series of batteries at Island No. 10, and with 8,000 Confederate troops at New Madrid, Madrid Bend, and Island No. 10, the general thought they could hold the line.[15]

By March 12, Foote felt prepared to move on Island No. 10, but the transports had not yet arrived at Cairo, and he considered it unsafe to move without troops to occupy the island if it were captured. Foote feared that if they succeeded in passing Island No. 10, then Confederate troops on the Tennessee side would return, man their batteries, and "thus shut up the river in our rear, as we should be short of coal and towboats to get back to re-attack No. 10 or the opposite shore." Halleck wired back immediately, telling Foote not to move until ordered to do so. Twenty-four hours later, Halleck gave the go-ahead: "You will proceed tomorrow with the gun and mortar boats to attack the batteries on Island No. 10." Halleck urged Foote not to expose his gunboats unnecessarily to close fire and to let the mortar boats do the main work.[16] Many in the flotilla had anticipated the order. "We're going down to Island No. 10 to attack the Rebs," Morison wrote in his diary on March 12. Rumor had it that the rebels had evacuated the island, and upon hearing this, "the crews of some of the [boats] cheered lustily."[17]

Workmen had swarmed over the *Carondelet* at the Mound City yard, patching decks and installing new chimneys. Walke welcomed efforts to remove the thin armor on the pilothouse, which could "hardly turn a Minie ball," and hammer down heavy oak timber to reinforce it. The gunboat also received a new cannon to replace the bow gun that had exploded at Donelson.[18]

Foote's flotilla left Cairo on March 14, 1862. The flagship *Benton* led the way, followed by the *St. Louis, Cincinnati, Pittsburg, Mound City,* and *Louisville.* The *Carondelet* joined them at Columbus. True to his word, Foote had arranged to have the ten little mortar boats towed downriver with the gunboats. When the flotilla arrived at Columbus, Foote paused to take on 1,200 men of Colonel Napoleon Buford's infantry brigade. That same day, the flag officer received encouraging news from Brigadier General John S. Pope, who reported that his forces had captured New Madrid. A West Point graduate, Pope had been a topographical engineer before the war and had surveyed routes for the railroad. In 1861 he had recruited Illinois volunteers for the army, and after a successful campaign against Sterling Price in Missouri, Halleck appointed him to command the Army of the Mississippi. Described as "aggressive, impatient, and boastful," Pope conjectured "that No. 10 also must be evacuated for it could not be reinforced or supplied from below."[19]

Buoyed by Pope's news, Foote ordered the flotilla to proceed down the river. The *Carondelet* chugged downstream to near Hickman, Tennessee. At Hickman, Commander Dove reported that the *Louisville* had developed leaks in its boilers, so it returned to Columbus for repairs. Early the next day the flotilla continued down the fog-shrouded river toward Island No. 10.[20]

As Foote's flotilla steamed along Seven Mile Stretch between Islands No. 8 and No. 10, Phelps ordered the *Benton* to occasionally fire a shell into the woods. This precaution failed to stir up any masked enemy batteries. From outside the *Carondelet*'s pilothouse, Walke could see that heavy rains had flooded the shoreline. Once the head of Island No. 10 appeared, Walke could make out a chain of forts extending along the shore. "The commodore fired several shots," Morison wrote on March 15, "which fell short, at long intervals at two white objects on the far shore, but no answer." After a while, Foote "placed two mortars, which began throwing their heavy shells. After they fired twice, we could see a flash from between two white objects."[21]

In a letter to his fiancée, Browne stated that on March 15 a tugboat went down to find a good position for the mortar boats. "No. 12 fired first shell at half past 2 o'clock, and from that time during the afternoon there was a continual fire kept up, being answered by the enemy at 2:30 by a single shot." At dark the mortars were towed upstream, "for fear of a surprise." Buffeted by the river's current, the bow-heavy ironclads had to tie up to the banks on either side. The *Carondelet* went upstream and "made fast to a tree." Morison observed, "I had often heard of anchoring in the wood but I never saw it verified until then."[22]

Private Francis Kilburn, a correspondent for the *Daily Evening Express* who used the byline "Ranger," witnessed the bombardment of Island No. 10 aboard Mortar Boat No. 12 and described the operation of the mortars: "The charge is from fifteen to twenty-two pounds. The shell weighs 230 pounds, and is thirteen inches in diameter. The size of a soup plate." Kilburn, who had joined the 5th Pennsylvania Reserves but had been transferred to the gunboat service in February 1862, explained that a derrick was set up onshore and positioned to drop the shell into the mouth of the mortar after a bag of powder had gone down its throat. "The boat is moored alongside the shore, so as to withstand the shock firmly, and the men go ashore when the mortar is to be fired. A pull of the string does the work, and the whole vicinity is shaken with the concussion. The report is deafening and the most enthusiastic person gets enough of it with one or two discharges."[23]

Early on Sunday, March 16, Foote placed the mortar boats, commanded by Maynadier, in position and ordered them moored to the Missouri shore. "At this time the mortars and 'Benton' opened a heavy fire on all their batteries, while the rest of us were compelled to lie by and keep quiet," Browne wrote. On Monday morning, Foote's flotilla commenced a long-range attack on the forts. "The Cincinnati, St. Louis, and Benton were lashed together," Morison wrote, "the Benton in the centre, and their heads turned downstream, where they took a position close into the Tennessee shore. The *Carondelet*'s orders were, I believe, to follow after some time."[24]

The federal vessels opened fire from 2,000 yards, for the rapid current made it impossible to get any nearer without the risk of being carried under the enemy's guns. Cautious after the pummeling his ironclads had taken at Fort Donelson, Foote feared a closer approach would expose the gunboats' most vulnerable points—their bows and quarters—to enemy fire from six other batteries mounting forty-three guns.

The *Carondelet* then commenced firing. Morison observed, "I could see the dirt fly in all directions around the fort. Every now and then, I could see a shell from a gun would go whizzing along and, falling short, would send huge jets of water high into the air." From the *Carondelet*'s hurricane deck, Walke watched the bombardment and called out to his gunners to elevate the guns to the maximum. Suddenly, Walke spotted a 128-pound shell arcing directly toward the *Carondelet*. With a piercing whine, the shell whizzed over the ironclad and plopped into the river with such force that the splash inundated the decks with muddy water. At noon, Foote's flotilla opened fire on the upper fort on the Tennessee shore and continued to receive brisk fire from this and four other batteries. Browne wrote, "At this time the bombardment became general from the three gunboats in the stream, the mortars (8 in number) and 'M. City.' I tell [you] it was [a] grand sight to see and hear, especially to me, for it was the first engagement I had ever seen."[25]

The bursting of a gun on *St. Louis* proved to be the day's most startling development. When the gunner pulled the lanyard to scrape the friction fuse and fire the rifled port gun, the barrel exploded with a loud bang that could be heard on both the *Benton* and the *Cincinnati*. Razor-sharp metal splinters flew in every direction, killing two seamen and wounding others in the gun crew and anyone standing near the old 42-pounder.[26] Over on the *Cincinnati,* Roger Stembel hailed the flagship and asked if the *St. Louis* needed assistance. He was told that two sailors had been killed and fifteen men wounded. Although the *Cincinnati* had been spared serious casualties, the ironclad had developed engine trouble, forcing Stembel to tell Foote that he might have to go to Cairo for repairs.[27]

Finally, when darkness had obscured the forts from view, Foote ordered a cease-fire. He was confident that the *Benton* and the others had damaged the upper fort. "We dismounted one of their guns, and the men at times ran from the batteries."[28]

Under orders to guard the mortar boats during the night, the *Carondelet* stood down toward the Missouri shore. The rebels had not quit for the night, however, and opened another couple of batteries on the *Benton.* "One shot—a 128 pounder, I believe—struck her, going through her deck and up again, lodging at last in a wash basin in the wardroom. Fortunately nobody was hurt." At last, all firing from the boats ceased, but the mortars kept firing through the night at short intervals.[29]

Later that evening, Foote wrote to Welles. He hoped to silence the upper battery the next day but cautioned, "This place is even stronger and better adapted for defense than Columbus ever was; each fortification commands the one above it. We can count forty nine guns in different batteries, where there are plausibly double the number, with 10,000 troops."[30]

On Tuesday morning, March 18, the *Carondelet* dropped down astern of the *Mound City* and opened fire with its port rifled gun. The shot fell short. "Then the starboard rifled gun threw one which landed plump into the fort and the clouds of dirt it threw up was truly enormous," Morison penned in his diary. Foote signaled the gunboat to stop firing. "We then sat watching the shells from the mortars dropping all round them. We did not fire anymore all day." Morison arose the next day "sick and miserable," suffering from chills and fever, but by Saturday, March 22, he was feeling fine. "We have been down here a week now and no further a head on the capture of this place than when we came down." The *Carondelet* and *Mound City* participated in another round of shelling the following day, and then Walke took his vessel down to guard the mortar boats.[31]

After three days of bombardment, Foote decided to call a council of war, the first since he had taken command of the flotilla. Pope had requested that the gunboats run past Island No. 10, but as Foote explained, the general had no transports and could not cross to the Tennessee side from New Madrid because the countryside was flooded. Concerned about the fate of towns on the river above No. 10 should they attack and fail, Foote asked Stembel to solicit the opinion of each of the ironclad captains. When Stembel returned to the *Benton,* he reported that all but one officer opposed running the blockade to help Pope. Phelps had offered to take the *Benton* down, and Foote considered it, as the *Benton* was the best protected of all his gunboats, despite being "slow and sluggish." Realizing that the *Benton's* loss would be a devastating one, however, Foote abandoned the idea.[32] Although Foote had temporarily given up the notion of running past Island No. 10, his mortar boats continued to bombard rebel fortifications.[33]

The *Carondelet* now joined the bombardment from a new position. At dawn on Sunday, March 23, its gun crews stood ready. "After breakfast, whilst kneeling by the mess chest, [I] heard some [thing] come crashing into our deck," Morison noted in his journal. "Thought it was a shell but found it was a tree which fell on us. After awhile another crash and shock far more severe than the former." Two cottonwood trees had fallen on the ironclad, their limbs and foliage covering the deck. Men were sent up to the deck with axes to remove the tangle of leaves and twigs. Then, without any warning, another enormous tree toppled over and crashed onto the port quarterdecks and wheelhouse. The tree, four feet in diameter, ripped through the portside boats, shattered a skylight, and tore up signal masts and rigging. Beneath the massive tree, the boatswain found four sailors bleeding and moaning. One was not breathing. Thankfully, the surgeon's assistant and others came to carry the wounded below. "Luckily," Morison wrote, "there was no one killed, but we had three wounded—one (a messmate of mine named Maguire) severely, the ship's cook slightly, and a colored cook cut over the eye." In the meantime, thinking they had hit the ironclad, Confederate gunners began firing at the *Carondelet,* only adding to the confusion. Finally, after appeals to the flagship for assistance, the *Alps* arrived to tow the *Carondelet* out of harm's way. It would take carpenters a week to repair the damage.[34]

Foote's mortar boats, ironclads, and gunboats continued to shell the rebels at a leisurely pace. With so little return fire from the rebel forts, the crew of the *Cincinnati* took to reading magazines and letters while sitting on deck. "It was more like a gunnery drill or the Fourth of July," one bluejacket remarked. Only the arrival of a flatboat carrying a gas balloon interrupted the routine. McClellan had sent Captain John H. Steiner of the army's balloon corps west, but when Halleck failed to be impressed, Steiner had offered the balloon to Foote. A correspondent to the *Daily Evening Express* wrote, "On Saturday the 'Dan Pollard' brought down Captain Steiner, with a new balloon, 'Eagle,' and on Sunday we commenced fitting her for the purpose of taking observations." Steiner, Mayor Julian O. Romsey of Chicago, a colonel of the 24th Illinois, and Maynadier stepped into the balloon's basket, and as the *Cincinnati*'s astonished crew watched, the balloon slowly ascended. Through the haze and smoke, the three officers could make out seven Confederate steamers at the end of Island No. 10 but not a single enemy gunboat. The following day they went up again and could clearly see mortar shells from Maynadier's mortar boats arcing toward the enemy forts but falling well behind them. These observations allowed Maynadier's mortar crews to correct the fuse settings.[35]

The balloonists' reports cheered Foote, but he remained concerned that even if they could shell the enemy out of his batteries, there were insufficient troops to occupy Island No. 10 without support from the army in the rear. Anxious to bypass the stubborn defenders, Pope latched on to an idea proposed by Colonel J. W. Bissel to dig a canal from the bend of the Mississippi River near Island No. 8 across a peninsula near New Madrid. The canal would be too shallow for the Union gunboats but could accommodate light-draft vessels and transports. Described by one historian as "one of the more innovative engineering achievements of the entire war," the work to cut a canal through six miles of timber was progressing, but not quickly enough for the general.[36]

Disappointment over the bombardment's ineffectiveness and their lack of progress extended to officers and men of the flotilla. "I still uphold that no attack will be made by the gunboats excepting at long range," Browne explained to his fiancée. "And as for running the blockade, I am sorry to say that this seems to have been given up entirely."[37]

On March 28 Halleck sent Foote a cryptic telegram: "General Pope is confident that he can turn the enemy's position by crossing below. Give him all the assistance in your power by the use of your gunboats. I think that by a combined operation the object can be accomplished."[38] Foote gathered his commanders in the *Benton*'s great stern cabin, read them the telegram, and asked them if they were willing to risk running past the rebel batteries. Then, ushering them into an adjoining cabin one at a time, Foote sought each captain's counsel.

Walke was the second officer interviewed. When Foote asked whether he would be willing to pass the enemy's batteries with the *Carondelet,* Walke recalled that he replied "in the affirmative. Foote accepted my advice, and expressed himself as greatly relieved from heavy responsibility, as he had determined to send none but volunteers on an expedition he regarded as perilous and of very doubtful success." The flag officer then told Walke that he "should or would be rewarded."[39]

Walke returned to the *Carondelet* to await orders and make preparations. At first, he shared his decision with no one. The rebels had nearly fifty guns that could be focused on the ironclad, and some would consider it a suicide mission. Everyone remembered what had happened at Fort Donelson, where the rebels had inflicted more than fifty hits on the *St. Louis* and *Carondelet.* Walke knew the stakes were high, but he also realized that unless they took No. 10, the war on the Mississippi might be lost. With rebel gunboats below No. 10 poised to ascend the river, time was of the essence. Rumors of one or more large, powerful Confederate boats under construction only added to Walke's concerns, but the risk had to be accepted.

On March 30 Foote issued specific instructions for what he called "this delicate and somewhat hazardous service." On the first foggy or rainy night, Walke was to drift the *Carondelet* down past the rebel batteries on the Tennessee shore and Island No. 10 until he reached New Madrid. If he had coal, and if the current allowed, Walke was to steam up the river and capture or destroy the rebel gunboat *Grampus* as the army moved to attack the rebel fortifications. Foote cautioned Walke to keep his lights "secreted in the hold or put out" and to forbid his men from speaking above a whisper, and then only if they were on duty. He urged Walke to use every other precaution to prevent the rebels from suspecting that he was dropping below their batteries. Foote told Walke that the government would fully appreciate and reward him "for a service which, I trust, will enable the army to cross the river and make a successful attack in rear while we storm the batteries in front of this stronghold of the rebels." After commending Walke and his crew to the "care and protection of God," Foote added a postscript: "Should you meet with disaster, you will, as a last resort, destroy the steam machinery, and, if possible to escape, set fire to your gunboat or sink her, and prevent her from falling into hands of the rebels."[40]

Knowing that the mission involved considerable risk, Walke asked for volunteers among the *Carondelet*'s officers. First master Richard K. Wade asked to be excused, but the others agreed to follow Walke. In an account written after the war, seaman John Ford noted that Wade "considered our captain a madman to attempt it." William R. Hoel, first master of the *Cincinnati,* volunteered to replace Wade. The thirty-eight-year-old Hoel, a native of Butler County, Ohio, had been a Mississippi steamboat pilot before entering the navy in 1861 and had run to New Orleans 194 times.[41]

The *Carondelet*'s crew finally learned of its mission on Friday, April 4. In his diary, Morison wrote, "I understand that the commodore asked the captains of the flotilla if any of them would under take to run the blockade of the island. They all refused except our captain, who said he would try it." Remembering the damage done at Fort Donelson, Walke tasked his crew with making the *Carondelet* better able to fend off enemy shot during the run past Island No. 10. Walke also had chief engineer William Faulkner and his men lead the escape steam through pipes and snake it through the wheelhouse, covering the paddle wheel to cut down on any loud puffing noises. The strongest deckhands and firemen were assigned to take large hoses topside to repel anyone who tried to board the boat with a blast of scalding water from the boilers. As one final task, Walke instructed head gunner Richard Adams and his crew to take the two 42-pounders from the bow and replace them with a 30- and a 50-pounder. Then the men on the *Carondelet* waited—and waited. They needed a foggy or rainy night, but every day dawned picture perfect. "The siege of Island No. 10 has become as tedious as a twice told tale," wrote a correspondent on board the steamer *V. F. Wilson.* "Each day drags on its heavy length more wearily than the one before. The gunboats maintain the same position they did a week ago."[42]

Observing the falling river level from the *Carondelet*'s quarterdeck, Walke grew more impatient. Finally, equally impatient army officials convinced Foote to organize an expedition to assault the guns of the enemy's upper or No. 1 fort on the Tennessee shore. When the landing party returned, Foote was undoubtedly relieved to see the *Benton*'s fourth master, George P. Lord, bound up the gunboat's side. He reported that they had spiked all eleven guns in the battery—one of them a Columbiad, which would have been a distinct danger if the federal boats had attempted to run past it. Foote inquired whether they had met any enemy opposition, and Lord replied, "The Reb sentinels fired on us, but they ran off." Foote was reportedly "delighted with the operation, which must have reminded him of his own assault on the Canton barrier forts." Then a ferocious blast of rain and wind drove them all from the deck as a squall hit.[43]

Two days later, Walke sent one of his officers to the flagship with a message for Foote: with Foote's approval, he intended to run the gauntlet that night. Earlier that morning at about 9:00, Hoel had come over from the *Cincinnati* to join the *Carondelet*. He and the other two pilots, Daniel Weaver and John Denning, huddled over the charts, plotting the ironclad's journey past the rebel batteries, as well as the river's notorious sandbars and wrecks. Much depended on the pilots' knowledge of the river, but as added protection, Walke asked his friend Colonel Buford to find a barge and have it filled with bales of hay. Deckhands lashed the barge to the ironclad's port side to protect the magazine and used the hay to cover the sill of the gun ports and to protect the fantail and casemate astern. Observing the *Carondelet* just prior to its run past the rebel batteries, Walke said, "The brave old 'Carondelet' looked like a farmer's team preparing for market."[44]

That evening, Colonel Buford came on board. At dusk, Captain Hottenstein and twenty-three sharpshooters of the 42nd Illinois arrived in the gunboat's cutters; they were mustered on deck, inspected, and instructed to cooperate with the crew in repelling boarders. It promised to be a clear night, and Walke reportedly told Buford, "We will wait until the moon is down and then go, whatever the chances." Buford stayed until the last moment and then shook hands with Walke, Hoel, and Hottenstein before departing. "No officers of the fleet were present," Walke recalled, "although by some of them it was said, the 'Carondelet' was going into the 'jaws of death,' and from them cheer was not expected."[45]

Walke then mustered his officers and crew on the darkened gun deck, lit now by only one lantern. He explained the importance of their mission and cautioned the men not to speak above a whisper, lest the rebels hear them. They greeted his brief speech with cheers. As the men went to their quarters, Walke ordered the master at arms to break out the pistols, cutlasses, boarding pikes, and hand grenades.

By 10:00 p.m., the sliver of moon had gone down, but "before that time," Morison explained, "the sky became overcast and got dark as pitch. Then rain began falling and the thunder to roll and the lightning to flash which made everything look weird-like and fantastic." In the darkness Walke, Hoel, and the two other pilots could see flashes of lightning as a thunderstorm approached. Casting off, the *Carondelet* headed downstream, enveloped in blackness and sheets of driving rain. "We beat to quarters and put out all lights and kept quiet as possible," Morison noted.[46]

Relieved to have sudden flashes of lightning to illuminate the dark river, Hoel and the pilots guided the *Carondelet* downstream. "With our bow pointing to the island, we passed the lowest point of land without being observed, it appears, by the enemy, " Walke recalled. "All speed was given to the vessel to drive her through the tempest." Below in the fire room, the sweating coal heavers worked furiously to feed the boilers as the *Carondelet* raced downriver. Except for the rumbles of thunder and the brilliant flashes of lightning, all remained quiet until the vessel came abreast of Battery No. 2. Suddenly, the *Carondelet*'s chimneys blazed up. Those in the pilothouse held their breath, fearing the red flame would alert the enemy ashore. Describing the *Carondelet*'s passage, a reporter for the *St. Louis Democrat* wrote, "The soot in the chimneys caught fire, and a blaze five feet high leaped out from their tops, lighting brightly the upper deck of the vessel, and everything around." Walke explained that the soot had become dry, since the escape steam that usually kept it wet had been diverted to the wheelhouse. Faulkner's men opened the flue caps, and the flame subsided. "Notwithstanding . . . no alarm among the rebels was discovered to follow, and we were consoling ourselves over the remissness of the rebel sentries, when to our great astonishment, the chimneys were fired again," the reporter wrote. Those on deck blamed the engineer for mismanagement, "and it was with no little emphasis that the executive officer [Hoel] demanded, 'why in h—l the flue caps were not kept open.'" This time, the rebels took notice, and the crackle of musket fire came from across the river. Five rockets shot up from shore to alert the Confederate defenders, followed by a cannon shot from Battery No. 2. With the rebel batteries expected to open fire from all their guns, "the engineroom was signaled and the gunboat raced ahead."[47]

To better guide the ironclad around shoals and obstacles in the river, Hoel turned the six-foot wheel over to Weaver, slipped below to the gun deck, and made his way out to the hurricane deck. From there, he could relay soundings from the boatswain on the forecastle to the man at the wheel. He brushed past a gun crew, ordered the gun port opened, and climbed out. From his exposed position, Hoel conned the Pook turtle downstream to the sound of rifle shells and claps of thunder. Suddenly he yelled, "Hard a' port!" In the pitch darkness, the *Carondelet* had narrowly avoided striking a shoal. As two more rebel batteries took aim at the gunboat, Hoel struggled to maneuver the ironclad and the cumbersome barge. Shells splashed into the river all around the *Carondelet,* and one struck the barge with a loud clank. Although the shots were alarmingly close, Walke assured Weaver that the rebels were firing at random.

After thirty long minutes, the *Carondelet* passed the batteries unscathed, much to the relief of the crew. Below in the darkness, the gun crews that had patiently endured the run in silence were elated, but the gun captain had to remind them to keep quiet, as they still had to pass the enemy's floating battery. Sure enough, as they came abreast of the battery, the rebels got off half a dozen rounds. One round smashed into the barge. The gun crews heard the sound and gritted their teeth—would the next shell find their gun port? But silence followed. The next day they found a 12-pound shot in a bale of hay on the barge.

The *Carondelet* now sped downstream and arrived off New Madrid around midnight. "We might have been destroyed," Morison penned in his diary, "but thank God we ran clear until we came close to New Madrid, where we ran aground, but after a little work she was got off again and we tied up close to the town." On the quarterdeck, Walke shook hands with Hoel and the two pilots. Nixon, the paymaster, asked Walke, "Splice the main brace, sir?" Walke granted permission, "and when the boatswain's mate sounded, 'grog, oh,' there was never a ship's crew merrier than the one on board the 'Carondelet.'"[48]

During the *Carondelet*'s run past Island No. 10's batteries, Foote and the men of the upper flotilla waited in suspense for news. Finally, they heard the prearranged signal announcing the ironclad's safe passage: three cannon shots one minute apart, repeated five minutes later. As the sounds alerting the flotilla of the *Carondelet*'s safe passage came up, a war correspondent noted, "There went up such a thunder of cheers and hurricanes of shots from the watching crowds that even the storm itself was outroared."[49]

At New Madrid, news of the *Carondelet*'s arrival brought a crowd of army officers and soldiers to the river. Walke went ashore to meet General Pope and Assistant Secretary of War Thomas Scott. A group of jubilant soldiers descended on the crew of Walke's gig, cheering, embracing the sailors, and shouting, "Hip hip hurrah for Commodore Foote, Captain Walke, and the navy!" The celebrations concluded, and the gig crew pulled the boat back to the *Carondelet*.[50]

On Saturday, April 5, Morison went ashore to help gather wood for the *Carondelet*. "Whilst wooding, I went ashore to look at the fortification which the rebels built and found the sandbags, in place of being filled with sand, were filled with corn which they had taken from the only Union farmer in the vicinity out of sheer wantonness and spite."[51]

At Pope's request, on April 6 Foote ordered Lieutenant Egbert Thompson to take the *Pittsburg* down and repeat the *Carondelet*'s dash past Island No. 10. The arrival of a second ironclad would give Pope two gunboats to cover his men when they crossed over to the Tennessee side.[52]

In the meantime, the *Carondelet* had gone down the river on a reconnaissance expedition, stopping at the military camp to pick up Brigadier General John M. Palmer. The gunboat then continued on to Meriweather's Landing, where Walke called for the gun captain to lob a few 42-pound shots at a small rebel battery there. When no return fire came, he decided to go back upstream and have the two bow guns shell another enemy battery opposite Point Pleasant. "They opened up on us from a three-gun batterie, of which we took no notice," Morison wrote, "more than returning their warm compliments in kind. We found that they had batteries mounting from one to three guns, scattered all along the Tennessee shore as far as Tipton, a distance of about 15 miles, with which they were in the habit of annoying our troops on the Missouri shore, and as they mounted heavier guns than our batteries did, they done so almost with impunity." After lying off Tipton for a while, the *Carondelet* went back upstream to shell the rebel batteries. The first one, Morison wrote, "fought well and obstinately," but they could not get the gunboat's range. The gunboat gunners then decreased the range to the battery to grape and canister.[53]

After quickly demolishing the Confederate battery's guns, Captain Hottenstein took a landing party of 42nd Illinois soldiers ashore to spike the guns and dump the ammunition in the river. The zing of rifle fire from a rebel sniper interrupted their efforts, provoking the soldiers and prompting the *Carondelet*'s gun crew to fire grape and canister into the woods. The sniper, hit in the nose, dropped his weapon and took off into the woods.[54]

From the riverbank, curious federal soldiers watched the black ironclad as it steamed up and down the river, shelling enemy batteries. They hollered and waved their caps as the ironclad passed by. The *Carondelet* returned to New Madrid in the predawn hours of April 7. Knowing that Pope's troops would soon begin crossing the river, Walke ordered the *Pittsburg*'s commander to prepare for action. Thompson sent back a puzzling reply: "*Pittsburg* is not ready." By 6:30 a.m., Walke could see federal transports poised to move across the river, so the *Carondelet* hoisted the signal "follow me" and got under way to support the army by shelling rebel batteries on the west bank and the two 8-inch siege howitzers and one 32-pounder at Watson's Landing.

While maneuvering to bring the *Carondelet*'s broadside battery to bear, however, the gunboat was hit by an enemy shot that cut the starboard wheel rope. Then a 64-pound shot smacked into the boat's port quarter, glancing off the stern gun and falling into the river. Just as the *Carondelet*'s gun crews returned to the fight, Walke heard shells whizzing overhead. It was the *Pittsburg.* Morison penned in his diary: "Determined to have a hand in, she ran across our bows and delivered her fire, with what effect we could not tell, as it was now drizzling rain and a damp kind of vapor had overspread the river, shutting the Tennessee shore out from our view." The *Pittsburg* dropped astern and took up a position by the Missouri shore, "from which she continued to heave shells, sometimes over us, in the direction of the fort." Furious, Walke raised his speaking trumpet and waved it at the ironclad. "After a time," Morison noted, "the mist cleared away and the sun shone in fine style." The *Carondelet* then closed the rebels and dosed them with short-range shells that compelled them to retreat. The gunboat sent a party ashore to spike the guns and take ammunition on board. It then left for the other shore, "well satisfied with our day's work of taking and destroying nine guns, besides breaking up a camp of three thousand men, which I think was a good day's work for one boat."[55]

Once Pope's troops had moved across, the *Pittsburg* came alongside the *Carondelet,* and Thompson called out from the deck, "Congratulations, Walke, we did it." Walke shouted back through his trumpet, "Damn you, I don't congratulate you. You sulked behind my boat and fired shots over my deck." Walke ignored the visitors and onlookers who could clearly hear his invective and angrily told Thompson, "Damn you, if you ever do such a thing again, I will turn my batteries on you and blow you out of the water."[56]

Late on April 8, realizing that Pope's troops had cut them off from below, the Confederates on Island No. 10 surrendered. When the *Carondelet* dropped down close to the island, Morison wrote, "We could see that our flag was waving over it. We then hurried down and heard the joyful news that Island No. 10 had been evacuated and that two thousand prisoners, including one general, had fallen into our hands." He proudly noted, "I think this achievement will compare favorably with any of the war, and in my opinion it is all attributable to the skill and courage of Captain Walke of this boat, because if he had not run the blockade and destroyed their batteries, Pope could never have landed his troops and so getting behind them, compelling them to evacuate and then taking them prisoners."[57]

With the navy's assistance, Pope had, in fact, bagged three generals,

4,500 rebel troops, twenty artillery pieces, and a large quantity of arms and ammunition. The Confederates had also failed to scuttle four steamers. For the Yankees, the cost was seven soldiers killed, fourteen wounded, and four missing. Hearing news of the victory at Island No. 10, Halleck wired his congratulations to Pope, saying, "It exceeds in boldness and brilliancy all other operations of the war."[58]

The Union navy had reason to boast as well. In addition to running the gauntlet past Island No. 10 and supporting the army's occupation of the Confederate stronghold, Captain Kilty of the *Mound City* had captured the enemy's signal book, signals, and telegraphic dictionary. The *Carondelet's* run past No. 10's batteries captured the nation's attention, but as the war progressed, the tactic of running under enemy guns became commonplace on western rivers. Less celebrated but equally important was the damage done to the Confederate batteries along the shore below No. 10. Disabling these 64-pounders was an important contribution to the Union seizure of the rebel stronghold and attested to the effectiveness of naval ordnance.

Navy Secretary Welles was less than enthusiastic about the seizure of Island No. 10, but he did tell Foote, "Your triumph is not the less appreciated because it was protracted and finally bloodless." The Mississippi River was now open to the federals all the way to Fort Pillow. With that position secured, Memphis became Foote's next important objective.[59]

5

Securing New Orleans

I see no want of determination on the part of our people. But I look for a bloody conflict.

—Francis Asbury Roe

From the beginning of the war, Union strategy had called for the capture of New Orleans, the South's largest city and leading port. In addition to being an important entry port for goods coming into the United States, New Orleans was the destination for goods being exported from farms and manufacturers served by the Mississippi River. Following the secession of states in the Mississippi Valley, the newly formed Confederate States of America came to depend on New Orleans for the importation of foodstuffs, beef, and war supplies. Confederate cities from Memphis to Baton Rouge also relied on the Mississippi River to ship cotton and other products to market in New Orleans. The Lincoln administration realized that seizing New Orleans and controlling the mouth of the Mississippi River would strike at the heart of the Confederacy, disrupting this flow of goods and seriously impacting the South's war-waging ability. As one military historian noted, "The river was also a major avenue of north-south communication from Tennessee to Louisiana and a bulwark against any attack for the west that might be mounted."[1] Securing New Orleans and the Mississippi line to Memphis would bisect the Confederacy, cutting the eastern states off from Arkansas and Texas. Furthermore, the loss of the city would have a positive impact on Northern morale and a negative one on the South.

Louisiana had seceded from the Union, and Confederate authorities were relying on the ironclad ram CSS *Manassas* and lightly armed gunboats

81

guarding the bayous and other water approaches to defend New Orleans. The Confederate government also looked to Fort St. Philip and Fort Jackson, located seventy miles below the city, to fend off Union naval forces. In addition, the *Louisiana* and the *Mississippi*, two large ironclads, were under construction but not yet completed. Assured that Forts Jackson and St. Philip would prevent any federal naval force from approaching New Orleans, the Confederates had sent most of their troops off to fight in Virginia or Tennessee, leaving just 4,000 local troops, commanded by Major General Mansfield Lovell, to defend the city.[2]

In September 1861 federal blockaders moved up the Mississippi River to Head of the Passes. A month later they became embroiled in a controversial engagement with Confederate navy vessels, including the *Manassas.* Mounting a surprise attack, the rebels damaged the USS *Richmond* and left the USS *Vincennes* aground on a bar. With a federal supply ship in tow, the Confederates then triumphantly retired up the river, rendering New Orleans safe, at least for the time being.[3]

Following this debacle, Union authorities had all but given up on attacking New Orleans—except for Commander David Dixon Porter. In the fall of 1861 he formulated a plan to ascend the Mississippi River and attack New Orleans. Porter had lived briefly in the city, and he knew that its approaches were guarded by two old forts that Union warships would have to get past. To Porter's mind, the old maxim still held true: a ship's a fool to fight a fort. However, the recent success of a joint Union army and navy expedition in taking Port Royal, South Carolina, had given him hope that modern warships could defeat shore fortifications without undue losses. Porter took his idea to Welles at the Navy Department: Union forces would first reduce Forts Jackson and St. Philip below New Orleans with a bombardment by a flotilla of mortar schooners. This would enable larger warships to proceed up the river to the city. Once New Orleans had been taken, Porter argued, the forts would surrender and could be garrisoned by a small force of army troops.

Welles found Porter's plan a sound one and presented it to the president. Lincoln then sent Welles, Fox, and Porter to confer with McClellan. The general took some convincing that wooden ships could indeed pass the forts, but in the end, Porter's argument that 13-inch mortars would reduce the forts prevailed. The War Department and Navy Department agreed on the plan, and Lincoln endorsed it.

To prepare for the New Orleans attack, Welles divided the federal blockading vessels into an East and a West Gulf Blockading Squadron. After much deliberation, and based on Porter's recommendation, he appointed David Glasgow Farragut to command the West Squadron and the operation against New Orleans. Porter deemed the sixty-year-old Farragut (who was, in fact, Porter's foster brother) better suited to command the expedition than most of the older, less aggressive captains on the navy's active list. Farragut's career in the navy began as a midshipman in 1810. He fought in the War of 1812, served in the West Indies, oversaw the building of the Mare Island navy yard, and earned promotions to lieutenant, commander, and captain. In 1861 he loyally offered his services to the Union navy. Porter was Welles's obvious choice to command the mortar flotilla, and he set off immediately to have mortars built, purchase schooners, and find light-draft steamers to tow them up the river.[4]

As his flagship, the navy assigned Farragut the USS *Hartford,* a wooden screw sloop of war with graceful lines and a full, square rig. Farragut's twelve ships had a detachment of 333 marines commanded by Captain John L. Broome, one of the few veteran Marine Corps officers who did not "go South." The marines under his command served as guards or sentries, in gun crews and armed landing parties, or as sharpshooters during battle. Richard Wainwright, the *Hartford*'s commanding officer, began his naval career as a midshipman in 1831. He quickly earned the respect and admiration of the US marines on board the *Hartford,* among them Private Oscar Smith, who had marched down to a local recruiting station in Portsmouth, New Hampshire, and volunteered in the fall of 1861. In a journal he kept while serving on the *Hartford,* Smith wrote, "Our captain is very fastidious. He had several men relieved for having their belts slightly soiled. Barr was triced up for half an hour and got a week extra duty."[5]

After being fitted out for wartime service, the *Hartford* went into commission on January 19, 1862. Following the noon meal, the marines formed up smartly on the starboard side of the ship, a signalman ran a pennant up the main mast, and the *Hartford* was declared in commission. "An imposing and solemn occasion," Smith told a fellow marine who joined the ship later. "The whole company took off their hats."[6] The *Hartford* then departed Philadelphia for the Gulf of Mexico, and the largely inexperienced crew endured a rough passage down the coast in wintry seas. On February 11 the *Hartford* arrived in Key West, Florida, joining the recommissioned steam sloop *Pensacola* and six of Porter's new mortar schooners. When the *Pensacola*'s commanding officer, Captain Henry W. Morris, reported to the flagship, Farragut asked him for his observations about the Southern coast. Morris, who had participated in the Coast Survey, reminded Farragut that the water was very shallow, and the *Pensacola* and *Hartford* were deep-draft vessels. He suggested that if they had vessels with a five-foot draft, they could go up the shallow bayous and creeks and catch rebel blockade runners off guard. Morris also noted that they would need more medical officers and mechanics and should make plans for coal delivery. Farragut agreed to ask Welles for shallow-draft vessels that could be armed with two or three 20-pounder rifles and then set about composing a letter to the navy secretary summarizing the squadron's needs.[7]

To whip his green crew into shape, the *Hartford*'s captain drilled his men in the use of the ship's guns. On February 20 Private Smith made a note in his journal: "After quarters we trained with the big gun. A second marine crew formed today." From Key West, the *Hartford* went on to Ship Island, Mississippi, the only deep-water harbor between Mobile Bay and the mouth of the Mississippi River. Troops of the 26th Massachusetts and 9th Connecticut Volunteers had occupied and secured the island, which was protected from the Gulf's most dangerous storms, as a base for Union navy vessels and a staging area for Union forces. Smith enjoyed the cool weather at Ship Island and noted that it looked "as if covered with snow, the sand is so white." Wainwright continued to drill his gun crews. Smith wrote, "After dinner continued practicing at all distances. I hit the barrel once at 150 yards and made all line shots. We afterward drilled a short time. Sailors drilled with small arms."[8]

In early March the *Pensacola* hove into view off Ship Island to join the *Hartford*, *Vincennes*, *Preble*, *Colorado*, *Brooklyn*, *Winona*, and *Kineo*. As he awaited the arrival of all his ships, including Porter's mortar schooners, Farragut kept himself busy. He asked the Navy Department to send more coal and machine tools, and he asked the Coast Survey to provide surveys of Pass a l'Outré and Southwest Pass into the Mississippi.

One March morning the newly commissioned Unadilla-class screw gunboat *Cayuga* arrived safely at Ship Island after a stormy passage. Twenty-six-year-old George Hamilton Perkins, the first lieutenant, wrote to his family that the *Cayuga* was "not very well fitted up for comfort, though she is a fine gunboat." Only the captain, Lieutenant Napoleon B. Harrison, had ever been to sea on a man-of-war. Most of the gunboat's ninety-five-man crew were green hands, causing Perkins to note, "My berth as first lieutenant is as onerous as honorary." Farragut's blockaders had gathered at Ship

Island to escort General Benjamin F. Butler's troops to the mouth of the Mississippi River for an attack against New Orleans. "General Butler is embarking his troops, and we all leave this evening for New Orleans," Perkins wrote on March 31, 1862. "Everything is all excitement. The attack will be made at once, and they say if we succeed it will end the war."[9]

Meanwhile, with the capable assistance of Captain Henry H. Bell, Porter had purchased his schooners and pushed the construction of their 13-inch mortars so that his flotilla now consisted of three divisions. The schooners varied in length from 87 to 121 feet and from 125 to 349 tons, and they had complements of less than fifty men. Each schooner carried a massive 13-inch mortar; fifteen of the vessels also had two 32-pounders each, and eleven others were armed with two 12-pound howitzers. As his flagship, Porter chose the *Harriet Lane,* a large side-wheel steamer built as a revenue cutter in 1857 and transferred to the navy in 1861.

Porter had arrived at Key West in his flagship *Harriet Lane* on the last day of February, only to learn to his dismay that Farragut had already proceeded to the mouth of the Mississippi. When the mortar schooners arrived at Ship Island on March 11, he had no vessels to tow them to the delta. After fretting for a week, Porter ordered the schooners to set sail for Ship Island, accompanied by his flagship and two steamers. The *Colorado, Pensacola,* and *Mississippi* had already joined the sloop of war *Brooklyn,* which had been blockading Pass a l'Outré off the mouth of the Mississippi since early February.[10]

Before ascending the Mississippi to attack Forts Jackson and St. Philip, Farragut's ships had to cross bars at the entrance to the delta. These bars had been created by a year of maritime inactivity; as a result of the cessation of dredging operations, the entrances to the five passes into the Mississippi River had filled with silt. Blessed with shallow drafts, the federal gunboats *Winona, Kineo,* and *Kennebec,* under the command of Bell, had crossed the bars and seized the small village of Pilot Town. From there they proceeded upriver toward the rebel forts. Of the deeper-draft vessels, the *Brooklyn* made the first attempt to negotiate the channel into Pass a l'Outre. "The Brooklyn is still trying to get over the bar, but doesn't succeed. She struck on the bar where she has been laying during the afternoon and night," Smith wrote. For seventeen agonizing hours, Commander Thomas T. Craven tried in vain to free his ship from the mud. Finally, the *Hartford* towed the vessel off, and Craven went around to Southwest Pass. Fortunately, Farragut had sent an assistant to sound and buoy Southwest Pass, so the *Brook-*

lyn made it on the first attempt, grounding for only an hour. The *Hartford* crossed the bar the next day, March 13. "Our flag is now, I hope, permanently hoisted on Louisiana soil," Farragut wrote to Welles.[11]

To Farragut's relief, Porter's tugboats *Clifton* and *Westfield* arrived at the mouth of the Mississippi on March 18 and immediately went to work towing the mortar flotilla across the bar. All this frantic activity should have provoked a response from the Confederates, but except for two side-wheelers that came downriver on March 12 and promptly turned around rather than face Farragut's gunboats, the federal squadron entered the Mississippi unopposed. Much to his disgust, however, Farragut's war with the mud of the Mississippi Delta had just begun. Concerned about their deep drafts, he had sent the *Mississippi, Pensacola,* and *Colorado* back to Ship Island to lighten their loads. When they arrived back off Southwest Pass on March 24 and the *Pensacola* attempted to cross the bar, the efforts only drove the ship deeper into the mud. Likewise, it would take ten days of arduous work to get the old *Mississippi* through the mud and over the bar. Farragut could not have predicted how difficult it would be to get his deep-draft wooden vessels up the Mississippi River and past New Orleans.[12]

Finally, on April 8, Private Smith made this cryptic journal entry: "The commodore went to Pilot Town this morning, returning in the evening. He said that 'things are in readiness.'" The following day Porter's mortar boats began coming in. "One brought us two nine inch guns," Smith noted. The *Harriet Lane* followed the next day with several more mortar schooners, and Porter went up with a surveying party to map the channels and mark anchorages.[13]

By now, all this activity had caught the Confederates' attention, and they sent down a fire raft with towering flames. On April 17 rebel steamers began taking potshots at the surveyors. By the next day, which was Good Friday, Porter's three divisions of mortar schooners were towed into position. Porter directed that the masts of the schooners be dressed with bushes "to make them invisible to the enemy and mingle with the thick forest of trees and matted vines behind which they were placed." Lieutenant Watson Smith's first division of seven boats opened the bombardment, firing 13-inch shells at Fort Jackson. Positioned behind the first division, Lieutenant Walter Queen's third division then took aim on the fort and set fire to the citadel, endangering the magazine. Confederate gunners at the fort returned fire, and when it grew "rather hot," Porter asked Farragut to send some of his gunboats up to draw their fire. A large 120-pound shell passed through the cabin of Queen's vessel, and another fell near the *George Mang-ham,* prompting Porter to move both boats astern. Unaware of the extent of the damage done to the fort, Porter called a cease-fire at sunset, and in the wee hours of the morning Queen's division moved from the northeast bank of the river to a less exposed position on the south shore.[14]

The mortar bombardment resumed on April 19, and Private Smith carefully noted its progress. "Mortars opened fire at six bells. 8:30 o'clock. Gunboats are going up the river, firing constantly." At noon "a mortar schooner commenced sinking from her own mortar, the concussion making her leak. Her crew had just come on board the Hartford." Porter reported that the schooner, *Maria J. Carlton,* had actually "been sunk by a rifle shot passing down through her deck, magazine, and bottom." Confederate gunfire was now having an effect. "A rebel shot struck the schooner's row boat and sank it. Five men were wounded on the Iroquois between twelve and two o'clock by a ten-inch shot. Three were dangerously wounded." After dinner, Smith went aloft to view the bombardment from the rigging. For two hours he watched shells fall from the federal mortars. "Only a few seemed to burst. Three bursted high in the air. The fort ceased firing about 8:30 o'clock. We bombarded all night."[15]

When fire from the rebel forts grew alarmingly severe, smashing into the first division's masts and rigging, Porter signaled Lieutenant Smith to fall back. But Smith, Porter wrote, "seemed determined not to withdraw until something was sunk." One of his vessels, the *Arletta,* had taken a 10-inch shot between the stop of the mortar bed and the mortar, disabling the latter. The captain had men working to repair it, but with the mortar out of service, his men were under fire without any distraction. Given Smith's reluctance to fall back, Porter relented and allowed his division to remain in place.

Bad fuses continued to plague the mortar schooners, so Porter ordered full-length fuses put in. To Porter's disappointment, the soft, wet ground absorbed the mortar rounds, which plunged twenty feet into the earth and exploded, throwing up mounds of dirt and causing little damage. The shots shook the ground like earthquakes, however, demoralizing the rebels. And Porter later learned that those hitting the fort's ramparts knocked off large pieces of parapet and casemate.[16]

Francis Asbury Roe, the *Pensacola*'s first lieutenant, assessed the success of the day's bombardment in his journal. "The bombs do not fall with accuracy, however but they land all about the fort, and occasionally strike it.

A barbette gun was dismounted by a XI-inch shell, from one of the gunboats."[17]

Two days of mortar bombardment had not silenced Fort Jackson, and Farragut was now faced with a crucial decision. Should he postpone the move to New Orleans until the forts had been "reduced," or should he leave Porter's mortar flotilla and Butler's troops behind and take his fleet past the forts to the Crescent City? Farragut chose the latter option and called a conference of his commanders. A lively discussion followed. Several argued that going above the forts would hazard being cut off from their supplies, but others pointed out that steamers could pass down at twelve miles per hour. Finally, Farragut agreed to allow Porter's mortars to pummel the forts for several more days before running his fleet past them. However, he warned that the fleet's ammunition was running low, and they would have to act soon. "I believe in celerity," he told his commanders.[18]

Roe observed, "the great problem of ships and forts is now to be solved." He assessed the situation as follows: "The enemy numbers the same number of guns as ourselves. But he has all bearing upon our ships, whereas our ships have only half of their guns to bear at once upon the enemy." He expected the chain to be cut that night, and then they would get under way and form a line of battle. "I am proud that the *Pensacola* is to lead the van of the second division and engage Fort [St.] Philip. The first division will engage [Fort] Jackson, while the second will deliver their fire and pass over to the east bank to Fort St. Philip."[19]

Before Farragut's ships could proceed upriver past the rebel forts, they would have to cut a boom comprised of chains and cables stretched across old hulks and placed across the river by the Confederates. On the evening of April 20, Captain Bell led the gunboats *Pinola* and *Itasca* in an attempt to sever the boom. Explosive charges set to break the barrier failed to explode, but Lieutenant Charles Caldwell's *Itasca* came alongside one of the hulks, and his crewmen unshackled the chains and opened up a channel.[20]

Despite their failure to blow up the chain, Bell's operation proved successful, prompting Perkins to write, "Today or to-morrow we start up the river. The chain across it was cut last night, and I have no doubt but that the forts will be ours before tomorrow evening." His prediction proved far too optimistic. After five days of bombardment and an expenditure of 16,800 rounds from the mortar schooners, the forts were damaged but still full of fight. The ongoing bombardment was wearing on the squadron's officers and men. "The rebels are continually sending down fire rafts, and the bombardment from the mortars goes on night and day, so that we have hardly had any sleep," Perkins explained. He remained optimistic, however. "Unless we meet some unforeseen obstacles, New Orleans must fall, though perhaps it will take a week's hard fighting."[21]

Finally, at 2:00 on the morning of April 24, the flagship hoisted Farragut's signal to get under way for the run past the enemy forts. On the *Pensacola*, Roe made a last-minute entry in his diary: "I see no want of determination on the part of our people. But I look for a bloody conflict." As Farragut's ships advanced, Porter's mortars threw shells at a furious rate. The *Cayuga* led Captain Bailey's division—the *Cayuga, Mississippi, Pensacola, Oneida, Varuna, Katahdin, Kineo,* and *Wissahickon.* The task of conning the *Pensacola* fell to Roe, the executive officer, who had taken his station on the bridge. By 3:00 the *Pensacola* was under way, with anchors secured. Bailey's division had formed in a close line, with "the gunboat *Cayuga* leading us like a pilot fish," but it was so far ahead that Roe considered the *Pensacola* to be in the van. It slowed as it neared the fort. A rifle shot whizzed overhead. "It was but a moment more when the battle was in full play," Roe wrote. "I had kept my people lying down flat until I was fairly in reach of our guns, when I ordered the division to open." Roe knew that order would save lives and not waste ammunition. As the ship neared the breach in the barricade, the forts opened fire, and the *Pensacola* replied with its bow guns. As a small space in the broken chain across the river opened up, the ship proceeded slowly in the darkness and in the smoke of burning powder.[22]

By now, a rebel gunboat squadron had the *Pensacola* in sight. "They kept ahead of us, firing a stream of rifle shot and shell from a raking position down upon us," Roe explained. Fire from the rebel forts gave the *Pensacola*'s officers and crew some close calls, but Roe ordered the ship's 80-pounder and 11-inch pivot guns trained nearly ahead and fought back. The *Pensacola*'s gun crews took several devastating hits that scattered splinters and bolts every which way. One shot cut acting master E. C. Weeks's sword belt from his waist in three pieces. A fragment struck boatswain Goodrich in his arm, but he remained at his station. The No. 5 gun crew suffered the most from enemy fire. John Ryan, the gun captain, was killed, and several others were injured by shell fragments. Rebel gunners seemed to aim for the *Pensacola*'s bridge, just abaft the mainmast. "My signal quartermaster [Murray] and my boy aid [Flood] were both swept away from my side," Roe recalled. To his amazement, the boy got the quartermaster below to the surgeon and then "returned to my side again, brave as a lion." Murray's leg had been shot away by a shell that burst near them, and as day broke, Roe discovered that splinters had cut his own pants away at the knee and stripped a piece off the bottom of his coat. At daylight, the *Pensacola* was past the enemy batteries and pursuing the retreating rebel gunboats. Roe noted that, "one after another," the rebel boats "were hulled by our guns, and ran ashore and burned or destroyed. Not one escaped."[23]

Farragut's flagship had gone ahead of the *Brooklyn*. "All Hands were called to quarters and lay down at the guns," Private Smith wrote. "While we lay thus the fort opened upon us, and shot whistled around us furiously. As soon as our guns could be brought to bear on the fort we opened fire." The *Hartford* commenced fire with its port guns, sending clouds of heavy smoke to shroud the decks. When a lookout spotted a rebel fire raft coming toward them, Farragut ordered "Hard port," but the current caught the ship and sent its bows so close to a mud bank that a sailor on the bowsprit could reach out and touch the tops of the bushes. Standing to his gun, Smith could hear rebel gunners on the casemates of Fort St. Philip giving orders. "Both sides fired incessantly and shot and shell flew around like hail," Smith wrote. "While this battle was raging fiercest a ram forced a fire raft against us, setting the ship on fire, while the heat drove us from our guns." The *Hartford* was aground, but as Smith explained, "By what seemed a miracle we got off the ground, cleared the raft, and put out the fire." They ran down the rebel boats wherever they found them. "The shore seemed lined with burning rafts and steamers. During the hottest part of the engagement a rebel gunboat came within pistol shot. Our Captain hailed her and asked the Captain if he wished to surrender. He answered, 'No, never.' 'Then fire upon her' said our Captain. A shower of grape from the top and a broadside dealt death among them."[24]

The *Brooklyn* pressed on at full speed to get beyond the forts, but the tide had carried it over to the other shore. The *Brooklyn* stood by the *Hartford,* despite the heavy enemy fire, and when Craven could see that the fire raft no longer threatened the flagship, he ordered, "Full steam ahead." Passing close to Fort St. Philip—some observers said only sixty yards—the *Brooklyn* got off three broadsides. Craven told his wife, "Pretty close work to fight our eleven guns against sixty, and that, too, entirely unsupported." The ship steamed so close to the fort that its barbette gunners could not depress their guns enough to score hits. Soldiers on the parapets fired their muskets at the ship, however, and one bullet found its mark on the port of the No. 1 gun, hitting Lieutenant O'Kane in the leg. He crumpled to the deck, but when several men raced to carry him below, O'Kane hollered, "Not until I fire back at those bastards."[25]

Led by the *Sciota*, Bell's third division now attempted to run past the forts. The *Sciota* slipped by with little damage, but the rebel CSS *McRae* took on the *Iroquois*. The federal sloop of war let go with its 11-inch Dahlgren and set the *McRae* ablaze. The *Pinola* followed up, forcing the little Confederate boat into the bank. With the exception of the *Kennebec, Itasca,* and *Winona,* Farragut now had all his vessels above the forts. Those three had been caught in a raft of logs, and enemy gunners took advantage of the daylight and drove the heavily damaged trio back.

With thirteen of his ships now above the forts, Farragut could take stock. Only three of the rebels' dozen vessels had engaged his fleet. The *McRae* had burned, the *Manassas* had been driven ashore and abandoned, and the *Varuna*'s duel with the *Governor Moore* had destroyed both of them. The casualty count was 184; of these, 37 had been killed. Below, Porter urged Butler to land his troops in the rear of Fort St. Philip. He had sent a surrender demand to the forts, which the rebels had refused.[26]

Farragut's saltwater fleet had run the gauntlet past Forts Jackson and St. Philip, but the forts remained in rebel hands. The Union ships steamed up to New Orleans on April 25, firing on two earthworks just below the city. Confederate militia fled, and thousands of bales of cotton were set aflame. When surrender negotiations failed, Farragut sent in the marines. They marched to city hall on April 29, hauled down the Louisiana flag, and hoisted the Stars and Stripes above the mint and the customhouse. In the meantime, as Butler's troops approached the forts on the evening of April 27, the 250 men of the Fort Jackson garrison mutinied. Both forts surrendered on April 28, 1862.[27]

6

The Battle of Plum Point Bend

We have now passed No. 10 and are on our way to New Orleans. We expect a warm reception at Fort Pillow, but as our cause is just we confidently expect to pass it.

—Lieutenant George Blodgett

Following the fall of Island No. 10, Foote moved the *Benton, Cincinnati, Mound City, Cairo,* and *St. Louis,* along with the mortar boats, tugs, towboats, and transports, downstream to New Madrid. His intention was to proceed to Fort Pillow, about eighty miles above Memphis. Foote had reliable intelligence that the rebels at Fort Pillow had constructed a long line of breastworks with a ditch and timber in front. At the top of the steep bluffs, they had placed some forty heavy guns, including 10-inch Columbiads. The rebels "had 1,200 negroes working on the batteries still, to strengthen this stronghold," Foote told Welles.[1]

When Foote arrived at New Madrid on the evening of April 11, 1862, Major General Pope informed him that seven Confederate gunboats had been seen anchored fifteen miles below. Pope also told Foote that some of his troops had not yet embarked on the transports, but he assured the flag officer that they would be aboard by April 13. The presence of enemy gunboats did not seem to ruffle Foote, who assumed they would "skeddadle" downstream to the protection of the rebel batteries. News that the troops had not embarked, however, displeased Foote. He refused to wait for the army and steamed downriver on April 12.[2]

In the forenoon the federal squadron passed the *Carondelet* and the *Pittsburg,* and Foote signaled for the *Carondelet* to get in line and follow the

93

flotilla downstream. "There was nothing to be seen except the same ever-lasting cottonwood bottom, flooded," *Carondelet* diarist John Morison wrote, "and here and there an old tumbledown shanty propped up like an old worn out stage horse on the verge of dissolution." A fleet of transports tagged along behind the gunboats. "About sundown we tied up abreast the mouth of the Ohio river, famous only as having been the theater of some of the adventures of the once celebrated Davy Crockett," Morison reported.[3]

The squadron steamed down to an anchorage at Hale's Point, some fifty miles below New Madrid. In the meantime, the *Cairo* had drawn an assignment, as explained by fourteen-year-old seaman George Yost: "At 12 left New Madrid and started down the river to guard the mortar fleet part of which are ahead of us and part astern, the other Gunboats have gone on ahead of us. Kept on down the river until 8 P.M. when we dropped anchor." The *Cairo* had just rejoined the flotilla after almost a week in Cairo undergoing modifications designed to better protect the gunboat's pilothouse from enemy shot and shell. Carpenters had lined the interior with pine paneling to absorb splinters, and workmen had installed iron flaps over the ports that could be closed, offering the pilots better protection. All these changes were based on lessons learned after the engagements with Forts Henry and Donelson.[4]

The *Carondelet*'s arrival farther south brought enemies of a different variety. "Here the approach of summer made itself rather severely felt in the shape of several 'skeeter' bites," Morison wrote. He had gone on deck "with the intention of enjoying the soft spring evening, but it was no use, as they drove me below." For those pondering the squadron's next move, Fort Pillow seemed a likely target. Its guns blocked any Union movement downstream toward Memphis, where the Memphis and Little Rock Railroad ended. The tracks continued on to Chattanooga and Savannah, acting as a lifeline and bringing an abundance of produce from Arkansas into the Confederacy. Other commanders shared Walke's expectation of an engagement with the rebels. In a letter to his aunt, the *Conestoga*'s commanding officer, Lieutenant Blodgett, explained, "We have now passed No. 10 and are on our way to New Orleans. We expect a warm reception at Fort Pillow, but as our cause is just we confidently expect to pass it."[5]

The *Carondelet*'s hands were called out to take in coal at 4:00 the next morning, April 13. In the early light just before dawn, transports bearing Pope's 20,000-man force hove into view, as did the first of five Confederate "cotton-clad" gunboats, so named because compressed cotton bales had been tucked around their vulnerable parts. Morison carefully recorded what happened next: "As the morning mist lifted off the face of the river, a rebel steamer could be described, apparently aground on the bend of the river a mile below us. She made no effort to get off." After a while, they could see the smoke of several other boats coming around the bend farther below. Soon there were four boats, and "they all set to work apparently to get the stranded one off. They plied and ran around as carelessly as if there wasn't a yankee gunboat on the Mississippi." Captain Thomas B. Huger, commanding the Confederate gunboat *General Sterling Price,* had spotted the federal vessels and decided to challenge them. "After watching them for about three hours, the commodore very 'leisurely' [signaled] to get under weigh and gave us orders to follow him," Morison wrote. The flagship *Benton* took half an hour to turn around, and by then, the five cotton-clads had gone down toward Fort Pillow. "Before they left, however, they sent us a few shell, which came a little nearer than was pleasant to contemplate. We also sent them a few, which helped to hurry them up." Morison reported that "the whole flotilla was now running downstream as fast as possible, the rebs ditto." About two miles above the fort, they all came to. "We lay still for a little, when the commodore sent orders to follow him." The gunboats then ran down to the bend, and as soon as they were in sight of Fort Pillow, the rebels began shelling them. "We took hasty look and departed in short order." At 11:00 Foote took his gunboats out of range of Fort Pillow and headed back upstream.[6]

All four of Foote's gunboats then headed for Plum Point. Pope's transports, crowded with troops, headed for the Tennessee shore. The *Cairo,* sent to guard the mortar scows, had missed out on the brief encounter with the cotton-clads. Yost noted that the *Benton* and *Mound City* had gone down the river to reconnoiter, holding out hope for action soon. "We will probably go down to Randolph tomorrow and will be likely to have stirring times."[7]

Blodgett, recently promoted to lieutenant, seemed pleased at the results of the flotilla's encounter. "When at a distance of about 2 miles, from them the Flag Steamer 'Benton' opened with her Dahlgren rifled guns, and made some very handsome shots for so long a range." He thought they had done some damage to the Confederate ships, given "the rapidity with which they got up steam, and put off down stream. We have not seen them since."[8]

After conferring with Pope about the plan to attack Fort Pillow, Foote sent tugs down with the mortar scows to within half a mile of Craigshead

Point on the morning of April 14. He instructed Maynadier to tie them up along the Arkansas shore in preparation for a bombardment of the fort. Pope's troops would land above Plum Point, cross a neck of land, and advance against the fort from the rear, while Foote's gunboats and mortar boats attacked them in the front.[9]

"Six mortar boats were placed in position this morning," Morison wrote in his diary. At 2:00 that afternoon, the mortars opened fire. "A flash and a roar and our first installment of our national debt is being paid," he noted. "The firing was kept up through the day and at short intervals through the night. Once in a while they returned fire, making good line shots, but none of them took effect."[10]

Protected, as planned, by Foote' gunboats, Pope's troops went ashore six miles above Craigshead Point. "I have no idea when an attack will be made," *Mound City* sailor Symmes Browne wrote a day later. "I do not think they will make much of a stand here for our mortars are too close to them and will be very destructive."[11]

For several days, Foote's mortars shelled Fort Pillow, to no avail. Young Yost watched the bombardment from the *Cairo* and penned a graphic description in his diary: "I frequently saw as many as a dozen shells in the air at one time, crossing each other's fiery tracks; some of them burst in mid air, some landing in the water, others in the heavy woods on the Arkansas shore."[12]

On the flagship *Benton,* Foote was still hobbling around on crutches—his recovery proving nearly as frustrating as the Western Flotilla's lack of progress against the rebel fort. He fully intended to coordinate a gunboat attack on Fort Pillow with Pope's troops, but at the time of their conference on the *Benton,* neither Foote nor Pope knew that the river had flooded the low ground behind the fort, making an assault by Pope's troops impossible. When a message arrived reporting that much of the land around the fort was under water, Foote called for assistance. "While he was preparing to attack Fort Pillow," Walke later wrote, "Foote sent his executive officer twice to me on the *Carondelet* to inquire whether I would undertake, with my vessel and two or three other gun-boats, to pass below the fort to cooperate with General Pope." Exuding confidence after the *Carondelet's* successful run past Island No. 10, Walke told Foote he "was ready at anytime to make the attempt."[13]

In the end, nothing came of Foote's request. A telegram from Pope arrived on the evening of April 16, enclosing a message from Halleck. Halleck had ordered Pope to move his troops immediately to Pittsburg Landing. "I will leave with you two strong regiments, sufficient to garrison Fort Pillow, when it is evacuated," Pope assured Foote. The departure of all but Colonel Graham Fitch's two volunteer regiments left Foote utterly dismayed that his "best matured and hopeful plans" to take Fort Pillow and go on to Memphis had been frustrated. Foote composed a letter to Welles, explaining that he now had just two land regiments of about 1,500 men, his seven ironclads, a wooden gunboat, and sixteen mortar boats. In contrast, "Ft. Pillow has for its defense at least forty heavy guns in position and nine ironclads, six of them, however, being wooden boats, but armed with heavy guns, and a force of 6,000 troops." This disparity made Foote reluctant to attack the fort directly.[14]

In the meantime, federal mortars continued bombarding Fort Pillow, annoying the enemy gun crews but not dislodging the guns. On April 15 the *Cairo*'s sailor-diarist recounted a near miss: "One shell, a very large one passed directly over our upper deck, where I was sitting, missing our wheel house about twenty feet, and dropping into the water twenty yards away, where it burst, making a tremendous splashing of the water."[15] The following day the commanding officers of the *Cairo, Carondelet,* and *St. Louis* were ordered to stand by six of the mortar boats while they fired off shells at a rate of one per minute. Rebel gunners on the bluff fired back, and a 128-pounder struck the hammock nettings of the *Carondelet* before falling into the river, drenching the sailors who were standing near the railing. Enemy shot inflicted a few hits on the *St. Louis* and *Cairo* but caused only minor damage. "There is but little firing on the other side today," Yost explained on April 18, but "the Rebels have the range of our flotilla very good."[16]

Although April 20 was Easter Sunday, Foote's flotilla enjoyed little in the way of celebration. "Indeed, dearest, this day has seemed the least like Sunday to me of any Sabbath since I left home," Browne told his fiancée. Morison, who was sick with ague, lamented, "No eggs around but a good supply of 'shell.'" And, in the way of an Easter gift, he noted that the *Carondelet* had received a draft of thirty men from Cairo. "The old messes were all broken up and reconstructed. I was placed in 7 mess, of which I am now cook."[17]

The siege of Fort Pillow went on relentlessly. Twice, heavy rain caused the mortars to recoil dangerously on their wet platforms, but little else broke the monotony, save the appearance of enemy deserters or fugitive blacks. As the days passed, Foote dutifully kept Welles informed of the situation. On April 23 Foote noted that his vessels had been assaulting the fort daily, except for two days when heavy rain precluded any mortar bombardment. Colonel Fitch's efforts to find a way to bring in heavy guns to blockade the river and prevent the enemy from coming up from New Orleans and Memphis had been unsuccessful. The disgruntled Foote blamed this lack of progress on Pope, who had left the army without any tools to cut through the swamps. However, Foote assured Welles that he would do everything in his power to capture Fort Pillow "and exert myself beyond my impaired health and strength toward the accomplishment of this great object."[18]

A week later the flag officer assured Welles that the flotilla was prepared for an attack by rebel gunboats "at any moment," but he doubted one would come. Foote hated just sitting around waiting to be attacked, so he proposed taking the initiative on "a dark night" and, "by running the blockade, get below the fort and attack the rebel boats and rams with our seven ironclad gunboats." After destroying the rebel fleet, the federal flotilla would attack the fort upstream and proceed to Memphis. There were some objections to this idea: namely, if Foote's vessels ran the blockade, they might leave one or two rebel steamers behind, which could destroy the federal transports and mortar boats and command the river above. This would leave the flotilla without coal or ammunition below. "We have but 1,200 troops," Foote explained, an insufficient number to hold the place if they went on to Memphis. "Had General Pope not been ordered away, with his 20,000 troops, we should, before this, humanly speaking [have] been in possession of Fort Pillow and Memphis."[19]

The expectation of a Confederate attack, based largely on information garnered from rebel deserters, seemed common knowledge in the squadron. In fact, in anticipation of the rebels coming up one evening, Foote had ordered the watches doubled, the sick removed, and the gunboats anchored with their bows facing downstream. "One of the late deserters states that the rebels intend making an attack on us some night this week with thirteen boats," Morison wrote in his diary on April 28, "in consequence of which report we get everything ready for action every night before turning in. We also keep watch, and watch and sleep with our side arms on. If they come up, they will have a good time, I don't think." The next day, however, Morison noted, "Nary [a] rebel last night. Nothing of any consequence going on." Unbeknownst to the diarist at the time, deserters had reported that the rebels would have attacked the Union flotilla the previous night if not for the fact that the Confederate commander, Captain James Edward Montgomery, was waiting for a new gunboat from Memphis.[20]

The gunboat *Cairo* had been preparing for action with the rebels as well. On April 27 a supply vessel had come down from Cairo with several Parrott rifle guns. "We received on board from the steamer 'De Soto' 1 30 pounder Parrott Rifle gun, in the afternoon," Yost wrote in his journal. The following day, a Monday, he noted, "The Parrott rifle was placed in position today on the Starboard Bow. I was stationed at the Parrott gun as Powder Boy." On the last day of April Yost reported that the "boilers [were] cleaned and repaired. . . . There is but little firing from the rebels today, the flag officer seems to be waiting for an attack and the rebels are in all probability waiting for an attack also. I went in the river bathing today, the first time this season." The next day he noted, "There is but very little firing on the other side today. . . . [We] had a roast pig today that was killed in the wilds of Arkansas. We are having fresh meat almost all the time since we lay alongside the mortar boats but we have to go some distance in boats as the river is out of its banks at this place."[21]

The mortar bombardment of Fort Pillow continued throughout April, and as the month came to an end, Maynadier reported to Foote that his mortars had fired a total of 531 13-inch shells at Fort Pillow since April 14.[22] The end of the month also brought good news from Farragut's squadron. "We have received news that Com. Porter has possession of New Orleans and Baton Rouge and is advancing up the river," Browne on the *Mound City* confidently told his fiancée. "If this is so, it will not require a great while to open his river, and then we will chase the enemy's gunboats up the smaller rivers and capture them."[23]

Anticipating an enemy attack that never came led many in the flotilla to doubt the rebels' intentions. "We have heard very little concerning new gunboats built by the rebels and apprehend very little danger from them," Browne wrote. His gunboat, the *Mound City*, remained on station off Fort Pillow. The bored officers occupied themselves with diversions such as deer hunting or rowing in a skiff with the ship's surgeon looking for specimens of worms, bugs, lizards, and insects.[24]

Then, on May 8, the *Carondelet*'s hands "were awakened about 4 a.m. with the cry of 'all hands' tumble out, lash and carry, three turns and run, the rebels are coming." As the men staggered out, "some were rubbing their eyes, some bundling their clothes on wrong side up without care, some already dressed but busy swearing," Morison noted. The drum beat quarters and "soon got everything quiet, cutlasses were buckled on, guns trained and the magazine and shell rooms opened in expectation of an attack." Morison went up on deck and found that a couple of rebel boats had gone around the elbow of the Arkansas shore with the "intention of stealing a couple of our mortars, which weren't there." The enemy's appearance roused the crews of all the gunboats. Browne wrote, "In fifteen minutes the ship [*Mound City*] was cleared and ready for action, and we gave the enemy a salute by a shell from our Dahlgren gun, and then one from our port rifle, and the 'Cincinnati' and 'Cairo,' which lay just above us, opened fire also."[25]

The rebel boats "buzzed around for an hour, taking good care, however, to keep out of the range of the rifled shell which were kept in waiting for them," Morison wrote. "One of them seemed to approach a little but she was warned off by a shell from the 'Benton,' which if it did not hurt her, it scared her badly, as she backed out in short order." The *Mound City* fired six shots, and the other boats together fired ten—"quite a nice little excitement for such an early hour, and we all enjoyed it." The federals kept a sharp lookout the following day, lest the enemy boats return, but they did not make an appearance. Finding no mortar boats to attack, the rebel *General Bragg, General Sumter,* and *General Van Dorn* had returned to base.[26]

Two weeks earlier, Foote had forwarded to Welles the report of three surgeons who had examined him and concluded that his injured foot would soon make him unfit to command. "His wounded foot, which has become no better, has affected his general health," Phelps wrote, "and left him prey to the prevalent disease of the locality, diarrhea and fever combined, and he is now very ill from these combination of evils." The medical board advised that Foote be sent home to rest and recuperate in a more temperate climate. Phelps had campaigned to succeed Foote, but the flag officer bowed to the navy's seniority system and recommended that Captain Charles H. Davis temporarily replace him.[27]

"The steamer from Cairo brought down Commodore Davis, who is to relieve Commodore Foote," Morison wrote on May 9. That same day, the ailing Foote departed for Cairo. "About one bell (12½ P.M.) all hands were called to cheer ship as the commodore was going away. We all tumbled up to get a parting look at the old man. He looked very pale and feeble as he was passing us," Morison noted. "He said, if he was able, he would come on aboard and shake hands with all of us and then he wished that God might bless and protect us. A few turns of the wheels and the western flotilla knew Commodore Foote no more."[28]

As he wistfully watched the *De Soto* pull away with the former Western Flotilla commander, Charles H. Davis must have felt the weight of command on his shoulders. A blue-water oceanographer for most of his naval career, Davis was more at home on the Coast Survey than on a gunboat on the Mississippi. Before Foote's departure, he and Phelps, who had assumed much of the responsibility for the flotilla's operations, had briefed Davis on the flotilla's routine and on the bombardment of Fort Pillow. Both men had warned the new commander that they expected the thirteen rebel gunboats and rams loitering a few miles below Pillow to make a run at the federal squadron.

Given an earlier foray by the rebels in April, it should have come as no surprise to Davis or his commanders that at about 6:30 on the morning of May 10, a sailor holystoning the *Benton*'s decks cried, "Smoke in sight!" Throwing their buckets aside, the wet, bare-legged sailors looked out to see several enemy vessels coming around Plum Point, belching dense smoke from their chimneys. Morison, who was in the *Carondelet*'s forecastle that morning, wrote, "I heard some of the rebels are coming and in looking towards the fort, I saw steamers rounding the point of the Arkansas shore and they were closely followed by several others, as we could see by their smoke." The gunboat beat to quarters, and by then, four or five of the enemy boats "had got round the point and were making for the 'Cincinnati' with the intention of either sinking her or capturing her and the mortar which she covered."[29]

At the time, Davis's flagship the *Benton,* the *Carondelet,* and the *Pittsburg* were tied up along the Tennessee side of the riverbank; the *Cincinnati, Mound City, St. Louis,* and *Cairo* were on the western or Arkansas side. By positioning his vessels on either side of the river, Davis had hoped to catch any rebel gunboats in a cross fire if they attempted to approach.

From the *Benton,* pilot Richard Birch could clearly see black smoke coming from the first of the rebel steamers chugging around the bend in the river. "No officer was on the deck of the *Benton* (flag-steamer) except the pilot, Mr. Birch," Walke later recalled, "who informed the flag-officer of the situation, and passed the order to the *Carondelet* and *Pittsburgh* to proceed without waiting for the flag-steamer." The signal to get under way was not visible on account of the light fog, so Birch took his speaking trumpet and hailed the *Carondelet* and *Pittsburg,* telling them to get under way.[30]

From Mortar Boat No. 16, acting master Gregory could see the approaching rebel steamers. His little mortar boat, more raft than vessel, had been towed by the *Cincinnati* into position early that morning to shell the fort. At 6:00 a.m. the No. 16 had opened fire, the gun crew elevating the 13-inch mortar to 41 degrees. Loaded with a 20-pound powder charge, the mortar could hurl a 204-pound shell a distance of 4,200 yards. After firing five shells, Gregory spotted the enemy rams in full view rounding Plum Point. As they closed the range, he could clearly make out that the lead vessel was heading straight for the No. 16. Lacking the motor power to withdraw or avoid the attacker, Gregory's boat had only one defense: its massive mortar. A high-trajectory weapon normally used to lob heavy shells over obstacles, the mortar was not designed to fire on enemy vessels, but Gregory had little choice. Calling out to the mortar's gun captain, Gregory hastily issued orders to decrease the elevation and reduce the charges. Using dangerously short fuses, No. 16's eleven-man mortar crew opened fire on its attacker at short range, bursting a shell directly over the rebels.[31]

From the *Cincinnati,* which had been lying close to the riverbank, Roger Stembel watched the huge mortar shell arc into the air. Without hesitation, Stembel ordered the gunboat to go to No. 16's assistance. "Eight minutes would bring them alongside," Eliot Callender, an ensign on the gunboat, recalled. "The 'Cincinnati,' with hardly enough steam to turn her wheel over, lay three miles away from the rest of the Union fleet, not one boat of which had enough steam up to hold itself against the current." The *Cincinnati* slipped its cables and slowly swung into the stream. "Her engineers were throwing oil and everything else inflammable into her fires, that the necessary head of steam might be obtained to handle the boat." The former side-wheel Gulf steamer *General Bragg,* considerably ahead of its consorts, steamed along the Arkansas shore perilously near the little mortar boat and then headed straight for the *Cincinnati* at full speed. "Her powerful engines were ploughing her along at a rate that raised a billow ten feet high at her bow," Callender recalled.[32]

From his station on the *Cincinnati,* Callender could observe the action and later described his gunboat's duel with the enemy ram. "At a distance of not over fifty yards, she received our full starboard battery of four thirty-two pound guns. Cotton bales were seen to tumble, and splinters fly; but on she came, her great walking-beam engine driving her at a fateful rate." Stembel ordered the helmsman to swing the bow, hoping to lessen the blow. As Stembel braced for impact, the ram struck the *Cincinnati* on its starboard quarter. "It was a glancing blow that the 'General Bragg' gave us, and not the one she intended," Callender explained. "A right-angle contact would have sunk us then and there; but glancing blow as it was, it took a piece out of our midships six feet deep and twelve feet long, throwing the magazine open to the inflow of water, and knocking everything down from one end of the boat to the other." Then the two vessels came together, and the *Bragg*'s wheelhouse rode up on the *Cincinnati*'s casemate. The muzzles of the *Cincinnati*'s guns almost touched the rebel ram's hull, and the Union gunners struggled to ram home powder and shot. "The men sprang with a cheer to their guns, and the entire broadside was emptied into the 'Bragg' with such close range the guns could not be run out of the ports. This broadside settled the 'Bragg,' for she lay careened up against us so that it tore an immense hole in her from side to side."[33]

Wreathed in smoke, the *General Bragg* swung away and slipped downstream, but two more rebel rams, the *General Price* and *General Sumter,* set their sights on the *Cincinnati*. They converged to strike and seriously damage the federal gunboat. The *Price* rammed the *Cincinnati*'s aft quarter, tearing away the sternpost and shoving the gunboat into the *Sumter*. "The water was pouring in from three directions," Callender wrote, "the engineers were standing waist deep in the engine-room, the fires being rapidly extinguished; and we had just one more round of ammunition in the guns, the magazine being flooded." As the Union gunboat took on water and drifted toward the bank, Stembel, fearing the rebels would board his boat, ordered his men on deck with cutlasses, carbines, and hand grenades. He too left the protection of the wheelhouse and went on deck, where he could see that the enemy vessel had turned just enough to expose the pilot in the pilothouse. Without hesitation, Stembel drew his revolver and shot the pilot dead. The *Cincinnati*'s pilot, William Hoel, saw an enemy sharpshooter in the pilothouse drawing a bead on Stembel and shouted a warning. Just as Stembel turned to step inside his own pilothouse, a shot from the *Sumter*'s deck struck him above the shoulder blade, passed through his neck, and exited his throat just under his chin. A sailor on *Cincinnati* quickly took aim on the shooter and killed him. Others rushed to aid Stembel, who was bleeding profusely from the throat and back, and carried him below. Fourth master Reynolds and a seaman on the *Cincinnati* also suffered serious wounds.[34]

Hoel came down on the gun deck and took command. According to Callender, he shouted, "'Boys, give 'em the best you've got! We ain't dead yet!' A cheer was his answer, and every gun on the boat poured its iron hail into one or another of the enemy, the 'Cincinnati' rolled first to one side and then the other, gave a convulsive shudder, and went down bow-first and head on to the enemy." Then the *Cincinnati* discharged its steam batteries, throwing steam and scalding water onto the *Sumter*'s deck, killing many rebel sailors, and forcing the boat to withdraw.[35]

In the meantime, the *Benton, Mound City,* and *Carondelet* had entered the fray, coming to the *Cincinnati*'s assistance. During this time, as Morison explained, the *Carondelet* "had been dropping down rapidly, and we got within range, we opened on them with our bow guns, but the range was rather high and did not seem to strike her." After a few minutes, "our starboard bow gun sent one through her starboard wheel house and (into her boilers, it is thought), as the steam gushed out in huge jets from an hundred places, I could also see her crew retreat to the fantail." The rebel boat dropped astern, and Morison had to go to his station as first sponger. From that position he had little opportunity to observe the battle, "except when I would be on the port loading, and then I would look around to see what was going on. I could see their boats and ours mixed up indiscriminately and the shot, shell, and grape flying about in a careless manner."[36]

The *Carondelet*'s captain had ample opportunity to observe the engagement. In his memoir Walke wrote:

> When the second ram, *General Price,* rammed *Cincinnati,* we fired our bow-guns into the *General Price,* and she backed off, disabled also. The *Cincinnati* was again struck by one of the enemy's rams, the *General Sumter.* Having pushed on with all speed to the rescue of the *Cincinnati, Carondelet* passed her in a sinking condition, and, rounding to, we fired our bow guns and starboard broadside guns into the retreating *General Bragg* and the advancing rams *General Jeff Thompson, General Beauregard,* and *General Lovell.*

Skirting a shoal, the *Carondelet* brought its port broadsides to bear on the *Sumter* and *Price.* "At this crisis the *Van Dorn* and *Little Rebel* had run above the *Carondelet,* [and] the *Bragg, Jeff Thompson, Beauregard* and *Lovell* were below her," Walke explained.[37]

The Confederate ram *General Van Dorn* had "kept close to the Arks. shore all the way up," *Mound City* sailor Browne noted, but then "headed from the shore toward us. [She] was now coming on our starboard (right) side as fast as she could travel, notwithstanding we were pouring broadside after broadside into her, and ran into us, so that we headed up stream; and she passed close in front of us, receiving the contents of our three bow guns, and then struck the Arks. shore which immediately stopped her." The *Van Dorn* backed upstream, out of the woods, and then came down at full speed on the *Mound City's* port side. "Here she received our whole port broadside, and then [when she missed our target] our aft guns opened on her after we had passed. Though nearly every one of our shot and shell struck her, strange to say she got off without sinking."[38]

Not so the *Mound City*. Although the *Van Dorn* had struck only a glancing blow, the impact cut a four-foot-hole in the hull and turned the *Mound City* around so that it was now headed upstream. When the *Van Dorn* passed by and went toward the Arkansas shore, the pilot asked Kilty if they might pursue the enemy, ram it, and push it into the bank. Kilty replied, "No, we're sinking. See the *Benton,* she'll finish her up." At this point, the *St. Louis* arrived to assist the *Cairo's* efforts to keep the *Mound City* afloat. "Our boat began to go down as soon as the 'Van Dorn' struck us," Browne admitted, "for she [tore] away nearly half of our forecastle [and] opened an awful hole in our bows, so we were compelled to run ashore on a bar about two miles above. I saved most of our clothing, but all our provisions were destroyed by getting wet." Symmes Browne and his brother Henry were on the upper deck during the whole engagement, but neither was hurt.[39]

The *Benton* had finally gotten up enough steam, and as it passed the half-sunken *Cincinnati,* Phelps could see the crew on top of the wheelhouse, "perched like so many turkeys on a cornfield." Taking on one of the enemy rams that had struck the *Cincinnati,* Phelps directed the pilot to turn the *Benton* in a tight circle. He then ordered the *Benton's* port bow 42-pounder gun crew to open fire, and they put a shot into the ram's boiler.

With trepidation, Walke now realized that only the *Carondelet* and the *Benton* were left to tackle the three remaining Confederate gunboats: *Thompson, Lovell,* and *Beauregard.* These three fired into the *Carondelet,* which returned fire with its stern guns. But "while in this position," Walke recalled, "I ordered the port rifled 50-pounder Dahlgren gun to be leveled and fired at the center of the *Sumter.* The shot struck the vessel just forward of her wheel-house, and the steam instantly poured out from her ports and all parts of her casemates, and we saw her men running out of them, and falling or lying down on the deck." The shot had struck the enemy's boilers, and Walke thought it caused an explosion; however, Confederate reports failed to mention any explosion. The disabled ram then dropped downstream.[40]

Peering through the dense smoke, Walke could barely make out the gunboats above the *Carondelet*. Strangely, none of the other federal boats had come to the aid of the *Carondelet,* which was caught in a cross fire between a federal boat above and the rebel gunboats below. "The upper deck of the *Carondelet* was swept with grape-shot and fragments of broken shell; some of the latter were picked up by one of the sharp-shooters, who told me they were obliged to lie down under shelter to save themselves from the grape and other shot of the *Pittsburg* above us, and from the shot and broken shell of the enemy below us." Two fragments of an exploded shell hit the *Carondelet*. Walke later learned that two grapeshot fired from the *Pittsburg* also struck his gunboat, and he reported that they had feared the *Pittsburg*'s fire more than that of the enemy. By now, the *Carondelet* had drifted down below the fleet, but it kept firing on the enemy until they were out of sight. The *Benton* steamed past the *Carondelet* in pursuit of the fleeing Confederate boats, which managed to gain the protection of Fort Pillow's guns. "They now began to fall down towards the fort and in a short time they were all under its guns leaving us masters of the field," Morison wrote in his diary. "I now looked at the cabin clock and found that the action had [lasted] one hour and ten minutes." Morison went on deck to see what damage had been done. The *Carondelet,* he noted, "had got struck with some grape shot and shell but without doing any material damage."[41]

While the *Benton* and *Carondelet* were fending off the remaining rebel gunboats, the *Pittsburg* and a tug took the disabled *Cincinnati* to the Tennessee shore, where it sank in eleven feet of water. The *Cincinnati*'s wounded commanding officer had regained consciousness, but he was having difficulty breathing. He would be transferred to a hospital boat for better care as soon as possible.

The battle of Plum Point Bend had ended. "This engagement was sharp, but not decisive," Walke wrote. "From the first to the last shot fired by the *Carondelet,* one hour and ten minutes elapsed." In what Phelps described as "the first purely naval fight of the war," six of Davis's vessels had engaged eight ironclad Confederate gunboats, four of them equipped with rams. The Confederates could claim a victory, for they had sunk two federal ironclads. But as Davis told Welles, his flotilla had "sustained some injury from the rams but will be in fighting condition to-morrow." Furthermore, the Union squadron had destroyed or disabled all the attacking vessels of the Confederate River Defense Force except for the *General Van Dorn*.[42]

Many Union naval officers concluded that they had been caught napping at Plum Point. They had not taken the precaution of stationing a picket boat or scout downriver to warn of approaching rebel vessels, nor did Mortar No. 16's guard, the *Cincinnati*, have steam up. Others argued that the rebel fleet had fallen back to Memphis and skedaddled, leaving numerous dead behind. They pointed out that the Confederate vessels had been torn to pieces by Yankee shot, some of which had punctured holes in their hulls large enough for a man to walk through. In reality, the Confederates had suffered just two killed, one seriously wounded, and eight to ten slightly wounded, including Captain Isaac Fulkerson of the *Van Dorn*. The Western Gunboat Flotilla had incurred damage as well. The *Carondelet* had escaped in remarkably fine shape, incurring just a few shrapnel hits, but the *Cincinnati* lay on the river bottom, and the damaged *Mound City* was on a bar. However, as Yost observed, "All the rest of the boats were uninjured, owing probably to the small number of shots that the rebels fired at us." The *Cincinnati* and *Mound City* were promptly refloated and sent north.[43]

The night after the battle of Plum Point, the *Carondelet*'s crew slept with their sidearms, hoping "to be ready in case of another attack." The next day, a Sunday, the gunboat held worship services and mustered as usual. The *Cairo* lay about a quarter of a mile from the mortar boats, which, according to Yost, "opened fire at 8 a.m. In the afternoon the rebels fired five or six times but their shots fell short." On Monday, May 13, Morison jotted, "Another alarm today. Thought they were coming, as they came up to the point, but concluded to go back. By a deserter we learn that two of their boats have gone under and one is so severely damaged as to be useless." The rebels kept up a steady fire from their heavy guns all night, he explained. "You could trace the course of their shell through the air by the twinkle of its firing eye as it revolved in its flight towards us." At 10:00 p.m. the flagship sent up a rocket, the signal for action. According to Yost, "In 10 minutes all hands had their hammocks lashed up and were at their quarters ready for action, but the rebels did not come."[44]

False alarms kept the officers and men of Davis's flotilla on edge for days. Deserters from Fort Pillow came in, reporting that the garrison had a food shortage and "cannot get any supplies, as the people of Memphis are not able to help them."[45]

No more attacks came, and life in the Western Flotilla returned to its normal. "Flotilla in status quo," Morison wrote. The flotilla continued to shell Fort Pillow, but Davis altered its operating procedures. He assigned a pair of ironclads to maneuver the mortar boats onto their stations each day, then drop down to guard them until sunset, when tugs towed them upstream for the night.[46]

Davis's gunboats took turns going up to the coal flats to take on coal, but without more firepower, Davis knew he could not push past the rebel fortifications. On May 12 he wrote to Welles and implored him to pressure the shipyards to finish several new vessels, including steam rams being converted from side-wheel steamers based on the designs of Charles Ellet Jr. Yards at Cincinnati were working on the *Queen of the West* and the *Lancaster,* while the *Switzerland* was being rebuilt at Madison and the *Monarch* at New Albany. The conversion included reinforcing the steamers' hulls and bulkheads and bracing the machinery in the holds, but the rams would not be armed with ordnance. Ellet believed in using steam propulsion to "make the warship into a guided missile more deadly than a ballistic projectile."[47]

7

The Battle of Memphis

A perfect hurricane of shot and shell.

—Roy Wisecarver III

With the damage done off Plum Point Bend repaired, the *Mound City* rejoined the flotilla above Fort Pillow. Its officers and crew were anxious to get back into the action. "The engagement has only served to make our crew hate the enemy all the more, and the next time, should it come, we will be at them with a double force," Symmes Browne wrote to his fiancée.[1]

Above Fort Pillow, Davis had assembled a collection of gunboats, mortar boats, and transports. In addition, his flotilla had been joined by the vessels of Colonel Charles Ellet Jr.'s "ram fleet." In late May the aggressive Ellet met with Davis on the flagship *Benton,* hoping to persuade the commodore to run below the rebel batteries at Fort Pillow with the joint force and surprise the enemy fleet. Davis listened to Ellet's proposal but cautiously deferred any decision.[2]

The *Carondelet* had been on station off Fort Pillow since early May, along with the *Cairo, Pittsburg, Louisville,* and *St. Louis.* The gunboats and mortar boats took turns going down to the point and firing a few rounds. For the most part, however, the rebels' return fire fell short, and no Confederate steamers appeared to engage the Yankee flotilla.

Then, on May 25, the *Mound City*'s crew thought they were getting another opportunity to lock horns with the enemy. A dozen voices called out, "Here they come. Here they come. Get ready boys, we're going to get another butting." Before Browne could get on deck, the drum beat to quarters. He reported, "I snatched my cutlas from the hook and buckled it on as

I ran to the deck, from which I saw a rebel gunboat off the point, Craigs-head, and heading towards us. In a few moments all was ready and anxious-ly awaiting the enemy's approach, but very much to our annoyance she now fell back below the point without a shot being fired."[3]

Over the next few days, the federal boats pursued several attempts by the rebels to come around the point. On the *Cairo,* young sailor Yost noted, "Considerable smoke was seen around the point this morning. One boat was seen at the point at 5 A.M." The *Carondelet* and *St. Louis* went down to the point with the mortar boats and opened fire, but their shots fell short.[4]

As Browne told his fiancée, "We are all 'hot'—to use one of your own expressions—for another engagement, the last being only a taste. We want to get this river clear, and then I for one will be satisfied to be transferred to my native state to wait the time when my services will again be required." Browne's sentiments were shared by other officers in the squadron. "As we have Corinth in our possession Fort Pillow, Fort Randolph and Memphis must soon fall and the Miss will be opened," Lieutenant Blodgett told his aunt in a letter dated the last day of May.[5]

For days, however, the enemy seemed reluctant to give the *Mound City* and the gunboats another opportunity for a fight. In the meantime, Browne and his fellow tars fought the mosquitoes and the heat. "Weather warm. Mosquitoes worse than the Rebels," Yost penned in his diary on May 13. The *Cairo* moved into midstream to avoid the pesky insects, which had made a number of sailors ill, many of them suffering from fever.[6]

On Tuesday, June 3, coxswain Morison finally had some news to write in the diary that he faithfully kept. "I think there is something of impor-tance taking place at the fort, as their steamers are continually going and coming." Not one to be intimidated by the supposed presence of rebel rams below Fort Pillow, Ellet had decided to take the *Queen of the West* and the *Monarch,* with his brother Alfred in command, down to reconnoiter. He wanted to test the strength of the enemy, especially a rebel steamer said to be around Craighead Point under the fort's guns. In Ellet's opinion, "an ex-aggerated view of the power of these rebel rams" had spread amongst the fleet, and he felt "the necessity of doing something to check the extension of the contagion." When his men expressed doubts about undertaking such a risky expedition, Ellet allowed the captain, two of the three pilots, and most of the crew to take their baggage and leave the *Queen.* Then he hastily organized a new volunteer crew and went downstream. "This evening the 'ram' Queen of the West went around the point to reconoitre," Morison wrote. "After she had got well round, they open fire on her, striking her twice, but without doing her any hurt. Two of their boats steamed up towards her, when she retired to the shelter of our gun boats, which opened fire on the enemy in return, when they retired quicker than they came." Ellet reported that although the fort's guns were overrated, the Confederate fleet of gunboats and rams was far larger than his own.[7]

Yost reported in his journal that smoke was seen at about 6:00. "In about ten minutes the rebel boats made their appearance around the point. There were three of them [and] several shots were fired at them . . . about ten minutes after they had made their appearance they went back around the point and smoke was seen." The *Cairo* then weighed anchor and joined the rest of the flotilla.[8]

The next day Morison jotted, "Rumors are afloat to the effect that the fort is evacuated. One of our tugs was sent to ascertain the truth of the matter. She did not return until evening when she confirmed it." Phelps went down the river in a tug to reconnoiter, a *New York Tribune* correspondent on one of the flotilla's vessels reported, "and discovered that the enemy had quitted Pillow, having previously set fire to the cotton bales they had used for breastworks, the barracks and gun-carriages, and such articles and stores as they could not remove."[9]

As it grew dark, the men on the federal gunboats could see clouds of smoke rising from the fort, followed, Morison noted, "by a bright glare in the sky, as if a heavy fire was raging beneath it. After a while a sullen boom came floating through the calm evening air, telling of a magazine blown up. All were impatient for the next day's sun that they might see [what] had detained us for fifty-two days doing nothing on Plum Point bend."[10]

Early on the morning of June 5, the sound of gunfire sent Alfred Ellet downstream in a yawl. He approached Fort Pillow and, finding it a smoking ruin, realized the Confederates had abandoned their stronghold. A reporter told *Tribune* readers that Ellet had landed and "planted the Stars and Stripes at the fort, much to the chagrin and indignation, I understand, of the Commodore." Ellet then signaled his brother, who came racing down with three of his rams. Scouting twelve miles below, Charles Ellet sent Alfred to demand the surrender of the fort at Randolph, which had also been abandoned.[11]

In the meantime, leaving the *Pittsburg* and Fitch's command to hold Fort Pillow and the *Mound City* to escort army transports, Davis's squadron, accompanied by the mortar fleet and ordnance ships, had turned their bows downstream. "At 5 a.m. the Gun Boat fleet passed the point and came in sight of the Fort with the rams alongside the Fort and the stars and stripes waving in triumph over Fort Pillow," Yost proudly noted.[12]

When the *Carondelet* came abreast of the fort, Morison observed that it consisted of about forty guns. "It was a splendid point of defense and would have cost us a vast amount of trouble and perhaps loss of life to capture it." After the troops were landed, the *Carondelet* got under way. "Passed Randolph," Morison noted. "There was never much of a fortification there. Saw piles of burning cotton just below it." The *Carondelet* continued downstream, and from the pilothouse, Walke watched the peaceful river slip by. Every so often he caught a glimpse of beautiful plantations, some of which appeared deserted. A few African Americans along the riverbanks stared curiously at the federal vessels and waved handkerchiefs or caps. When the squadron passed Fort Randolph, Walke could see through his spyglass the Stars and Stripes flying above it. Two hours later a Confederate steamer appeared "which had been destroying everything along the bank," Morison wrote. "We opened fire on her. Two of our shots were seen to strike her, but she did not hold up, and as she steamed faster than we did, she was likely to get away, but the commodore sent the armed tug 'Spitfire' after her. We soon lost sight of both of them in the crooks of the river but every few minutes the report of the tug's gun came to our ears, telling us that she was closing in with her chase."[13]

From the *Carondelet*'s quarterdeck Walke watched the race between the fast, nimble tug and the rebel steamer. Lieutenant Joshua Bishop ably steered the tug, cutting corners until he gained on the steamer and could open fire with his 12-pounder howitzer. Pursued by shot, the steamer *Sovereign* ran into the bank, and Bishop took it as a prize. Concluding his diary entry, Morison wrote, "At last, after about twenty minutes, we came in sight of them and found that the tug had captured her. There was a cheer went up from every boat in the fleet at the sight." The prize was soon following in the *Carondelet*'s wake, heading for Memphis, Tennessee. "Sic transit mundi," Morison quipped.[14]

Davis's vessels chugged downstream and anchored in a line of battle across the river at the lower end of Island No. 45, just above Memphis. The *Carondelet* anchored nearest the Tennessee shore; the *Benton, St. Louis, Cairo,* and *Louisville* were just west of it. When Walke arrived on deck in the predawn hours of June 6, he could see the city lights only two miles away.

The gunboats were within signaling distance, so at daybreak, all Davis had to do was hoist a signal for the *Louisville* to weigh anchor and join the *Benton* to search for the rebel fleet. They discovered that Captain James Montgomery's Confederate River Defense Force, numbering eight vessels, had taken up positions to defend Memphis. When the *Benton* and *Louisville* returned, Davis allowed the crews to finish their breakfast; then, at 4:20 a.m., he signaled his gunboats to get under way. "We then went to quarters and awaited a demonstration on their part, which they did not seem inclined to make. We could see that they had nine boats to our four," the *Carondelet*'s coxswain explained.[15]

The *Benton, Louisville, Carondelet, Cairo,* and *St. Louis* drifted down the river stern first. The commodore chose this tactic so that if any of his boats were damaged or disabled in the engagement, they could more easily head upstream and out of harm's way. "Gunboat 'Cairo' was in front of all the rest going head down stream," Yost proudly penned in his journal.[16]

Half an hour later, Montgomery's rams and gunboats opened fire. "About 5½ A.M., the Bragg came up towards us and opened fire," Morison wrote. "It was answered by us instantly." In his report to Welles, Davis carefully noted, "The rebels, still lying in front of the town, opened fire with the intention of exposing the city to injury from our shot. The fire was returned on our part with due care in this regard." Morison continued: "The commodore now signaled the whole fleet to drop down and engage them. We crowded steam on and got right on amongst them and fired our bow broadside and stern guns as the occasion demanded." Walke watched the rebels' first shot whiz over the gunboats and plop into the river near the tugs. The next, fired by the Confederate *General M. Jeff Thompson*, almost found its mark, splashing into the water near the *Benton*. "'Benton,' 'Cairo,' and 'Carondelet' let loose their fiery dogs," Yost wrote, "the 'Cairo' firing the first shot. The other boats soon turned around head down and then shot and shell flew around like hail while the fight was kept up in front of the city of Memphis."[17]

For another fifteen minutes, Walke watched the Union stern gunners continue to fire at the advancing rebel fleet. The sulfurous smoke from the cannon filled the air and mingled with black smoke from the steamboats' chimneys, forming a cloud that moved toward the middle of the river. Suddenly, the flagship turned downstream to attack and signaled: "Follow my motions." To Walke's surprise, out of the smoke came two of Ellet's ram fleet, the *Queen of the West* and the *Monarch*. "These vessels fearlessly dashed ahead of our gun-boats," Walke wrote, "ran for the enemy's fleet, and at the first plunge succeeded sinking one vessel, and disabling another."[18]

The *Queen of the West* aimed for the *Colonel Lovell,* but the rebel ship veered at the last moment, and the ram struck it just forward of the wheelhouse. The impact sent the *Queen*'s tables and pantry ware and the crew's half-eaten breakfasts crashing to the decks, but it crushed the *Lovell*'s hull and sent its chimneys toppling over. Almost cut in two, but still clinging to Ellet's ram, the *Lovell* started to sink. Just then the *Beauregard* slammed into the *Queen*'s wheelhouse, damaging the wheel and the tiller ropes. Ellet emerged from the pilothouse to survey the damage but was cut down by a bullet to his knee. Carried to safety, the colonel continued to call out orders to the helmsman to point the *Queen* into the Arkansas riverbank.[19]

A crowd of spectators had gathered on the bluff above the river to watch the battle, and they cheered with joy when the *Beauregard* plowed into the *Queen of the West.* "Glory, Glory, Glory!" they screamed, but they soon fell quiet as the crippled *Lovell* approached shore. The crowd had caught sight of the horror-stricken face of one of the crewman, his arm severed by a cannonball, beckoning for help. A cloud of steam rose from the rebel boat's boilers, and the crowd watched as men jumped into the river to escape being scalded. Many drowned in plain sight of the ladies on the bluff.

With the *Queen* now out of action, the momentum of the federal attack passed to Alfred Ellet and the *Monarch.* After giving the *Lovell* another blow, the *Monarch* became the target of the rebels' *General Beauregard* and *General Price,* "which made a dash at the *Monarch* as she approached them," Walke recalled. When the *Beauregard* took aim on the *Monarch,* the ram's sharpshooters forced the rebel wheelmen to lose control of the vessel, allowing the federal ram to slip away. "The *Beauregard* . . . missed the *Monarch* and struck the *General Price* instead on her portside, placing her *hors de combat,*" Walke reported. With its bow caved in, the *Price* began to take on water. After the *Beauregard* collided with the *Price,* Ellet saw his chance. Before the two could entangle, "the *Monarch* then rammed the *Beauregard,* which had several times been raked fore and aft by the shot and shell of the ironclads and she quickly sank in the river opposite Memphis." Ellet finished up by running into the *Little Rebel,* "just as our fleet was passing her in pursuit."[20]

Taking advantage of their greater speed, the rebel rams went downriver, pursued by Davis's vessels. As the *Carondelet* steamed past the disabled *Queen* and the two rebel boats, Walke could see how much damage the collisions had caused. His bow gunners kept firing at the fleeing rebels, but when a heavy shot struck the *Carondelet* on the forecastle, it carried away the port iron anchor chock, the sheave, and the ring of the anchor. Walke saw the shot pass across the temporary barricade on the upper deck and over the boat. Splinters wounded three men slightly, but to Walke's relief, they suffered no other casualties. "We had two wounded slightly by a shot striking us on the ring of the anchor and chocks, sending the fragments on board. A shell also burst over us, a small fragment striking me but doing no harm." Walke reported that the *Carondelet* had fired fifty-two solid shots (rifled and round) and ten rifled fifteen-second shells.[21]

"We chased them about ten miles below the city," Morison wrote. "As we returned, we could see the hull of a boat on the stocks which had been set on fire by them to keep her from falling into our hands." The rebels had run two others ashore, and Yankee shells had set fire to the *Jeff Thompson*. "Just as we got past the burning one, she blew up with a terrible report which sent all hands for their guns, as the bursting of the shells in her magazine sounded as if they had opened a battery on us."[22]

"The battle lasted about 1½ hours. The last boat was captured at 7 A.M.," Yost explained. The *Cairo* started up, intending to put a prize crew on board the *Jeff Thompson*, "but when we came in sight of her she was in flames, just as we passed her she blew up with a tremendous explosion. Nothing could be saved of her except a small boat which was saved by some of the 'Cairo' crew."[23]

The federal squadron had captured or destroyed four of the five remaining rebel ships. Only the *General Van Dorn* escaped, pursued for a while by the *Monarch* and the *Lancaster*. Pleased with the performance of his ironclads and Ellet's rams, Davis reported the outcome to Welles: "The *Colonel Lovell*, was sunk in the beginning of the action by the *Queen of the West*; she went down in deep water. The *General Beauregard*, blown up by her boilers and otherwise injured by shot, went down near shore." The enemy had run the *Little Rebel* on the riverbank and abandoned it. Set on fire by federal shells, the *Jeff Thompson* blew up. The *General Price* went into the Arkansas shore, but the *Sumter* was still afloat. The final steamer, the *General Bragg*, Davis reported, "is also above water, though a good deal shattered in her upper works and hull. The *Van Dorn* escaped." The engagement also prompted the rebels to destroy the *Tennessee*, an ironclad they were building at Memphis, and to send the *Arkansas* downstream to prevent its capture.[24]

The *Carondelet* arrived in front of Memphis at 9:30 p.m. Seeing that the rebel flag was still flying, Davis "sent a flag of truce ashore demanding the surrender of the city," Morison wrote. "But as the mob had put the mayor in jail (for fear he should surrender it), nothing could be done, as the people were in a terrible state of excitement. Matters remained so until three P.M., when a party of soldiers went ashore and cut it [the flag] down. So here we are with Memphis in our possession." At supper, the *Carondelet*'s crew was treated to grog to celebrate the victory.[25]

Davis's squadron had scored a victory. "Few Northern triumphs in the Civil War were more complete or one-sided than the Battle of Memphis," historian John Milligan noted. "The Confederate ram fleet had been destroyed, the city captured, and the great river opened to Vicksburg, Mississippi, directly through enemy-held territory." The victory at Memphis capped a spring of Union successes in the West following the capture of Fort Donelson. Nashville had fallen, a small Union army in northwestern Arkansas had routed the Confederates at the battle of Pea Ridge in March, Grant's army had beaten back a rebel attack at Shiloh, and Farragut's squadron had ascended the Mississippi after securing New Orleans, Baton Rouge, and Natchez. In the eastern theater, Union forces had captured sea islands from South Carolina to Florida, along with the harbors at New Berne and Beaufort. Only McClellan's Peninsular Campaign in Virginia had failed to produce a Union victory.[26]

"The Mississippi is comparatively open, and there is no more fighting for the gunboats," a relieved Symmes Browne told his fiancée. Although the Mississippi River now lay open to Vicksburg, the ever-cautious Davis had no intention of steaming into harm's way until he was sure the Confederates posed no real threat to his flotilla. Well aware that the *General Van Dorn* had escaped following the battle off Memphis, Davis suspected the enemy had ascended either the White or the Arkansas River, waiting to emerge and make a run at his vessels. So when Halleck asked Davis to provide support for General Samuel Curtis, who was fighting the rebels in northern Arkansas, he was only too happy to oblige. Curtis, ensconced at Batesville, was convinced that rebel troops from Texas had reinforced Major General Thomas C. Hindman, and he pleaded for support. If Davis would send his gunboats up the White River, Halleck told Secretary of War Edwin Stanton, then Curtis could be supplied by that route. According to Halleck, "The roads are so bad in Missouri that it is almost impossible to reach him by land."[27]

Davis immediately set about preparing for an expedition up the White River, in cooperation with Ellet's ram fleet. Ellet agreed to contribute the side-wheel steamer *Lancaster;* two stern-wheel rams, the *Mingo* and the *Lioness;* and the tug *Horner.* Two days later, Davis informed Colonel G. N. Fitch that he had ordered the *Conestoga* to accompany the steamer *White Cloud,* which was laden with stores for Jacksonport. He asked Fitch to join the expedition with an Indiana regiment to assist in removing a raft sunk in the lower part of the White River and to protect his seamen from attacks by rebel guerrillas.[28]

On June 13 Davis could report that a detachment of the squadron composed of the *Mound City, St. Louis,* and *Lexington* had sailed for the White River and Jacksonport, followed that same day by a transport bearing Fitch and the 46th Indiana Regiment convoyed by the *Conestoga,* Lieutenant George M. Blodgett commanding. The veteran timberclad had not been at Memphis, Blodgett explained to his aunt. "I did not have the pleasure of participating in the last engagement as I was on the river on detached service, but soon after received orders to come down, and upon my arrival received orders to get the 'Conestoga' ready and then to join the expedition going up the White River."[29]

After a pleasant voyage downriver, they came to Helena, Arkansas. "As we rounded the point above Helena, we discovered a steamboat at the wharf," Browne wrote, "and putting on a full head of steam, bore down upon the place as fast as possible, thinking they might start down the river or burn her." A few minutes later, they saw the steamboat backing out from shore and heading down the river. "We immediately fired our Dahlgren gun ahead of her to bring her to, but she only went the faster." Captain Kilty sent the tug after the steamer, identified as the *Clara Dolsen,* "and at the same time continued our firing, tho' she was entirely out of range." Kilty then ordered Shirk to take the *Lexington* and pursue the rebel gunboat.[30]

Browne, who been on duty in the gig, watched the chase from the deck of the *St. Louis.* "The 'Mound City' and 'Lexington' seemed to be running a race, for it was hard to tell which was making the fastest time." Finally, "the 'Lextn' got ahead, and the steamer and tug both ran out of sight around a bend. It was very evident that the gunboats could not come near the [steamer] although [they] ran out of sight of the 'St. Louis' except once in awhile we could see them six or eight miles off." The pursuit continued until dark, when the *Mound City* and *St. Louis* dropped anchor, joined later by the *Lexington*. The next morning the gunboats ran six miles upriver in search of the steamer and anchored. Kilty sent a tug with fifty men after the *Clara Dolsen*, which they located in a creek and took as a prize. "She is said to be worth seventy-five thousand dollars. Pretty good day's work, isn't it?" Browne wrote.[31]

In the meantime, the *Conestoga* had been escorting the *White Cloud* upriver, and by June 15 they had gone about fifty miles. "We are now on our way and as yet have met no resistance," Blodgett wrote, "but learn that the Rebels have got two Gun Boats and three transports about 80 miles up from here, where they have also blockaded the river by falling trees and rafts etc." Blodgett assured his aunt that they "will however make short work of these slight obstructions and in all probability will be able to communicate with Gen. Curtis who is about 200 miles up." Concluding his letter on an optimistic note, the young lieutenant wrote, "The Mississippi River will soon be opened."[32]

The *Conestoga* and the transports continued upstream. On the morning of June 16 they reached the other federal gunboats at a point called the Arkansas cutoff. From there, the expedition continued up the river to within five miles of St. Charles, Arkansas, and anchored for the night. The following morning the flotilla, including the *Mound City, St. Louis, Lexington, Conestoga,* and the transports, got under way to support an attack by federal troops on some enemy fortifications at Devil's Hill, above St. Charles. "After consultation we determined to attack the forts on Tuesday morning the 17th. This we did," Blodgett told his aunt.[33]

When the boats got to within two miles of the enemy fortifications, Fitch landed his regiment, and the *Mound City* and the gunboats opened fire on rebel pickets. "We continued to stand on, firing on either side and ahead as we went," the *St. Louis*'s commanding officer, Lieutenant Wilson McGunnegle, reported. As they approached a bend in the river, they saw three boats sunk across the river; they assumed the rebels had a battery located on a bluff abreast of these obstructions, but trees obscured their view. Undeterred, Kilty led his gunboats up. The Confederates opened fire, the federal boats responded, and "the cannonading from our side became terrific."[34]

"We had passed the lower batteries and progressed as far as we could without running on the bar under the point, and let the boat swing near the shore," Browne wrote, "when a shot from a masked battery entered our port bow, passed through the steam drum, thence against the heater, and then lodged in the steerage cupboard." Escaping steam enveloped the *Mound City,* "and before men could jump out of the ports, over a hundred poor creatures were either scalded to death or so badly that they will never recover."[35]

Describing their plight, Blodgett wrote, "25 were either drowned or shot by the enemy while in the water struggling for life—boats were sent to the rescue of those in the water who were being . . . murdered by the sharpshooters from shore." Boats from the *Conestoga,* he claimed, "took the lead and arrived first and had commenced picking up the men; but while engaged in this duty a 42 pdr ball from the enemy struck both boats one of which was shattered to pieces, the other made out to return."[36]

"Only the Ex Officer, Mr. Dominy, and myself of all the officers [are] unhurt," Browne explained. "Only twenty-three men out of the whole crew of sailors were able to muster after the disaster." He then told his fiancée the sad news about his brother: "Among the dead, I am pained to say, is dear Henry. Poor boy was badly scalded over head and arms but lived in little pain until 9½ P.M. 13th [17th], yesterday."[37]

Also severely burned in the explosion was the gunboat's captain, Augustus Kilty. When he opened the trapdoor to the gun room, a blast of steam came rushing into the pilothouse, tossing him back and blinding the pilot. A 32-pounder shot had evidently passed through the steam drum and heater.

"The 'Mound City' was still under fire of the upper battery and was drifting in toward shore," Blodgett explained, "where I could see the rebels coming down the bluff for the purpose I suppose of boarding her—I then determined to proceed up and haul her out of action." Blodgett ordered the *Conestoga* to tow the disabled gunboat clear. When he boarded the vessel, an awful scene greeted him. "I immediately sent all the medical assistance at my command who did everything in their power to relieve the wounded, still 50 died with in 4 hours after the accident happened. I had removed to my cabin Capt. Kilty the two drs and paymaster from the 'Mound City' also the Rebel Col. Frey, who was wounded and had been taken prisoner." Blodgett received orders to proceed to Memphis in the company of a transport loaded with the wounded, but, he wrote, "on our way up 33 men died and were buried on the banks of the Miss."[38]

Ten minutes after the explosion on the *Mound City,* Colonel Fitch signaled the gunboats to cease firing. The infantry then charged the rebels and carried the battery without losing a single man; they captured twenty-nine of the enemy. As soon as McGunnegle was certain they had gained a victory, he went over to the *Mound City* and placed First Master John Duble in command. Told by the surgeons that any delay might prove fatal to the wounded, McGunnegle decided to send the *Conestoga* and the steamer *Musselman* to Memphis with the surgeons and the wounded on board.[39]

On Thursday, June 19, the *Conestoga* landed at Memphis. Dr. William H. Wilson, the assistant surgeon, had done his best to care for the wounded but was eager to transfer them to the hospital boat. As soon as the *Conestoga* had tied up, the hospital boat's nurses and sailors prepared to receive the *Mound City's* burn victims, who had been placed on beds of cotton gathered from the river by the *Lexington* after the engagement. Gingerly, the sailors carried each of the thirty-eight wounded over to the hospital boat on makeshift stretchers. "Pop, I saw some of the *Mound City's* men the day after the fight," Preston Bishop, a surgeon's assistant on the *Carondelet,* wrote. "They were brought up here to the Hospital Boat, and a more pitiful sight, I hope I may never witness again. They were scalded awfully." He told his father, "Many died on the way up and out of about 25 that were brought here there are about 10 or 15 yet alive, there will be but 15 or 20 out of her crew to tell the tale." Bishop was under the impression that the *Mound City's* wounded had not received any medical care following the incident, but McGunnegle told Davis that Dr. William H. Wilson of the *Conestoga* and Dr. George W. Garver of the *Lexington* "were untiring in their attention to the wounded."[40]

Some of the *Mound City* crew had reportedly jumped overboard to escape the steam, "only to be shot down by the rebels while in the water." Reacting to this news, Bishop told his father, "[if] this is their style of warfare, it is high time we were hoisting the Black Flag, for they have . . . never to show us Gun Boat Boys any quarters. I helped to save the Pilot of the Sumter in the other action, but I will never do such an act again, they would not do it for me." In his report to Davis, McGunnegle confirmed the reports of other witnesses: "Many, very many, must have been killed by the enemy while they were struggling in the water. I was quite close to the spot and distinctly remarked on the cowardly act at the moment they were perpetrating it."[41]

As soon as he could, Phelps boarded the *Conestoga,* anxious for news of his mentor and the crew of the *Mound City.* Phelps was fond of Kilty, who had taken Phelps under his wing in 1842 while on the frigate *Columbus.* Phelps learned that Kilty had been badly burned but was doing well. One hundred thirteen of the gunboat's crew had been killed by the explosion or died later; only twenty-five men had escaped unharmed. Shaken by the news, Phelps took pen in hand and wrote to Elisha Whittlesey: "A more piteous sight than that presented by the wounded on the Hospital Boat no man ever saw. The one shot doing all this harm, was the only one that injured any of the four vessels." As Phelps had to admit, however, "The wonder is that a similar accident has not happened long ago & one I think our Naval Constructor, Mr. Pook—who devised these miserable craft called in the country 'Iron Clad'—but far from being such in fact, should be hanged for this mischief."[42]

8

On to Vicksburg!

Flag Officer believes the defenses will be abandoned if he shows an imposing force there.

—Henry Bell

While Davis's flotilla was making its way down the Mississippi River past Fort Pillow to Memphis, Farragut's West Gulf Blockading Squadron had been steaming up the Old Muddy toward Vicksburg to join him. The passage of federal ships past Forts St. Philip and Jackson and the capture of Memphis had been a triumph for Farragut, but now he faced a difficult decision. His original intention had been "not to stop until I meet Foote," but now he seemed to favor taking his squadron back down the Mississippi River to the Gulf of Mexico and on to Mobile, Alabama. Pondering his next move, Farragut may have recalled Welles's orders in January: if Foote had not moved down from Cairo, Farragut should secure New Orleans and then take advantage of the enemy's panic and push a strong force up the Mississippi. However, Farragut's squadron of seagoing, wooden warships comprised deep-draft vessels, not flat-bottomed, shallow-draft river steamers designed for the Mississippi's snags and sandbars.[1]

Farragut kept the squadron at or below New Orleans until May 1, 1862, when Commander Porter and a flotilla of mortar schooners came in with the *Harriet Lane,* and General Benjamin F. Butler arrived with troops to occupy the forts. Farragut then sent the *Richmond* north to the Confederate river town of Baton Rouge, but the steam sloop ran aground. Even though he had not found a pilot, Captain Thomas T. Craven volunteered to take the *Brooklyn,* along with the *Sciota, Winona,* and *Itasca,* ahead to

Baton Rouge. A career naval officer, Craven had served in the West Indies and Brazil Squadrons and had commanded the frigate *Congress* in the Mediterranean Squadron. He had been promoted to captain in 1861.[2]

One of the three gunboats accompanying Craven up the river was the 1,370-ton Unadilla-class screw gunboat *Winona.* Anthony O'Neil faithfully recorded daily events during the *Winona's* journey up the Mississippi. His diary entries offer a contemporary view not only of the West Gulf Squadron's operations that spring but also of life aboard the little gunboat; observations of the towns and the people, white and black, who lived along the river; and their response to the Yankees' arrival. On April 30, 1862, O'Neil noted that the *Winona* had arrived at New Orleans, "where we found our fleet anchored and the American flag flying over the Custom House." On May 2 the "*Brooklyn* made signal to get underway which we did & followed her up the river." Two hours later they found the *Sciota* some twelve miles up the river and anchored for the night. "At midnight sent [a] boat ashore & obtained from some niggers on a plantation, some chicken, eggs, milk, etc." The next day they passed St. James Landing and anchored on the left bank of the river, astern of the *Brooklyn.*[3]

The gunboats continued up the Mississippi past Point Pleasant, and early on May 5 O'Neil went ashore to get fresh provisions. "Found an old creole at home a conservative man with some very pretty, well educated daughters. Talked a little French with them, gave them some papers and in return received fish eggs & milk & a handsome bouquet." O'Neil returned to the *Winona,* and as the gunboats passed Baton Rouge, he observed, "Everybody here on the river seem to be rabid 'secesh.' We continually pass large quantities of cotton both on fire and floating down the river. Have seen no rebel flags however except one yesterday. On the Arsenal at Baton Rouge the authorities had hung the state flag from one of the towers." By 7:00 the following evening the federal vessels had reached Natchez. The *Sciota* had experienced engine trouble, however, and O'Neil noted that the *Itasca* was also "in very bad order." He explained, "Our object in coming up the river was to go up to Vicksburg & cut off the railroad communication at that point. Having ascertained however that there were a large number of troops at that place & the gunboats being almost out of coal & two disabled, it was deemed prudent to return down the river & so we steamed back."[4]

The *Brooklyn* took the *Sciota* in tow, and at 1:00 p.m. on May 7 they met the *Oneida* coming up the river. The *Oneida* sent a boat to communicate with the *Brooklyn* and then accompanied the other boats downstream. That night, O'Neil and the crew of the *Winona* encountered their first group of runaway slaves; seeing the Yankee gunboats' approach, they had seized the opportunity to flee their masters. "At midnight a boat with 3 'darks' came alongside. They had run away from a plantation 3 miles below us. Sent them on board Brooklyn." As commander of the Potomac Flotilla, Craven had experience dealing with fugitive slaves as well as free blacks. On August 30, 1861, he had personally taken four runaways on board off Upper Cedar Point. Mindful of the First Confiscation Act, rather than returning them to their Southern owners, he had sent them to the Washington Navy Yard. As Craven had learned, these contrabands often willingly provided valuable intelligence about Confederate activities.[5]

The *Winona* spent the day coaling, and that evening it sent a boat up to Clarksville to obtain fresh provisions. But because the inhabitants were "all rabid secessionists, we were unable to obtain anything so gave them a good leave & returned." The next day, May 9, the *Brooklyn* went downriver, while the *Winona, Oneida, Sciota, Pinola,* and *Kennebec* headed upriver. When the *Pinola* signaled that its engines were disabled, they all dropped down to the landing at the Red River.[6]

In the meantime, the rest of Farragut's squadron had begun moving up to Baton Rouge, the capital of Louisiana and a thriving river port. As the *Hartford* steamed upriver, Fleet Captain Henry Bell carefully observed the shoreline from the poop deck. "Here and there little knots of people, both white and black, lined the banks, but none waved or greeted the passing federal vessels."[7]

Late on May 8 the *Itasca* steamed into view, and Lieutenant Charles Caldwell boarded the *Hartford* and reported that all the advance vessels except for the *Iroquois* were sixty miles below Natchez but short on coal. Caldwell advised Bell that the rebels had sunk all the coal on the banks as they advanced. The river above Baton Rouge was rife with sandbars and snags, he told Bell, and every one of their boats had grounded at least once. According to Caldwell, refugees from Vicksburg claimed the rebels were evacuating Fort Pillow but fortifying Memphis. This came as no surprise to Bell, confirming information he had received several days earlier from a carpenter in New Orleans. Caldwell then left the flagship and took the *Itasca* down to Pilot Town, where he ordered some coal vessels to come up to replenish the fleet. That evening the *Hartford* anchored below Donaldsonville, off the plantation belonging to South Carolina governor Manning.

Seeing an opportunity to procure fresh provisions, Bell sent the steward ashore, and he returned with beef, mutton, fowl, and eggs.[8]

The following day the ships continued to steam upriver, arriving off Baton Rouge late on the afternoon of May 9. There, they found that Craven had repaired his disabled vessels and then taken the *Brooklyn* back downriver, sending the *Winona, Sciota, Pinola, Kennebec,* and *Oneida* upstream. Upon his arrival at Baton Rouge, Craven had discovered that the commanding officer of the *Iroquois,* Commander James E. Palmer, had demanded the city's surrender, but the stubborn rebels had refused. Nonplussed, Palmer had promptly landed a party of seamen and marines, and they raised the flag over the former federal arsenal.[9]

Late in the afternoon the *Hartford, Richmond,* and *Wissahickon* arrived from New Orleans, where Farragut found that Samuel Phillips Lee had asked for and been granted permission to take the *Oneida* and *Pinola* up to Baton Rouge, leaving on May 3. After struggling against the current for three days, the *Pinola's* engines gave out, and Lee left it behind and continued up to Baton Rouge. Farragut now instructed Lee to press on to Natchez. "We've no support for you beyond here. You'll have to find pilots where you can," Farragut wrote, "and scavenge coal as you go."[10]

The weather had turned warm and sultry, a foretaste of the hot, humid summer to come. May 11 being a Sunday, Captain Wainwright held worship services on deck, "himself officiating in excellent style, reading some of the psalms and prayers," Bell jotted in his diary. "This day, I rejoice to see, is given to the crew for rest." That same day, Palmer received orders from Farragut, who was still at Baton Rouge, to take the *Iroquois* and proceed to Natchez, secure the city, and await his arrival. Late that afternoon Palmer met Lee, and they both steamed to Natchez and anchored. On May 12 Palmer sent a message to the mayor, demanding the city's surrender, but the authorities refused to accept it. Irritated, Palmer seized a ferryboat and ordered a landing party of seamen and marines aboard, under the command of Lieutenant Harmony. He told Harmony that if there were no authorities to receive his communication, he should "land his force, march up to the town, which was about a half mile distant, with colors flying, and there cause the mayor to take receive and read my letter." After a tense wait, Harmony returned with the welcome news that two members of the city council had cordially received him at the landing, with apologies from the mayor, and assured him that they would offer no resistance. The following morning the mayor replied to Palmer's message and sent a copy of his proclamation surrendering Natchez. The mayor assured Palmer that the Confederate flag had never officially flown in Natchez and that the Confederate States of America owned no property in the town.[11]

When Farragut reached Natchez, he learned that Lee had gone to Vicksburg with the *Winona* and the other gunboats, escorting the steamers *Ceres* and *Burton* carrying Brigadier General Thomas Williams's troops. According to O'Neil, the boats anchored for the night abreast a plantation, giving the sailors an opportunity to forage for supplies; they "went ashore and purchased a lot of bucks, chickens and eggs." The following day the *Winona* and the other gunboats continued upriver. "The country on both sides of the river for a number of miles appeared to be completely inundated, the houses near the levees being submerged up to the roof," O'Neil observed. At 11:00 a.m. on Sunday, May 18, the four gunboats came within sight of Vicksburg. "Saw a large battery on the bluff below the city, containing approximately 5 or 6 guns," O'Neil wrote. They also observed "a number of Rebel Flags were flying in different parts of the City."[12]

Lee's ships dropped anchor just below Vicksburg, and he conferred with Williams. "We should call for the city's surrender," Lee told the general, who observed that it had certainly worked in Baton Rouge and Natchez. Lee then sent a flag-of-truce boat ashore with a letter to the Vicksburg authorities, demanding that they surrender the city. The boat returned with a reply from Colonel James Autry, the military governor: "I have to state that Mississippians don't know, and refuse to learn, how to surrender to an enemy. If Commodore Farragut or Brigadier-General Butler can teach them, let them come and try." Lee pondered the situation, called for his gunboat commanders, and explained to them that Vicksburg was clearly not Baton Rouge or Natchez. The man in charge was a military governor, not a civilian mayor. "We have demanded they surrender, they have refused," Lee said. Lee's captains all agreed they did not have the force to seize Vicksburg, and the gunboats' guns could not reach the heights of the rebel batteries. After warning the Vicksburg authorities to remove all the women and children from the town, lest they be injured by gunfire, Lee waited. A standoff ensued. Lee's gunboats did not attack Vicksburg, and the rebel batteries on the bluffs did not fire on the federal gunboats.[13]

After weeks of duty with the advance squadron on the Mississippi, Lee and his men were feeling the strain. "For a month passed I have slept most of the time with my clothes on—the men of the watch below have sometimes slept on their arms; the men of the watch on deck are nearly always armed at night. The battery is kept ready for instant use," Lee wrote to his wife on May 11, 1862.[14]

Operations on the Mississippi River were proving to be a challenge for all of Farragut's squadron, including his flagship *Hartford,* which had been struggling upstream since May 14. Although the Mississippi appeared to have plenty of water, the deep-draft *Hartford* ran aground. The frigate backed off, but that evening it ran aground again at the lower end of Tunica Bend. Bell ordered the entire crew to line up on the port side and then, at his command, run to the starboard side, but the *Hartford* still refused to budge. As darkness fell, the *Itasca* came up with a hawser to drag the *Hartford* off. The flagship backed, but to no avail. To lighten the *Hartford,* Bell ordered coal transferred to the *Itasca.*[15]

When dawn came, Bell could see the extensive mudflats around the ship. Knowing the river was at its highest, he began to worry. If the water level fell, the *Hartford* could be in serious trouble. The flagship's sailors had spent the evening removing coal from the vessel. Oscar Smith and his fellow marines had been sent over to post a guard on the ferryboat. Rumor had it that there were rebel guerrillas along the riverbanks, just waiting for the Yankees to turn their backs. Contending with guerrillas would become an ongoing concern for both Farragut's men and those of Davis's Western Gunboat Flotilla.

On May 16 the *Itasca* made several more attempts to pull the flagship off the mud. Finally, after an hour, the ship came free, to lusty cheers from the *Hartford*'s crew. Private Smith noted, "Got afloat about one o'clock and anchored in the stream." Bell and Farragut were greatly relieved, but for the crew it meant more hours of backbreaking work to haul the ammunition, coal, and guns back on board. Had it not been for the *Itasca* pulling it off the mud at Tunica Bend, the *Hartford* might not have gotten as far as Natchez, let alone Vicksburg.[16]

Before dawn on May 17 the *Hartford* resumed its journey upstream, accompanied by the *Itasca.* That evening they anchored off a plantation, giving some of the crew an opportunity to take a boat ashore to acquire provisions. The men killed a cow and loaded the boat with fresh fruits and other foodstuffs. The following day they reached Natchez and found the *Brooklyn, Iroquois,* and *Richmond* there. Farragut learned that Lee had departed two days earlier for Vicksburg with five gunboats and two steamboats bearing Williams's 1,200 troops. Early on May 19 Farragut's vessels resumed their journey upstream. That night they anchored twenty miles above Natchez, Bell explained, "to await the coming of troops." He also jubilantly reported, "Good news! Boats ashore this morning heard reports that Norfolk was taken by General Burnside and *Merrimack* blown up. All hands happy!" As he did every evening before retiring, Bell recorded the day's events in his journal. "Yesterday and last night the flag-officer expressed much disappointment at the delay attending the capture of Vicksburg, & the dilatory movements of the officer having it in charge." Then, in a telling comment, Bell wrote, "Flag Officer believes the defenses will be abandoned if he shows an imposing force there, and hence wants to take up all the ships." But some of Farragut's officers thought the larger ships, many without regular pilots, had gone high enough, "considering the dangers of navigation in the river at all times, and particularly after it shall have fallen." They expected a decisive battle "hourly" at Corinth, which, Bell wrote, "if gained by us, will clear the Southwest of all serious opposition to our arms." Halleck had finally planned an assault against Beauregard's troops (those who had survived the battle of Shiloh) at the small railroad town of Corinth, Mississippi. As commander of the Union army in the West, Halleck now had three armies: Grant's Army of Tennessee, Buell's Army of the Ohio, and Pope's Army of the Mississippi. Farragut and his commanders fully expected the federals to trounce Beauregard's rebels.[17]

That evening the *Kennebec* came down from Vicksburg with a dispatch from Lee, who had been appointed to command the blockade there. Farragut had instructed Lee to keep up a strict offensive blockade on Vicksburg, fire on any rebels he discovered working on batteries, and keep a lookout for enemy gunboats and destroy them. General Williams had gone up the river, Lee informed Farragut, but he had an inadequate force to accomplish anything. Lee also reported that the rebels had mounted a strong defense on the bluffs above Vicksburg and that the current in the river was very rapid. Urged by Bell to confer with Williams and see the situation for himself, Farragut departed at 5:00 a.m. on May 20 in the *Kennebec* and joined Lee, instructing Bell to follow with the fleet only as far as Grand Gulf.[18]

When the *Kennebec* returned from Vicksburg just after midday on May 23, Bell jotted in his journal that Farragut was "much disturbed by the state of things above and the feeling among the gunboats." From Lee, the flag officer had learned that two enemy gunboats were lying under the upper battery. Farragut wanted Lee, Caldwell, Nichols, De Camp, and Donaldson to cut the rebel gunboats out, but as Bell explained, "The first three considered it impractical or madness, while the other two are willing to try the enterprise. Lee carried his objection so far as to say any one who would undertake it might have his vessel."[19]

Preparations for a cutting-out operation were evidently under way. O'Neil carefully recorded the *Winona*'s preparations in his diary. "At dark received orders to dress all hands, officers and all, in such a manner as to have the [illegible] in white and body dark. The [illegible] . . . was to go up the river at midnight and board some rebel gunboats known to be lying at Vicksburg. At 11 p.m. however, when all were rejoicing at the prospect of doing something as last, the order was countermanded. I was never so disgusted in all my life."[20]

When Palmer arrived off Vicksburg on May 22, he assumed command of the squadron there and volunteered for the mission. According to Bell's diary, "Palmer promised to undertake the cutting out to night with the aid of De Camp and Donaldson. Flag-Officer was indignant at the opposition and defiance of the enemy and thought they should be 'chastised,' and that the gunboats were sufficient for it if the officers had the will."[21]

A contentious debate ensued about whether to cut out the enemy gunboats and bombard the city prior to an army assault. In the end, after two days of discussion, Farragut decided they did not have a large enough force to take Vicksburg, making a bombardment unnecessary. He would leave the gunboats behind to blockade the river below and go back downriver in the *Kennebec*.[22]

Farragut reached the fleet below Grand Gulf just before noon on May 23, but only a few hours later he changed his mind and decided to go back to Vicksburg. At 4:30 p.m., accompanied by the *Brooklyn, Richmond,* and *Kennebec,* the *Hartford* got under way and headed up the Mississippi River again. When Farragut arrived, he called for his captains to join him on the *Kennebec* for a reconnaissance of Vicksburg. Approaching to within two miles of the Confederate bastion, the commanders craned their necks to see the tops of the high bluffs. About halfway up they could clearly see a battery of three or four guns that commanded the entire bend of the river. As the officers surveyed the rebel town's defenses, their faces told the story. The rebels had mounted at least six large guns on the hilltops and stationed a rebel gunboat under a bluff at the upper end of the town. Just before dusk, the *Kennebec* steamed back down. Suddenly, an enemy gunboat appeared and fired at the *Oneida,* but the shot missed, falling harmlessly several hundred yards ahead. That evening Williams boarded the *Hartford* and conferred with the commanding officers about using his troops to reduce the forts. Both Bell and Craven advised Williams to make his own reconnaissance of Vicksburg the next day.[23]

Farragut had taken ill, so the following day Bell accompanied Williams and his staff on the *Kennebec* to reconnoiter the rebels' defenses. They went within 300 yards of the wharf boat opposite Vicksburg, noting that the river had overflowed its banks and levees. At sunset the general and all the captains met with Farragut on board the *Hartford*. Williams opined that he could not land and make his way to the batteries on the hill. He had only 1,400 effective troops, and his spies had informed him that the enemy had 8,000 men at Vicksburg and more troops at Jackson, just forty miles distant by railroad. The general insisted he could not bring up the steam transports carrying his troops unless the ships first silenced the batteries.

Bell dutifully recorded the entire, undoubtedly heated discussion in his journal. Captains Bell, Craven, Wainwright, Lee, Russell, Nichols, and Donaldson all agreed that the ships' guns could not reach the highest batteries where the heaviest rebel guns were mounted and from which they could deliver a plunging fire. They advised against an attack. But, Bell noted, "De Camp thought they should go with it as the enemy had answered Capt. Lee's demand for surrender 'insultingly,'" and Palmer wanted "to go in and 'smash them up' (the bluffs, I presume), and thought we should not, if we could not!" Alden kept changing his mind, and Caldwell "thought we should attack and destroy the town, as did Palmer & De Camp." Farragut "clearly wanted to chastise the enemy by destroying the town—but was restrained by his better judgment, as the troops could not cooperate by land attack and spiking his guns." In the end, Bell explained, Farragut "acquiesced to the opinion of the majority, made 'unanimous,' and ordered a blockade of the river below."[24]

With the conference concluded, Farragut announced that he was going back down the Mississippi, leaving the transports and six gunboats to blockade the river. He then directed the *Iroquois, Oneida, Wissahickon, Sciota, Winona,* and *Itasca* to carry out the bombardments; issued orders to Lee; and sent his ships, with the *Kennebec,* the *Kineo,* and the troop transports, downstream. Bell explained, "Some of the ships reporting only five days' provisions on board, and the river beginning to fall, it was expedient to descend the river without delay, as their grounding while the water is falling would be fatal to them."[25]

Meanwhile, in late May, Beauregard had withdrawn his Confederate forces from Corinth and retreated south, but his army remained a threat to middle Tennessee and Kentucky. Instead of going after and engaging the Confederates, however, Halleck had contented himself with fortifying Corinth, in the expectation that the rebels would come at him there.

On the morning of May 26 the *Richmond, Kineo,* and *Brooklyn* weighed anchor and steamed downriver, followed by the *Kennebec* and *Hartford.* "It seems that no attack is to be made in consequence of the river falling," marine private Smith wrote in his diary. "Weighed anchor at one o'clock and started down the river."[26]

The *Hartford* steamed back down the Old Muddy toward New Orleans. At about 9:00 a.m. on May 28 the ship dropped anchor off Baton Rouge. "A small boat (Dinkey) with the chief engineer, four boys and steward were going ashore when they were fired on by a band of guerillas from the shore," Smith noted. The steward intended to go ashore to fetch some clothes that had been left there on the journey upriver to be washed. As Bell explained, "The boat grounded on touching the landing, and whilst the boys were shoving her off, and before Mr. Kimball could leave the boat, some 30 or 50 horsemen rode toward him, firing on the boat with buckshot, and wounded Mr. Kimball and two boys severely, though not mortally." The nearly disabled dinghy pulled down to the *Kennebec,* and at 10:30 Wainwright ordered, "Beat to quarters." The flagship's gun crews ran to their guns, but the coal vessel *Althea,* which was lashed to the ship's side, had to be cleared away before the flagship could drop down and open fire. Fifteen minutes later the *Hartford* went down below the arsenal and fired about twenty shells. According to Bell, "most of the sailors blazed away right into the houses without regard to the position of the foe." Farragut saw this and called "Cease firing!" The enemy had fled.[27]

That afternoon the mayor of Baton Rouge arrived and reassured Farragut that there would be no recurrence of such attacks, which some blamed on the guerrillas. Without further ado, the *Hartford* and the other federal gunboats proceeded downriver, leaving the occupation of Baton Rouge to the 4th Wisconsin and a Michigan army regiment.[28]

While Farragut took the West Gulf Blockading Squadron back down the Mississippi River, the *Winona* remained behind at Vicksburg to perform picket duty and harass the rebel batteries. Crewman O'Neil faithfully recorded the gunboat's participation in the blockade near Vicksburg. Before the flagship departed, the *Winona* received various stores from the ship, including apples, whiskey, soap, and two kegs of pickles. Late in the day on May 26, the gunboat, accompanied by the *Iroquois,* skirmished with the rebel batteries. "When within 2 miles of the town, we opened upon the batteries with our pivot gun & rifle—Batteries replied without effect." The rebels had not given up the fight. The next evening the *Oneida* and *Itasca,* joined later by the *Katahdin* and *Sciota,* steamed up to engage the rebel batteries. From the *Winona,* Lieutenant Nichols observed "a good deal of firing on shore between the gunboats and batteries," and then he saw a small fire raft drifting downriver. The gunboat continued patrolling the Mississippi, where it encountered refugees, deserters, and fugitive slaves. As O'Neil noted, "At 8 a.m. saw a man paddling up the river close to shore. Fired a rifle and brought him to." The *Winona* sent a boat to pick him up and bring him on board, but Nichols turned the man over to the *Iroquois.* Two days later the gunboat picked up two skiffs containing four contrabands and sent them to the *Iroquois* as well. The *Winona* then went upriver, keeping close to the left bank, and fired five 11-inch shells and two Parrott shells at rebel soldiers on the brow of a hill.[29]

During the first week of June 1862, the *Winona* and the other gunboats took turns on picket duty, patrolling the river as far down as Warrenton. Then the *Winona* received orders to proceed to Natchez. "We sent to the 'Iroquois,' 'Oneida,' and 'Katahdin' for a pilot but could not get one," O'Neil lamented. Obtaining river pilots had been an ongoing problem on the Mississippi. Nonetheless, at 5:50 a.m. the gunboat weighed anchor and proceeded down the Mississippi, passing New Carthage and arriving off Natchez in the early afternoon. The next day, June 4, the *Winona* passed Grand Gulf, where Nichols spotted a large number of men throwing up earthworks, presumably for a battery. About three miles below the town of Rodney, the gunboat grounded on a bar. When efforts to free it failed, Nichols set the crew to lightening ship by throwing precious coal overboard.[30]

Without a launch to pull the gunboat off the bar, the *Winona* remained firmly aground, so Nichols sent a three-boat party out to find a vessel to tow the ship off. Master Charles Hatchett commanded one boat, and Anthony O'Neil led another. "Our orders were to go up under cover of darkness to the town of Rodney to seize the steamer 'Ruby,' supposed to be at that place." Keeping close to the right bank, they proceeded about three miles and then crossed the river. When they were opposite the upper part of the town, they approached the shore with muffled oars. They came across a black man and asked him where they could find the *Ruby.* "He informed us that she was now in a bayou," O'Neil explained. So the boats entered the shallow bayou, where they grounded once but managed to free themselves. They located the *Ruby* and boarded it. "We found only one person on board, a boy attached to the steamer who we pressed into service. The young scamp was frightened and would have run away had I not caught him in time & showed him the muzzle of a Pistol, unpleasantly close to his ear." The boy told them where the pilot lived, and three sailors went to find the man and bring him aboard. The men then fired up the *Ruby*'s boilers, and at 4:30 a.m. the ship steamed out into the river. "All the inhabitants were soon up and no doubt much surprised to see their only steamer in possession of officers of the United States Navy."[31]

With the pilot's assistance, they returned to the *Winona,* brought the captured *Ruby* alongside, and attempted once again to get the gunboat off the bar, but to no avail. Then they tied the port bower anchor to the ferryboat, hove it taut, and "at 10:15 a.m. the vessel slid off the Bar into 8½ fathoms of water." With an engineer and firemen on board the *Ruby,* the two ships got under way and steamed upriver. As they passed Grand Gulf, "we spliced the main brace," O'Neil cheerfully noted. The *Winona* anchored at about 7:00 on the left bank and sent the *Lark* to a large plantation on the opposite side. "I took the gig & went to one on the left side for Provisions," O'Neil wrote. "Shortly after anchoring we passed a boat containing a number of men, but supposed from the appearance that it was merely a pleasure party," so they took no notice and let it pass. "What was our chagrin to find, from information afterwards obtained by me on shore that the Boat contained Jeff Davis' Brother & children—Arch traitors all!"[32]

Just after noon on the following day, June 6, the *Winona* anchored with the *Iroquois, Oneida, Wissahickon, Sciota, Katahdin,* and *Itasca* below Vicksburg. The next afternoon the *Winona* and *Wissahickon* dropped down to Grand Gulf and sent a flag of truce ashore, ordering all workmen from the earthworks discovered there. Just for good measure, the *Wissahickon* and *Itasca* fired their howitzers at the earthworks before steaming back up the river. They returned to Grand Gulf, and O'Neil explained what happened next: "On the morning of the 8th about 4 o'clock while at anchor off the town the gunboats were opened [on] from the town by two batt. of field pieces." The Confederates had moved 6- and 12-pounders into position on the ridge behind Grand Gulf. "The 'Wissahickon' slipped her cable but then 'Itasca' was unable to do so, the . . . bolt being rusty, and she had to heave up anchor under . . . fire at close range." Finally, the gunboats engaged the batteries for four hours, driving the rebels from their position.

"The 'Itasca' was struck 30 times 1 man being killed & 52 wounded. The 'Wissahickon' suffered less having several wounded."[33]

While the *Winona* and the gunboats patrolled the river between Vicksburg and Grand Gulf, the *Hartford* continued downriver and arrived back in New Orleans at 2:00 p.m. on May 30. The *Hartford*'s officers and men enjoyed the pleasures of that city, including a theatrical performance on the *Pensacola*. On June 5 Private Smith wrote, "The mail steamer Connecticut left for New York with the mail and the sick and wounded. We gave her three cheers on leaving the harbor." Two days later, when General Butler sent a number of pilots aboard, Smith suspected a fleet movement was in the offing and noted, "Captain Porter was on board today."[34]

Porter had returned to New Orleans from Ship Island at the suggestion of Butler, who surmised that Porter's mortars might be able to reach the Confederate batteries above Vicksburg. In early May, Farragut had sent Porter and his mortar flotilla to Ship Island to await the commodore's anticipated operation on Mobile Bay—an attack that never materialized. Farragut welcomed Butler's suggestion, as well as his offer to allocate 7,000 troops for an attack on the rebel stronghold at Vicksburg. Farragut had been under increasing pressure from the Navy Department to send a more substantial force to open the Mississippi River. Learning that Farragut had abandoned his first attempt to eliminate the enemy stronghold at Vicksburg, Welles had fired off a pointed message, stating, "It is of paramount importance that you go up and clear the river with utmost expedition." With little choice but to comply with the Navy Department's wishes, which were shared by President Lincoln, Farragut set about organizing a stronger force to renew operations against Vicksburg. He immediately asked Porter to send him ten mortar boats with steamers to tow them up the river. Although Porter believed this renewed movement up the Mississippi was a diversion from the more important objective of taking Mobile, he dutifully ordered not ten but twenty of his mortar boats to New Orleans.[35]

When Porter arrived in New Orleans, he discovered that Farragut had every intention of going up the Mississippi. Although Porter was "decidedly against" going to Memphis to join Davis, Bell noted in his diary that Porter "acquiesces like the rest of us." Always an optimist, Porter predicted, "On the 20th Vicksburg will be on fire, I hope."[36]

On June 8, after spending a week in New Orleans, Farragut boarded his flagship, and at 6:00 a.m. it began the journey north to Vicksburg. The summer heat had taken hold, and Smith noted in his diary, "Wore white pants today for the first time."[37]

Just below Vicksburg, a few miles above Grand Gulf, O'Neil witnessed the squadron's arrival from the deck of the *Winona*. "At 10:25 the fleet anchored about 2 miles above that place," he noted in his entry for June 10. That evening, the *Winona* opened fire on the town of Grand Gulf, expending twelve 10-inch shells, seven Parrott rifle percussion shells, and some shrapnel from its howitzer. The *Wissahickon* joined in the bombardment, and the following day the *Winona* moved abreast of the town of Grand Gulf. "At 6 P.M. opened fire on the town & batteries," O'Neil noted. "Quite a number of men were driven out of the hill battery into the woods, which were also shelled." The *Wissahickon* and *Winona* then sent two armed boats ashore led by Lieutenant Walker and accompanied by master's mate Hunt and third assistant engineer Hatfield. Their mission, to burn down the town of Grand Gulf, suggests that the war had become increasingly contentious by June 1862. Before returning to their ships at 7:00 p.m., the sailors started fires in Grand Gulf at eight different places.[38]

In the morning the Yankee gunboats continued down the river. The *Winona* passed Natchez on the afternoon of June 12 but then turned around, passed Natchez again, and anchored for the night some five miles above the city. Two days later the fleet went back upstream to Grand Gulf. The town, O'Neil noted, "was nearly all in ashes & was still smoking." They anchored below Vicksburg that evening, and O'Neil observed, "River falling very fast."[39]

On board the *Hartford*, Farragut had been making slow progress up the Mississippi, which, as O'Neil noted, continued to fall steadily. Federal troops had also started up for Vicksburg. Sixteen of Porter's mortar boats had already left New Orleans, and another five were under tow by June 15. The next day Porter followed in the *Octorara*. With food supplies at a minimum in New Orleans, the ships, gunboats, and mortar boats of the flotilla had inadequate provisions and would have to rely on plantations along the way for fresh meat, fruit, and vegetables. Consequently, when the *Hartford* arrived at Waterloo, south of Grand Gulf, on June 19, some of the crew were allowed ashore to buy fresh meat and other food from the locals. "Men went ashore and were treated coldly," Smith wrote. "The inhabitants refused to sell anything or allow us to bury our dead." The locals' chilly reception extended to one of the *Hartford*'s lieutenants, who politely requested permission to bring a deceased bluejacket ashore for burial. An older, obviously influential gentleman in the little settlement stoutly refused. The landing party returned to the *Hartford* empty-handed, which prompted Bell to send an armed landing party of marines ashore the next day with orders to bury the dead sailor. A day later the *Hartford* anchored off a plantation below Fort Adams, and Bell sent the purser and one sailor to shore to procure fresh meat. On this occasion the Yankees encountered pro-Union locals, including "a wealthy Union planter, who gave meat for nothing," Smith noted.[40]

The rebels at Grand Gulf had other intentions, however. The *Winona* remained anchored below Vicksburg, and the crew members spent their time holystoning the decks and scrubbing the paintwork. On June 21 O'Neil heard heavy firing from the direction of Grand Gulf, and when the *Winona* passed the town, he learned that federal steamers and four mortar schooners had been fired on by a rebel artillery company. "At 7 p.m. being in sight of Grand Gulf we beat to quarters and cleared for action." Three of Porter's mortar schooners had come up and were towed into position; they fired shells into the town, dislodging the rebel artillery company.[41]

On June 21 the *Pinola* appeared, towing a schooner. It was followed by river steamers carrying Williams's troops. They had negotiated the current, bars, and snags of the Mississippi well, but the *Hartford* had run aground and remained stuck fast until morning. "Worked all night trying to get off but did not succeed 'til ten o'clock this morning," Smith wrote. With a manila stream cable discovered in the hold, the troopships had pulled the *Hartford* free, and a relieved Bell wrote, "All Hands in high glee. I felt sure the ship was here til next winter, as the river is falling fast, and there were no means of lightening ship as fast as the water falls."[42]

The federal vessels and the nine transports continued up the river, with the *Winona* and *Pinola* going on ahead. In the midafternoon, about twenty miles below Natchez, "Beat to quarters" sounded, bringing the *Hartford*'s men to their guns. Smith took up his position at a 9-inch broadside gun, one of two manned by marines. Suddenly they heard the crack of two cannon shots. "*Oneida* fired two shots over the bluff. The fire was not returned. General Williams landed some troops."[43]

The *Hartford* anchored for the night, and Farragut retired to his cabin. All but those on watch tried to get some rest, but Smith spent the night on guard. "Anchored a short distance above the bluffs," he wrote. "Since dark a bright light is seen, supposed to be a campfire. Had no hammocks last night." The *Hartford*'s crew remained on alert, worried the Confederates might be watching them from the bluffs. They had heard rumors that rebel riflemen had fired on the mortar boats from the cliffs. The flagship steamed up the Mississippi the next day, with Williams's troops in the lead. The *Winona* took Mortar No. 10 in tow, and the *Oneida* and *Pinola* towed the bark *Sea Bride*. The following day the *Hartford* passed Grand Gulf with the crew at general quarters. To Farragut and Bell's relief, there were no more signs of enemy activity, and they dropped anchor "at dark in a lonesome place about 12 miles below Vicksburg."[44]

On June 25 Farragut's flagship anchored below the Confederate stronghold. The federal squadron there included the *Brooklyn, Richmond, Iroquois, Sciota, Wissahickon, Winona, Harriet Lane, Octorara, Miami, Westfield, Clifton,* and *Jackson*. Always conscious of the ships around the *Hartford,* Private Smith observed that Porter's sixteen mortar boats had joined them. "A few shots were fired by Porter's fleet between four and six o'clock," he wrote. General Williams boarded the *Hartford* and explained to Farragut that he now had only 3,500 troops and, using contrabands as a labor force, had been digging a canal across the peninsula by the bend at Vicksburg. Williams had landed in the rear of Grand Gulf, entered the town through a bayou, and torched it. The flag officer also learned from a messenger sent by Lieutenant Colonel Alfred Ellet that the Mississippi River was clear from Memphis to Vicksburg and that the colonel now had four rams and a tender positioned on the other side of the peninsula, almost bisecting the river. On a less auspicious note, Farragut received a report from Lee that the river had fallen eighteen inches in just three days.[45]

Meanwhile, the *Hartford*'s captain, Wainwright, had his own responsibilities, and he quickly set his crew to preparing for the battle to come. "The main hold was cleared out today and ropes and stuff layed on the deck to protect the boilers," Smith wrote.[46]

The previous evening, Porter had placed eight mortars and three steamers on the right bank and another nine mortars and three steamers on the left bank. At about 4:30 a.m. on June 26, Porter came down in his gig and reported that he was nearly ready, but he wanted assurances that the ships would support him. Farragut replied affirmatively and told Porter that after a one-hour bombardment, he would sail with the fleet. Farragut asked Porter to signal him when he was ready.[47]

At 5:00 a.m. Farragut called his captains to the flagship for orders. They were to attack in two lines, with the *Richmond* leading the starboard line, as its chase guns were better placed and of better caliber for attacking the forts. The *Hartford* and *Brooklyn* were to follow. The *Iroquois* would lead the port line, followed by the *Oneida, Wissahickon, Sciota, Winona, Pinola,* and *Kennebec.* The captains departed, and Farragut spent the day waiting for the signal from Porter. When none came, he sent Bell to inquire about the delay. Bell reported, "Found that officer resting himself, he and his people being thoroughly fagged out by working all last night and to-day." Porter had his men computing the distances, the mortars' charges, and the fuses. He told Bell he would let Farragut know as soon as the mortars were ready, but it would not be before the next morning.[48]

Porter's mortar vessel crews labored to finish their preparations. That afternoon they opened fire and kept up a steady bombardment until dusk. At sunrise the following day, Smith took his guard post and watched the big mortar shells arc toward the Vicksburg bluffs. "Mortars resumed firing at sunrise. The fire was returned occasionally by the batteries. Some shots were fired by the *Westfield* and *Octorara.* Ceased bombarding about nine o'clock P.M."[49]

That night, Farragut called his captains back to the flagship and explained his plan of attack for the run past the Vicksburg batteries. "At 2 a.m., 28th (to-morrow), he will hoist two vertical red lights as the signal to get underway," Bell wrote.[50]

On the *Hartford,* Wainwright mustered his officers and crew to address them before the coming battle, a responsibility usually assigned to the first lieutenant. He explained that they would face murderous fire as they passed the rebel batteries at Vicksburg and asked for their approval. The *Hartford's* bluejackets greeted Wainwright's unprecedented request with loud cheering. "We will follow you anywhere," the sailors shouted, "we go to Vicksburg."

At 2:00 a.m. on June 28 the flagship signaled for the squadron to get under way. An hour later the *Hartford* weighed anchor; all the vessels hoisted their colors at the mastheads and took up their stations in two columns. The *Winona,* O'Neil wrote, "steamed ahead slowly into our position on Port quarter of Flagship. All the fleet underway and heading slowly up the river in the following order: Iroquois, Oneida, Richmond, Wissahickon, Sciota, Hartford, Winona, Pinola, Brooklyn, Kennebec and Katahdin." Concealed from rebel eyes by the darkness, Farragut's ships steamed slowly toward the mortar vessels and the enemy batteries, but as the *Iroquois* neared the lower battery, the Confederates gave the alarm. Soon the rebels' large rifles and heavy-caliber guns opened fire, the red flashes illuminating the night. In the face of heavy raking fire from the town and plunging fire from the hills, Palmer coolly took the *Iroquois* toward the town. To his surprise and relief, despite this furious fusillade, only one enemy shell burst on board, scattering metal fragments in all directions. Beginning at 4:00 a.m. and throughout the run past Vicksburg, Porter's mortars kept up a constant fire. In his diary O'Neil carefully noted the course of the squadron's passage. "At 4 a.m. the ball opened with a gun from rebel water battery in front of the Marine Hospital. The fire was immediately returned by the leading ships and by Porter's steamers with long range rifle guns and by the mortars." At exactly 4:27 a.m., he wrote, "the Flagship opened with her bow guns and immediately afterwards at 4:30 a.m. we opened with our XI inch rifle gun."[51]

On the *Hartford,* Smith had been standing ready at the broadside gun, tense from the waiting. Two or three enemy guns just eighty feet above the water took aim on the flagship. "Many of their shot passed through the rigging and into the bulwarks of our ship. One shot cut the main topsail yard in two," Smith observed. The *Hartford* drew ahead, and its broadside guns were brought to bear, with "excellent execution. One division of the great guns was assigned to take care of the batteries on the ridge. It was thought they could not reach that battery. They did, however, just reach it with all the elevation they could get, and we plainly saw the shot (shell) against the sky until they struck the batteries there, some going over." Seeing that some of the *Hartford*'s guns were pouring fire into the hills where no batteries were located, Wainwright ordered the other two gun divisions to silence the lower batteries. By now, a dense smoke had drifted over the scene, obscuring the view. The shells burst in the air, but no one knew for certain whether they hit the enemy batteries or exploded harmlessly. The federal gunners kept up their fire, but Bell thought they were sometimes firing at bombshells, thinking them gun flashes.[52]

After the Union ships had passed by half a mile, two "saucy" rebel guns opened up again, "their shot striking astern and ricocheting over us and cutting our lower rigging severely, and boats." To Bell's consternation, "During this time not a gun could be brought to bear on this battery, the rifle gun on the poop being on the quarter could not be trained on them."[53]

When the *Winona* came abreast of the upper battery, it was entirely clear of men, dispersed by the guns of the flagship. But, the *Winona*'s captain noted, "as soon as I passed, they returned and opened a very spiteful fire upon the flagship *Iroquois, Pinola,* and this vessel until beyond range."

The *Winona* kept its position close to the flagship, O'Neil explained, "and as soon as we could bring them to bear we opened with our howitzer."[54]

As they approached the fort, the sun rose red and fiery, just to the right of it. By now, the *Richmond, Wissahickon,* and *Sciota* were safely out of sight above the bend; having passed the city, the *Winona* ceased firing at 5:15 a.m. The gunboat had expended seventeen Parrott rifle shells, seven shrapnel for the howitzer, and shell, grape, and shrapnel for the 11-inch pivot guns. The *Winona* had suffered little damage. "Examined the vessel and found two small holes in starboard forward bulwark—either grape or small field pieces," O'Neil recorded. "At 12:30 P.M. Flagship signaled to report killed and wounded. Signaled in reply—'None.'"[55]

The *Hartford* had also made it past the Vicksburg batteries. Private Smith summed up the day's events: "The firing was hot and lasted about two hours. We did not succeed in silencing the batteries. Our loss was one killed and ten wounded."[56]

The sense of relief was short lived. The *Richmond, Wissahickon,* and *Sciota* had made it above the bend, but Bell could not see the gunboats *Katahdin* and *Kennebec*—nor, he suddenly realized, the man-of-war *Brooklyn.* When Bell informed Farragut that the *Brooklyn* was nowhere in sight, the flag officer ordered a messenger sent through the swamps to locate the ship.[57] Within the hour, Farragut summoned Palmer, Lee, Alden, Donaldson, Nichols, and Crosby to the flagship to report. Bell did not record their conversation, but Palmer of the *Iroquois* wrote in his official report, "We fought our way up running close in to the town having raking fire from the fort above and plunging fire from the batteries on the hill, together with broadsides from the cannon planted in the streets." Despite this heavy concentrated fire, the lucky *Iroquois* escaped without injury. "One shell burst on board of us, scattering its fragments around us, and yet no casualty."[58]

Although still suffering from a fever that had confined him to bed for several days prior to the attack, De Camp had stood on the *Wissahickon*'s deck to encourage his men. However, he gave full credit to the executive officer, Lieutenant E. E. Potter, for taking charge during the passing of the Vicksburg batteries. The gunboat received four hits. One entered the berth deck, killing one sailor and wounding others who had been stationed there to pass shot and shell.[59]

The *Pinola,* the last vessel to run past the enemy batteries, was the target of heavy fire but suffered only a few hits. One enemy shot, however, struck a seaman at the 11-inch gun, severely wounding him; another

50-pounder rifle shot slammed into the howitzer and carriage, killing the gun captain and a nearby landsman.[60]

Lee's *Oneida* also suffered casualties. Rebel gunners scored four hits. One 8-inch rifle shell came through the starboard after-pivot port, killing a seaman and wounding the third assistant engineer. The shell then passed through the engine room hatch and picked up three loaded muskets, severely wounding a seaman and another man.[61]

Three shots struck the *Sciota*, Donaldson reported, killing a seaman. One man lost his arm above the elbow, and two others were slightly wounded.[62]

In his initial report, Wainwright explained that the rebel batteries had been scattered on the hills, and the federal gunners could discover them only by the flash or smoke of their guns. "Some were also on high bluffs rendering it difficult to elevate our guns to reach them." Wainwright noted that they might have run past the batteries under full steam, but their objective had been to drive the enemy from their guns. The *Hartford* had endured heavy fire, and one man was wounded by a musket ball while working a howitzer in the top. Edward E. Jennings was killed, and a seaman and a few others were slightly wounded. Farragut suffered a slight contusion.[63]

The *Winona*'s Nichols spoke for many: "Taking all things into consideration, it seems miraculous that no more damage was sustained by the fleet." The run past Vicksburg had convinced Nichols that ships could clear batteries placed on a level with them, but, he argued, "the men return to them as soon as the ships' guns cease to bear; but as to batteries placed on hills and bluffs, ships are almost useless against them."[64]

Above the Vicksburg batteries, Farragut found Ellet's rams and told one to take dispatches to Memphis for Captain Davis and General Halleck. In a letter to Welles, Farragut announced that he had run past the Vicksburg batteries but, he opined, "to no purpose. The enemy leave their guns for the moment, but return to them as soon as we have passed and rake us." Farragut now concluded, "It is not possible for us to take Vicksburg without an army force of twelve to fifteen thousand men."[65]

The *Brooklyn, Katahdin,* and *Kennebec* were still missing, but those on the *Hartford* could hear the sound of firing from below. Evening came, and the sound of gunfire ceased. Finally, a messenger arrived with word from the *Brooklyn* and the mortar fleet. Lieutenant Woodworth, commanding the *J. P. Jackson,* reported that his vessel had been hit by an 8-inch rifle shell on the starboard side, forward of the bulkhead. The shot had passed through the wheelhouse and out through the hurricane deck, taking off the right foot of a steersman and wounding his left foot. Loss of steering left the *Jackson* unmanageable for a time, but they rigged a tiller and headed downriver. Woodworth noted that the *Jackson* had fired 117 shot, shell, grape, and shrapnel during the battle. When the *Clifton* went to its assistance, it was struck in the boilers. Six men were scalded to death, and two were forced to jump overboard.[66]

Although Farragut gave Porter's mortars due credit for their service at Vicksburg, Porter himself insisted they had silenced "every battery." He claimed, "But for the mortars we would all have been sunk." The Confederates denied that any of their guns had been disabled, and they claimed they had suffered just thirteen casualties. In a telegram to President Jefferson Davis, General Van Dorn acknowledged a heavy bombardment of Vicksburg but wrote, "No flinching. Houses perforated; none burned yet. Contest will commence when the enemy attempt to land; he will probably try it." As one historian commented, "the mortar bombardment was a waste of ammunition."[67]

With most of his fleet now safely above Vicksburg, Farragut chose to observe June 29, 1862, the Sabbath, with a "blessed day of rest." According to O'Neil, "Flagship telegraphed—'Eleven,' return thanks for God's mercy."[68]

9

CSS *Arkansas*

Gentlemen, in seeking combat as we now do we must win or perish.
—Lieutenant Isaac Brown

The officers and men of Farragut's fleet, anchored above Vicksburg, were at breakfast on Tuesday, July 1, 1862, when Charles Davis's squadron hove into sight. *Winona* crewman O'Neil noted its arrival in his diary: "At 6:25 a.m. during a thunder storm Capt. Davis' ironclads Benton (F.S.) Cincinnati, Carondelet, Louisville came down river with steamers towing mortar boats." Farragut had asked Davis, who had recently been appointed the flag officer in command of US naval forces on the Mississippi and its tributaries, to assemble all the vessels he could, steam down from Memphis, and join him in reducing the Confederate defenses at Vicksburg.[1]

Word spread quickly, and Farragut's men rushed to the decks to see the strange new river craft of Davis's flotilla. Marine private Smith's duty on board the *Hartford* gave him an opportunity to see Davis's arrival. "Today has been an eventful day," Smith penned in his diary. "The marines fell out and saluted Commodore Davis when coming and going. Captain Davis dined with our Commodore and left the ship at 1:15 o'clock."[2]

When the *Carondelet* came to anchor, coxswain Morison caught his first glimpse of Vicksburg. "From where we were lying the dome of the courthouse and the spires of two churches are to be seen. The Louisiana shore in front of the city assumes the form of two sides of a triangle (owing to the sinuous course of the river)." Morison also observed the position of Porter's mortar boats. "Along the lower side Porter's mortars are placed, and

145

along the upper are ours, so that the city is placed between two fires which must eventually drive them out."[3]

The joining of these two federal squadrons gave rise to loud cheering from Farragut's West Gulf Blockading Squadron and joyous celebrations by both officers and enlisted men. Most of the officers of the two squadrons had been shipmates before the war, and they welcomed the opportunity to catch up on war news and family events. However, it soon became apparent that all was not well with Farragut's squadron. "There's a great deal of gossip among the officers," Phelps explained in a letter to Foote. "The lower fleet is rent with criminations and recriminations."[4]

Bell confided his distress about the situation to his journal. "Visited the fleet below. Bad state of feeling there. C— had received a sharp reprimand from flag-officer, which he considered unmerited and insulting, and would not be comforted." Farragut informed Bell that he was to replace Craven and assume command of the *Brooklyn*. "This is a heavy blow, and interferes with my calculations for getting free of the river, for there is every prospect of the fleet summering between its steep banks, smitten with insects, heat intolerable, fevers, chills, and dysentery, and inglorious inactivity, losing all that the fleet has won in honor and reputation." The word of Craven's departure spread quickly among the crews of both fleets. Bell reluctantly packed his uniforms and personal gear and made a brief but poignant entry in his journal: "Found an order for me to relieve Captain Craven in command of the Brooklyn; went to bed with a heavy heart."[5]

Farragut's requests that Halleck send troops to attack Vicksburg had gone unanswered, leaving only Williams's 3,000 troops to take the Confederate stronghold defended by 12,000 rebels. Halleck could have committed his entire federal force to the taking of Vicksburg before leaving for Washington to replace George McClellan as general in chief, a change in command prompted by McClellan's humiliating defeat before Richmond. Instead, Halleck chose to dismantle "his grand army piecemeal." He sent Buell's Army of the Ohio eastward toward Chattanooga, sent Grant's Army of the Tennessee west to occupy Memphis, and recalled Pope's army to defend Corinth.[6]

Too few to mount a direct assault, Williams's soldiers, assisted by a large number of slaves, were put to work digging a twelve-foot-wide canal across the peninsula opposite Vicksburg. But in the hot, dry summer weather, the Mississippi River continued to fall, and prospects for the canal project's success dwindled.[7]

Without the means to assault Vicksburg, Farragut had to rely on a bombardment of rebel defenses by his mortars and four mortar scows sent down by Davis. "Our mortars opened on the city this morning," Morison wrote on July 3. "It was soon returned in the shape of a large rifled shell which came whirling through the air like a gigantic quail. Burst short, doing no harm. The firing was carried on by both parties at intervals all day. No harm to our side."[8]

At midnight, thirty-four guns from the big mortars began a Fourth of July greeting. They were joined by all the vessels of the fleet except for the *Richmond.* That ship's sick bay and all available spaces had been taken up by the growing number of ill sailors, most of them suffering from chills, fever, and dysentery. On the morning of July 4, O'Neil wrote, "8 a.m. dressed ship as did the other vessels in the fleet in honor of the day." Lending a sense of patriotic festivity to the day, several army bands toured the fleet in boats, playing national airs. Each federal ship flew a large American flag at the masthead in celebration of the Fourth. "Independence Day. We are fighting today for what we fought eighty-six years ago—our national existence then against King George, now King Cotton," Morison quipped. In honor of the glorious Fourth, "the main brace was spliced on board every craft of the two fleets," he noted, "with the exception of this one miserabile."[9]

Farragut and Davis celebrated the holiday by going downstream in the *Benton* to reconnoiter the Confederate batteries. A formidable gunboat armed with seven 32-pounders and two 11-inch and seven 8-inch rifles, the *Benton* could challenge the rebel batteries, in Davis's opinion. But to his surprise, when the gunboat opened fire on the upper battery, the rebels shot back with a new Whitworth rifle. One shot went clean through the *Benton*'s bow gun port, exploding with a bang and injuring several sailors.[10]

Much as Bell had feared, the hot summer of 1862 continued to generate a steady supply of sick soldiers and sailors. On July 9 a correspondent reporting from Farragut's fleet off Vicksburg told readers: "Considerable indisposition prevails among the fleet, chiefly arising from the excessively hot weather. Bowel complaints, and various forms of bilious diseases affect all, more or less, but no deaths occur from these causes." In his diary Bell noted the prevalence of illness: "A large sick list, the cases being a type of dengue fever (fever and chills)."[11]

Federal gunboats plying the Mississippi also had to contend with rebel guerrillas lurking along the shore and taking potshots at passing vessels. A correspondent on board the ram *Queen of the West,* en route from Memphis to join the flotilla at Vicksburg, told readers: "Occasionally along the shores the dreaded guerrillas stealthily gliding from tree to tree, with the deadly intent of 'picking off' some of our crew, but the bright muzzle of a brace of 12 pound howitzers flashing defiance from the hurricane deck admonished the reptiles of terrible retribution." The correspondent reported that they had met the ram *Lancaster* on its way up, and "she had fired into a band of guerrillas a few miles further down, wounding some and causing all to scatter."[12]

Off Vicksburg, Farragut and Davis's men sweltered in the heat, pestered by swarms of mosquitoes. Canvas awnings draped over the gunboats' spar decks provided some relief from the broiling sun, but the iron-plated decks shimmered with the heat. On July 13, a Sunday, Morison noted in his journal: "Am twenty-four years old today and the hottest this summer, the glass standing at 110 degrees in the shade." Desperate to ease the suffering of a growing number of sailors with prickly heat, the *Benton*'s surgeon ordered them bathed in vinegar, and soon the pungent odor permeated the entire gunboat.[13]

With the river level steadily falling, numerous men succumbing to illness, and his coal and provisions dwindling, Farragut began to despair. On July 4, confiding his frustrations to Welles, he wrote that he had "almost abandoned the idea of getting the ships down the river unless this place is either taken possession of or cut off."[14] Less than a week later, Farragut received a telegram from Welles, asking him to send twelve mortar boats and the *Octorara* with Porter to Hampton Roads. Porter wasted little time. He left Commander Renshaw in the *Westfield* with the remaining mortar vessels and departed the following afternoon. Porter ordered the vessels' shot holes patched and painted over to conceal any damage. Then, with his officers resplendent in their full dress uniforms and the enlisted men dressed in whites, Porter took his mortar schooners downstream in parade formation, past the curious Confederate onlookers lining the riverbanks to watch what they called a "retreat."[15] The following day, a Thursday, O'Neil received an appointment "as an Acting Master in the U.S. Gunboat Service" and was ordered to report to the USS *Cincinnati*. He bid his shipmates on the *Winona* farewell and joined the city-class gunboat, where he took the morning and dog watches on Saturday, July 12.[16]

The meeting of Davis's flotilla and Farragut's fleet above Vicksburg had forced the Confederate commander, General Van Dorn, to reassess the city's defenses. He then made a straightforward choice, ordering that the ram *Arkansas* be completed, put under his orders, and sent to attack the Yankee fleets. "It was better to die in action," he argued, "than to be buried up at Yazoo City." The ram's new commander, Lieutenant Isaac N. Brown, a forty-five-year-old navy veteran from Kentucky, had towed the unfinished vessel down the Yazoo River from Greenwood to Yazoo City. There, Brown pressed ahead with almost superhuman effort to turn the hulk into a powerful ram. He procured workmen and supplies to finish the vessel, which had been labeled a "bucket of bolts" by its crew, in part because Brown had plated its 18-inch-thick wooden casemate, which sloped at a 45-degree angle, with railroad iron. The 165-foot *Arkansas* had a lethal 16-foot-long ram, two 9-inch smoothbores, two 64-pounders, two 7-inch rifles, and two 32-pounder smoothbores for armament. A pair of unreliable low-pressure engines salvaged from the sunken *Natchez* powered its twin screws, giving the ram a speed of 8 knots, but with a 12-foot draft, even Brown doubted the ram's suitability for the West's shallow, narrow rivers.

On July 14, ordered into action prematurely, the *Arkansas* and its 100-man crew started down the Yazoo, stopping at Satartia to dry powder from the forward magazine that had been dampened by steam from the old, leaky boilers. The next day, which one of the sailors described as "bucolic, warm and calm," with good visibility, the *Arkansas* approached the Old River channel near the Mississippi with the men at battle stations.[17]

Late the previous evening, Phelps had come aboard the *Carondelet* to deliver what Walke later described as "formal, brief, and verbal" orders from Davis to make a reconnaissance up the Yazoo the following morning. Walke, who had been plagued by a fever off and on, replied that many of his crew were ill, and he could man only one division of guns. Brushing aside Walke's objections, Phelps explained that based on information from deserters, the rebel ram would come down on July 15. Davis had dismissed these reports earlier, but now, Phelps felt, Davis believed them.[18]

The *Carondelet* departed before dawn the next morning, and two hours later, with a pilot on board, it entered the Old River. To Walke's surprise, he spotted the faster *Tyler* and *Queen of the West* passing him.[19] They steamed a mile or so ahead of Walke's ironclad. At about 7:00 the call "Boat in sight" interrupted the *Tyler* crew's breakfast of coffee and hard biscuits. Squinting in an attempt to make out the vessel's identity, the *Tyler*'s pilot exclaimed, "Looks like a 'chocolate brown' house." The captain, Lieutenant William Gwin, focused on the steamer's huge smokestack through his spyglass and immediately recognized the vessel as the rebel ram *Arkansas*. Through the ram's two gun ports, Gwin could clearly see heavy guns. "The ram not having any colors flying, we fired a shot at her," Gwin wrote in his initial report.[20]

From the ram's shield, Brown saw the federal timberclad and, in the light of the rising sun, two more vessels. Gathering his officers, he said, "Gentlemen, in seeking combat as we now do we must win or perish." Admonishing them to fight their way through the enemy fleet and on no account allow the *Arkansas* to be taken by the Yankees, Brown told them, "Go to your guns!"[21]

A puff of powder, followed by a cannonball whizzing over the pilothouse, prompted Gwin to order the *Tyler*'s forward gun deck to open fire on the rebel ram. From half a mile off, the *Tyler*'s gunners took aim on the *Arkansas,* which returned fire from a pair of bow guns. Gwin had stopped the *Tyler*'s engines, but he now called down to chief engineer Goble in the engine room for full speed astern. "I then commenced backing down the river, hoping that I would have speed enough to keep ahead of her and be able to fight most of my battery," Gwin explained, "but finding she was approaching me rapidly, I rounded down the river and took a position about 100 yards distant on the port bow of the *Carondelet,* which vessel was standing down."[22]

The *Carondelet*'s crew had also been piped to breakfast when they heard the report of a gun. Morison recalled, "I looked through a port to see what caused all the commotion and I beheld our gunboat and ram retreating from a most formidable-looking monster which was coming down river in style, at the same time keeping up a steady fire on the Tylor."[23] Walke barked at the gun captain to fire a bow gun at the rebel ram, then paused to decide whether to advance or retreat. If he fought the rebel ram bow on, he risked being outmaneuvered; if he backed down, he exposed the gunboat's vulnerable stern. Walke turned to the helmsman and ordered him to go back down the river. The *Carondelet*'s engines churned, and it sped down the Yazoo as fast as the stokers could feed the boilers.[24]

When the *Tyler* neared the *Carondelet,* Walke hailed Gwin and ordered him to report the approach of the *Arkansas* to Davis. The *Tyler*'s captain shook his head and kept the timberclad's 30-pounder stern rifle blasting away at the *Arkansas.* Occasionally, the *Tyler*'s broadside battery joined in to support the embattled *Carondelet.*[25]

For the next hour, the *Arkansas* pursued all three federal vessels, pummeling them with fire from its bow guns. "I had got my gun cast loose and ready as I could, which I did," Morison wrote. "I now became very warm, so I pulled my shirt and hat off, which made me feel better. The decks were very slippery and I asked for sand, which was not to be had, but I soon got a substitute in the shape of a flood of water which came pouring in through a hole in the wheelhouse, caused by an eight-inch solid shot which came through our stern, gutted the captain's cabin, passed through the wheelhouse, steerage and several steam pipes, and knocked a twelve inch oak log into splinters and then rolled out on deck." The *Arkansas* was close astern of the *Carondelet* now and "steadily gaining on us," the diarist noted. When Walke saw the ram headed straight for the *Carondelet,* raking the gunboat with its 64-pounder guns, he explained, "I avoided her prow, and as she came up we exchanged broadsides." As the ram swept by, the *Carondelet's* bow gunners gave the rebel a few rounds. "I got several good shots at her," Morison claimed, "but I imagine without effect, as her iron-cased sides did not look as if they were broached. She mounted ten heavy guns, three on each side and two forward and aft. Altogether she was a mighty unpleasant looking critter to be closing you up and at the same time throwing solid shot through you." As the *Arkansas* steamed past, Walke could see two holes in its side and the crew frantically pumping and bailing.[26]

"At last she touched our stern and then ranged up on our starboard side," gunner Morison wrote. "As she touched our stern, I fired the last shot I could at her and came forward just as she poured her broadside guns into us, which stove in our plating as if it were glass." The ram then ran across *Carondelet's* bows, and Morison "fired a sixty-eight into her at less than two yards distance, with what effect I don't know. We then tried to bring our port broadside to bear on her but she was not in range." Fire from the *Arkansas* had, however, cut the federal gunboat's wheel ropes and destroyed steam gauges and water pipes. "We had got aground, but after some work we got afloat and followed her down as fast as our disabled condition would permit us. I now had time to look around and I found that we had four killed, sixteen wounded (some very severely) and twelve missing, all in one short hour's fight." Many had leaped overboard to escape the steam and the enemy fire.[27]

From the *Tyler,* acting master Coleman, signal officer for the day, caught a final glimpse of the *Carondelet* up against the bank in a cloud of enveloping smoke, "with steam escaping from her ports and . . . men jumping overboard." Coleman and Gwin both assumed the *Arkansas* would pause to take the Pook turtle as a prize, but instead the ram pressed downstream. They all remembered what had happened to the *Mound City* on the White River, when one shot to the steam chest had inflicted so many casualties. "There was nothing reassuring in the present situation," Coleman noted, "for we were even more vulnerable than the 'Mound City,' and it was evident that the 'Tyler' was no match for an armored vessel such as was her antagonist."[28]

Gwin managed to keep a lead of 200 or 300 yards on the *Arkansas* for a time, but then the ram began to gain on the *Tyler,* its bow guns raking the timberclad's stern. Gunner Herman Peters's stern gun crew kept firing on the rebel ironclad, but their shots merely bounced off the ram's sloping sides. Gwin remained grimly determined to outrun the *Arkansas,* but shot and shell from his pursuer began to take a toll. A detachment of army sharpshooters from the 4th Wisconsin Regiment bore the brunt of the enemy fire, which killed the sharpshooters' captain early in the engagement. Five soldiers were also killed, and another five wounded. Then, as Gwin watched, a rebel shot took pilot John Sebastian's left arm clean off. He crumpled to the deck in a pool of blood, but the second pilot, David Hiner, took the wheel. As several crewmen carried Sebastian below to the surgeon, Gwin and Coleman realized that, with the *Carondelet* now out of the fight, the only other federal vessel able to fend off the rebel ram was the *Queen of the West,* which had been hanging back several hundred yards astern of the *Tyler.* Gwin "called out to her commander to move up, and ram the 'Arkansas,'" Coleman wrote. "His only response to this was to commence backing vigorously out of range, while Gwin was expressing his opinion of him through the trumpet in that vigorous English a commander in battle sometimes uses, when thing do not go altogether right."[29]

Although struck eleven times by enemy shot and shell and pummeled by grape from the rebel ram, the *Tyler* continued moving downstream. The timberclad's stern gun crew blazed away at the rebel ram, but many of the crewmen stood helplessly by their posts, unable to fight back. "Things looked squally," Coleman wrote. "Blood was flowing freely on board, and the crash of timbers from time to time as the 'Arkansas' riddled us seemed to indicate that some vital part would be soon struck. In fact our steering apparatus was shot away, and we handled the vessel for some time soley with the engine[s] until repairs could be made." The killed and wounded, four of them headless, lay everywhere on the *Tyler*'s deck, and the woodwork was spattered with blood and shreds of flesh and hair. Few of the *Tyler*'s crewmen escaped without bloody evidence on their clothing. A cut in the port safe pipe had enveloped the timberclad's after section in steam. "All knew that the vessel might go down and all of us be killed, but there would be no surrender," Coleman recalled. Gwin "made that reassuring remark to the first lieutenant in my presence, when the officer suggested such a possibility. We were fighting for existence and we all knew it."[30]

Below, assistant surgeon Cadwallader and his men worked feverishly to care for the men wounded by grape and shrapnel, many of them army sharpshooters. So far, the *Tyler* had lost thirteen men killed, thirty-four wounded, and ten missing in the fight with the *Arkansas.*

Early that morning, when the *Tyler* finally turned out into the Mississippi River at Tuscumbia Bend, O'Neil recorded the moment the *Cincinnati* sighted it. "At 5:15 heavy firing was heard up the Yazoo river which increased and apparently drew near until 7:21 when the 'Queen' came out of the Yazoo, followed immediately by the 'Tyler,' firing her stern guns and flying signal 'I Have seen the Enemy.'"[31]

When Gwin ducked out of the *Tyler*'s pilothouse to the welcome sight of the federal fleet, he supposed "they would be in readiness to give her [*Arkansas*] a warm reception," Coleman recalled. "This was not the case. The heavy firing had been heard of course but it was supposed that the expedition was on its return and shelling the woods and no preparations were made to meet the emergency."[32]

As the *Tyler* and *Queen of the West* came closer and the gunfire grew louder, other officers in the fleet realized the *Tyler*'s dilemma, and cries of "Clear for action!" and "Beat to quarters" rang out. Crews raced to man their guns, and exasperated commanders swore and called down to their engine rooms to raise steam. None of the commanding officers of Farragut's ships, Davis's ironclads, or Ellet's rams had anticipated the arrival of the *Arkansas.* Most had only enough steam up to maintain their engines. The *Arkansas* had caught them all napping. "Got steam up and slipped our cable immediately, stood in towards the Mississippi shore," O'Neil noted. "No other vessel in either fleet, was yet underway with the exception of the 'Tyler' & 'Queen of the West.' Farragut made signal to two of his vessels the 'Oneida' & 'Winona' to get underway when the 'Tyler' first made her appearance but unfortunately he [came] upon the only two of his boats that had no steam."[33]

The rebel ram also surprised the men of Lieutenant Kidder Breese's five mortar vessels, anchored just out of gunshot range on the right bank of the river. Although Breese had heard gunfire up the river, he did not raise the alarm until an officer came to the bank and hailed him. "[He] stated that the rebel ram *Arkansas* was attempting to run through the fleet, and she would probably succeed." Breese immediately passed the word to the division to heave short.[34]

Swept along by the Mississippi's current, the *Arkansas* approached the federal fleet. Vicksburg was still a ways off, but Brown's eyes rested on the enemy in every direction. "It seemed at a glance as if the whole navy has come to keep me away from that heroic city." Observing federal rams and ironclads poised to oppose the *Arkansas,* Brown told the pilot, "Brady, shave that line of men-of-war as close as you can, so that the rams will not have room to gather head-way in coming out to strike us."[35]

As the *Arkansas* rounded the point at about 8:00, the mortar flotilla's Second Division commander, William B. Renshaw, signaled the mortar schooners to get under way. They all dropped down close to the bank, except for the *Sidney C. Jones,* which was aground and had been left in a defenseless position. The *Jones's* commander, acting master Charles Jack, signaled Renshaw, "Shall I destroy her?" Renshaw told Jack to "get ready" to blow up the *Jones,* but not until he received orders to do so "or the ram was actually coming down upon him." Renshaw then went to see Bell, who reported that Farragut had directed him to bring the mortars to bear on the rebel batteries. Meanwhile, the *Jones's* crew spiked the mortar and two 32-pounder guns and detonated the explosives, blowing the schooner up in a shower of fragments. It burned to the water's edge. Despite a hail of enemy fire from guns and sharpshooters on the opposite bank, the schooners *John Griffith, Oliver H. Lee,* and *Henry Jones* managed to open fire with their mortars on the rebel batteries.[36]

Hoping to reach the shelter of the rebel batteries on the bluffs, the captain of the *Arkansas* had decided to steam rapidly through the Yankee fleet. "The 'Arkansas,' as the Rebel Ram proved to be, held her course steadily along the Louisiana shore," O'Neil explained, "between the fleet & the transports along the banks, firing briskly in all directions, but with apparently little effect except in one or two instances." In the first instance, the *Arkansas* "got a shot into the Boilers of the ram 'Lancaster' killing or wounding many by escaping steam."[37]

The *Lancaster,* anchored above the fleet with some steam up, claimed to be the first to see the danger. Colonel Ellet signaled the ship to attack the rebel ram. "As she rounded to give her a little of our kind of warfare, a 64 pound ball came through our bulwarks and steam drum," a correspondent told readers. "Our lead engineer, John Wybrant, was knocked down and badly scalded inwardly; second engineer, John Goshorn, badly scalded, jumped overboard, and missing." Enemy fire also injured three soldiers and seven black deckhands and coal heavers. "One contraband had both arms and a leg shot off, badly scalded besides; he died a few minutes later."[38]

From the *Richmond,* Commander Alden could see the *Lancaster* just astern. The scalded men "jumped overboard, and some of them never came to the surface again," he recalled. Ten or twelve men began swimming, but some just held on to the rudder. The *Lancaster* ordered a boat to rescue the men, but according to Alden, "By this time she had drifted astern of us, and the 'Arkansas' came on down, and as she passed we fired our whole broadside!" One shot knocked Brown off the platform where he stood, breaking a marine glass in his hand. Without flinching, Brown resumed his place directing the ram's movements. When a seaman called out that the colors had been shot way, midshipman Dabney Scales dashed up a ladder, ignoring a hail of fire, to bend on the colors again. Keeping to midstream, the *Arkansas* ran the gauntlet of federal vessels anchored on either side and seemingly escaped damage. The *Richmond* fired a broadside at the ram, which momentarily disappeared in the smoke. The *Hartford*'s gunners eagerly watched for the smoke to lift so they could take a shot, but the *Arkansas* passed by the flagship and then turned to. Suddenly, when it was a half mile astern, the *Arkansas* fired two shots at the flagship, which missed, and the ram steamed downriver.[39]

"The fleet kept up a brisk fire on her as she passed with all the guns practicable," the *Cincinnati*'s O'Neil explained. "Our fire was, however, necessarily limited owing to the great danger of hitting our Transports ranged along the bank." The *Cincinnati,* below the fleet on picket duty, still kept its position. The ram steamed off toward the *Cincinnati* "as if going to ram us, but probably finding the water too shoal for her continued on her former course. We opened a heavy fire on her, with apparently good effect and which she returned."[40]

When the *Arkansas* came to the end of the line of enemy ships, Brown recalled, "I now called the officers up to take a look at what we had just come through and to get the fresh air, and as the little group of heroes closed around me with their friendly words of congratulations, a heavy rifle-shot passed close over our heads; it was a parting salutation, and if aimed two feet lower would have been to us the most injurious of the battle." To Farragut's "mortification," the battered *Arkansas* steamed on to the Vicksburg wharf and the protection of the Confederate batteries.[41]

The *Arkansas* had "successfully run through a fleet of sixteen men of war, six of them ironclad, and mounting in the aggregate not less than one hundred & sixty guns," O'Neil commented. "A far more brilliant achievement than that accomplished by the 'Virginia' at Hampton Roads."[42]

Visibly shaken by the rebel ram's success, Farragut immediately called for a conference with Davis. In the *Hartford*'s cabin the flag officer told Davis that he intended to have his fleet raise steam and immediately go down to destroy the ram. Davis tried to dissuade the irate Farragut from this rash and dangerous action, arguing that the *Arkansas* was comparatively harmless where it was. When Davis declined to attack the ram, Farragut reluctantly agreed to wait until late afternoon to run past the rebel batteries. Davis then returned to his flagship.[43]

The soldiers and citizens of Vicksburg greeted the *Arkansas*'s arrival with shouts of joy. General Van Dorn dashed off a telegram to President Jefferson Davis, announcing the ram's safe arrival and assuring him that it would "soon be repaired, and then ho! for New Orleans."[44]

Late in the afternoon the rumble of thunder and a cool breeze announced the arrival of a storm. The ensuing rain and wind delayed the fleet's preparation to run past Vicksburg, but just before 7:00 p.m. Farragut's ships got under way in two columns. Farragut's parting signal left no doubt about their mission: "The ram must be destroyed." Davis sent the *Sumter* down to Farragut and instructed the *Benton, Louisville,* and *Cincinnati* to draw fire from the upper rebel battery.[45]

Darkness fell as Farragut's ships neared the upper battery. When the Confederate gunners opened fire, the *Hartford*'s gun crews returned fire, aiming at the gun flashes. As the ship approached the enemy, shot and shell began whistling overhead. Several enemy shots struck the flagship's hull, and one 9-inch shell carried away the starboard fore-topsail bitts on the berth deck but did not explode. Marines stood by their gun and did not suffer any injuries, but they heard the disturbing news that their commanding officer, Captain John Broome, had suffered a bruised head and shoulder. He would recover, but master's mate George Lounsberry; Charles Jackson, the officers' cook; and seaman Cameron were killed by a cannonball. Six others were wounded.

Passing the rebel battery had inflicted a few casualties on the crews of the *Richmond, Sciota,* and *Winona* as well. A shell explosion killed one man on the *Winona,* and to keep it from sinking, the ship had to be run on shore.[46]

As Farragut's port column passed just thirty yards from shore, he strained to see the rebel ram in the darkness but could only make out the enemy's gun flashes. Lee claimed he had seen the *Arkansas* lying under a bank in an exposed position and had fired two solid shots at it from the *Oneida*'s 11-inch pivot guns.

When Farragut's vessels returned, Bell, now commanding the *Brooklyn,* boarded the *Hartford* and found a dispirited Farragut. They had not destroyed the rebel ram, and Farragut's fleet had suffered five killed and sixteen wounded. Davis's squadron had thirteen killed and thirty-four wounded. Bell recalled that Farragut vented his anger and disappointment, saying, "The ram must be attacked with resolution and be destroyed, or she will destroy us."[47]

That evening, one of the *Hartford*'s officers put pen to paper and wrote a letter to his family. "The fight was a hard one," he told them, "and the firing on both sides was terrific. . . . Our decks were slippery, and in some places, fairly swimming with blood." He revealed that in the morning he would have to bury a shipmate. "I hope and pray this war may soon be ended; but God's will be done. This rebellion must be crushed if it costs the life of every loyal citizen in the country. The ram can be seen lying off Vicksburg, and it is expected that she will come down. But we are ready for her now, and will not be caught napping again."[48]

The morning of July 16 dawned cold and rainy. "Some of our missing has turned up and report three of their number drowned in endeavoring to swim ashore," the *Carondelet*'s Morison wrote. "Our dead were taken ashore at noon and burned. A great many of our crew sick with the ague. In fact, all hands look dull and stupid." Many of the *Hartford*'s crew had taken ill as well. "Half of the marine guard is on the medical list," Private Smith noted. "Fifty odd are on the list." The *Carondelet* remained with the fleet for several days, awaiting repairs to its steam pipes. "The number of our sick still increasing," Morison reported, "the captain being amongst the number." On Sunday he delivered a message to Walke, who had gone to the hospital boat *Red Rover* that morning. "Saw some of our wounded and sick. All seemed to be doing well. Found that some 'Sisters of Charity' were stationed on the boat and all the patients spoke very highly of their patience and self-denial."[49]

On July 21 the *Carondelet* began taking on coal for the journey to Cairo. "Thirty contrabands were sent to coal her and help work her to Cairo," Morison wrote. He was put in charge of some of the contrabands "to see that they worked and to remain until the job was finished." Supervising the coaling kept Morison up until 3:30 a.m., when he got his grog and turned in for a short nap. The next day, "the first cutter also brought whatever of our sick were able to stand the journey to Cairo. Twenty five of the contrabands were kept on aboard, the remainder being sent back to their quarters about 2 P.M. *Carondelet* then got under way and headed toward Cairo."[50]

Still smarting from his failure to destroy the *Arkansas,* Farragut gathered Bell, Alden, De Camp, and Renshaw the following morning for a conference. He proposed to take the three larger ships and attack at night. Bell wrote in his journal, "I was opposed to the night attack for the reason that the one just made was a failure; that a low object against the bank could not be seen." Bell favored a daytime attack, and Alden agreed, suggesting that Davis's ironclads and rams be given the mission. According to Bell, Farragut responded that he could not control Davis's ships and could trust only his own vessels.[51]

Now determined to attack the *Arkansas* during daylight, Farragut ordered preparations made and the *Sumter* fitted out to ram the rebel ironclad. On July 16 the *Arkansas* moved into the river, turned, and went back to the Vicksburg wharf, as if taunting the federal fleet. Farragut fired off a message to Davis, reminding him that the country would blame both of them for any disaster that occurred if the ram escaped. He proposed a combined attack on the rebel ram. Farragut promised his full support if Davis would come down with his ironclad vessels past the first enemy battery and meet him off Vicksburg to fight both the batteries and the ram.[52]

In his usual calm, thoughtful manner, Davis replied to Farragut's proposed attack by arguing that the *Arkansas* was "harmless in her present position" and would be more easily destroyed if it came out from under the protection of the batteries. Explaining that he was as eager as Farragut to "put an end to this impudent rascal's existence," Davis advised vigilance and self-control, "pursuing the course that was adopted at Fort Columbus, Island No. 10, and Fort Pillow." After reading Davis's reply, Farragut called for another council with his commanders, explaining that he had tried to prod Davis into action, sending him two more messages suggesting that a few shells might disturb the people at work on the ram, but Davis refused to move.[53]

This council of war resolved nothing, and the *Arkansas* remained off Vicksburg, an ever-present reminder of Yankee ineptness. For days Farragut and Davis engaged in a back-and-forth debate on a course of action to destroy the *Arkansas,* but they were unable to resolve their differences. On a scorching hot July morning, Farragut crossed the peninsula to see Davis, who informed him that Colonel Ellet had agreed to have one of his rams attack the *Arkansas* if the navy would attack the batteries. Chagrined at his rams' inability to resolve the situation, Ellet had written to Davis on July 20, arguing that the *Arkansas's* presence "so near us, is exerting a very pernicious influence upon the confidence of our crews, and even on the commanders of our boats." He urged that some risk be taken to destroy the ram and to "reestablish our own prestige over the Mississippi River." Farragut then reconsidered Ellet's proposal to have Davis's fleet engage the Confederate batteries while he sent one of his rams to attack the *Arkansas* at the wharf.[54]

An article in the *Cincinnati Daily Gazette* offered additional details about the plan. On Monday morning, Davis, Farragut, and Ellet had met for an hour on board the ram *Switzerland,* the newspaper claimed, where Ellet's daring plan "was fully discussed and explicitly agreed upon." According to this article, "The Commanders agreed that the *Essex* which is regarded as little less than invulnerable, should go ahead of the ram and attack the *Arkansas,* grapple her, and so distract her attention as to give the ram the least possible opportunity of butting her." Ellet agreed to furnish the *Queen of the West* for the enterprise, which was set to commence the next morning, July 22, at daybreak.[55]

The success of the attack depended primarily on Davis's flotilla, especially Porter's ironclad *Essex* and Ellet's ram *Queen of the West.* Davis's fleet would bombard the upper batteries at Vicksburg, while the lower fleet under Farragut attacked the lower batteries. "The *Essex* was to push on, strike the rebel ram, deliver her fire, and then fall behind the lower fleet," Porter explained. With the *Sumter* in the lead, Farragut's vessels would get in position to cover the lower Confederate batteries and await the *Arkansas,* which Davis expected would be driven down or destroyed by the shot-proof *Essex.* Davis wanted the *Sumter* to attack and ram the *Arkansas* as well, and he rejected a last-minute message from Farragut suggesting that his fleet come up past the lower batteries to assist.[56]

The *Essex* took on coal and sent its crew ashore to fill sandbags, which were packed on the upper deck over the boilers. The *Louisville, Cincinnati, Benton,* and *Bragg* also prepared for the attack. Ellet selected a volunteer crew for the *Queen of the West* "and told his men in plain terms that he wanted no man to accompany him that was not ready to risk his life in the project."[57]

On Tuesday morning, July 22, Davis's three gunboats, the *Benton,* the *Cincinnati,* and the *Louisville,* steamed down the Mississippi to shell the upper rebel batteries as the *Essex* and the *Queen of the West* got under way to make their assault on the *Arkansas,* which was moored that morning to the riverbank with its head facing upriver. "We were at anchor with only enough men to fight two of our guns," Brown recalled, "but by the zeal of our officers, who mixed in with these men, as part of the guns' crews, we were able to train at the right moment and fire all the guns which could be brought to bear upon our cautiously coming assailants."[58]

In his recollections of the engagement, Lieutenant George W. Gift wrote, "In a few minutes we observed the ironclad steamer *Essex* steaming around the point and steering for us." As the *Essex* and *Queen* approached the upper battery, the rebel gunners opened fire. The ram took aim at the *Essex* with its Columbiad, but the *Essex* pressed on toward the *Arkansas.* Gift's gun crew got off a shot that struck the federal ironclad, but "on she came like a mad bull, nothing daunted or overawed." Watching the *Essex* head toward his vessel, with the *Queen of the West* following, Brown realized that Porter's plan was to have the *Queen* run into the *Arkansas* with its flat bow and shove it aground so that his ram could butt a hole in Brown's ram.[59]

Porter did just as Brown expected. He brought the *Essex* abreast of the *Arkansas,* turned, and attempted to ram the rebel amidships. Brown, however, had cut the bow hawser, hoping to let the current swing the bow toward the federal ironclad. Every minute counted, and with its speed decreased by the turn, the *Essex* missed the lethal, pointed ram and slammed into the *Arkansas* at an angle. "At the moment of collision, when our guns were muzzle to muzzle," a shot from one of the *Essex*'s bow guns struck the *Arkansas* a foot forward of the forward broadside port, "breaking off the ends of the railroad bars and driving them in among our people," Brown wrote. The shot crossed the gun deck and hit the breech of a starboard gun, cutting down eight of Brown's men and wounding six more. Splinters flew in every direction. As Porter brought the *Essex* alongside the *Arkansas,* the ram poured out a broadside. Brown went ahead on the port screw, turned, and brought his stern guns to bear. In the face of murderous fire from rebel batteries and riflemen, some of them only 100 feet away, Porter's men could not board the *Arkansas,* so he ordered the *Essex* to back off and drift downstream.[60]

On the *Queen of the West,* correspondent Dungannon had a ringside seat for the encounter with the rebel ram. He watched the *Essex* about a mile ahead of him reply to the rebel's fire and then speed past. "This disconcerted Col. Ellet considerably for he expected to find the iron-clad vessel in close quarters with the rebel gunboat. Just at this critical moment, too, the Flag-Officer Davis waved his hand from the *Benton,* to Ellet and shouted, 'Good luck, good luck!' which Ellet understood to be, 'Go back Go back!' and immediately gave orders for the engines to be reversed." When Ellet realized his mistake, he ordered the *Queen* to head for the *Arkansas,* which lay with its prow upstream. Ellet and his son Edward stood on the upper deck of the *Queen of the West,* and as it approached the *Arkansas,* a shower of bullets from sharpshooters along the shore whistled around their heads. The sound of shattering hull timbers followed as the rebel ram fired its forward and larboard guns. Dungannon braced himself as the ship struck the *Arkansas* just aft of the third gun on the port side. Delayed by the confusing signal, the *Queen of the West* managed to strike only a glancing blow on the *Arkansas,* stripping some of its railroad irons half off but not seriously damaging the ram. The *Queen of the West* drifted astern, pummeled by fire from the rebel ram, and Ellet saw that he faced a "fiery gauntlet of a mile of batteries to be run." Newsman Dungannon gave the colonel credit as a "courageous commander" who "nerved himself to the terrible task," coolly giving orders for the direction of his vessel and finally reaching the turning point in safety, "amid a perfect hurricane of shot and shell."[61]

To cover the run past the batteries by the *Essex* and *Queen of the West,* the gunboats *Benton, Cincinnati,* and *Louisville* had engaged the upper rebel batteries. According to O'Neil on the *Cincinnati,* "In this engagement our upper works were badly cut up, but no one on board was injured."[62]

Damaged but still afloat, the *Arkansas* slipped away upstream. The contest with the *Essex* had been so close that unburned powder coming through the ram's gun ports had blackened and burned the faces of some of the surviving crewmen. And, to Gift's astonishment, he discovered the ram's forecastle littered with hundreds of unbroken glass marbles—the kind boys play with—fired from one of the *Essex*'s guns. The *Essex* and *Sumter* fled downstream, now cut off from Davis's command. To Davis's consternation, the *Sumter* had not participated at all.[63]

This failed attempt to destroy the *Arkansas* brought recriminations from all sides. Ellet laid the blame on Davis, who in turn pointed the finger at Farragut. Davis argued that Farragut had not cooperated with his efforts above the upper batteries and had withheld his squadron's support. Nettled,

Farragut defended himself, reminding Bell of the letter received from Davis the night before the battle in which "he specifically told me that the lower fleet were to have no share in the affair until the ram was driven down to us."[64]

Davis focused his displeasure on the *Sumter,* which had failed to come up. In a petulant letter to Foote, Phelps argued that Farragut should have advised the *Sumter*'s commander that his plans had changed and allowed him to act independently. "Because the lower fleet failed to act the whole affair failed of its purpose though the attempt was a gallant one," Phelps told Foote. "The whole thing was a fizzle. Every day we heard great things threatened only to realize fizzles." Phelps was not optimistic about the situation of the lower flotilla: five of the thirteen vessels were undergoing repairs, 40 percent of the men were sick, and the vessels on the river were being fired on by enemy batteries. Amidst all this, the officers and men of the two squadrons could agree on only one important fact: the second attempt to take Vicksburg had failed dismally.[65]

With the water level in the Mississippi falling, threatening to strand his larger vessels, Farragut was eager to move downstream, so he welcomed a telegram from Welles the next day that read: "Go down river at discretion. Not expected to remain up during the season." Farragut then called Bell, Alden, Lee, and Crosby to the flagship for a council, informing them that the Navy Department had given him permission to go downriver. The *Arkansas* still posed a threat, but former fleet captain Bell argued that mounting another attack with so many vessels in need of repair and so many men sick would be inadvisable. When all his commanders had spoken their mind, advising him to abandon the pursuit of the *Arkansas* and the Vicksburg operation, Farragut dismissed the four officers and sat down to pen a letter to Welles. He told the secretary that to attack the ram "under the forts with the present amount of work before us would be madness."[66]

The following day, July 24, as the thermometer climbed toward ninety degrees, Private Smith watched from his station on the forecastle as Farragut's ships weighed anchor. "At two o'clock the whole fleet got in line and proceeded down the river. The river boats carry the troops and also tow the mortar schooners. The Richmond, Hartford and Brooklyn bring up the rear, the Brooklyn last." No one regretted leaving Vicksburg and its debilitating climate, especially Farragut. Left behind were the slaves who had toiled in the heat and malarial swamps to dig the canal, denied their promised freedom. Their frantic, tearful pleas to be taken on board fell on deaf ears but tugged at the heartstrings of the bluejackets who had shared the arduous work with them. Farragut intended to drop Williams's troops off at Baton Rouge and then take his fleet into the Gulf of Mexico.[67]

Farragut was relieved to be leaving Mississippi's infernal heat and mosquitoes, but he remained despondent over his failure to destroy the *Arkansas*. In his diary, Welles expressed his own opinion of the saga: "The most disreputable naval affair of the War was the descent of the steam ram *Arkansas* through both squadrons till she hauled in under the batteries of Vicksburg, and there the two flag officers abandoned the place and the ironclad ram, Farragut and his force going down to New Orleans, and Davis proceeding with his flotilla up the river."[68]

With the lower fleet gone, Davis had decided it would be safe to send his squadron away from Vicksburg. With 40 percent of his men ill with malaria and scurvy, Davis knew he had to move to a healthier climate. In his diary he wrote, "Sickness had made sudden and terrible havoc with my people. It came, as it were, all at once." A request for gunboats from General Samuel Curtis at Helena, Arkansas, offered further enticement, and Davis knew his withdrawal "would not involve any loss of control over the river." Davis explained that he could not have taken Vicksburg without troops, and "this being so I am as well at Helena as at any point lower down." Recent reports from transports and towing vessels confirmed that if Davis had remained at Vicksburg any longer, he would not "have had engineers nor firemen enough to bring the vessels up. As it is we have depended very much on the contrabands to do the work in front of the fires." A reporter also noted, "It has become an absolute necessity to employ negroes in almost every capacity in the flotilla, for they alone seemed adapted to endure the rigors of this plague-infested atmosphere."[69]

Illness had deprived Ellet of many of his men as well, and he told Secretary of War Edwin Stanton that he had "to employ large numbers of blacks, who came to me asking protection." Some of these were the African Americans employed by General Williams and left on the Louisiana shore. Stanton instructed Ellet to employ "such negroes as you require on your boats, and send the others who are under your protection to Memphis to be employed by General Sherman."[70]

Struggling against the current, the flagship *Benton,* assisted by the *General Bragg* and the *Switzerland,* made it to Helena on the last day of July. After only a few days, however, Davis decided to go to Cairo, leaving Phelps in command at Helena.

10

The Mississippi Squadron

If we can get our forces down here in time enough, we might make a
good haul on them.

—Henry Walke

The *Carondelet* had gone upriver to Memphis, and en route, Walke had
picked up a man named Lucas. "About 7 P.M., a man in a skiff came alongside and hailed us," Morison wrote. "Picked him up and found that he was
the pilot of the transport Sallie Wood (which left Vicksburg on Sunday
with our mail). She had been fired onto by rebels at Island 82 and sunk. She
had some passengers on her, both men, women, and children." When the
steamer began to sink, "all managed to escape and took to the woods. He
(the pilot) got a skiff and some of his luggage, jumped into skiff and started
downstream for the fleet. He lay still daytimes and went on his way at
night. He was first starting out when we ran across him."[1]

Determined to find those who had fired on the *Sallie Wood,* Walke
took the *Carondelet* up the river, firing on several possible rebel locations.
Abreast of Greenville he opened fire on the houses and woods but elicited
no response. At 4:00 the gunboat arrived at the place where rebel guns had
first shot at the *Sallie Wood.* The *Carondelet* "fired about fifteen shots and
left, as there was nothing to be seen." In a vain attempt to locate those taken
prisoner from the *Sallie Wood,* Walke landed men at Island No. 82. "About
8 P.M.," Morison wrote, they "came to off the island where the boat had
been sunk. Blew our whistle but no one came. A boat's crew, armed, were
now sent ashore to a house on the island to look for traces of the lost ones."
Eventually, the whistle did elicit a response: a "Lieut. of the Wis. 4th and a

165

darkie that were on the Sallie Wood." The lieutenant, who said his name was Wing, told them his companions had been captured and he had been three days without food, hidden in driftwood.[2]

That same day, July 25, 1862, the *Carondelet* took on board a man named Montague, a deserter from a guerrilla band. He informed Walke that the rebels had batteries composed of four guns. "Negroes," the man said, "did not work the guns," contrary to what the pilot had claimed; they drove the teams and dug the rifle pits and trenches.[3]

On the trip up to Helena, Arkansas, the *Carondelet* also picked up one contraband and seven refugees. Four of the refugees "had fled from Miss. to avoid conscription," Morison explained. The other three, picked up in a skiff, had "left Ark. to avoid conscription too. They had rowed 800 miles before reaching us."[4]

In the afternoon the *Carondelet* came across the ram *Lioness* and took on coal from a coal barge being towed by the transport *Lady Pike*. Both the transport and the ram had been targeted by the increasingly bold rebels lurking along the riverbanks. Just below Island No. 82, about fifteen miles above Greenville, the *Lioness* and the *Lady Pike* had been attacked by a rebel battery of flying artillery, and one man had been killed. When the *Queen of the West* met the two boats and discovered they had been attacked, the ram shelled the woods before continuing upstream. At Greenville, rebel sharpshooters and a rebel battery opened fire on them. "The [*Queen's*] gunners were driven from the deck, and for nearly half an hour we were subjected to their annoying fire," a correspondent reported. Some of the *Queen's* crew remained on the boiler deck, "thinking that the musket-proof bulkheads for sharpshooters would protect them, but a shell passed through, and striking Thomas W. Spencer in the back, cut him almost in twain." A severed steam pipe was repaired, and the ram went on to Napoleon without further incident. The growing number of rebel attacks on transports and other vessels on the river threatened communication and made armed escorts necessary. But finding crews to man his gunboats was a problem for Davis, who needed 500 sailors to fill existing vacancies.[5]

At 6:00 on the morning of July 27, the *Queen of the West* overtook the *Carondelet* above Napoleon and took on board Lieutenant Wing of the 4th Wisconsin Regiment and the prisoner E. D. Montague. At Greenville, the *Carondelet* had shelled the woods, "but the skulking ruffians had laid low, reserving their attacks for unprotected vessels passing by." The *Carondelet* had sent an armed party ashore, which returned with a rebel cavalryman who stated that the rebels had a battery of four fieldpieces and about 200 cavalry. They had chosen the position at Greenville, the man said, "because they can travel across the bends and attack boats from three points."[6]

On July 28 the *Carondelet* arrived at Helena, where General Curtis and his army were located. "Made Helena and Gen'l Curtis' army," Morison noted in his diary. "The captain went ashore and held a short confab with him. He (Curtis) is a short, slight man with a blonde goatee and moustache." Curtis had been forced from the interior of Arkansas back to the Mississippi River at Helena. He reported to Walke that he had some 25,000 men at Helena but needed a fast gunboat or two to keep the river clear and prevent the rebels from crossing over to his rear.[7]

The *Carondelet*'s officers and crew found Helena abuzz with news that Davis had been ordered to return to the Navy Department as chief of the Bureau of Navigation. On August 3 he departed for Cairo, leaving Phelps in command to prepare for an expedition down to the White River. In the meantime, Farragut had gone down the Mississippi as planned, dropping off Williams's troops at Baton Rouge, along with the remaining mortar boats. Porter's *Essex* and *Sumter* also came down to Baton Rouge from Grand Gulf to assist Davis's gunboats *Kineo, Cayuga,* and *Katahdin* in supporting and defending the troops "and keep[ing] a careful watch over the rebel gunboat *Arkansas*."[8]

The *Arkansas* had, in fact, started downriver to support a Confederate attempt to recapture Baton Rouge. After months of efforts to prepare the *Arkansas* for combat and the ram's engagements with the federals, an exhausted Isaac Brown had taken leave and fallen ill, leaving Lieutenant Henry Stevens in command. The chief engineer, George W. City, had also left, entirely broken down from his exertions to keep the ram's engines running. "We soon began to feel his loss," Lieutenant Gift recalled. "The engineer in charge, a volunteer from the army had recently joined us, and though a young man of pluck and gallantry, and possessed of great will and determination to make the engines work, yet was unequal to the task."[9]

The *Arkansas* churned down the river, but just short of Baton Rouge, Gift learned that the Union navy had the *Essex* and two wooden gunboats there, and the Confederate forces planned to commence their attack the next morning. At daylight, the *Arkansas* cast off and started down the river. Within sight of Baton Rouge, Stevens mustered his officers and crew, poised to attack the *Essex*. Then the rebel ram's starboard engine suddenly quit, and it ran hard aground. Being unfamiliar with screw vessels or single-stroke engines, the new engineer had pushed the machinery too hard. Throwing railroad iron overboard to lighten the ram, they refloated *Arkansas,* and at dark the engineer reported to Stevens that the ram could move. After going less than 100 yards, however, the same engine broke again, forcing the crew to spend the night repairing it. "Meantime, the enemy became aware of our crippled condition, and at daylight moved up to the attack," Gift recalled. The *Arkansas*'s misfortune had given Porter's *Essex* a golden opportunity to go after the ram.[10]

When Porter's first officer fell ill, the *Essex*'s second master, David Porter Rosenmiller, a native of Lancaster, Pennsylvania, assumed his duties. Rosenmiller gave readers of the *Lancaster Daily Inquirer* a detailed account of the gunboat's engagement with the *Arkansas.* The *Essex,* he wrote, "was in sight of the *Arkansas,* which was now streaming down towards us. We kept up a continual firing at her, and forced her to retreat into a small bayou." They continued the attack until an explosive shell entered one of the ram's ports and ignited some cotton and wool, "and the glad news was announced, that the rebel vessel was on fire. In five minutes after we fired the shell, we saw the crew rushing on deck, and in ten minutes she was reported to be unmistakenly on fire." Fearful of an explosion, Porter kept the *Essex* clear of the burning ram, which swung out into the current. "Onward she went, sending high in the air, huge volumes of smoke and flame," Rosenmiller told readers, "whilst every second, shell after shell on board of her became ignited and exploded. All her guns, likewise, were loaded, and these discharged from the same cause." The *Essex* followed the *Arkansas* until the fire reached the magazine, and it exploded. "And such a sight! It was the grandest ever beheld," he wrote.[11]

According to Gift, who was present, Charles Read "kept firing at the *Essex* until Stevens had set fire to the ward-room and cabin, then all jumped on shore, and in a few moments the flames burst up the hatches. Loaded shells had been placed at all the guns, which commenced exploding as soon as the fire reached the gun deck. This was the last of the *Arkansas.*"[12]

With the rebel ram destroyed, the Union navy had a tenuous hold on the Mississippi River north from New Orleans to Port Hudson and from Cairo down to Helena. Confederate forces still controlled a 400-mile section of the river from Helena to their stronghold at Vicksburg and down to Port Hudson, where they had constructed strong defenses. Hoping to take Baton Rouge back from the Union, Van Dorn had ordered Confederate troops under Major General John C. Breckenridge to advance on the city, but on August 4 the alert Yankee sentries discovered the rebels and gave the alarm. The bluecoats retired to defensive works protected by Union gunboats. An assault by Confederate troops the following morning almost succeeded, but fire from federal gunboats forced them to withdraw. Had the ram *Arkansas* been able to support the Confederate attack, then Baton Rouge might have been retaken.

Farragut explained to Welles that he had taken his fleet to New Orleans and set his sights on attacking Mobile. Davis had sent much of his flotilla with Phelps to Helena, 160 miles north of Vicksburg, to close up his lines, which were now too extended to open the sources of communication and supply. Rebel guerrillas operating along the river, sometimes supported by mobile artillery, had threatened to cut Davis's flotilla off from its supply of mail, coal, and provisions, forcing him to detail gunboats to convoy steamers up and down the Mississippi.

On August 5, not content to sit idle, the aggressive Phelps took the *Benton, Louisville, Mound City,* and *Bragg,* along with two of Ellet's rams and three transports with army troops, on an expedition down to the mouth of the White River. Finding no sign of the enemy, and failing to locate and destroy a rebel battery, the expedition returned to Helena. Phelps enjoyed better success on his next movement, which netted him the *Fair Play* carrying a trove of Enfield rifles and muskets for the rebels.

The capture of the *Fair Play* and some $300,000 worth of weapons delighted Davis, who praised Phelps's accomplishment. This also encouraged Phelps to continue his campaign to be named Davis's successor in command of the flotilla. Change was in the wind that August, not only in terms of promotions but also in terms of the flotilla's organization. Efforts to persuade Generals Halleck and Butler to support naval operations had failed, prompting Welles and Fox to press President Lincoln and Congress to transfer the Western Gunboat Flotilla to the navy. Congress agreed and passed legislation giving the navy control of the flotilla, to be renamed the Mississippi Squadron, effective on October 1, 1862.[13]

The officers and men of the Union navy welcomed this transfer of the flotilla, but another announcement from the Navy Department caused howls of dismay. Congress had passed a reform act in July, amending navy regulations on a number of issues related to gambling, lying, cruelty, swearing, and drinking. Effective September 1, 1862, alcohol would be prohibited on all navy ships, thus banning spirits from the officers' wardroom and ending the sailors' beloved grog ration. "Curses not so loud, but deep, were indulged in by old tars, some of whom had seen years of service, and who, by custom, had become habituated to their allowance of grog, that the very expectation of it was accompanied by a feeling of pleasure," one sailor recalled. Others exclaimed, "The country will go to dogs!"[14]

After less than four months commanding the Western Gunboat Flotilla, Charles Davis departed for his new post at the Bureau of Navigation. Despite Phelps's campaign to be named commander of the new squadron, on September 22, 1862, Welles informed David Dixon Porter that he would replace Davis as flag officer of the newly renamed Mississippi Squadron, with the temporary rank of acting rear admiral. Porter's mission was to renew the campaign to capture Vicksburg. In his diary, Welles wrote, "Davis, whom he [Porter] succeeds, . . . is kind and affable, but has not the vim, dash—recklessness perhaps is the better word—of Porter." The secretary knew Porter well and noted, "[He] is fertile in resources, has great energy, excessive and sometimes not over scrupulous ambition." Welles believed the command needed a young, active officer like Porter, and since Phelps was only a lieutenant commander, he lacked the necessary rank.[15]

Undoubtedly, Porter's appointment took some officers by surprise, for he was a junior commander. He did, however, come from a notable naval family. The Porters had served the nation for five generations. David Porter the elder had fought during the war with Tripoli and in 1812, taking prizes and bringing glory to the navy. His son, David Dixon Porter, had joined the navy as an eleven-year-old and had made a name for himself in the Mexican War.[16]

On October 1, 1862, the navy quietly took over the Mississippi Squadron, formerly the Western Gunboat Flotilla. Porter bade farewell to his wife Georgy and his young children and headed west to assume command of the squadron. He stopped in Cincinnati to inspect the *Indianola,* which was nearing completion at Brown's yard, and then inspected the new vessels being built in St. Louis. From there, Porter hurried on to Cairo. On October 15 the *Benton*'s officers and crew mustered on the deck for the customary change-of-command ceremony. As Porter came up the gangway, sailors in crisp whites saluted, and Davis greeted Porter. Then, following the boom of a gun salute, a midshipman solemnly hauled down Davis's pennant, snapped on Porter's white-starred blue flag, and ran it up the masthead.[17]

In his history of the war, Porter explained, "Up to this time the gunboats had strictly speaking, been under the control of the Army; but now all this was changed, and the Mississippi Squadron, like all the other naval forces, was brought directly under the supervision of the Secretary of the Navy. The Commander-in-Chief of the squadron had no longer to receive orders from General Halleck or Army headquarters, but was left to manage his command to the best of his ability, and to co-operate with the Army whenever he could do so." This new arrangement allowed Porter "to exercise his judgment, instead of being handicapped as Foote and Davis were."[18]

Captain A. M. Pennock, commandant of the naval station, and Walke of the *Carondelet* welcomed the new Mississippi Squadron commander. Although no records survive of their first meeting, Porter reportedly found Walke "an active, impatient man" with ideas similar to his own. The squadron needed attention. The army had signed up many recruits at ratings and pay levels higher than they deserved, causing old hands to grumble. Porter would have to ease some of those men out and discharge hundreds who had come down with river fevers. The squadron's leaky, makeshift vessels were overdue for repairs, and poor conditions aboard had undoubtedly contributed to the number of ill sailors. Clearly, commanding the Mississippi Squadron would be no easy task.[19]

In his cabin on the *Benton*, Porter assessed the squadron's resources for fighting the war on western waters and found them wanting. He told the Navy Department he needed more of everything—gunboats, auxiliary craft, artillery, officers, crewmen, and, most of all, river craft suited for narrow, shallow rivers. Porter would retain the city-class ironclads, but to escort convoys and support the infantry, his squadron needed more versatile vessels. To meet Porter's demands, the navy built dozens of what became known as tinclads, as well as two stern-wheeled monitors, the *Neosho* and *Osage*. The navy would also commission three ironclads, the *Tuscumbia, Indianola,* and *Chillicothe,* all launched in 1862, and convert the captured *Eastport* to carry 6.5-inch armor and eight guns. For his flagship, however, Porter chose the 260-foot tinclad *Black Hawk,* a former luxury cruise boat converted to carry thirteen guns. Never one to pass up an opportunity for amenities, Porter kept the rich wood paneling and chandeliers in the *Black Hawk*'s officers' quarters and installed stalls for horses.[20]

Just prior to the change of command, and for weeks afterward, Phelps carried on the squadron's active operations at Helena. Without Kilty, Stembel, and Paulding, he had only Walke, Winslow, Dove, Bryant, and Thompson as captains. Phelps thought Winslow and Dove inefficient commanders but considered Walke a "fighting captain." Fortuitously for Phelps, Winslow asked for a transfer, and Phelps managed to replace Dove with Richard

W. Meade as captain of the *Louisville*. Bryant had fallen ill, so the *Cairo* also received a new captain, twenty-six-year-old Lieutenant Commander Thomas O. Selfridge Jr. "Received on board Commander Selfridge as our captain," George Yost wrote on September 12, 1862. "Capt. Bryant being in ill health he was sent home."[21]

The state of the flotilla's gunboats appalled Phelps. The *Cincinnati* had sprung countless leaks, and its engines needed repair. The *Carondelet* had gone to the yard in Cairo after the engagement with the *Arkansas*. A survey had found the *Louisville* in a "disgraceful and dirty condition" and its executive officer, two masters, and surgeons incompetent. The situation in Ellet's ram fleet was even worse. Disputes were rife, and the rams' men had taken to plundering, stealing, and luring blacks from plantations. Fortunately, Lincoln realized the ram fleet needed to be under the Navy Department's command. Consequently, on November 8, 1862, Alfred Ellet was promoted to brigadier general, and his rams were renamed the Mississippi Marine Brigade.[22]

On October 19, with its engines repaired, the *Carondelet* headed downriver to Helena. It passed Island No. 10 on October 21 and then took on coal at Memphis. Bright and early on October 23, the *Carondelet* took a pilot on board and, Morison noted, "dropped down amongst the fleet. Came to anchor abreast the city. Here we found Benton, Bragg, Mound City, Louisville, and Cairo." All the gunboat captains, including Selfridge, the *Cairo*'s new commanding officer, came on board and visited with Walke. According to Yost, Selfridge had clearly set out to make the *Cairo* a proper man-of-war with a regular routine. "We drilled considerable to day and I think that our Captain intends to try to soon have the best drilled crew in the fleet," he wrote in his diary on October 13. "The boat looks much cleaner and nicer now than it ever did before."[23]

Meanwhile, the *Cincinnati* had completed repairs at Cairo and had received some new recruits, among them Daniel F. Kemp. On September 16, 1862, Kemp had enlisted in the navy for one year. Rated a landsman, he went by rail to Cairo, Illinois, to the receiving ship *Clara Dolsen*. Most of the recruits, Kemp recalled, were made guards, as the ship had no marines "to keep the crew in order." Then, he wrote, "a gunboat came up the river one day. . . . This was the gunboat Cincinnati. We were taken on board the Cincinnati on November 6, 1862." The new recruits' first assignment was to take on coal. Kemp observed, "This was a hard, unpleasant job as none of us boys had been used to hard work. However, we were in Uncle Sam's

Navy now, and had to do whatever we were told to do whether we liked it or not. We were getting ready to go down to Vicksburg, and the firemen had to have coal." Kemp vividly recalled their trip downstream: "We left Cairo one Sunday and started down the Mississippi for our destination, but the river was very low and our progress was very slow, for we had to take soundings quite often so as not to run aground." The gunboat anchored a short distance from Island No. 10 for several days, due to low water and heavy fog. Then, as the gunboat steamed down the Mississippi, Kemp explained that they "took on board a lot of contrabands, and they were a jolly lot of darkies right from the plantation. They would get together at night and give us a gay old time, a regular plantation jig. The names of their leaders were Alex, Charley, and Black Hawk. Alex would do the patting, and Charley and Black Hawk would do the dancing and the usual shouting and yah yahing." The *Cincinnati* continued past Columbus, Hickman, Fort Pillow, Memphis, and Napoleon before arriving at Helena. "We finally reached the fleet, and found anchored there, the Signal, Marmora (Mosquito), Mound City, Carondelet, and Pittsburgh. Also a packet boat and the Lexington, a wooden gunboat."[24]

The *Carondelet* had spent the first part of November at Helena, tasked to convoy any vessels running between Memphis and Helena, provided there was sufficient depth of water. Navigating the Mississippi River still proved a challenge, for there was barely enough water for his ironclad boats to move up or down the river, Walke reported to Porter on November 8. He requested any light-draft, armed steamers that were available. He had sent a number of sick sailors to Cairo but cautioned the admiral, "There is still quite a number of officers and men who are very much debilitated by the fever and ague this fall, and I am afraid they will not be fit for duty this winter."[25]

By the fall of 1862, officials in Washington had grown weary with the lack of progress in the West. Generals Buell and McClellan had been pursuing a style of warfare that reflected their limited war aims. The halting Union advances had prolonged the fighting, and now the president resolved to prosecute the war more aggressively. "The army, like the nation, has become demoralized by the idea that the war is to be ended, the nation reunited, and peace restored by *strategy*, and not by hard, desperate fighting," Lincoln said. In late October he replaced Buell with William S. Rosecrans as commander of the Army of the Cumberland, and on November 7 he informed McClellan that Ambrose Burnside would supersede him. Lincoln urged his generals to renew the attack on Vicksburg, which had been delayed by military crises in Kentucky and Maryland and by a Confederate attempt to lever Grant's forces out of northern Mississippi. Grant had initially declined to renew operations against Vicksburg, citing the need to rebuild railroads in northern Mississippi and Tennessee. In November, however, Lincoln replaced Butler with Nathaniel P. Banks as commander of Union forces in southern Louisiana and gave him the mission of opening the Mississippi River by coordinating an attack on Vicksburg and Port Hudson. Finally, Grant proposed a move south to Grenada, Mississippi, which he expected would engage Confederate forces and enable Sherman to make an amphibious assault downstream from Memphis to Vicksburg.[26]

Naturally, Porter knew the reputation of the man everyone now called U. S., or "Unconditional Surrender," Grant, but he had never met the general and knew nothing of his plans. One evening, the admiral attended a dinner party on board an army quartermaster's riverboat. When a man in a rumpled brown coat and gray trousers appeared, the host said, "Admiral Porter, meet General Grant." The two found a table away from the party guests and sat down. Without fanfare, Grant explained his plan to take Vicksburg. "I need your assistance, Porter," Grant said, "all you can provide." Impressed with Grant's calm demeanor and his determination, Porter pledged his full support for the coming campaign. Then, without taking a bite of supper, Grant rose, clamped down on the cigar in his mouth, and announced he was going to ride back the way he had come.[27]

Back on board the *Black Hawk,* Porter finalized the squadron's plans to support Sherman's expedition up the Yazoo River. Walke, who was now in charge of the Mississippi Squadron's vessels based at Helena, was given the mission of securing all the landings on the Yazoo where the Confederates could erect batteries, determining the water's depth, and dragging the river for mines. Porter then sent orders to his commanders to proceed to Helena and report to Walke.[28]

On November 21 Walke, who was still suffering from what he called "Yazoo fever," received orders to leave for the Yazoo as soon as possible. He was supposed to prevent the erection of batteries at the mouth of the river, or as far as federal guns would reach. If there was insufficient water in the Yazoo for his large vessels, he was instructed to send the *Signal* and *Marmora* with some good marksmen to secure a landing for General McClernand's troops. The admiral also ordered Walke to take all the ironclads at Helena, except for the *Benton* and the former Confederate *Bragg,* plus the

Lexington and *Tyler,* and secure control of as much of the Yazoo as possible. "Pick up all the good contrabands you can get, and something may be learned from the most intelligent of them and dispatch it to me," Porter instructed. He explained that in about ten days he would be pushing down-river with all the light-draft boats he could get finished. Selfridge in the *Cairo* would be joining Walke at Memphis. The *Cincinnati, Pittsburg,* and *Baron de Kalb,* Porter wrote, "will be off on Monday." With the *Carondelet* short fifty men, Walke realized he would have to take men from the *Mound City* and the *Benton* to fill his complement.[29]

On November 24 the gunboat *Marmora* arrived with mail, and Morison reported that "dispatches also came in for our captain and immediately all hands were in motion, getting ready for a start down river to Vicksburg." The next day Walke left Helena in the *Carondelet* with the *Mound City, Signal,* and *Marmora.* The *Lexington,* led by Lieutenant Commander James W. Shirk, was on its way to Helena with some refugee families. After dropping them off, the *Lexington* went down to Ashton, Louisiana, destroying every ferryboat it came across. Shirk brought back twenty-four contrabands, all of whom told him "that they are to be free on the 1st of January, but that their owners are getting ready to move them back from the river as soon as possible." Lincoln's Emancipation Proclamation would go into effect on New Year's Day 1863.[30]

The *Carondelet* headed downstream accompanied by the *Marmora* and *Signal,* each towing a coal barge. On Wednesday, November 26, they met the *Lexington,* which followed them. The next day Morison wrote, "Picked [up] some more 'contrabands,' one of them having lived in the woods for over five months. Passed one plantation where all the slaves on it apparently wanted to come off, but being rather short of provisions, had to decline the honor." The contrabands claimed that rebel troops had gone to Holly Springs and that all the blacks employed there had been sent to work on the forts at Vicksburg, as well as at another fort about forty miles below it.[31]

The federal gunboats came to anchor off Milliken's Bend at 4:00 p.m. on November 28, and Walke sent an armed boat crew from the *Marmora* on a tug. "As they landed, some guerillas in the woods fired on them and wounded one of 'Marmora's' officers in the right side." After this, they kept a lookout for enemy batteries along the shore. When the little flotilla reached the mouth of the Yazoo the next day, Walke sent the *Marmora* and *Signal* up to reconnoiter, accompanied by twenty men and the gunner from the *Carondelet.* The expedition ascended the Yazoo about forty miles but returned after encountering a masked battery. Although they did not engage the enemy battery, "they shelled the woods, thereby driving in the pickets from the river banks and killing a few of them," Morison explained. They took two prisoners and a contraband on board and "found that the rebs were busy erecting some more batteries down towards the mouth of the river."[32]

Observing the water level, Walke decided not to take his ironclads up the river; instead, he sent the tinclads *Marmora* and *Signal* to sound the river and look for rebel activity. Suspecting rebel guerrillas in the area, Walke then sent a detachment of twenty armed men, under the command of gunner William Beaufort, to the *Marmora* to protect the crew while they sounded the river. At 2:15 p.m. his suspicions were confirmed when a party of men fired a volley of musketry at the *Carondelet* from shore. The gunboat immediately replied with four solid shots and two five-second shells.

Lieutenant Robert Getty took the *Marmora* and *Signal* up the Yazoo, and at Twelve Mile Bayou guerrillas fired down on the federal gunboats from the high banks. Getty shelled them, and they disappeared. Upon reaching Anthony's Ferry, some twenty-one miles up the Yazoo, Getty reported, "I was again subjected to a severe and rapid guerilla fire, which was promptly returned with howitzers and rifles, silencing the enemy." Finally, at Drumgould's Bluff, Getty found the enemy's fortifications. He studied them through his spyglass, determined they were indeed formidable, and then steamed back down to the mouth of the Yazoo. In his report to Walke, Getty claimed that his reconnaissance had confirmed the presence of rebel pickets and some cavalry. The guerrillas were active, he told Walke, but the Confederates had no batteries for twenty-three miles up the Yazoo from its mouth.[33]

On December 1 Walke issued special orders to his commanders. He told them to keep a quarter watch during the night and to maintain sufficient steam to work their engines. Should the enemy fire on any of the vessels, the nearest one would fire immediately. If fired upon by a battery or field battery, then all vessels should go to quarters and place themselves in a position to engage the enemy to the best advantage. Recalling the friendly fire taken by the *Carondelet* after running past Island No. 10, Walke instructed his commanders to engage any enemy gunboat approaching the squadron with their bow guns in the first order of sailing, "being careful not to fire into each other."[34]

Walke also sat down to write a report to Porter. He informed Porter that the Confederate fort on the Yazoo "was said to be on a very high bluff concealed from view by another high point." The passage up the Yazoo was clear to the fort, but he noted that "a land force would be needed to capture it." He told Porter that he really needed more rams and noted, "The rebels have some good, large steamers at Vicksburg, and I suppose they will come out and surprise us, if they can, but I will keep a bright lookout for that. They can not attack us except with rams, or by boarding in the fog with large steamers." Walke commented that the weather was "quite pleasant" but added that, having been on blockade duty on the Mississippi since September 1861, he would be happy to see the river open again, "as the ague and fever of this country is, like the rebels themselves, obstinate and treacherous."[35]

USS *Tyler*

Henry Walke

Andrew Hull Foote

USS *Carondelet*

William Gwin

De Kalb, Mound City, and *Cincinnati*

USS *Benton*

David Glasgow Farragut

Charles H. Davis

David Dixon Porter

USS *Essex*

William D. Porter

USS *Black Hawk*

Augustus Kilty

Gunboat USS *Cairo*

USS *Lafayette*

Crew of the USS *Lafayette*

USS *Cincinnati*

11

The First Vicksburg Campaign

I can't blame an officer who seeks to put his ship close to the enemy.
—David Dixon Porter

In early December the weather turned rainy just above the mouth of the Yazoo at Milliken's Bend. Worried about a possible threat from Confederate rams, Walke anxiously awaited the arrival of Colonel Charles Ellet's rams. At the time, Ellet commanded seven rams: *Switzerland, Queen of the West, Monarch, Lancaster, Lioness, Horner,* and *Fulton.*[1]

Late on the afternoon of December 5, the *Switzerland* finally arrived at Milliken's Bend, and commanding officer Major J. W. Lawrence reported immediately to Walke. Lawrence told Ellet that Walke had given him "very concise" instructions to be on the alert, "as he expects a rebel ram, and if one comes in sight, to 'pitch in.'" The major informed Walke that he had procured enough contrabands for deckhands but could use an anchor, as the *Switzerland* had lost its the previous night.[2]

The arrival of the rams *Queen of the West* and *Switzerland* certainly eased Walke's concerns about a rebel attack, as did a report from a contraband claiming that the rebels had neither rams nor gunboats up the Yazoo. The man reported that the Confederates had erected a heavy timber barricade at or near a fort armed with ten guns about twenty-three miles upstream. Before ascending the Yazoo, Walke dispatched Lieutenant Robert Getty with the *Marmora* and a tug up the Yazoo to sound the river. When Getty returned, he reported seven feet of water on the bar, but no change along the banks.

Getty's report prompted Walke to write to Porter on December 8: "I expect the river to be high enough in a day or two to go up the Yazoo with some of the ironclads." Walke continued to keep the admiral informed of conditions. That very morning, he told Porter, a white resident of Yazoo had come on board the *Carondelet* claiming, contrary to earlier reports, that the rebels had built or were building two or three ram gunboats at Yazoo City. "We shall require some land force to clear the Yazoo, I think," Walke observed.[3]

During the early part of December, while Walke supervised the squadron's operations at Milliken's Bend, Porter was in Cairo conducting squadron business and communicating with Generals Grant and Sherman. "Grant has called on me to assist him; he is marching on to Vicksburg," Porter told Welles. Grant's forces had moved down directly on the Confederates' strong lines behind the Tallahatchie River, but when a rebel force from Helena appeared unexpectedly on their flank, they had retreated in confusion. "I think [the rebels did so] for the purpose of drawing him (General Grant) away from his supplies," Porter explained. "It is expected they will halt and reform behind Yalobusha River, at which place (if we can get our light-drafts up the Yazoo) we will cut them off from Vicksburg." Grant had ordered Sherman to go back to Memphis with one division and augment it with men from Helena and with McClernand's troops coming down from the north. Although Porter had not heard from McClernand, he expressed a willingness to work with the general and claimed that Sherman and his troops would leave Memphis for Vicksburg by December 20, land up the Yazoo, and then attack the rebel stronghold. "He asks the navy's cooperation and I am ready to give [it to] him," Porter told Welles.[4]

On December 8 Sherman informed Porter that he would be leaving soon for Memphis, and he asked Porter to send light drafts down with Phelps, Gwin, and Shirk to assist him in the preliminary work. "Of course Vicksburg can not be reduced till you arrived with the large gunboats," he added.[5]

Porter promised to be in Memphis in a day or two and assured Sherman that he had sent down every vessel he had, including Ellet's rams. Concluding his letter to the general, Porter offhandedly dismissed the navy's role: "The naval attack on Vicksburg will not amount to much. It will be mostly an army affair, for they will evacuate, if your force is at all what I suppose it will be." The squadron's manpower shortages weighed on Porter's mind, however, and he lamented to Assistant Secretary Fox, "Some are 50 men short. I'm sending away 600 sick and broken-down men in the squadron, turning away lazy deck hands on transports at $30 a month, and substituting ordinary seamen and contrabands." Nevertheless, Porter told Fox, "I send the vessels out if they can only man one gun." Explaining that the men sent from New York were all boys and ordinary landsmen, Porter confessed, "All the old sailors are mostly broke down."[6]

Taking Vicksburg and opening the Mississippi remained a top priority for the Mississippi Squadron, and to that end, Porter sent additional vessels to Walke's naval forces off the mouth of the Yazoo. But plans to ascend the river had been postponed. As the *Carondelet*'s coxswain Morison explained, "Capt. Walke being sick . . . the expedition was deferred until he got well."[7]

The gunboat *Cairo* had dropped anchor off the mouth of the Yazoo River on December 8. "We have a pretty formidable fleet here," sailor Yost observed, "now composed of the flagship 'Carondelet,' and the 'Cincinnati,' the 'Baron DeKalb,' the 'Mound City,' the 'Cairo,' the 'Pittsburgh,' the U.S. rams 'Switzerland,' 'Queen of the West,' also the store boat 'David Tatum.'" At 8:00 that evening the *Lexington, Tecumseh, Metropolitan, Dacotah,* and *Sallie List* came up from Vicksburg.[8]

The officers and men of Walke's flotilla continued to be on the alert for guerrilla attacks—a distinct possibility, given earlier incidents and one on December 8 involving the *Cairo.* The gunboat had arrived from above and "reported being fired into by guerillas at Milliken's Landing," Morison wrote. "A quartermaster named William Smith was wounded in the arm so that it was found necessary to amputate it. She shelled the woods where the guerillas were and also blew down a couple of houses in the village." In his diary, Yost explained that six of his shipmates had placed Smith on a litter and had taken him to the *Lexington* to go north.[9]

Farragut's vessels on duty in the lower Mississippi were also fired on by rebels. "On our way the two hindermost gunboats were fired into by musketeers from shore, but without inflicting any injury to anyone," surgeon Aaron Oberly wrote. "This is commencing to be the Southern mode of warfare with the vessels on the river."[10]

Anticipating action with the enemy, Selfridge kept the *Cairo*'s crew busy with preparations. "At 10 a.m. beat to quarters and at 10:15 a.m. drilled at the great guns, small arms, Boarders, Pikemen, Firemen as in action," Yost noted on December 9. The drills continued the following day, and "men called to quarters to see how soon we could get ready for action. It took the first division 3½ minutes, the 2nd and the rest almost 10 minutes. I belong to the No. 3 gun [42] pdr rifle."[11]

Two days later, Walke sent the *Marmora* and *Signal* twenty miles up the Yazoo on a reconnaissance to confirm the presence of an enemy barricade near the rebel fort. When the tinclads returned in the afternoon, Lieutenants Getty and Scott reported that they had discovered the presence of a number of "torpedoes," or mines. One had exploded near the *Signal.* On their return, the *Marmora* had spotted another torpedo visible above the water; a sailor had fired at it with his musket, and it exploded. Getty assured Walke that they could safely clear the river of all these mines if he would provide one or two gunboats to "keep down the sharpshooters." There were rebel rifle pits all along the south bank of the Yazoo, as well as some light artillery.[12]

After consulting with Walker of the *Baron De Kalb,* Selfridge of the *Cairo,* and Hoel of the *Pittsburg,* Walke agreed to Selfridge's request to clear the river of mines. Selfridge had argued that the *Cairo,* the fastest and lightest of the three gunboats, should be sent on the mission. Concerned about rebel opposition, Walke ordered the *Pittsburg* and the *Queen of the West* to accompany the *Marmora* and *Signal* while they swept for mines. Although he might have wished to go himself, Walke was still weak from a recent bout of malaria and chose to remain behind.[13]

Walke did, however, take pains to caution all the commanding officers—and Selfridge in particular—"to be very careful not to run their vessels in among the torpedoes, but to avoid the channel where they were set; to scour the shore with small boats and haul the torpedoes on shore, and destroy them before proceeding farther up the river." Walke later insisted that he had "repeated positively" these instructions and had told his commanders that the *Marmora* and *Signal* were to destroy the mines, "the ram should follow astern of them and the gunboats should be kept in the rear of all of them, so that they could shell the river banks if necessary." Before dismissing his officers, Walke admonished them, "If there is any apparent danger you are to relinquish the project and return until we can find better means to scour the shores and drag out the torpedoes."[14]

At 8:00 on the morning of December 12, the *Cairo, Pittsburg, Marmora, Signal,* and *Queen of the West* proceeded carefully up the Yazoo River to where the mines had been discovered the previous day. Selfridge's mission, as he understood it, was to destroy as many of these mines as possible. The light gunboats would go ahead, followed by the *Cairo* and *Pittsburg,* which would protect them by shelling the woods on the riverbank.[15]

Ensign Walter E. H. Fentress commanded the *Marmora*'s sharpshooter detachment, consisting of twenty men chosen from the crew of the *Caron-delet*. "We proceeded up the river very slowly and met no resistance," Fentress explained in his report to Walke. They steamed twelve miles upriver, occasionally shelling suspected rebel sharpshooter positions in the woods. At 10:00 a.m. they came across a skiff containing a white man and an African American. Getty questioned the white man, Jonathan Williams, who claimed to be the overseer on Blake's plantation. "Williams acknowledged, with reluctance, full knowledge of the location of the torpedoes. On discovering this fact, I immediately placed him in irons, as also the negro, who stated at the time of his arrest that Williams knew of the existence and location of the torpedoes." At Porter's orders, both men were to be turned over to Pennock, kept in irons, and fed on bread and water.[16]

The *Marmora* continued to lead the flotilla upstream, and at 11:00 the tinclad hove in sight of the sunken enemy mines. A hundred yards in advance of the other gunboats, the *Marmora* stopped its engines, and the rest of the fleet closed up. "I lowered my cutter and made it pull along the shore to reconnoiter and destroy the lines and cords which held the torpedoes," Getty reported.[17]

As the *Cairo* neared the spot indicated as the torpedo location, Selfridge strained his eyes and tried to spot the *Marmora,* which was partially hidden by a bend in the river. Suddenly, he heard the crackle of heavy musketry. In his report, Selfridge claimed that when he heard the sound of gunfire and saw the *Marmora* backing down, it led him to "suppose she was attacked for shore. I hastened up to her support, when I found the firing was from the *Marmora* at an object—a block of wood—floating in the river." As the *Cairo* came alongside the *Marmora,* Selfridge hailed Getty and asked why the vessel had stopped. "Here is where the torpedoes are," Getty replied.[18]

In his version of the incident, Fentress claimed the *Cairo* steamed up nearly abreast of the *Marmora* and an officer hailed "to go ahead." As the *Marmora* moved very slowly forward, Fentress could clearly see an object resembling a small buoy floating in the river. He asked Getty if he might examine it. With Getty's permission, Fentress took a boat and approached the buoy. He wrote, "I found a boat from the *Cairo* on the same errand, and I pushed forward to reach a line that I saw on the bank. As soon as I could I severed the line with my sword, and a large object immediately rose in the middle of river. Pulling to it by the line, I soon discovered it to be some 'infernal machine.'" Looking closely at the mine, the ensign saw a wire running from the object to the shore. "Cut it," cried an officer from *Cairo.* Obeying the order, Fentress began to break the mine into pieces, when a loud explosion startled him. Looking up, he saw an anchor tossed several feet in the air and then watched as the *Cairo* began to settle into the muddy Yazoo.[19]

Realizing that the *Cairo* had gone in toward the shore, Selfridge had backed out to go upstream and ordered the *Marmora* to go ahead slowly. "I had made but half a dozen revolutions of the wheel and gone ahead perhaps half a length," he wrote, "the *Marmora* a little ahead, leading, when two sudden explosions in quick succession occurred, one close to my port quarter and another under the port bow—the latter so severe as to raise the guns under it some distance from the deck." In the diary he saved after the *Cairo* sank, fifteen-year-old George Yost wrote, "The explosion dismounted one of our heaviest guns which was in the Port bow severely injuring 3 men one of whom was an engineer (Mr. Wilkins)." The young sailor explained, "We were struck by a Torpedo which exploded under the Forward part of our boat crushing in the bottom of the boat so that in 5 minutes after the explosion took place the whole forward part of the Hold was full of water and it was running over the deck forward."[20]

Brown river water poured into a gaping hole in the gunboat's hull, flooding the forward shell room, and the *Cairo* began to settle by the bow. "She commenced filling so rapidly that in two or three minutes the water was over the forecastle," Selfridge explained. The boat was run ashore as soon as possible to prevent it from sinking in deep water. Selfridge ordered a hawser tied to a tree, hoping to keep the *Cairo* from sliding off into deep water, and he had the crew man the steam and hand pumps.[21]

On board the *Pittsburg,* some 200 yards astern of the *Cairo,* Lieutenant Hoel heard the explosion, looked toward the *Cairo,* and saw a puff of smoke. Neither he nor A. J. Wilson, his executive officer, suspected that any damage had been done until they heard Selfridge hailing the *Signal* to come alongside, "as he was sinking." Hoel sent one of his cutters to the *Cairo*'s assistance, but the gunboat was going down so fast that Selfridge gave the order to abandon ship. He also called for the *Queen of the West* to come alongside. The ram's captain, Edwin Sutherland, immediately brought his vessel to the sinking *Cairo* and lowered the boats.[22] Under the supervision of surgeon's steward John Gerten, sailors began passing injured men, sea bags, hammocks, and other articles over to the ram. "The water was across the gun deck when the Ram Queen of the West came alongside to take us off. We were then told to leave quarters and take all the small arms we could and go on board the Ram which we did in double quick time," Yost recalled. "I can tell you, we fired one Gun at the fort just as she was sinking. I saved 2 Revolvers and most of us saved something some of us saved our bags some Hammocks and several saved nothing but themselves." The *Queen of the West* rescued some of the *Cairo*'s sailors while other crewmen took to the remaining boats. When they looked back, the *Cairo* had settled in six fathoms of water, with just its tall, black smokestacks visible. "Executive Officer Hiram K. Hazlett, and the writer were the last two persons to leave the sinking vessel," Yost explained, "which we did by jumping into the 'Dingey' which was manned by two sailors, and awaiting us at the stern; we moved off just in time to escape being swallowed up in the seething cauldron of foaming water." Fortunately, the *Cairo* suffered no fatalities as a result of the explosion, but six men were injured.[23]

In the meantime, on Selfridge's orders, Hoel had sent the *Pittsburg*'s boats to search for and destroy any remaining mines. As the gunboat threw shell, grape, and canister into the banks, the boat crews discovered mines being constructed behind every nearby levee and destroyed them. The *Queen of the West*'s boats also picked up floating wreckage, and the captain sent some bluejackets to pull down the *Cairo*'s smokestacks. "Nothing of the *Cairo* could be seen 12 minutes after the first explosion, excepting the smokestacks and the flag staff from which still floated the flag above the troubled waters," Yost recalled.[24]

Hoel's gunners expended sixty shells and four solid shots before Selfridge signaled, "Will return." Unable to ascend any farther up the Yazoo, the *Pittsburg, Marmora, Signal,* and *Queen of the West* headed back downstream, shelling wherever they spotted enemy pickets. The following day Walke ordered Selfridge to take the officers and crew of the *Cairo* on board the *Marmora* and report to Porter at Cairo.[25]

While Walke's vessels had been moving up the Yazoo River, Porter had been steaming down to Memphis on the *Black Hawk,* leaving Pennock in Cairo to tend to the squadron's administrative affairs. He knew that Walke had been up the Yazoo but had received no reports from him.[26] At about 10:00 on the morning of December 17, the *Marmora* came up the river, and the flagship lowered a boat, picked up Selfridge, and brought him aboard to see Porter. Selfridge related the story of the *Cairo*'s demise to the admiral and then asked if he was going to order a court of inquiry. "Court! I have no time to order courts!" Porter reportedly replied. "I can't blame an officer who seeks to put his ship close to the enemy. Is there any other vessel you would like to have?" Before Selfridge could reply, Porter turned to Fleet Captain Breese and told him that Selfridge would command the *Conestoga*. With that, Porter dismissed Selfridge and went back to what he clearly thought were more important matters. As the *Black Hawk* got under way for Memphis, Porter told his fleet captain to instruct the gunboats to clear the Yazoo of those "infernal machines." Federal vessels, including the *Lexington*, *Tyler*, and *Benton*, quickly set to work dragging for mines all the way to Haynes' Bluff, less than fifteen miles north of Vicksburg.[27]

When Porter arrived at Memphis on December 18, he called on General Sherman at his headquarters. Consulting a map, the general explained the army's plans. Grant was anxious to get moving and would be off to Holly Springs and then to Grenada, Sherman said, with a large force to engage General Pemberton or prevent him from reinforcing Vicksburg. Major General Nathaniel P. Banks, now in command at New Orleans, was expected to move up the Mississippi River, take Port Hudson, and then advance on Vicksburg. He and Porter would push down the Mississippi from the north and land on the Yazoo. "Grant says the garrison at Vicksburg is small," Sherman noted, "and you would have no difficulty getting inside the works. He seemed sure that when we occupy Vicksburg, Johnston will retreat via Jackson." With that, Porter returned to the *Black Hawk* and ordered Walke to proceed with several vessels to the Yazoo River, seize the landings to prevent the erection of batteries, and drag the river above Chickasaw Bayou for mines. He directed Walke "to use all possible expedition, so as to reach the Yazoo at least a day in advance of us."[28]

Conferencing with Breese, Porter explained that he would use the squadron to clear the way for Sherman's fifty-nine troop transports, which were bringing men and supplies to mount the assault on Chickasaw Bluffs. Porter had two divisions to support the operation. Walke's first division consisted of the *Carondelet;* the new ironclad *Chillicothe;* the timberclad *Lexington;* and the city-class gunboats *Cincinnati, Louisville,* and *Baron De Kalb* (formerly the *St. Louis*). Gwin, in the *Pittsburg,* commanded the second division with the *Tyler, Conestoga, Indianola,* and *Mound City.*[29]

On Wednesday, December 17, with stores running low, the *Carondelet* had gone up the river, Morison explained, "to see what had detained the store ship." The following morning the gunboat weighed anchor. "As some guerillas were hovering about, we went to quarters but they did not deem it prudent to fire on us." When the *Lexington* hove in sight with the *Sover-*

eign in convoy, "We immediately tuned about and proceeded down river again."[30]

The *Carondelet* arrived at the mouth of the Yazoo on Friday morning, December 19. On Saturday the ram *Lioness* and transport *City of Madison* came down with prisoners to be exchanged. "The rebel pickets, taking advantage of the presence of the flag of truce which accompanied the prisoners, showed themselves in groups along the levee," Morison wrote, "smoking and lounging about in the most nonchalant manner imaginable." The prisoners were exchanged and left for Vicksburg, with the *Lexington* acting as convoy. "Queer war, this, when a man has to be protected from his own friends," Morison observed.[31]

Sherman's troop transports were poised to begin making their way downstream. After loading all their baggage and train on the stern-wheeler *Dacotah,* the 3rd Infantry, Missouri Volunteers, was ready to go on December 20. Sergeant Major E. P. Reichhelm wrote in his diary that the fleet "had assumed really Grand proportions there being now assembled before Helena at least 70 transports and 6–8 gunboats, the former not only filled but crowded with troops. The monster 'Imperial' for instance, having on board 1500 men, 600 mules and horses, 80 wagons and a battery of artillery." This grand sight "inspired us all with the greatest confidence of success, and even fears were uttered 'that we would again be disappointed in the expectation of a fight, and that the rebels would skedaddle at our approach!'"[32]

The following day the *Black Hawk,* leading Sherman's transports downriver, arrived at Helena. As the flagship drew near the town, Porter could hear singing and shouting. A sizable crowd of African Americans had gathered and pushed through the lines of soldiers; they were singing "Jubilo," a popular tune among the black community in Mississippi. The joyous, singing contrabands—men, women, and children—were looking forward to what they called "Mancipation"—Lincoln's promised Emancipation Proclamation, set for January 1, 1863, just weeks away. Many of the most able-bodied male contrabands would be going on the transports to labor for the army, but on Sherman's orders, all the female camp followers who had traveled with the army from Memphis had been rousted off the transports and out of the tent camps and waterfront dives. Scores of laundresses, nurses, sutlers, and steamboat captains' wives could be seen bidding their men tearful good-byes. They would not be spending Christmas with them or going to Vicksburg.[33]

The troop-laden transports started out from Helena at 3:00 on December 22, Reichhelm explained, and steamed down to a rendezvous point. Their advance was "considerably annoyed by guerilla parties, stationed on the bends and narrow places of the river, and firing to our transports with cannon." To put a stop to this, "a brigade was here and there landed to pursue the Guerillas but mostly without avail and all the revenge we could take was to burn the houses, plantations and villages near which such depredations had been committed." The sergeant lamented, "The wanton destruction of homes and splendid farms not being a 'military necessity,' but originating merely in a thirst for vengeance, and licentious desire to sack and burn, filled me with sorrow."[34]

Protecting transports and other shipping in the river from guerrilla attacks had become a necessary precaution. When the transport *Champion No. 3* arrived on December 20, along with the ram *Switzerland,* the transport reported "being fired into by guerillas at Milliken's Landing, one shot (a 6 Pr) passing through her pilot house."[35]

Orders from Porter had arrived that day, informing Walke that Gwin would take charge of the expedition consisting of the *Benton, Lexington, Tyler, Lioness, Queen of the West,* and three light drafts. They were to proceed up the Yazoo, clear out mines, and secure a landing place for federal troops. "You will furnish him [Gwin] with anything he requires," the admiral instructed Walke. "I expect to find the landing in possession of our vessels when I arrive."[36]

Mindful that the *Cairo* had been lost to mines, Porter warned Gwin, "You will have to proceed with much care." He gave Gwin specific instructions about positioning his boats, dragging for torpedoes, keeping a chart, and myriad other details. Porter also admonished Gwin to keep a bright lookout but not to engage any rebel batteries unless they barred the federal vessels' passage.[37]

By the time Porter arrived at Helena, Walke's intermittent fever had returned. Too ill to personally go up the Yazoo to reconnoiter, he ordered on December 23 the *Baron De Kalb, Queen of the West,* and *Signal,* as well as the tug *Laurel,* up the rapidly rising river. He gave Walker, the *Baron De Kalb*'s commanding officer, specific instructions to ascend the river only ten to fifteen miles and to let the *Signal* take the lead. He was to send small boats in advance along the banks, each with a grapnel towing astern to catch any mines.[38]

In the evening the *Baron De Kalb* and the tug returned, leaving Gwin and the *Signal* up the Yazoo. They had seen nothing to excite suspicion, Walker reported, until they came abreast of Johnson's plantation about a mile up the Yazoo, where they found buoys with wires attached. While examining the devices and dragging with boats, they were fired on from both banks. Proceeding with caution, Walker had reached a point twelve to fourteen miles from the mouth of the river "under a galling fire of musketry." Encountering more mines, he decided they could not pass without dragging for them, so he returned. About a mile above Johnson's plantation, he met Gwin with his expedition. Concluding his report to Walke, Walker noted that one man had been killed and one severely wounded, both belonging to the tug.[39]

The day before Christmas Eve, the *Carondelet*'s officers and men learned more news. "One of the rams came down the Yazoo this morning and reports one killed and three wounded on the 'Benton.' The tug 'Intrepid' came down also, she being disabled." Morison reported that they buried the *Erebus*'s cook that afternoon. Then he soulfully penned, "Christmas Eve. I wonder how my wife is spending it. Better than me, I hope."[40]

That same day, Porter arrived at Milliken's Bend. "A merry Christmas to you all! A queer place this, to wish a merry Christmas from, and not less peculiar are the surroundings," veteran reporter Franc Wilkie wrote.[41]

"Christmas Eve was spent and celebrated by carrying a rail fence on board to be used as fuel which article had commenced to become scarce," Reichhelm wrote in his diary. "Nevertheless the officers amused themselves till late at night by song and speeches, tobacco and some little whiskey punch, and being invited to partake of all those luxuries I spent, at least part of the evening, very agreeably." Then, leaving the "merry crowd," Reichhelm went up to the pilothouse and was soon consumed by thoughts of home and happier Christmases. "I soon found myself musing over the hard and rough life of a soldier, and the sad disappointments that had been my lot since leaving home to serve my country." His transport continued downriver all night and landed at Milliken's Bend at 3:00 a.m.[42]

Walke and the men of the *Carondelet* spent an uneventful Christmas Day. "Christmas Day. 'Oh' What. Visions of roast turkey and sech-like the name recalls," Morison wrote in his diary. At about 1:30 that afternoon a steamer hove in sight, with Porter on board. "Close behind came a fleet of transports, ninety-two in number, carrying McClernand's army and bringing up the rear came the gunboat 'Louisville.'"[43]

Porter had arrived off the mouth of the Yazoo the previous evening, and early on Christmas Day he and Sherman met at Johnson's plantation, opposite Steele's Bayou. They mounted horses and set off to explore the area. Sherman and Porter rode across the dry fields and surveyed the ground until it became swampy, their mounts sinking into the muck. Across the swamp and a small lake, the two men could see the foothills of the Walnut Hills. The sound of rifle fire coming from that direction alerted Sherman that the enemy had occupied the hills, where they could observe the federals' every movement.[44]

Both Sherman and Porter remained hopeful that Union troops could take Chickasaw Bluffs and Haynes' Bluff before the rebels could reinforce them. This would draw enemy units away from Vicksburg, allowing Grant's men to take the rebel stronghold. Sherman asked Porter to move his gunboats convoying the transports up the Yazoo the next morning at 8:00. He planned to land his troops at Johnson's plantation, thirteen miles up the Yazoo. The men would ford the Chickasaw Bayou and assault the heights of the Walnuts Hills.[45]

All of Porter's vessels had been ordered to darken ship and to refrain from any Christmas night celebrations that would bring attention to them—the blowing of whistles, the ringing of bells, or the lighting of lanterns. Porter spent the evening in his cabin, answering correspondence and writing orders. Earlier, he had issued specific orders dividing the Mississippi Squadron into two divisions commanded by Walke and Gwin. That same day, the admiral told Brown in the *Forest Rose* to get under way and convoy the *Great Western* and the mortar boats to Milliken's Bend.[46]

As planned, the day after Christmas, Sherman's transports landed men, artillery, gear, and horses. "The flagship (bearing the admiral), accompanied by the gunboats 'DeKalb,' 'Cincinnati,' and a few mosquitoes with fifty transports, ascended the Yazoo," the *Carondelet*'s coxswain noted. "About noon the gunboat 'Louisville' also went up."[47] Fortunately for Vicksburg's Confederate defenders, Sherman had taken his time moving up the Yazoo and landing his troops, giving General Stephen D. Lee ample opportunity to move his fieldpieces and wagons of ammunition to Chickasaw Bluffs.

The *Tyler* accompanied the troops, and in a letter to his fiancée, Symmes Browne explained, "Three regiments proceeded up the right [left] bank and completely [chased] the enemy out as far as Chickasaw creek, at the mouth of which they had a breastwork for infantry from which the 'Butternuts' fairly ran for dear life." The *Tyler* shelled the woods beyond the federal troops, "thus making it hot for them for over a mile back from the river bank." At 2:00 the troops returned to the landing, and the *Tyler* steamed back to the mouth of the Yazoo. Morison noted, "The gunboat 'Taylor' [*Tyler*] came back down to get coal and brought news that after destroying several torpedoes, they got within range of a battery at Snyder's Mills. They opened fire on it but received no answer."[48]

Sergeant Reichhelm's transport was among those entering the Yazoo. On the morning of December 26, after loading up on fences to fuel the boat, they started up the river. After proceeding about eight miles they landed "near the grand and splendid plantation of Sidney A. Johnson, the great rebel, now destroyed and leveled to the ground by our troops." At 4:00 the troops disembarked and marched into a nearby cornfield. Just as they set out from the boat, "a cold piercing rain started to fall," Reichhelm wrote, and "increased to an awful rain pouring down upon us in torrents." Their baggage remained on the boat, so the soldiers spent the evening "exposed to the most horrible storm and cold rain. . . . Not even fire was allowed, for fear of betraying to the . . . enemy our position and no wonder that some of the boys got sick in consequence."[49]

In the wee hours of December 27, Sherman, on the *Forest Queen,* sent a message to Porter, on the *Black Hawk.* "The commencement of rain and nonarrival of General A. J. Smith's division makes modification of my plan necessary," he wrote. He had sent three brigades out to reconnoiter the enemy defenses, and they had skirmished with General Stephen D. Lee's men. Sherman still intended to send the three columns, as previously planned, but he ordered Steele's two brigades to Blake's Levee at the mouth of Chickasaw Creek, "to follow the levee along Chickasaw Bayou back to the hills to secure a lodgment; the gunboats could then threaten Haynes' Bluff battery."[50]

Reichhelm's Missouri Volunteers, "soaken wet and blue with frost," reboarded their transport that morning and were taken four miles farther up the river. The regiment formed and then advanced a mile in the opposite direction from the river. Once they had made it through some prickly berry patches, they took a position in a cornfield, but except for a little skirmishing at about 11:00, they did little battle. At 4:00 they were ordered to fall back and join the brigade.[51]

By late morning, Sherman had his army deployed on a front running north to south some five miles facing Chickasaw Bluffs. From high on the bluffs, Confederate commander Lee observed the bluecoats landing in droves. The Yankees had done just as he had predicted—come ashore at

Johnson's place. But his men were ready—guns sighted, ammunition up, and fields of fire cleared. Now all they needed were the promised reinforcements from Pemberton and Bragg. With only one brigade of 2,300 men and four artillery batteries to defend his position on Chickasaw Bluffs against Sherman's more than 20,000 men, Lee could only hope and pray that the additional troops would arrive in time. If they did not, Sherman's troops could advance and push Lee's men back to Vicksburg.[52]

Porter's ironclads had moved up the Yazoo to support Sherman's troops, following the admiral's specific instructions. He told Gwin, the *Benton's* commander, to move up again "and prepare to go on fishing up torpedoes." The *Cincinnati* and *Louisville* would proceed as "if going to attack Haynes Bluff." The rebels had gun batteries at Drum Gould's Bluff, Snyder's Bluff, and Haynes' Bluff along the Yazoo, north of Chickasaw Bluffs.[53]

Porter instructed Lieutenant George M. Bache, commanding the *Cincinnati,* to follow 400 yards astern of the *Benton,* taking care not to fire into the Union soldiers moving up the right bank. As usual, the admiral gave very detailed instructions. In this case, he instructed all the ironclads to fire at the highest elevation with the longest fuses "to prevent the enemy at the forts from reinforcing the troops at Vicksburg by the Mill Dale road." Porter also instructed Walker in the *Baron De Kalb* to move up after the *Benton* and anchor 100 yards astern.[54]

According to plan, Porter's boats began removing mines from the Yazoo River that morning. The boats worked under a steady fire from riflemen concealed in pits, but the Confederates gradually fell back. By 3:00 that afternoon, Porter's vessels had advanced to within three-quarters of a mile of the rebel batteries.

With the way clear of mines, Gwin had advanced his vessels up the narrow channel in a single file against a strong current. The *Benton* took the lead, followed by the *De Kalb, Cincinnati, Louisville, Queen of the West, Marmora,* and *Lexington.* The *Black Hawk* remained behind, and if Porter felt anxious about his first major engagement as squadron commander, he did not show it. To his commanders, Porter appeared superbly confident. "My object," Porter explained, "was to draw off a large portion of the troops from Vicksburg and to guard Sherman's left against a flank attack."[55]

As the *Benton* came up within range of the rebel batteries on Drum Gould's Bluff, Gwin found it impossible to work his gun batteries, so he ordered the vessel to move to the left bank. In this position, in full view of the enemy, the *Benton's* gunners could work the bow or starboard batteries by slacking or tautening the lines. Mines made it unsafe to engage the batteries farther up the river or at closer quarters. At 3:35 p.m. the *Benton* opened with its bow guns and bombarded the rebel batteries for an hour. At first, the rebel gunners aimed for all the federal gunboats, one shot striking the *Cincinnati* but causing no damage. Rebel gunners then realized that the *Benton* offered the most visible target. Shots began striking its sloping casemate, and several came thudding down on the deck. Amidst it all, Gwin stood on the forward part of the quarterdeck, looking with his spyglass toward the hills and the rebel guns. With the other gunboats concealed behind trees, the *Benton* was fully exposed to the rebel gunners, and three rifled shells whizzed through one of the gunboat's open gun ports. Still, Gwin coolly remained on the quarterdeck. As Porter explained in his report, Gwin "refused to enter the shot-proof pilot house, saying that a captain's place is on the quarter-deck."[56]

Realizing that the rebels had "a dead range" on his vessel, Gwin ordered the *Benton* to the opposite side of the river. The words had barely left his lips when a shot struck the ship's armor and bounced off, hitting Gwin and gouging a terrible wound in his chest and right arm. While nearby crewmen carried the bleeding Gwin down to paymaster Lownds, who was tending the wounded in the wardroom, the *Benton*'s executive officer, George Lord, took command. He had Morton, the pilot, handle the gunboat while he gave orders, hopping about on a wounded foot. Lord then communicated with Lieutenant Commander E. K. Owen on the *Louisville,* asking him whether he should anchor. Owen told Lord to proceed down the river and report to Porter. The *Benton* had been hit twenty-four times; master-at-arms Robert Royal was killed, and a seaman named Smith was mortally wounded.

After what seemed a long time, Lord received permission to go back downriver with the wounded, now numbering ten men, including Gwin. When they arrived alongside the flagship *Black Hawk,* Porter came on deck and saw Gwin, lying on a stretcher looking frail and in pain; he insisted that the wounded lieutenant be carried to his own cabin. Porter then went to the wardroom and sent a message to Pennock: "We have had stirring times today, engaging the Yazoo batteries and taking up the torpedoes. The old war horse, *Benton,* has been much cut up, and the gallant, noble Gwin, I fear, mortally wounded . . . *Benton* has 10 wounded, but though hit often is still good for a fight . . . I am anxiously looking for the hospital boat. Send her down under convoy."[57]

Porter's next communiqué was to Secretary Welles. "I had three of the ironclads, *Lexington, Marmora* and ram *Queen of the West* lying as reserve, but none of them were struck, though in action, except *Cincinnati,* Lieutenant Bache, by which no material damage occurred to the vessel. The Army advanced at same time we were attacking forts, making the enemy believe we were going to force the river forts. This induced them to draw off a large part of their force from Vicksburg." Encouraged by the day's action, that evening Porter ordered the *Baron De Kalb* to come up and take the *Benton's* place. He instructed Brown to take the *Forest Rose* and *Marmora* up the Old River channel to the head of False River the next morning and briskly lob some shells and shots toward the rebels at Vicksburg.[58]

Reichhelm's Missourians had spent a cold night on wet, swampy ground "directly opposite and not 300 yards distant from the rebel fortifications, from which every now and then a shell or solid shot would whistle over our heads, completely driving sleep from our eyes." With a thankful heart, he wrote, "We greeted daylight, slowly dawning through the trees. A large kettle of coffee having meanwhile arrived from the river bank prepared there by the Colonel's Negro, was a welcome beverage as ever was consumed." That got his spirits back "into fighting trim."[59]

When the fog lifted on December 28, the *Marmora* and *Forest Rose* got under way and went three miles up Old River to shell the bank. At noon they ceased firing. The *Forest Rose* went aground, but the *Marmora* managed to tow it clear. By 1:00, both had come back down.

Reichhelm's regiment had advanced that morning to a position directly opposite a high bluff. "A little to the left we could distinctly see the glistening of gun-barrels through the thicket, and toward our right the solid earthworks of a fort were plainly visible through the tree tops." The regiment halted, and heavy skirmishing broke out on its right as the Missourians encountered enemy pickets. A "storm of shot and shell [came] from Fort Morgan" and then opened up on their left as well. Reichhelm's unit spent the day in the front, "under a constant and heavy fire of artillery," but it suffered fewer casualties than those in the rear—the "shot mostly going over us and far too high." They had no word about the battle to their left. After what Reichhelm called "an ominous pause" around noontime, the strife began again at 1:30. At 4:00 the fire slackened and "appeared to draw back from the bluffs indicating a 'retrograde advance' on our side." The day's fighting ended at nightfall.[60]

About noon that same day, the *Rocket* had arrived, bringing news of the engagement to the *Carondelet,* whose men had "heard the sound of heavy firing through the night." It slackened at 4:00 and then resumed at 8:00 the next morning "and was kept up until 1 P.M. with a fierceness and regularity that told of hot work." The *Rocket* reported taking three earthworks that commanded the approaches to Vicksburg on one side. "The rebels fought well and contested every inch of the ground," Morison wrote.[61]

That evening, Porter composed a letter to Foote: "We have had a lively time up the Yazoo. Imagine the Yazoo becoming the theater of war! We waded through 16 miles of torpedoes to get at the forts (seven in number), but when we got that far the fire from the boats from the riflemen in pits dug for miles along the river and from the batteries became very annoying." That "gallant fellow Gwin thought he could check them, which he did until he was knocked over with the most fearful wound I ever saw." He could not advance, Porter confessed to Foote, with "the torpedoes popping up ahead as thick as mushrooms, and we have had pretty good evidence of their power to do mischief." The forts on the high bluffs were powerful works and out of reach of the ships, he explained, and their plunging fire shot through the gunboats' upper decks. "The river is so narrow only one vessel could engage them until the torpedoes could all be removed." Of Gwin, Porter wrote, "there is little hope for; no man could live with such a wound. He is a noble, gallant fellow. I have him in my cabin and do all I can for him; his sufferings are terrible."[62]

Having failed to turn the Confederates' lines on December 28, Sherman decided to launch a frontal assault on Chickasaw Bluffs the next day, a Monday. He would attack across a narrow corduroy road running along Chickasaw Bayou, the only passable route. In his diary, Corporal William Reid recorded a soldier's perspective of the battle of Chickasaw Bluffs: "We were to take the rebel works on the bluff. . . . We formed in a double line of Companies and started forward at the signal, through a perfect shower of shot and shell from the enemy batteries." The woods offered some protection, "but on getting on open ground the enemy made havoc in our ranks. . . . We were forced to retire. . . . A terrific fire was kept up until after dark by infantry and artillery," he wrote. "The loss on our side was very heavy. We retired from our positions ¾ mile and lay in corn field. It rained all night and we got wet, a great many took colds from which they never recovered."[63]

Porter's gunboats had shelled rebel positions all day, but Sherman's troops were now beyond the effective range of the federal vessels. Two mortar boats had, however, lobbed shells into the woods on either side of the army's advance. As Morison noted: "The fighting is still going on. We are beating them back slowly but at the same time surely. We have taken 1000 prisoners already. Our two mortars are at work at the Yazoo fort steadily but seem to make no impression."[64]

On his flagship *Black Hawk,* Porter paced and waited for Sherman's report. Before twilight, the rain began to fall. "Then rain came on, and such a rain!" Porter wrote in his postwar account. When Sherman arrived, dripping wet and covered in mud, the two men took shelter from the deluge in Porter's cabin. In a whisper, so as not to disturb the wounded Gwin, Porter asked the wardroom steward to fetch the ingredients for whiskey punch. Porter knew Sherman could use a drink. He had encountered unexpected obstacles when the rebels had felled trees in the line of Chickasaw Bayou. One brigade had reached the top and held it for a time, but without reinforcements, it had fallen back down under murderous enemy fire. Writing after the war, Sherman admitted, "Our loss had been pretty heavy, and we had accomplished nothing, and had inflicted little loss on our enemy."[65]

In his recounting of their conversation, Porter asked Sherman, "You are out of sorts. What is the matter?" The general replied, "I have lost seventeen hundred men, and those infernal machines will publish all over the country their ridiculous stories about Sherman being whipped, etc." Nonplussed, Porter responded, "Only seventeen hundred men! Pshaw! that's nothing; simply an episode in the war. You'll lose seventeen thousand before the war is over, and will think nothing of it. We'll have Vicksburg yet before we die." To this Sherman exclaimed, "That's good sense, Porter! and I am glad to see you are not disheartened, but what shall we do now? I must take my boys somewhere and wipe this out." Porter wrote, "I informed the general that I was ready to go anywhere." To which Sherman replied, "Then, let's go and thrash out Arkansas Post." Before they gave up on defeating the rebels at Chickasaw Bluffs, Porter suggested they try to secure a foothold farther up at Haynes' Bluff.[66]

As December drew to a close, a pea-soup fog enveloped the federal gunboats, keeping them at anchor. Reichhelm's regiment had been removed to a safer distance from enemy lines, and he was "enjoying the luxury of a fire. Coffee was also in process of boiling, and with the prospect of such good things as rest and something to eat, good spirits returned." On the morning of December 31, hostilities having ceased, the rebels consented to a flag of truce to bury the dead.[67]

The foggy weather had postponed Sherman's planned assault on the rebels at Haynes' Bluff, set for the night of December 31. The following day Porter advised Sherman that a late moonset would compel them to make a daylight landing, which was, in his opinion, "too hazardous to try."[68]

During the last few days of December, the *Carondelet* remained off the Yazoo, and Walke tended to some mundane business. He told Porter that he had sent the *Pittsburg* to guard the ordnance boats and had arranged for the officer in charge of prisoners to get provisions from the *Sovereign*. They were anxious to have a gunboat to convoy them, but, he told Porter, he "did not feel authorized to send one." On December 30 Porter informed Walke that all the gunboats would be needed the next evening and asked him to send the *Great Western,* the *Sovereign,* and the army store vessels up to Old River. He then invited Walke to visit him on the *Black Hawk.* "I have some plans to arrange with you," he told Walke. At about 7:00 on New Year's Eve, Morison noted, the *Carondelet* "weighed anchor and in company with 'Mound City' and 'Pittsburgh' steamed up the Yazoo to Johnson's Landing where the flag was lying." The *Carondelet* anchored at about 8:30 p.m., and Walke went to see Porter. They shared coffee, and the admiral gave Walke some wonderful news: his request for command of a larger ironclad had been granted.[69]

The year ended on a sour note, however, for Porter and Sherman. Heavy fog and inclement weather had convinced both men that a renewed assault on Vicksburg was out of the question. In one historian's view, Sherman's "costly and abortive frontal assault" on the rebel batteries below Drum Gould's Bluff had had "no chance whatever for success." Even if Porter's gunboats had risked the minefields in the river below the bluffs, they could not have provided the necessary fire support, and the swampy ground had kept the army's artillery on the riverbanks. In the end, Sherman wrote, "I became convinced the part of wisdom was to withdraw." Grant was not pressing Vicksburg from the rear, Porter had just learned, and Van Dorn's cavalry had raided Holly Springs, destroying Grant's supplies. Grant's communications to Columbus had been severed by Bedford Forrest's men, and General Banks had not even started to advance on Port Hudson. Sherman, Grant, and Porter's plan to capture the "Gibraltar of the West" had failed. As Sherman wrote to his wife, "Well, we have been to Vicksburg, and it was too much for us, and we have backed out."[70]

On the one hand, 1862 had been a disappointing year for the Union navy and the Union war effort. At sea, the Confederate raider *Alabama* had burned dozens of ships and whalers. General George McClellan's Peninsular Campaign had failed to reach the Confederate capital at Richmond, and he had withdrawn his army, leaving the rebels in control of the James River. Furthermore, the blockade of the southern coast, a critical component of the Union's war strategy, had not achieved the desired result of denying the Confederacy access to ports through which to import and export goods. From September 1861 through December 1862, blockade runners had successfully breached the blockade 72 times out of 105 attempts.

On the other hand, there had been some bright spots for the Union navy's western squadrons. Farragut's fleet had taken New Orleans and moved up the Mississippi River, seizing Baton Rouge and Natchez. Foote's Western Gunboat Flotilla had steamed down the Mississippi, and although it had been stalled for a time at Island No. 10, it had prevailed, thanks to the *Carondelet*'s run past the island. Following this triumph, the Western Gunboat Flotilla had snatched Memphis, crushed the rebel river defense force, and knocked out the ram *Arkansas*. Nonetheless, as 1862 drew to a close, Union forces had been unable to lever the secesh out of Vicksburg. The tenacity of Vicksburg's defenders frustrated and angered Walke and his fellow naval officers, but the *Carondelet*'s coxswain John Morison viewed the year more philosophically. On New Year's Eve, he penned, "Turned in soon after and so ended the year 1862. I am thankful that I have lived to see the end of it."[71]

12

Arkansas Post and Fort Hindman

This was a most beautiful fight.

—David Dixon Porter

"Hail to the New Year," John Morison wrote in his diary on January 1, 1863. On that very cold morning, the *Carondelet* and *Pittsburg* had weighed anchor and started upstream, followed by the *Mound City*. "We started up to the batteries (7 miles) but owing to a dense fog we did not make much headway, as it was a go-ahead slow, stop, back her all the time." Suddenly, a tug came in and ordered the gunboats back to the landing. According to Morison, the crew "lay still all day surmising why we were ordered back." The assault on Drum Gould's Bluffs, scheduled for 4:00 a.m., had been abruptly canceled.[1]

The *Carondelet* remained in the Yazoo, lying off Johnson's plantation. Later that afternoon a tug came down with orders from Porter. Concerned about reported Confederate activity across the Mississippi from New Madrid, the admiral wanted the ironclad to go up and secure Island No. 10. At about 8:00 p.m. the *Carondelet* weighed anchor and went down the Yazoo to the Mississippi, "bound for Island 10."[2]

The *Carondelet* proceeded up the Mississippi uneventfully, passing Napoleon, but while steaming close to shore, a boy on the bank hailed the boat. Walke asked what he wanted. "He said that his sister and himself were left alone and they had nothing to eat, whereupon our captain ordered the purser to give him some of his own private stores, 'for which may his shadow never grow less.'"[3]

After stopping near Island No. 89 to carry off a few wooden fence rails to use as fuel, the *Carondelet* continued past the mouth of the White River. The next day Walke ordered the red flag hoisted, indicating that he needed a tow. The tinclad *Marmora* took the gunboat in tow, and the little *Juliet* joined them, taking up a hawser. They arrived off Helena at about 8:30 p.m. and tied up to one of the coal barges.[4]

The *Carondelet* spent January 8 coaling ship, but at around 3:00 in the afternoon the *V. F. Wilson* came along to tow the ironclad up the river in yet another effort to conserve the gunboat's precious coal supply. Thomas Lyons, Walke's clerk, kept a journal while serving on the *Carondelet,* and in his entry for January 8 he noted that he had spent some of the evening "studying the President's message." News of the Emancipation Proclamation had spread far and wide.[5]

On Saturday, January 10, the *Chillicothe* arrived. "She rounded to and Capt. Walke went on board," Lyons wrote. "All eyes were turned to this new novelty of naval architecture which appeared to be nothing but a scow with a steam engine on board, and a pilot-house with 2 eleven inch guns mounted inside." The ironclad gunboat's arrival also provoked a comment from Morison. "In the forenoon we met the new style gunboat 'Chillicothe' on her way down to join the fleet. She is the queerest-looking specimen of a war ship that I ever seen. She may be a useful boat but I vow she is not a handsome one." A lightly armored ironclad, the *Chillicothe* had been built at Brown's yard in Cincinnati. The 162-foot gunboat had side wheels and two screws and carried a pair of 11-inch smoothbores.[6]

When the *Carondelet* arrived off Memphis, Tennessee, Walke sent the tug alongside the *General Bragg* and brought Commander Bishop on board. Bishop informed Walke that rebel guerrillas continued to plague the vessels of the Mississippi Squadron. Lyons wrote in his journal, "Captain Bishop reports that the Memphis Customs officers permit about 20 to 40 lbs of salt to pass across the river each day so that it will reach the rebel forces and that the guerrillas visit the river bank opposite Memphis with impunity, take a look and leave every four days."[7]

The captains concluded their conference, and the *Carondelet* continued up the river. As Walke had learned, the federal gunboats were exposed to more dangers than just guerrilla attacks. There was always the threat of a collision with a passing vessel, especially in foggy weather, and the sudden appearance of snags or "sawyers" could seriously damage even an ironclad. On January 11, for example, the *Carondelet* narrowly avoided colliding with another steamer. "During the night met the Tinclad 'Brilliant' coming down and barely escaped a collision with her," Lyons wrote. "Mr. Donelson [*sic*] being 'Officer-of-the-deck' at the time was put under arrest immediately." Less than a week later, Walke must have considered Ensign Oliver Donaldson sufficiently chastised, for Lyons noted on January 16, "Mr. Donelson [*sic*] reinstated and placed upon duty."[8]

After a brief stop at Fulton, the *Carondelet* passed Fort Pillow at 2:30 p.m. Its journey was not without further incident, however. After barely avoiding a collision earlier, the Pook turtle encountered another obstacle. "About 11½ last night I was awakened by a violent concussion," Morison wrote. He sprang out of his hammock but could not get on deck "to see what had caused such an uproar. It seemed as if the boat was going to pieces, glass falling and timber cracking and splitting to which were added the noise of falling bodies." At first, Morison thought they had encountered another accident like the one at Island No. 10. "Then I thought that a snap [snag] had run through her bottom. I had my mind to swim ashore as I came to the conclusion that the old 'Carondelet's' time had come." He tried the ports, but they were all closed. "After a while, as I did not hear the water running into her, I knew there was no danger and I returned to my hammock." As it turned out, a large snag had risen up and hit the *Carondelet* in the port bow. "It slid up the iron faced casemate and ripped off our hammock nettings, tearing down our awning stanchions and breaking our hog chain and its supports. The boat sank down about four inches on the port side." The crew rolled all the shot amidships, Morison explained, and the *Carondelet* proceeded on its way, slowly, passing Point Pleasant and Tiptonville in the afternoon. At 8:00 p.m. they tied up at New Madrid.[9]

After Walke visited the garrison at New Madrid, the gunboat continued on its way, arriving at Island No. 10 at about 2:30 in the afternoon. There, Walke learned that the rebels had abandoned plans to attack New Madrid or Island No. 10—the very reason his vessel had been summoned in the first place.[10]

The following day the weather turned stormy and cold, and a heavy rain turned to snow—yet another challenge for Union gunboats on the Mississippi. Lyons recorded: "7:30 all hands piped up to clear snow from decks. River rising at rate of 6 inches in 24 hrs." On January 15 a strong wind from the northeast brought more snow. Morison noted the intense cold as well: "Water freezing very rapidly. No difference between here and the banks of the Hudson today."[11]

Lyons spent his time productively, buying eggs and butter for the captain's mess from two contrabands who had come from the Kentucky shore. Three days later Lyons was awakened with a surprise announcement from the captain. "4 a.m. Captain Walke called me up and ordered me to pack the mess things and get ready to go up to Cairo on the U.S. Tinclad 'New Era.' She came alongside last night direct from Arkansas Post where the Union forces have just gained a victory over the 'Rebels.'"[12]

While the *Carondelet* had been slowly making its way up the Mississippi, Sherman had taken his troops up the Arkansas River to attack Fort Hindman, a Confederate installation at Arkansas Post. Porter's biographer, Richard West, surmised that Sherman's choice reflected, in part, his need to salvage the Union failure at Chickasaw Bluffs.[13] Sherman's troops had abandoned the ground on the Yazoo on January 1, 1863. "We evacuated our positions as quietly as possible and returned to the fleet. Embarked and moved down river a few miles," Corporal Reid of the 16th Ohio Volunteer Infantry wrote in his diary. The next day, he noted, "The fleet moved down to the Mississippi River and up to Milliken's Bend, where we were joined by General McClernand. A council of war was held and the expedition to Arkansas Post was formed accordingly. The fleet moved up the Mississippi River to the White River."[14]

That same day, a Friday, the *Tigress* had come down with General John A. McClernand and his staff on board. McClernand, an amateur general, had arrived to take charge of the campaign. "A couple of his staff came on board and held a pow-wow with our captain," the *Carondelet*'s Morison wrote.[15]

McClernand's success at raising troops in Illinois had given him enormous political influence with the Lincoln administration, but Sherman knew he needed more men to renew the assault on Vicksburg. The general also believed that Fort Hindman was a convenient base for rebels bent on attacking unescorted Union shipping on the Mississippi. On a bluff twenty-five feet above the north side of the Arkansas River, the Confederates had erected a four-sided earthwork to protect the river and discourage federal gunboats from using the river to attack Little Rock. Named in honor of General Thomas C. Hindman, the fort had a sophisticated design, but unlike Fort Donelson and many other rebel forts, it could not deliver plunging fire down on federal warships. Five thousand men, mostly dismounted Texas cavalrymen and three brigades of infantry under Confederate brigadier general Thomas Churchill, garrisoned the fort. However, by the end of 1862, disease and a tenuous supply chain had left it in a weakened state.[16]

Initially, McClernand objected to the idea of attacking Arkansas Post, but Sherman convinced him to ask Porter's opinion. Despite their failed attempt to take Chickasaw Bluffs, Porter had forged an amiable working relationship with Sherman, who, one historian wrote, "damned politics, damned the newspapers, and believed in fighting hard." Near midnight on January 4 the two generals went to the *Black Hawk* to see Porter, who had just donned his nightgown. They gathered at a table in Porter's cabin, not far from where Gwin still lay gravely wounded. The previous day, Sherman had written to Porter, "Am pained beyond measure to hear of poor Gwin's state; don't believe a single Catholic priest is in our fleet; have sent to enquire, but the answer comes back from each division, None."[17]

Sherman, McClernand, and Porter began to discuss their next plan of action. Sherman's men lay in Milliken's Bend, arranged in brigades and divisions, but where to deploy them was the question. Sherman sketched two possible courses of action. The second option was to "go right up and clear out Post of Arkansas and Little Rock." Porter refused to cooperate with such an operation unless McClernand named Sherman as commander. "To this McClernand agreed," the admiral later wrote, "only stipulating that he [McClernand] should accompany the expedition. So the matter was arranged, and the expedition started."[18]

On January 4 Porter assembled his ironclads and light drafts. He gave Lieutenant Commander Watson Smith command of the first division of light-draft gunboats, consisting of the *Rattler, Marmora, Romeo, Juliet, Glide, Springfield, New Era, Signal,* and, for this operation, *Forest Rose.* Porter also ordered Colonel Charles Ellet in the *Monarch* to join him at the mouth of the White River for the expedition and to leave Lieutenant Commander Prichett of the *Tyler* in charge of the rest of the rams.

They departed Milliken's Bend that same day, with transports towing Porter's gunboats to save fuel. In a letter written from the gunboat *Baron De Kalb,* young Frederic C. Davis described their journey up the river: "Saturday January 4th after arriving at mouth of Yazoo river, we got orders on Sunday to move up the river. All the fleet got underway, and we started up in tow of two transports."[19]

To deceive the rebels, Porter planned to take the expedition up the White River and over to the Arkansas River through a connecting channel. But first he sent the *Conestoga* on a reconnaissance up the Arkansas and down into the White River by this cutoff. On January 7 Porter issued his general order for the operation against Arkansas Post. Smith would go ahead in the *Rattler* to sound the depth of the water. If he could go through, he would hoist the blue jack. The *Romeo, Juliet,* and *Forest Rose* would then follow, with the *Marmora* going on ahead and sounding. "Commanders will look out for torpedoes or floats or wires extending from the bank. Boats will be kept manned to remove them," Porter instructed. The *Louisville, Baron De Kalb,* and *Cincinnati* would follow Porter's flagship, and the *Signal* would cover the transports. He gave the *Lexington* the mission of bringing up the rear, and he ordered the *Red Rover* and *Torrence* to guard the mouth of the White River.[20]

The *Cincinnati* had departed the Yazoo with a transport lashed to its side, "helping us along," Daniel Kemp recalled. "The crew, of course, did not know our destination, but when we reached the mouth of the White River, we laid up over night and started up the river the next morning. I thought the White River, as I now remember it, was one of the crookiest I ever saw, for our unwieldy gunboat had a hard time making the trip, as the river was very high and the current very swift."[21]

On January 8 Porter informed McClernand that he was ready to move. The signal officer on board the *Black Hawk* would communicate with the one on board Sherman's vessel. Porter's Arkansas pilot did not recommend steaming upriver all night, so the general agreed to stop with Porter's boats at the cutoff. McClernand reported that General Morgan had found a suitable landing site at Notrib's farm, just below Arkansas Post.[22]

"We steamed up the river until we came to the cut off, which took us into the Arkansas," the *Cincinnati*'s Kemp wrote in his memoirs. "This river, if I remember it rightly, was wider and much shallower than the White River. All, or nearly all, the transports accompanied us. The gunboats accompanying us were the Louisville, DeKalb, and also the Flag Ship and a number of Tinclads (The Mosquito Fleet)."[23]

When the transports reached Notrib's plantation, a few miles below Arkansas Post, McClernand ordered his troops ashore. They bivouacked for the night and then invested the rebel position. Sherman took his men around the fort to attack the rebel trenches in the rear, while Morgan's corps advanced along the river toward a levee. McClernand also ordered one brigade across the river.

The following morning, January 10, while the troops made their detour to surround the fort, Porter sent his ironclads up to try the range of the enemy's guns. He withdrew after a few rounds but ordered Smith to take the *Rattler* up to clear the rifle pits and force out the enemy soldiers hunkered down behind an extensive breastwork in front of the Union troops. The *Black Hawk* opened fire as well on the enemy rifle pits, and according to Porter, the rebels fled and the federal troops marched in.[24]

At 2:00 p.m. McClernand announced that he was ready to attack. Two hours later Porter informed the general that he was moving nearer the fort, but he received no reply. At 5:30 p.m. McClernand finally signaled Porter that he was ready to commence his assault. Just before sunset the admiral, expecting the troops to advance, ordered the ironclads *De Kalb, Louisville,* and *Cincinnati* to move to within 400 yards of Fort Hindman and open fire on the fort.[25]

For two hours the gunboats exchanged fire with the fort's gunners, and Porter brought the light-draft gunboats, as well as the *Lexington* and *Black Hawk,* to join in the engagement. Breese ordered the *Black Hawk* to throw in shrapnel and rifle fire, which proved very destructive, "killing nearly all the artillery horses in and about the fort."[26]

The officers and crew of the *Cincinnati* also participated in the attack. "We reached there one Saturday afternoon about half past five and began an attack," Kemp recalled. "We steamed close up to the battery, and bullets as well as shells fell about us like hail. We fought until it was dark so we couldn't tell where the battery was, except by the flash from their guns." Kemp reported that the *Cincinnati* was struck several times. "Once on the forecastle, tearing up a portion of the timbers and bursting in the port. Another struck the hammock netting, going through a ventilator, then on through our smoke stack, and down through the cook's galley, knocking down a slush barrel and spilling grease over the deck, then through the hawser box, and across to the other hammock netting and out to the bank. No one was hurt on our boat."[27]

When the battery had been pretty well silenced, Porter ordered Smith to take the *Rattler* past the fort to enfilade the rebels. Unfortunately for Smith, the fort's guns were not silenced, and they raked his vessel. "All his cabin works were knocked to pieces, and a heavy shell raked him from stem to stern in the hull." The *Rattler* made it past Fort Hindman but became ensnared in snags, forcing Smith to retire. McClernand never attacked. Once darkness fell, Porter took his vessels downriver and tied up to the bank for the night.[28]

That evening, Churchill, the Arkansas Post commander, asked his superior for reinforcements. However, he was told to "hold out til help arrived or until all dead."[29]

Sunday, January 11, dawned clear and pleasant. McClernand sent a message to Porter, requesting that the gunboats shell the rebel works to support an advance by Sherman's troops. Porter suggested that the general place some artillery along the riverbank, and McClernand agreed. Then about noon he told the admiral, "Please advance to the attack immediately."[30]

Porter's ironclads *Baron De Kalb, Cincinnati,* and *Louisville* moved up, followed by the light drafts. Ellet's ram remained to protect the rear. "This morning we heard firing at the battery. ½ past 1 received orders to move up," the *De Kalb*'s Davis wrote. "At 1 oc. got within 150 yds of the batteries and opened fire. It was returned. We have fought them for 4 hours to day. Our Army on the bank, and the Baron DeKalb (ahead) Louisville and Cincinnati on the river. It has been a most desperate fight. A harder fought battle than Fort Donaldson according to the strength of force & c."[31]

In his reminiscences, Kemp described the *Cincinnati*'s duel with the rebel batteries: "Next afternoon about one o'clock, we again opened fire on the battery, and the fight raged fiercely until about 4:30 o'clock. The guerillas kept up a continual fight, trying to pick off our men. The Tinclads in our rear kept pouring in shells and doing their best to help and look after the guerillas." Kemp noted that the *Louisville* was on fire at one point, "but the fire was soon put out. Our boat was again struck a number of times. Two shots struck our bow casemate, making a couple of dents in the iron plating. Another struck the Pilot house, making a dent through the Wheel house, through the Ward Room into the Captain's cabin, and lodged into the casemate. Not a man on the 'Cincinnati' was hurt, although shot and shell were flying all around us." Then he added, "We gave much credit to the way our Pilot handled our boat, as he kept her bow on the batteries during the whole fight."[32]

In his official report, George Bache, the *Cincinnati*'s commanding officer, confirmed Kemp's observations. Although it had been struck nine times on the bow, casemate, pilothouse, and upper works, the *Cincinnati* suffered no serious damage. Porter and Bache both attributed this to the application of a tallow coating to the vessels' iron plating, pilothouses, and casemates prior to the action. "The *Cincinnati* was struck eight times on her pilothouse with IX-inch shells, which glanced off like peas against glass," Porter noted. Of all the ironclads engaged, only the *De Kalb* suffered a broken casemate in three hours of "continuous hammering."[33]

The *Louisville* sustained six direct hits—one through the starboard side aft of its No. 2 gun, and one on the port side amidships, which exploded on the spar deck. Another struck the captain's gig, carrying away light iron, and the officers' quarters on the spar deck. One went through the smokestack, and two others struck light work on the spar deck. According to Kemp's memory, "One young man, I think he was from the Louisville, was so crazed with fear during the fight that when their boat was alongside of ours, he jumped on board our boat and ran back and hid in the Captain's cabin."[34]

When Porter received word that McClernand's men were retreating, he took the *Black Hawk* past the fort to land on the opposite bank and deposit a regiment of troops on shore to make another assault on the fort. Porter had also sent Ellet with the *Monarch, Rattler,* and *Glide* to open a cross fire. "Just before the surrender of the enemy," Ellet wrote, "I received orders to pass the fort, and cut off the retreat of the enemy. This was done, and I kept on up the river for 12 miles—the water then being so shallow as to render it impossible to proceed farther. The *Monarch* got aground four times as it was." Ellet then had to return.[35]

In the meantime, by 4:00, intense fire from the federal ironclads and gunboats had forced the fort to surrender. "As the gunboats got closer up I saw their flags actually over the parapet of Fort Hindman," Sherman later wrote, "and the rebel gunners scamper out of the embrasures and run down into the ditch behind. About the time a man jumped up on the rebel parapet just where the road entered, waving a large white flag." Other smaller flags appeared, and Sherman ordered a cease-fire. When Porter scrambled ashore, a rebel soldier told him that the post commander, Colonel Dunnington, wished to surrender to the naval commander, so Porter received the fort's surrender. Churchill later insisted that he had not ordered white flags flown but was helpless to prevent it.[36]

At 4:30 the enemy surrendered, "and such cheers after cheer you never heard. All hands were piped on deck to cheer ship and we gave 9 hearty ones," Frederic Davis recalled. "The 'Louisville' cheered the 'deKalb' and the Stars and Stripes were seen floating from the Batteries. We have fought a hard fight, have gained the victory, have between 6 and 7000 prisoners. . . . The rebels were Texans and fought desparatley [*sic*]. The[y] said they never would have surrendered to the Army but the[y] surrendered to the gunboats. They hardly know what to do when 'them dam'd gunboats appear,' they say." Davis wrote to his mother: "Before we left Memphis the people (nearly all Secesh) told us that when we got to 'Arkansas Post' we would find out that we could not gain the Victory every time. The result has shown that we can gain the day, no matter what the Memphis people say, or brag." After the gunboat's engineers and men had burned buildings and destroyed railcars, they would "go down and cut into the Mississippi; and soon shall be on our way to Vicksburg, that stronghold, which will give us the hardest battle of the War. If we are, the Mississippi will be open, for I hear that Genl Banks has taken Port Hudson." When Vicksburg falls, Davis explained, "with it falls the whole South West. I pray God that we may be successful." Davis then lamented the length of the war. At that point, he had spent ten months in the navy. "Little did I think that as I traveled down Westminster St. that this cruel strife would last so long. . . . Oh! where and when will it end?" But he assured his mother that he was not disheartened. "I shall try to do my Duty to my Country, whether the war last one year or five longer. This rebellion must soon cease, the West is clamoring for her rivers to be open, she must have her commerce, the Mississippi is what she depends up on and if we do not open it soon, she will go with the South and then open it by compromise."[37]

The victory at Arkansas Post elicited glowing comments from Porter. "This was a most beautiful fight," he told Pennock in a letter written just after the engagement. "We used up the Post of Arkansas fort to-day in three hours, dismounting every gun in the fort, eleven in all, and such destruction of men, horses, and guns you never saw." In reality, the Union victory was a combined operation by both the navy and the army, but a victory nonetheless.[38]

In his memoirs, Sherman argued that Arkansas Post was a tactical success but a poor strategic choice. Grant wired Halleck that McClernand had left Vicksburg to "go on a wild goose chase"; he suspected the political general might go as far as Little Rock or even beyond. This, Grant argued, would be an attempt by McClernand to initiate an independent command in Arkansas, not to mention a serious distraction from his campaign against Vicksburg. A fort forty miles inland did not threaten control of the Mississippi River.[39]

Although he had expected to go ashore the next day and see the fort, Kemp never had the opportunity. "Those of the Starboard watch, who had been ashore in the morning, said that the battlefield where our men had been fighting presented some horrible sights. Most of the dead were shot through the head, others had their breasts shot away. We had taken about 7, 000 prisoners. Both sides suffered terribly. I do not know how many were killed and wounded, but it was supposed our loss was the greater." McClernand's casualty list, in fact, included 129 men killed, 831 wounded, and 17 missing; Porter's had 31 killed and wounded. The Confederates lost about 200 men and had 4,791 taken prisoner. According to Kemp, the rebel prisoners "told us if it hadn't been for our gunboats they could have held out against fifty thousand men. They claimed the Cincinnati did them more damage than all the rest as one of our shots went through a port hole of the fort, knocking their gun to pieces and killing every man upon it."[40]

Porter ordered the *New Era* to take the wounded from the *De Kalb* and *Cincinnati* and carry them to the hospital ship at the mouth of the White River. Meanwhile, the prisoners were taken up the river to Cairo. After three days spent destroying the enemy fortifications and sorting through booty, the federals retired downriver and anchored off Napoleon. McClernand then gave his men leave to go ashore and celebrate their victory. The jubilant bluecoats evidently went berserk and burned half the town.[41]

Following the seizure of Arkansas Post, Porter sent federal gunboats to operate on the White River. Under the command of Walker, the *Baron De Kalb* and *Cincinnati* left Arkansas Post on January 12 and proceeded to the White River to cooperate with General Gorman's army troops in a movement to "clean out" St. Charles. Porter sent the little *Romeo,* with Acting Ensign R. B. Smith commanding, up to Walker with coal and thirty boxes of ammunition. The gunboats and transports bearing Gorman's soldiers reached St. Charles a couple of days later. For two days, a heavy rain fell and then turned to snow. "My! but it was cold, and as the snow was several inches thick on our deck, we poor wretches had to clean it off," Kemp recalled. "We were wishing we were back on the Yazoo River, away from this dreary lonesome cold White River." They had expected a hard fight at Fort St. Charles but "found that the rebels had skeddadled and found our own troops occupying the place, as they got there before we did. They burned nearly all the houses in the vicinity." The rebels did, however, carry off two 8-inch guns in an army transport named the *Blue Wing,* and Porter sent two light-draft gunboats to Walker in the hope of pursuing it. Porter then ordered Walker to push up the White River with a detachment of troops. "Get information from the negroes on the plantations as to where the *Blue Wing* has gone," he instructed him. Walker diligently pushed up the river in the *Baron De Kalb,* accompanied by the *Forest Rose* and *Romeo* and a transport carrying troops. They captured Devall's Bluff, along with two 8-inch guns with carriages and ammunition.[42]

In the meantime, Grant had decided to focus yet again on taking the Confederate stronghold at Vicksburg. Porter concurred that Vicksburg had to be the main Union objective, but to support the operation, he needed to recall his gunboats from their various missions on the White, Ohio, Tennessee, and Cumberland Rivers. Consequently, on January 19 Porter ordered Walker to wind up his operations on the White River. Leaving his gunboats there would be a "waste of time and money" and against the Navy Department's instructions to follow General Gorman's army down the river, Porter explained. In a report to Secretary Welles, the admiral praised Walker's efforts. "He performed the duty I sent him on much to my satisfaction, and deserves all the credit for the capture of the guns, other rebel property, and rebel prisoners."[43]

Porter's orders brought Walker's boats back down the White River to the Mississippi. Teenaged sailor Yost, having survived the sinking of the *Cairo* in December, had joined the crew of the *Forest Rose*. In company with the *Magnolia*, the *Forest Rose* passed the gunboat *Tyler* and nine troop transports. "At 7 P.M. arrived at the mouth of the Yazoo where we found a large fleet of transports and gunboats," Yost wrote in his journal on January 28, 1863. The following morning the men of the *Forest Rose* heard the sound of heavy firing coming from the direction of Vicksburg. "It is the mortars shelling the city," Yost noted.[44]

13

The Steele's Bayou Expedition

The Army is not equal to the occasion. It rests with the Naval Adml.
to reduce Vicksburg; if he cannot succeed in the scheme he has
entered upon, there is no hope of success from any other quarter.
—Nimian Pinckney

On January 30, 1863, the *Forest Rose* met the gunboat *Carondelet,* which had recently experienced a change of command. In early September 1862 Walke had asked to be considered an applicant for the command of one of the two rams being built at St Louis. Months later, Walke learned that he had been assigned to command the new gunboat USS *Lafayette.*[1]

"The 'Lafayette' was over two hundred and eighty feet long, and about forty feet beam," Walke recalled, "with a heavy sharp, iron prow or ram. Her armament consisted of two 11-inch Dahlgren bow guns, four 9-inch broadside guns, two 24-pounder howitzers, and two 100-pounder Parrott rifled stern guns." The *Lafayette* was a side-wheel steamer, Walke wrote, "but floated so deep that her guards were in the water, obstructing her speed, and rendering her almost unmanageable when she started down the river. Her speed afterwards increased very much by lightening her and cutting away some of the wheel guards."[2]

In his diary entry for January 18, Morison, the *Carondelet*'s coxswain, described his reaction to the news of Walke's appointment. "About 5½ this morning I was awakened by the captain's steward, having been sent for by the capt. I turned out double quick and went into the cabin. The captain informed me that he had been ordered to Cairo to take charge of the new gunboat 'Lafayette' and he wanted to know if I would go with him. I told

211

him I would be very glad to [go] with him. So he told me to pack up my things and be ready to go on board the mosquito boat, 'New Era' which was lying ashore of us."[3]

Walke also brought his clerk, Thomas Lyons, to the *Lafayette.* Lyons wrote in his diary on January 18: "8 o.c. AM we are all packed and on board of the 'New Era.' Officers of the 'Carondelet' mustered on the quarterdeck to bid Captain Walke good bye. The squad of Marines was drawn up in line on the fan-tail of the Gunboat to present arms, while Drumsticks beat the retreat." According to Morison, "There were five of us come with the captain—namely, John Ford, Terry P. Robinson, Maurice Phillips, Benjamin Holmes and myself." After helping to pack, Morison wrote, "At 8 A.M., all being ready, we went aboard and we were soon after underweigh for Cairo." Lyons noted, "As we shoved off, our friends on board of the 'Carondelet' gave us three cheers." The *New Era* went upriver, stopped to take on coal at Columbus, arrived at Cairo at 8:30 p.m., and made fast alongside the steamer *General Sterling Price.*[4]

January 20 dawned foggy and cloudy, but at first light, Lyons could see his new ship, "the new Iron-clad U.S. Steamer Ram and Gunboat 'Lafayette' lying at anchor near our port bow." Morison elaborated, "All our traps were placed on board and about 11 a.m. we went on board of the 'Lafayette.'" He found the new gunboat less than shipshape. "Everything was in the utmost confusion on board of her and four only of her eight guns being mounted. Got a fire started in the cabin. The captain got disgusted at the appearance of things and left for shore." Morison discovered about thirty men on board. "We made ourselves as comfortable as the circumstances would admit," he noted. In the evening he wrote a letter to his wife and went to bed at about 10:00. "I turned in on the cabin floor as it was the best place to be had."[5]

On Thursday, Walke returned and went over to the receiving ship *Clara Dolsen* "to get a few men if possible so that he could get a boat's crew as there were not enough men on board that knew how to pull an oar to man his gig," the coxswain noted. Manning new vessels continued to be a challenge for the Union navy, and Morison's diary provides valuable details about the manpower available to officers in early 1863. "Picked out twenty-five men, most of them being of our old crew which we left behind us in the hospital last fall," he wrote. When Morison went over to get them, however, only ten were allowed to go. Several days later the *Lafayette* went alongside the *Clara Dolsen* so Walke could look over a draft of new men from New

York. "Found most of them all boys. All are landsmen," Morison explained. Walke selected a hundred of the men, and the new gunboat also received thirty men from the USS *Eastport*.[6]

In April 1863 Ensign Elias Smith described the *Lafayette*'s officers, who hailed from various parts of the country. "Captain Walke is a post captain in the regular Navy, and won great credit by his conduct at Island 10, in command of the 'Carondelet.' The first lieutenant, or executive officer, Edward Morgan, is from St. Louis, and a very capable officer. The surgeon, Dr. Beauchamp, one of the ablest in the flotilla, is a western man." The *Lafayette*'s paymaster, he wrote, was "Mr. Jas P. Kelly, son of the well-known rector of St. Bartholomew's church in New York, but now of Chicago." The paymaster looked after the pecuniary interests of the officers and crew and "is observedly one of the most popular officers on board." The new ironclad's ensigns were, with one exception, from the East Coast. In addition, Smith noted that the ship had eight master mates, all from the West and Pennsylvania. Several had served in the army.[7]

As January drew to a close, the weather continued cold, and on February 4 a heavy snow fell. The *Lafayette*'s crew was anxious to complete fitting out and have the new gunboat put into commission, but the stern ports were found to be too small, so new ones had to be cut, "which will delay us some days yet," Morison wrote. Finally, on February 27, "the officers and crew all being on board, the 'Lafayette' was placed in commission." A final draft of seventy-five men had been taken aboard the previous day from the receiving ship.[8]

On the first day of March the *Lafayette* weighed anchor. The crew went to quarters, and Walke held worship services, read the Articles of War, and held a general muster of hands. The newly commissioned ironclad then steamed downriver. Accompanying them on the journey was McLeod Murphy, the new captain of the *Carondelet,* and two new 9-inch guns for his ship.[9]

On the way downriver they met the *V. F. Wilson* above Memphis, and Walke received Porter's orders to proceed immediately to the Yazoo. On March 3 the *Lafayette* arrived at the mouth of the Yazoo River, four days down from Cairo, where the gunboat's arrival must have provoked some comment. "The *Lafayette* is one of our newer style of gunboats," Daniel Kemp explained, "with an immense ram on her bow. A very formidable gunboat, and different entirely from the turtle-shaped boats like the *Cincinnati* and others."[10]

At the mouth of the Yazoo the *Lafayette* received some twenty soldiers from a broken-up Illinois regiment. The crew delivered the *Carondelet*'s two new guns and began moving *Lafayette*'s own two Parrott guns aft. Newly commissioned, the *Lafayette* was still in the shakedown phase, giving the ship's coxswain plenty of work. Although feeling ill, Morison wrote, "Had considerable boating to do, practising the crew."[11]

On March 9 Porter and Sherman arrived on board at about 11:30. The *Lafayette* backed out into the Mississippi; after dinner it backed down below the Williams Canal and came to. "All hands were beat to quarters and we opened fire on Vicksburg with our rifled Parrotts and fired eleven shots without eliciting a reply. We then left for the Yazoo again." At about 7:00 p.m., while passing the *Louisville,* Morison "noticed that they had a sham gunboat made for the purpose of sending down past the rebel batteries." Later that night the sound of a gun roused Morison from sleep. He went on deck to find it intensely dark and raining heavily. "About 1½ A.M.— bang—went a gun from Vicksburg and we knew that the 'Dumby' [the sham gunboat] was drifting past the batteries. Bang, went another, and so it was kept up until they fired ninety three shots. All hands slept on their arms all night to be ready in case of an emergency as a large bright light was seen up the river."[12]

This first sham gunboat was followed by a second. Walke reported, "Night before last I sent off another terrific monster, a perfect imitation of our 'Lafayette,' which latter vessel dropped down towards the turn of the river in the afternoon, and shelled the fortifications with a few 100-pounders." At 11:00 the "dummy namesake made her appearance before the batteries, belching out huge volumes of smoke through her beef-barrel chimneys, and the way the rebels peppered her was a caution to all dummies." Porter claimed the "little artillery sport must have cost the rebels a thousand charges of powder and the bursting and dismounting of five or six guns."[13]

The city of Vicksburg, as strongly fortified as ever, remained a thorn in the Union navy's side, blocking free passage up and down the Mississippi River. Grant had taken personal command of army operations against Vicksburg in January, but by then, high water and flooding had made approaching the city from the Mississippi River side virtually impossible. Unwilling to pull his forces back to Memphis and attack Vicksburg from the east, Grant chose instead to order water passages cut around Vicksburg and the city's formidable gun batteries. When this proved impractical, Grant turned to the intricate network of bayous and lakes that flowed into the Mississippi River. One natural passage in particular, from the Mississippi into the Yazoo River above Vicksburg, caught Porter's attention.[14]

In a letter to his wife Mary, fleet surgeon Nimian Pinckney described Porter's plan: "The object of the Admiral is to pass into the Yazoo above Haynes' Bluff. Here there is a heavy fortified point to pass. This bluff is seven miles from Vicksburg and in its rear. This once taken, Vicksburg must of necessity fall." To seize this fortification, "the adml has devised a plan by which he can get above the battery, without having to pass in front of it to thereby be exposed to its galling fire." The admiral and his ironclads would enter Steele's Bayou, pass into Deer Creek, and then into the Yazoo above the Haynes' Bluff battery. "If he succeeds in getting his vessels this far, he can attack the fortification so doubtless will take it." The water in these bayous was very shallow, Pinckney told his wife, and only small vessels of very light draft had passed through them. "The Confederate never dreamed of an attack in this way." Porter's plan entailed risks, Pinckney explained, for "if the river falls before he can reduce the fort, he will be caught in a complete net. No supplies could reach him. He is a shrewd man so no doubt has considered carefully all the difficulties. If this fails, there is no probability of the fall of Vicksburg; for it is enormously fortified & heavily garrisoned." Pinckney opined, "The Army is not equal to the occasion. It rests with the Naval Adml. to reduce Vicksburg; if he cannot succeed in the scheme he has entered upon, there is no hope of success from any other quarter."[15]

At the time, Porter had five of the 512-ton city-class ironclad gunboats available to him for a joint expedition: *Cincinnati, Louisville, Mound City, Pittsburg,* and *Carondelet.* In his memoirs, Porter explained the suitability of the city-class gunboats: "The ironclads drew only seven feet of water and had not masts or yards to encumber them, and but little about their decks that could be swept away by the bushes or lower branches of the trees."[16]

Before implementing the plan, Porter and Grant went about thirty miles up Steele's Bayou and found the route practical. However, Black Bayou was far less so, until "on further examination we found that by removing the trees we could heave the vessels around the bends, which were very short and left us not a foot to spare."[17] Grant approved Porter's plan and ordered Sherman to make a reconnaissance with the gunboats to ascertain the possibility of "a landing with troops on high ground on the east bank of the Yazoo, and from there to attack Haynes' Bluff."[18]

Reluctant to trust the success of the expedition to subordinates, Porter wisely chose to go himself. He obtained a pilot who was well acquainted with the country, and on March 14, 1863, he set out with the *Louisville, Cincinnati, Mound City, Carondelet, Pittsburg,* and four tugs towing mortar boats. A cutter manned and armed under the command of Ensign Bryant of the *Lafayette* and acting engineer Caven preceded them into Steele's Bayou.[19]

"It was all very pleasant at first, skimming along over summer seas, under the shade of stalwart oaks, but we had no conception of what we had before us," Porter recalled. "We had succeeded in getting well into the heart of the country before we were discovered. No one would believe that anything in the shape of a vessel could get through Black Bayou, or anywhere on the route." As they "molested no one, the inhabitants looked on in wonder and astonishment, and the negroes flocked in hundreds down the banks of the creek, to see the novel sight."[20]

The following day, under cloudy skies, the squadron continued up the bayou. In a journal he kept, an officer on the *Cincinnati* described their journey: "Sunday, March 15: At 9:30 a.m. entered among the willows in Steele's Bayou. The bottoms on both sides are inundated a long distance. Our decks are covered with limbs broken from trees by the pressure of our boats crushing their way along." At 11:00 a.m. a tug went ahead, and they began cutting away timber with axes. An hour and a half later they entered Muddy Bayou, a wider and freer stream edged with trees covered with Spanish moss. "We have made 28 miles to-day and are within 3½ miles of Black Bayou."[21]

At 11:00 the next morning Porter boarded the *Carondelet,* and they continued up Black Bayou, cutting through heavy timber. "The expedition went along finely until it reached Black Bayou," Porter noted. When they came to the passage leading into Deer Creek, however, "the crews of the vessels had to go to work to clear the way, pulling up trees by the roots or pushing them over with the ironclads, and cutting away branches above. It was terrible work, but in twenty four hours we succeeded in getting through these four miles and found ourselves in Deer Creek, where we were told there would be no more difficulties." Porter pushed on and was soon inside the bayou. "It was exactly forty-six feet wide. My vessel was forty-two feet wide, and that was the average width of the others."[22]

Earlier, Porter had asked Grant for at least 3,000 troops to hold his position. "If the enemy should throw in troops, they could stop our work and put us in a pretty tight place," he explained. "Please send them [the troops] at once, if with only one day's ration." In fact, Grant had already sent troops, and he quickly ordered Sherman to ascend Steele's Bayou with the steamers *Silver Lake* and *Diligent* and find the gunboats. Sherman was then instructed to go into the Yazoo to determine the feasibility of finding a route to get the army to the east bank of the river for an attack on Vicksburg.[23]

Following Grant's orders, Sherman sent Lieutenant Colonel David C. Coleman with a detail of fifty men up to Steele's Bayou in the *Diligent.* Sherman vowed to follow and to stay in communication with Coleman.[24] As promised, Sherman found Porter's ironclads just before they reached Deer Creek. Sherman knew every bayou and stream and warned the admiral, "You think it's all very fine just now, don't you; but, before you fellows get through, you won't have a smokestack or a boat among you." The general agreed to hold the position at Deer Creek, adding that he did not expect the rebels at Haynes' Bluff to do more than send out a scouting force. As Porter later explained, their intention was to advance together for mutual support: "we to transport him across the rivers and marshes, he to keep off sharp-shooters, whom we could not reach with our guns on account of the high banks."[25]

That same day the *Cincinnati* came up. "We entered Black Bayou at half past 6; found the water very black, and that we had literally to cut our way through about the same variety of timber, but of much more dense growth," an officer noted in his journal. "We are knocking down trees (by the concussion of the boat simply) which are 2 feet in diameter." Local African Americans told them that the rebels had seen smoke from the gunboats' chimneys and fled the day before, "leaving all their negroes and most of their valuables. The negroes say the whites had no idea of our coming." Early on March 17 the *Cincinnati* resumed its journey down the bayou, "making but slow progress."[26]

In his recollections of the war, Kemp wrote: "At one plantation, some distance off, a large fire was burning, showing us that the Rebels were burning their cotton to keep it from falling into our hands." When clouds of smoke appeared, Porter, now on board the *Cincinnati,* saw that cotton bales stacked on the levees had been set on fire. "Suddenly I saw two men rush up from each side of the bayou and apply a lighted pine-knot to each pile," Porter remembered. When an officer asked Porter if he should fire a howitzer shell at the arsonists to drive them away, the admiral replied, "No, that might kill them, and we don't want to do that except in battle."[27]

Porter ordered his vessels ahead through the smoke and fire. Porter, Bache, and the wheelman remained on the *Cincinnati*'s deck, but the heat was so intense that Porter jumped inside a small house covered with iron. Bache followed, and "the helmsman covered himself up with an old flag that lay in the wheel-house. The hose was pointed up the hatch to the upper deck and everything drenched with water, but it did not render the heat less intolerable." From the banks they heard "a yell from the negroes . . . who looked on with amazement at the doings of Mas' Linkum's gun-boats."[28]

By sunset, Porter's little flotilla had gone eight miles. That night the gunboat tied up to a bank, allowing the men to get some rest. At about 8:00 Porter heard the sound of chopping wood in the forest. This puzzled him, because they had seen no one along the stream. Determined to discover the source, Porter ordered Lieutenant Murphy to board the tug with a 12-pound howitzer and "see what was going on." The sound of howitzer fire followed by three blasts from the tug's whistle told the admiral the situation was under control. When Murphy returned, he reported that he "had suddenly come upon a large body of negroes under the charge of some white men carrying lanterns, cutting trees on the banks of the stream we were in." They had felled a tree measuring three feet in diameter, which had fallen across the bayou, "closing the stream completely against our advance." After his men cleared the channel, Porter told Murphy, "Go ahead with all the speed you have, and see that no more trees are cut down tonight." The admiral had little or no sympathy for anyone who opposed his operations, and he told Murphy that although he would be sorry to harm "that faithful friend and brother, the contraband, if he continues to chop at any one's dictates, you must give him shrapnel."[29]

Meanwhile, the *Carondelet* had gone on ahead and spent the night at Watson's lower plantation. Early the next morning, March 18, Porter came on board, and the gunboat made "good headway" up Deer Creek until about 8:00 that night, when the crew came upon felled trees obstructing the creek.[30]

"March 18, 1863 still found us battling our way through the woods knocking down trees pulling down bridges and in fact everything else that came in our way," the *Cincinnati*'s Kemp recalled. Happily for the gunboat's exhausted crewmen, local African Americans offered fresh provisions. As the *Cincinnati* passed Dr. Moore's large plantation, "the negroes had turkeys and chickens to sell, at $4 each for the former and 50 cents for the latter. Our boys traded with them tobacco at $20 per pound." Hard times must have befallen the white plantation owners along the bayou, for the slaves seemed desperate for certain items, including biscuits and tobacco. "During the morning the negroes followed us for miles, begging for biscuit and tobacco, which they eagerly eat, even when they had to pick it out of the backwater," an officer on the *Cincinnati* wrote. Clearly, the Union blockade of the southern coast was finally having an effect on imports and finances in Mississippi. Harsh conditions often prompted slaves to flee their masters, as did fear of being conscripted as laborers for the Confederacy; however, most slaves sought sanctuary on Union gunboats simply because they wanted to be free. Their desire to escape bondage could be intense, as the *Cincinnati*'s experience in the bayous shows. "We passed Williams' plantation and reached George Messenger's, where we took 12 negroes, who parted with their relatives and friends without a tear, others begging to be taken also." Not surprisingly, the slaves' owner sent for them. "At 5 o'clock a negro driver rode up to the vicinity of the ship and claimed four of the African Americans on the ship be returned to him. Our captain told him to get a written order from the admiral for them." Later in his journal the officer wrote, "The negro driver returned this morning, when we were at Woolfolks (having passed Butler's), and saw the admiral, but failed to get his men."[31]

Late on Thursday, March 19, as the gunboats neared Rolling Fork, Porter observed smoke. Fearing that the rebels might be advancing, he signaled Murphy to take the tug and reconnoiter. Spotting some old Indian mounds that would make good observations posts, Murphy went back to the admiral and suggested they send sailors to occupy one of them. Porter reluctantly agreed, and Murphy shoved off with 300 men and two howitzers.[32] Early the next morning a party from the *Carondelet* took possession of the Indian mound. As Kemp wrote, "Our men stationed themselves on a mound (supposed to be thrown up by the Indians) about a mile from where our gunboats were located, near a bridge a short distance ahead of the mound."[33] While the sailors got in position, rebel sharpshooters kept up a steady harassing fire on the federal gunboats from the right bank of the bayou. Four men on the *Carondelet*—assistant engineer Huff, seaman Thomas Graham, S. P. Strunk, and a marine—were hit by enemy fire. Then, to everyone's relief, at 2:45 p.m. the gunboat's crew saw the welcome sight of Colonel Smith and forward units of the 8th Missouri coming up the bank.[34]

At 3:00 that morning, a black messenger sent by Porter had reached Sherman, who ordered Smith and 800 men up to support the navy. Smith had set out at daybreak "with a negro guide. We had proceeded about 6 miles when we found the enemy had been very busy felling trees to obstruct the creek," Smith wrote in his official report. "I ordered all able-bodied negroes to be taken along, and warned some of the principal inhabitants that they would be held responsible for any more obstructions being placed along the creek." Smith reached the admiral at about 4:00 p.m., unopposed except for a skirmish between the rebels and his advance guard, during which one man was wounded and another killed. "I found the fleet obstructed by fallen trees and in the rear by a sunken coal-barge," he wrote. A large rebel force supplied with artillery was out of range of the admiral's guns, but according to Smith, "Every tree and stump covered a sharp-shooter, ready to pick off any luckless marine who showed his head above decks, and entirely preventing working parties from removing obstructions."[35]

In the meantime, Murphy and his sailors had been keeping a vigil on the Indian mound. Then, Kemp recalled, "About 5 o'clock P.M. the Rebels opened a heavy fire of shell and grape from seven pieces of artillery which they had stationed in the woods. As soon as the Rebels commenced to fire, our men commenced to run. I have heard of the retreat from Bull Run, but the retreat from the mound on Green Creek beats anything I ever knew anything about." The sailors left their muskets and cartridge boxes behind, and each man "ran like deer for his boat." To the *Cincinnati* sailors' credit, Kemp wrote, they were the last to leave the mound and left not one musket behind. From the *Carondelet,* Porter watched as the Union officers and men tumbled down the mound. The admiral later called it a "regular stampede."[36]

With the rebels harassing them, Porter realized that the best course of action was retreat. "The game was up, and we bumped on homeward," he wrote. After a quiet night, at 4:00 a.m. on March 22 the *Carondelet* began backing down Deer Creek. In a sharp contest between the rebel sharpshooters and the federal infantry on shore, the gunboat fired several "effective shots at the retreating enemy." The Pook turtle then resumed backing down the creek in the rain.[37]

The *Cincinnati* headed downstream as well. Assisted by the sailors, Smith's 8th Missourians got to work on the obstructions and had cleared the channel by 10:30 p.m., allowing Porter's vessels to continue their journey downstream, accompanied by the troops on the bank. The admiral went on ahead to the Yazoo. A steady rain fell, but the rebels did not annoy the *Cincinnati*. Obstructions slowed its progress, but by evening, the gunboat had reached Colonel Hunt's plantation, seven miles above Black Bayou.

On March 24 the *Carondelet* resumed its journey downstream, stopping at Foster's plantation at 8:00 a.m. to take aboard 125 sick soldiers from Sherman's brigade. That day the *Cincinnati* picked up a few of Sherman's ill and exhausted men as well. Other soldiers were covered with cotton stuck to their hair and clothes. They had spent the night in a cotton gin. Given that two of its men had been wounded by enemy fire, it is no surprise that the *Cincinnati*'s captain ordered his crew to burn buildings on Moore's plantation. By 1863, retaliating against those who had fired on federal vessels had become a common navy tactic.[38]

"The rebels follow and shoot at us," an officer from the *Cincinnati* confided in his journal on March 24. "The negroes, too, are following closer to us than the whites, and they form a motley group indeed, of all ages and sexes, the male, the halt, and the blind, as well as the stalwart and active." They are in all kinds of vehicles "and on horses, mules, and afoot, in high glee—'going to freedom, sure,' they say. Their antics and expressions are most amusing. Some shout to the animals they are driving, 'Go, 'long, dar old fool, hoss, dont know nothing; your's gwine to freedom, too.'"[39]

The *Carondelet* spent the night at the mouth of Black Bayou. The next morning, which was cool and dry, it moved down to Hill's on Black Bayou. The *Cincinnati* also continued its journey. "Thursday, March 26: A cool, clear night, the men slept on the gun decks, with the ports open, and got a good night's rest. One soldier died on board and was buried. At 9 a.m. the soldiers embarked on the gunboats. The negroes are bringing on board cotton in sacks." Making good headway, the *Cincinnati* passed Muddy Bayou at 9:30 a.m., entered the Yazoo at 4:10 p.m., and arrived at the mouth of the Yazoo at 5:30 p.m. on Friday, March 27. Concluding his chronicle of the Steele's Bayou expedition, the gunboat's officer wrote, "The *Cincinnati* has had her usual fortune—more unlucky in the damages received by the ship, and very lucky as to the amount of injuries received by her crew."[40]

In his report on the Steele's Bayou expedition, Porter tried to cast the operation in a positive light: "We destroyed a large amount of Confederate corn and captured a large number of mules, horses, and cattle. The rebels themselves burnt over 20,000 bales of cotton, and we burned all that we found marked 'C.S.A.' having taken on our deck and on mortar boats enough to pay for the building of a good gunboat." Had they succeeded, the admiral explained, "it would have dealt a severe blow to this part of the country, but it was not to be, and we must console ourselves with the damage we did the enemy and the morale effect of penetrating into a country deemed inaccessible. There will be no more planting in these regions for a long time to come. The able-bodied negroes left with our army, carrying with them all the stores laid up by their masters—for whom they showed little affection—for harder times."[41]

14

The Yazoo Pass Expedition of 1863

There were difficulties in the why of an assault, but whether they were sufficient to stop the troops when the fort was silenced I am unable to say.

—David Dixon Porter

While Porter was struggling to extract his gunboats from the bayous, Farragut's squadron had been ascending the Mississippi River toward Vicksburg. However, Confederate fortifications at Port Hudson hindered his passage upstream. Having control of the stretch of the Mississippi from Vicksburg south to Port Hudson allowed the rebel steamboats to bring cattle, provisions, and ammunition down the Red River to landings on the east bank. Hoping to damage one of the rebels' supply vessels, Porter ordered Colonel Charles Ellet on January 31, 1863, to take the *Queen of the West* down past the Vicksburg batteries and ram one of the large steamers unloading stores. He warned Ellet that the enemy had a potentially dangerous armored vessel on the river, the CSS *Webb,* and wrote, "if you get a first crack at her, you will sink her, and if she gets the first crack at you, she will sink you." Ellet obeyed the admiral's order with his usual élan, but the strong currents dashed his attempt to butt the rebel steamer *City of Vicksburg.* Harassed by fire from the Vicksburg batteries, Ellet decided to steam below the Confederate stronghold to the mouth of the Red River. On a ten-day spree, *Queen of the West* captured and then burned three steamers and destroyed quantities of cotton near the mouth of the Red River.[1]

Pleased by the *Queen's* success at passing the rebel batteries, Porter decided to risk sending an ironclad to assist in blockading the Red River. He

223

chose the *Indianola,* with Lieutenant Commander George Brown commanding. A recent addition to the squadron, the *Indianola* boasted two powerful 11-inch Dahlgren rifles and two 9-inch Dahlgren smoothbores. On February 13 Brown took the new ironclad down past Vicksburg to join the *Queen of the West.*

In the meantime, Ellet had gone up the Red River to attack an enemy battery at Fort De Russey, snagging the Confederates' *New Era No. 5* on his way up. Just short of the fortification, however, the *Queen* was driven aground by a disloyal pilot. Confederate gunners opened fire on the ram, compelling Ellet and his crew to abandon ship. They floated downstream on cotton bales and were rescued by the *De Soto.* Ellet then took command of the *New Era No. 5* and went down the Red River to the Mississippi. To Ellet's relief, not far from Natchez they met the *Indianola.* Together they chugged downstream, briefly encountering the CSS *Webb* in a thick fog. Porter had received no reports about the *Queen of the West*'s grounding, nor had he heard from the *Indianola.* On February 18 Ellet reported to Porter onboard the *Black Hawk.*[2]

When the admiral learned that *Queen of the West* had been seized by the Confederates, he called a conference of his officers. The ram's loss put the *Indianola* in jeopardy, but he had no suitable ironclad that he could send to aid the vessel. Porter decided to dispatch a fake monitor to threaten the rebels—the "Dumby" seen by George Yost and others. The trick worked superbly. The rebel gunboats panicked at the fake monitor's approach, getting under way in a hurry and abandoning salvage work on the *Indianola,* which had been captured below Grand Gulf by three rebel steamers—the hastily repaired *Queen of the West,* the *Webb,* and the *Dr. Beatty.* The old *Queen,* now in rebel hands, had opened fire on the *Indianola,* which was encumbered by two coal barges. Brown reversed his engines and foiled an attempt to ram him, but the *Webb* closed in, butting the *Indianola*'s bow. The Yankee gunners kept up a steady fire with the 11-inch bow guns. It proved a valiant but futile effort as both rebel boats struck repeated blows at the *Indianola*'s wheels and stern quarters, opening a gaping hole in the stern. Brown managed to nudge his sinking vessel onto the Louisiana shore, but when threatened with a boarding party from the *Dr. Beatty,* Brown surrendered, and the rebels captured almost the entire crew. The Confederate commander, Major Joseph L. Brent, put a prize master aboard the federal ironclad, had it towed to the eastern riverbank, and ordered a salvage crew to save the vessel. The following day, the rebels blew up the captured ironclad. "The fate of the *Indianola* was even more disgraceful than farcical," crowed the *Richmond Examiner*. "Here was perhaps the finest ironclad in western waters, captured after a heroic struggle, rapidly repaired, and destined to join the *Queen of the West* in a series of victories." But, the paper lamented, it had been blown up because a flatboat or mud scow "floated down the river, before the frightened eyes of the Partisan Rangers."[3]

Porter first heard about the *Indianola*'s fate on February 27, when a black coal passer from the vessel reported that the *Indianola* had been attacked and captured by the Confederates. Thus ended Porter's attempt to gain control of the river between Vicksburg and Port Hudson.[4]

Porter had now made three separate attempts to secure free passage of the Mississippi River. Just prior to the Steele's Bayou expedition, Porter's gunboats had ventured into the Yazoo Pass in yet another attempt, this one prompted by Grant's determination to outflank the Confederate stronghold at Vicksburg.

To pave the way for the proposed Yazoo Pass expedition, on Monday, February 1, the little 260-ton *Forest Rose* went downriver to a plantation and "destroyed all the skiffs and canoes that were there," Yost noted in his diary. The stern-wheeler then proceeded to the mouth of the Yazoo Pass, where commanding officer George W. Brown and Grant's engineer, Lieutenant Colonel J. H. Wilson, examined the area. In the 1850s a flood-control levee had been erected over the canal entrance to the pass, about six miles below Helena, and according to Yost, "The troops went to work cutting the levee." On February 3 Brown took powder, buried it under the levee between the ditches, and blew it up. "This loosened the dirt so that the water ran through at a terrible rate. It has 9 feet fall," Yost noted. By 11:00 p.m. an opening some forty yards wide had been made, "with the water pouring through like nothing else I ever saw except Niagara Falls," Wilson wrote. Wilson considered the work a perfect success, but it took weeks to flood the lowlands sufficiently to create a navigable pass. During this interval the Confederates discerned the Union plan and felled trees in the channel to block the federal flotilla's passage.[5]

In the meantime, the *Forest Rose* continued to probe the fifteen-foot-wide pass. Yost wrote, "After going down the Pass about 1½ miles we entered Moon Lake so called from its shape which is nearly in the form of a crescent." They went up the lake about four miles, where they found the mouth of another pass from Moon Lake to Cold Water River, a distance of eighteen miles. As Yost explained, "It is nothing more than a creek which will have to be well cleared before boats can enter." Grant set his men to work clearing the pass.[6]

Porter made the expedition's mission quite clear to the commander, Watson Smith. A Naval Academy graduate, Smith had served in European waters prior to the war and had commanded Mortar Schooner No 1. in Porter's mortar flotilla. Porter told Smith to obtain pilots and coal at Helena for all his vessels and to tow as much coal as needed in barges. Provided the current was "quite slack," Smith was to proceed into the Yazoo cut. "Proceed carefully, and only in the daytime; 600 or 800 soldiers will be detached to accompany you and will take 100 on aboard of each light-draft." When the expedition reached the Tallahatchie River, Smith was to ascend it as far as the railroad crossing, destroy the bridge, and go down to the mouth of the Yalobusha. Porter instructed Smith to coal his vessels there, leave the barges, and then "dash on to Grenada." From there, he was to move down the Yazoo River, enter the Sunflower River, and attempt to destroy the rebel steamers and ironclads reported to be in that river. If he found Honey Island fortified, then Smith was to destroy the guns and blow up the fort. Porter concluded his instructions by writing, "Do not engage batteries with the light vessels. The *Chillicothe* will do the fighting."[7]

When Smith reached Helena on February 13, however, he learned that clearing the Yazoo Pass would take weeks longer than anticipated. Realizing that this would eliminate the element of surprise, Porter sent reinforcements—additional ordnance, the *Baron De Kalb,* and the light-draft *Marmora.* A week later, believing the pass to be cleared of obstructions, Smith entered Moon Lake in the *Rattler,* accompanied by the new *Chillicothe* (Lieutenant James P. Foster), the old *Baron De Kalb* (Lieutenant Commander John G. Walker), the four tinclads (*Marmora, Forest Rose, Romeo,* and *Signal*), and the tugboat *S. Bayard,* with three coal barges in tow. They were to escort Brigadier General Leonard F. Ross's division in thirteen transports—*Small, Lawyer, Lebanon No. 2, Citizen, Lebanon, Cheesman, Mariner, Saint Louis, Volunteer, Lavinia Logan, John Bell, Key West No. 2,* and *Signal.*[8]

The *Forest Rose* had a new commanding officer. The tinclad's former captain, George W. Brown, had departed, and "Lieut. Johnston of the 'Baron De Kalb' came on board and took charge," young Yost recorded in his diary. "He [Brown] gave me a splendid enfield Rifle before leaving which was captured at Arkansas Post."[9]

At Moon Lake, Smith waited to hear from the officer in charge of clearing the pass and for the arrival of the troop transports. Then, on February 26, the expedition entered the narrow pass in line, with 100 soldiers assigned to each of the light drafts. The *Chillicothe* had the lead, followed by the *Baron De Kalb* and the light-draft gunboats. The *Forest Rose* entered the pass in "the rear of the last transport," Yost penned. The following day, a Friday, Yost noted, "We would stop for the transports to get untangled from the cane and underhanging limbs into which they would occasionally run." "All promises well," Smith assured Porter. The expedition proceeded slowly, reaching Coldwater, Mississippi, on February 28. There, Smith waited for the transports to come up.[10]

According to a correspondent for the *Detroit Free Press,* the expedition reached the end of the pass at noon on February 28. "The boats are much broken in the light upperworks, but not one is damaged in hull or machinery." The men were all in fine spirits. "We get all manner of reports of rebel preparations to receive us, but are only the cause of laughter." On March 1 the reporter noted that the expedition had advanced twenty miles since his last report. "The country is entirely destitute of population." The rams *Lioness* and *Fulton* had joined them, but they had heard no news. "We hope to reach Tallahatchie to-morrow, when we shall begin to make better progress."[11]

Later in the morning, the steamer *Emma,* loaded with troops, got fouled in a tree and lay helpless for several hours, "completely blocking up the pass." The *Forest Rose* finally got under way at 3:00, and "as we were now advancing into the Enemy's territory it must be done with caution," Yost reported.[12]

Two days later, Smith reported to Porter that their progress was slow because they could only advance with the current—any "faster than that brings us foul. Our speed is not more than 1½ miles per hour, if that." By the evening of March 6, they were twelve miles from the Coldwater at the Tallahatchie River. At this point, Smith set his men to work at night repairing damage done to the vessels in the narrow stream. He described some of his vessels as "being without smokestacks and with damaged wheels, and the woodwork of the light-drafts being much torn."[13]

A *New York Herald* correspondent blamed the delays on the poor quality of the transports hired by the government. "One or two of them have been condemned and sent back to Helena." He accused the government agents of chartering "old, broken down, water logged boats that can scarcely be kept afloat in any water."[14]

The *Forest Rose* finished coaling on March 8 and dropped down ahead of the coal barges to repair its wheel, which had been damaged while navigating the Yazoo Pass and Coldwater River. "The other boats were all worse torn up than we were," young Yost conceded. The following day the tinclad got under way, with the transports bringing up the rear. A day later, just at the edge of the water, they saw a cotton gin on fire. Because the river was only about sixty yards wide, they were compelled to pass very close to it. The tinclad's roof caught fire several times, "but we kept it from doing any harm." A blazing shingle fell into the muzzle of one of the *Forest Rose*'s guns, "and had it not been for the presence of mind and quick eye of one of our seamen it would in all probability have bursted and wounded several persons perhaps killing some of them."[15]

After traveling forty or fifty miles in a wilderness, with no sign of life on either side, they had finally emerged and were steaming along "at a fair rate of speed, in a moderately wide and straight river, with frequent plantations of considerable pretensions along the banks." At nearly every one they found a huge, smoldering pile of cotton, which they considered evidence that the enemy "was close in front of us, most probably falling back before us to lure us on to what they may consider our sure destruction." As the flotilla approached a neck of land, African Americans informed Smith that the rebels had mounted guns at that spot and had placed a raft in the river to obstruct the federals' passage. In fact, General Pemberton had sent men under General Loring down from Grenada to improvise a breastwork of earth and cotton on the right bank of the Tallahatchie, up from the Yalobusha juncture. The rebels called it Fort Pemberton.[16]

On the morning of March 11, General Ross boarded the *Chillicothe* to join Smith for a reconnaissance. The *Chillicothe* ran down to within a quarter of a mile of the rebel battery. The rebels sighted the ironclad and fired about twenty-five rounds, striking the *Chillicothe* twice in the turret and bow. Their shots rang true, pummeling the Union boat repeatedly and, according to Smith, "seriously damaging the forward face of the casemate, starting the iron plates and bolts, and driving back the 9-inch white-pine backing." The *Chillicothe* returned fire with its two 11-inch guns, but having concluded their observations of the enemy position, Smith ordered the ironclad to retire. After slushing the turret and piling bales of cotton against it to protect it from shot, the *Chillicothe* went back down to within 800 yards of the rebel battery and opened a brisk fire on a steamer. Return fire struck the gunboat four times, and it withdrew with the loss of three killed and ten wounded.[17]

In the afternoon, fearing that the rebels might be leaving their battery, Smith sent the *Chillicothe* and *De Kalb* forward to shell the enemy position. Rebel gunners opened fire, and heavy solid shot from the rebel guns nearly destroyed the forward face of the *Chillicothe.* According to the *Herald* correspondent, "At this juncture she met with a most unfortunate and disastrous accident. Her men were just loading her port gun . . . when a sixty-four pound shell from the rebels struck directly in her half open port, throwing apart and unshipping the heavy iron port shutters." One shutter was thrown overboard and, "lighting directly on the muzzle of the gun, exploded simultaneously with the shell that was being put in the piece." Foster ordered his men to remain quiet, bring the starboard gun into range, and continue the engagement until ordered to withdraw. The *Chillicothe* suffered four killed—three marines and the quarter gunner. The pilot, J. F. Morgan, was blown by the explosion but was not seriously hurt and returned to duty.[18]

Ordered by Porter not to use his light tinclads against enemy batteries, Smith had only the *Chillicothe* and *De Kalb,* but this did not prevent him from landing a 30-pound Parrott gun from the *Rattler* and another from the *Forest Rose.* Ross reported that they also put a 12-pound howitzer ashore. Parties of soldiers then went to work throwing up a battery facing the enemy's position. The soldiers covered the work, built of two tiers of cotton bales, with earth and mounted the 30-pounder from the *Rattler* in it, manned by a crew from the gunboats.[19]

Federal forces intended to attack the enemy fortification on the morning of March 12, but "the non-arrival of our mortar fleet, together with the incompleteness of certain preparations on the gunboats, made it advisable to postpone the attack," the *Herald's* reporter explained. That evening, he noted that Lieutenant Colonel Wilson had men place another Parrott rifle, taken from the *Forest Rose,* in position on the shore. March 13 dawned "like a June morning in the Northern States." The *Chillicothe* and *De Kalb,* "the mainstays of this expedition," had been covered with cotton bales to ensure their safety, the correspondent explained, "and should we lose one of them we would probably be required to abandon the whole movement."[20]

At first, Smith announced that he was not ready to commence the attack, but at 10:30 a.m. he gave the go-ahead. Both of the ironclad gunboats were to go down together, within close range of the batteries, and bring the mortars and land battery into play at the same time. Acting Lieutenant W. E. H. Fentress, the *Rattler's* executive officer, commanded the mortar crew, and Lieutenant Domine of the *Signal* had charge of the land battery.

The light-draft gunboats and the rams were ordered to remain about three-quarters of a mile above the rebel fortifications, protected by a bend in the river.

Domine's land battery opened fire at 10:30 a.m., just as Smith's ironclads prepared to get under way. The ironclads then closed the rebel fort to within 800 yards, but the rebels singled out the *Chillicothe* and "peppered her well." As Smith told Porter, "The rebels fired with great accuracy, especially from one gun or two, the shots of which struck with telling effect." Although hit thirty-four times with shot and shell that riddled the *Chillicothe*'s storm roof and wheelhouses and dented the iron plating, the ironclad had only two casualties. Seaman Francis O'Neal suffered a compound fracture of his arm, and Sergeant Leopold Trott of the 12th Missouri Regiment had his face badly burned.[21]

At 12:58 p.m. the *Chillicothe* withdrew from the action for want of ammunition, leaving the *De Kalb* alone to bombard the fort. The *De Kalb* had gone into action at 10:45 a.m. and engaged the fort until 2:00 p.m., when it was forced to retire. Hit at least a dozen times, the ironclad was, in Walker's words, "considerably cut up, . . . but nothing to render her unserviceable." In this March 13 action, the ironclad's quartermaster, John O'Neil, was killed, as was seaman Robert Murphy. Master's mate F. E. Davis was mortally wounded, a seaman lost a leg, and two others suffered minor injuries.[22]

According to Smith, the enemy guns had fallen silent before the *Chillicothe* and *De Kalb* were withdrawn, the former to "fill shells." During this engagement, the *Chillicothe* had, in fact, used up all the ordnance with five-second fuses in its magazine, a total of fifty-four shots. The *Chillicothe*'s captain, James Foster, praised the port gun crew, who, "although never drilled until the morning of the action, and who were never under fire before, behaved remarkably well."[23]

Smith claimed that Ross had proposed he wait for the arrival of reinforcements before assaulting the Confederate position. He spent two days making repairs to the *Chillicothe* and strengthening both it and the *De Kalb* with additional bales of cotton. Suffering from an unspecified illness, which may have affected his ability to make decisions, Smith had grown increasingly cautious. Twice his ironclads had dueled with the fort from 800 yards and had failed to silence the enemy guns. Both boats had suffered multiple hits. The *Chillicothe* proved especially vulnerable, its wooden bulwarks too thin to support the armor. To inflict a direct hit on the enemy batteries with its 11-inch guns, the *Chillicothe* would have to close to within a few hundred yards of the rebel fort. Smith had refused to send the *De Kalb* in alone, and he spent the following day repairing the *Chillicothe.* Then, out of respect for the Sabbath, Smith did not attack, allowing the rebels more time to bring in 8-inch smoothbores.[24]

On March 16 Smith and Ross agreed to a joint attack on the fort, "the intention being to attack the fort at a less distance," Smith wrote, "and if successful in silencing the enemy to advance three of the light-drafts with all the troops they could carry." The 8-inch and two 30-pounder federal batteries on land opened fire on Fort Pemberton at 11:30 a.m., followed by the *Chillicothe* and *De Kalb.* Smith agreed to close the range, and the *Chillicothe* advanced, in Smith's words, "to a closer position than before." Foster had the ironclad's stern tied to a tree on the right bank to keep it in position. In reality, the ironclad closed just 200 yards closer than before. After firing seven five-second fuse shells at the rebel fort, the *Chillicothe* was struck simultaneously by four shots battering its plates. According to Foster, the heavy projectiles penetrated or smashed in all the forward slide ports or drove the armor bolts out, making it "impossible to run out the guns." Foster ordered the starboard gun run out, but when its port remained hopelessly stuck, he decided to withdraw out of range and repair the damage. By then, in the bombardments of March 11, 13, and 16, the ironclad had suffered a total of twenty-two casualties. Smith ordered the undamaged *De Kalb* to break off.[25]

A day of inaction followed. Still unwell, Smith wrote to Porter and assured him that they had rations for thirteen days and 21,000 bushels of coal; however, foraging had not augmented their supplies. Personnel issues only added to Smith's worries. He wrote, "We are in want of ensigns and mates. The *DeKalb* is very deficient, one officer having been arrested for drunkenness on duty, in action; another wounded, it is feared mortally, another sick." He asked for five ensigns and eight mates to fill the vacancies. That same day, Smith's ill health created a vacancy at the top of the Yazoo expedition's command structure. "My health has failed under the influences of this climate until I am compelled to report myself as no longer fit for duty," he wrote. He had avoided relinquishing command and had hoped treatment by the physician might enable him to continue, but he now bowed to the surgeon's report.[26]

As the *Rattler* headed back toward Helena carrying the ill Watson Smith, it had several encounters with rebel guerrillas. According to Yost (who was headed back to Cairo on the *Rattler*), on the night of March 18 they were hailed from shore by someone "saying he had a letter for Captain B—this was followed by a volley of musket balls which flew around us pretty lively I can tell you—then we went up in a very few minutes and were shelling the woods and cane breaks at a terrible rate—but do not know that this hurt them any they having in all probability got out of harm's way."[27]

By then, Foster had assumed command of the expedition, and "believing the fort too strong for the forces there engaged and being short of ammunition," the force had retired. He informed Porter that he thought they were in imminent danger of being outflanked and cut off by rebel forces coming down the mouth of the Coldwater. Early on March 19 Foster took the federal flotilla back up the Tallahatchie. Fortunately, the Confederates did not realize the enemy had packed up and left.[28]

Returning to Helena, the federal flotilla met Brigadier General Quimby's reinforcements on transports coming down the Tallahatchie. Foster told Quimby it would be impossible to take the fort without heavy siege guns, and Quimby responded that he had a number of heavy 24-pounders and would procure others without delay. Quimby convinced Ross and Foster to go back to Fort Pemberton, and at about 3:00 on the afternoon of March 23, at the general's suggestion, Foster took his ironclad and the *De Kalb* down to draw the fire of the rebel fort. "*Chillicothe* took her old position before the fort, firing three shots for the purpose of drawing the enemy's fire," he explained. "Failing in this, she withdrew."[29]

For days, Quimby tried to come up with a plan. Foster reported, "We remained twelve days awaiting for the army to do something, and when General Quimby was ordered to withdraw his forces we brought up the rear." Grant had ordered the expedition to return, as he needed the troops for the Vicksburg campaign.[30]

The failure of the Yazoo expedition evoked recriminations from all sides. Foster believed that if Smith had carried out his orders to push on, "as the success of the expedition depended entirely on the rapidity of the movement," the expedition would have been successful. Deserters and prisoners reported that the fort's guns had been silenced and the federals might have taken the fort if they had advanced. Endorsing Foster's assessment of the Yazoo expedition, Porter wrote, "There were difficulties in the why of an assault, but whether they were sufficient to stop the troops when the fort was silenced I am unable to say."[31]

15

Port Hudson

The time has come; there can be no more delay. I must go—Army,
or no Army.

—Admiral David Farragut

When word reached Farragut that neither the *Queen of the West* nor the
Indianola had succeeded in blockading the Red River, he decided to steam
up the Mississippi, convince General Nathaniel Banks to cooperate, run
the batteries at Port Hudson, and take charge of the blockade himself.[1]
Leaving Commodore Henry Morris in command at New Orleans and in
the lower Mississippi, Farragut ordered Commander Charles H. E. Caldwell
to steam to Baton Rouge in the *Essex* and round up the mortars. On March
11, 1863, Farragut headed upstream in the *Hartford* with the *Richmond* and
Monongahela. His orders were "to communicate with the army and the fleet
of gunboats investing Vicksburg, some four hundred miles above New
Orleans by the river," according to Thomas Scott Bacon. A civilian, Bacon
had been invited to accompany the *Richmond* as a guest of Captain Alden.[2]

The Confederates had erected a series of batteries along a bluff just below Port Hudson, on the Mississippi's east bank some fifteen miles above
Baton Rouge. On the morning of March 13, off Baton Rouge, Farragut inspected his ships and "found everything well arranged and the ships well
prepared in every respect" for the run past Port Hudson. The *Richmond's*
crew had worked diligently and quietly to get ready. "All the brass railings
and other such ornaments were unscrewed and stowed below to remove everything which might possibly be struck by the enemy's shot and shell and
driven across the deck as deadly missiles," Bacon recalled. Alden had also

233

ordered his men to whitewash the bulwarks to provide some light when the ship was blacked out.[3]

Having been assured by Banks that his troops were ready to move against Port Hudson and create a diversion for Farragut's ships, the admiral signaled the fleet to head for Profit Island. "At 4 PM the vessel got underway and steamed slowly up the river in the following order to wit: Hartford, Richmond, Kineo, Monongahela + Mississippi. Came to anchor about two miles from Baton Rouge at 10 PM," the *Kineo's* surgeon Aaron Oberly wrote in his diary. According to Oberly, the *Laurel Hill* had gone ahead that afternoon, towing four mortar schooners. The following day, March 14, they steamed up to the upper end of Profit Island and found the *Essex, Genesee, Sachem,* and *Albatross* with the mortar schooners. Farragut called for his captains, and they "conversed freely as to the arrangements." He explained that "every commander arranged his ship in accordance with his own ideas."[4]

By March 1863 the Confederates had more than twenty cannon in eleven batteries on the bluffs just below the town of Port Hudson, and they had assembled a garrison of 16,000 troops. To incur the least damage running the gauntlet of these Confederate guns, Farragut ordered his three larger vessels—the *Hartford, Richmond,* and *Monongahela*—to lash a gunboat to their port sides aft, leaving the port guns clear to fire on the enemy batteries on that side of the river. He had just three gunboats available—the *Kineo, Albatross,* and *Genesee*—and because its side wheels could not accommodate a gunboat, Farragut did not assign one to the *Mississippi.* Farragut's general order also called for each ship to keep slightly on the starboard quarter of the next one ahead, "so as to give free range to her chase guns without risk of damage from premature explosion of shrapnel or shells." When the ships had run past the enemy batteries, the gunboats would steam up to the mouth of the Red River and police it between there and Port Hudson. A fourth gunboat, the *Pinola,* remained behind to defend Baton Rouge.[5]

On board the *Kineo,* the crew spent the day preparing for the upcoming engagement. "At 2:30 PM mortar schooners opened fire and continued until towards evening," Oberly jotted in his diary entry. "At 6:30 Albatross + Kineo got underway, the Albatross to come along port side of the Hartford. The Genesee along port side of Richmond, and the Kineo along the port side of the Monongahela. All hands prepared and arranged matters and things for a severe engagement. After supper the officers dressed themselves with a clean suit. All seemed cheerily with no forbodings of sorrow."

Oberly, however, wrote a letter "stating my wishes to those who might be saved in case it should be my misfortune to be killed. Put all my photographs in my coat pocket during the evening."[6]

Late on March 14 a message arrived from Banks indicating that he was at the crossroads and prepared to advance on Port Hudson. Farragut replied that he hoped to be past the enemy batteries by midnight. At dusk, he and his son Loyall went on deck to observe the final preparations, and at 9:00 p.m. he told Loyall "to go below and inform Captain Jenkins and Captain Palmer, with my compliments, that I am ready to get under way."[7]

On the *Richmond,* Bacon had asked to be allowed to observe the run past the enemy guns from the bridge. At 9:30 the officer of the deck reported seeing the admiral's signal—two red lights under the stern of the flagship. Bacon and the men assigned to the bridge went to their stations. The ship's executive officer, Commander A. Boyd Cummings, "who was to be in charge of the broadside firing, stood at the end of the bridge and gave the guns' crews general instructions as to deliberation, precision, accuracy of aim and firing the guns in rapid succession from bow to stern . . . —all in a very firm and distinct but low and quiet tone," Bacon told readers.[8]

To the admiral's annoyance, the *Mississippi* and *Monongahela* failed to take their stations, so at 10:00 p.m. he sent the tug *Reliance* to order them to close up. Farragut then signaled Caldwell in the *Essex* and the mortar boats to hold their fire until the enemy commenced firing at his ships. After a tense hour of waiting, they saw rockets go up. A rebel lookout had sighted the federal ships and given the alarm. When Confederate guns opened fire, Caldwell and his mortar boats commenced their bombardment.

The *Kineo*'s surgeon recorded the action in his diary: "After steaming slowly we arrived in reach of the batteries the Hartford opening fire about 11:15 P.M. Mortar schooners opened fire also, and continued until the action was over." During the first part of the engagement, Oberly passed his time on deck, "witnessing the firing on both sides, which was grand." Opposite the last battery, enemy shot disabled the *Monongahela*'s steerage apparatus and it ran aground; the sudden stop tore the *Kineo* from the larger vessel. Those of the *Monongahela*'s officers and crew who could, got ashore. "The Kineo being under her lee escaped being hit while there save once or twice," Oberly explained. With its rudder disabled and a propeller entangled with a hawser, the *Kineo* could steam only with difficulty, but after an hour it got afloat and pulled off the *Monongahela.* Both vessels then drifted downstream with the current.[9]

The *Hartford,* ably conned by pilots Thomas R. Carrell and I. B. Hamilton, had continued up the river, firing its guns and "stopping when the smoke became too dense to see and reopening whenever a fresh battery fired upon us," Farragut reported, "but we always silenced their battery when we fired." Confederate gunners manning the upper batteries now took aim on the *Hartford,* which returned fire with its 9-inch and 30-pounder Parrott rifles. Four shells struck the flagship, killing one man and wounding two others. Farragut thought he had seen the *Richmond* following the flagship, but as they rounded the bend he could not see it. The admiral now concluded that one or more of his vessels had met with disaster and the remainder had dropped downriver.[10]

The *Richmond,* second in line, had indeed followed the flagship upstream. On the bridge, Bacon could clearly hear "the strong and steady voice of Cummings giving his last orders, to this effect: You will fire the whole starboard battery, one gun at a time, from the bow-gun aft." Cummings then gave the order to open fire with the starboard battery. "Don't fire too fast. Aim carefully at the flashes of the enemy's guns. *Fire!*"[11]

The *Genesee,* lashed along the *Richmond*'s port quarter, opened fire as well with all its guns. When they had passed the enemy batteries at Thomas Point, they turned to follow the river's westward bend, but a shot struck the *Richmond*'s steam pipe near the safety valves, letting off steam. With the engine disabled, the ship could not make headway against the strong current and was caught in a cross fire of rebel batteries, compelling Alden to reluctantly order the *Richmond* to turn back. The *Genesee* turned the *Richmond* around, towed it down the river, and anchored out of range of enemy fire. In the process, the *Genesee* was struck by rifled shot passing through the side of the ship and igniting a 10-inch shell, causing a fire. Standing at Alden's side during the engagement, Cummings had his leg shot off below the knee by a cannonball. Eleven other crewmen suffered injuries, and two marines and a boatswain's mate were killed by enemy fire. They transferred Cummings to New Orleans, where he appeared to be doing well, but he died three days later.[12]

The *Mississippi* went upriver as ordered, but in the darkness and smoke, Commander Melancton Smith could not make out the *Monongahela* ahead of him, so he ordered "go ahead fast" to close the distance. First Lieutenant George Dewey recalled that their fate was in the hands of the pilot, who had never guided "a heavy-draught ocean-going ship in the midst of battle smoke, with the shells shrieking in his ears." According to Smith, "We had now reached the last and most formidable batteries, and were congratulating ourselves upon having gained the turn, when the *Mississippi* grounded and heeled over three streaks to port." Smith had the engine reversed and the port guns run in to put the ship on an even keel, but the situation was not encouraging. "We were being more frequently hit; the toll of our dead and wounded was increasing," Dewey wrote. However, "there was remarkably little confusion, thanks to the long drills which we had had off New Orleans, and to the fact that all but a few of the crew had already been under fire in passing forts Jackson and St. Philip."[13]

After thirty-five minutes of backing, the pilot determined it would be impossible to get the vessel off. Smith ordered the port battery spiked and the pivot gun thrown overboard, but before the latter could be accomplished, he changed his mind. "I deemed it most judicious and humane to abandon the vessel, as the enemy had obtained our range and we were exposed to the galling and cross fire of three batteries, their shot hulling us frequently," he wrote. The *Mississippi* ceased firing, and Smith ordered the wounded brought up and placed in the first of three small boats—the only ones not smashed to pieces by enemy fire. Dewey and Ensign O. A. Batcheller went below to start a fire in the wardroom and were in the last boat to leave the *Mississippi*. "They all left with just the clothes on their backs, but Smith had buckled on his sword and a pair of revolvers. He still had a cigar in his mouth, and was as calm as ever," Dewey wrote. Suddenly, Smith threw the sword and pistols overboard, stating, "I am not going to surrender them to any rebel." As the fast current swept them downstream, Dewey could see the fire break through the wardroom skylight, illuminating the ship to the rebels on the bluff, "who broke into that rebel yell which I then heard in full chorus of victory for the first and only time in my life." Assured that his ship, which had been set ablaze in four places, would be destroyed, Smith left with Dewey and went down to the *Richmond*. At 3:00 p.m., however, the *Mississippi* was still afloat. It finally slid off the shoal, and at 5:30 p.m. it blew up, "producing an awful concussion which was felt for miles around."[14]

At about 2:30 a.m. the *Kineo* came to anchor below the mortar schooners, but it could not use either its machinery or its steering apparatus. The *Richmond* and *Genesee* had come down, and the *Monongahela* followed. The *Kineo* had sustained a broken cathead and smashed bulwarks, but according to Oberly, "The officers and men acted as men and are deserving of consideration." He praised the captain, John Watters, who "acted coolly." He reported that "the Executive Officer Fred R. Rodgers and the steerage boy were considerably below, the latter frightened and the former dreading the shot as they screamed overhead. Paymaster was frightened and the hospital nurse was very much agitated."[15]

Of Farragut's ships, only the *Hartford* and *Albatross* made it past the Port Hudson defenses, prompting the admiral to meet with Walke, who, in Porter's absence, was the naval commander off Vicksburg. He asked Walke to send an ironclad and two rams down past the Vicksburg batteries to support him, but Walke wisely demurred. General Alfred W. Ellet, however, had recently arrived at Young's Point to take charge of the ram fleet from his nephew Charles. Ellet had eight large rams at his disposal, and he had no qualms about ordering two, the *Lancaster* and *Switzerland,* down past Vicksburg to support Farragut's ships if they were attacked by Confederate raiders coming from the Red River. On March 25 the *Lancaster* and *Switzerland* started down the river to run the gauntlet of the Vicksburg batteries. At 5:30 a.m. they came abreast of the batteries, which opened fire on them. "A large number of our officers and men saw the flashes of the rebel guns distinctly, but heard no sound whatever," the *Lafayette*'s diarist Thomas Lyons wrote. "The boats passed on out of sight and as far as our observers could tell they were safe."[16]

Observing from the riverbank, General Ellet heard the enemy guns and the sound of rebels cheering. Fearing that a disaster had befallen his boats, Ellet immediately took to a yawl and pulled into the river. To his horror, he saw the *Switzerland* drift into view, stern first. Steam poured from the ram, and flames licked near the pilothouse. Shouts from the hurricane deck assured the general that the men were safe and warned him to go back. Ellet ignored them and boarded the disabled ram. The *Lancaster* had fared no better, a plunging shot going clean through its stern, opening up the hull and forcing the crew to abandon ship.

Word that the two federal rams had been disabled reached the *Lafayette,* above Vicksburg, at 9:50 a.m. When three forlorn-looking soldiers appeared on the shore, "we hastened to get them on board and learned their adventures," Lyons explained. "They had come from one of the rams and told us that the rebels had opened fire on them from all the Batteries that were in range at once. And that two shots hit the Ram 'Lancaster' 'Blew her up,' 'Set her on fire' and that 'She sunk' in a few minutes." The ram *Switzerland,* Lyons added, "got one shot through her boiler which allowed all the steam to escape, but she drifted down under the guns of the 'Flagship Hartford' without further damage." According to Morison, "none were killed but several drowned, and the pilot and engineer of the 'Switzerland' were severely wounded." At 10:15 a.m. the survivors who had been rescued by the *Lafayette* left the ship to return to army headquarters. "One of the two men had swum over a mile in the river before being picked up."[17]

Porter returned to the Mississippi from the Steele's Bayou expedition on March 25, just two hours after the *Lancaster* sank. When he heard that, contrary to his orders, Ellet had sent the two rams to run the gauntlet past Vicksburg in broad daylight, Porter flew into a rage. He would have preferred to arrest Ellet but instead relieved him of his command.[18]

For the next few weeks, until the river fell, Porter focused his attention on repairing the gunboats from the Yazoo. "The fleet came down looking awfully used up," Morison noted in his diary, "some of the boats being minus their smokestacks, hammock nettings, and boats, the old 'Carondelet' as usual being the worst, she having had the lead."[19]

Preparations were already under way for the Mississippi Squadron's next operation—yet another attempt to eliminate the Confederate stronghold at Vicksburg and an effort to seize Port Hudson, both of which continued to block free navigation of the Mississippi. Although Farragut had run the *Hartford* and *Albatross* past the Port Hudson batteries, the town and its defenses remained firmly in enemy hands. Two weeks before the return of the Yazoo Pass expedition, Halleck had informed Grant that President Lincoln "seems to be rather impatient" about the Vicksburg campaign. Halleck urged Grant to link his army with one commanded by Banks below Vicksburg and accomplish the long-delayed mission of opening the muddy Mississippi. Given the continuous high water and the nature of the country, Grant doubted the feasibility of landing troops on the east side of the river above Vicksburg. He concluded that he had little choice but to use an alternative route south from Milliken's Bend and cross his army over the Mississippi below Vicksburg. Before attempting this new route, however, Grant needed transports, so he asked Porter to send his ironclads downstream to escort a number of empty transports past the rebel batteries at Vicksburg. Porter agreed to the general's request but reminded him that if he sent vessels to cooperate with an operation against Grand Gulf, then "there will be nothing left to attack Haynes Bluff, in case it should be deemed necessary to try it." The admiral was willing to send his best gunboats down past Vicksburg, but first he wanted to get his vessels back from the Yazoo, and he needed time to prepare and acquire coal and provisions.[20]

At this point, Grant called a council of war and proposed to send gunboats below Vicksburg with a sufficient number of transports packed with cotton to protect their boilers and machinery. The army would then march over to Carthage and be transported to the Vicksburg side as circumstance warranted. Most of the officers present at this council of war considered the plan too dangerous, but Grant announced, "My mind is made up."[21]

Preparations to run Porter's ironclads past the Vicksburg batteries began immediately. Porter called his captains to the *Benton* and explained that he was sending seven ironclads and gunboats down past Vicksburg with three transports. Each vessel was to take a coal barge in tow, secured to its starboard side. They would move at night in the following order: *Benton, Lafayette, Price, Louisville, Mound City, Pittsburg, Carondelet*. Commanders were to take every precaution to protect their ship's hulls and machinery against accidental shots. Porter advised his commanders that their gun crews would have to work in the dark on deck and set the range for 900 yards. "Fire shell, and sometimes grape. Don't fire after passing the town—the lower batteries are not worth noticing."[22]

On April 14 the *Carondelet* and *Price* went alongside a hay barge and took bales on board to protect their machinery. The following day the *Lafayette*'s crew "covered the forecastle with ranges of chain and greased our port side with a heavy coat of pork grease," coxswain Morison wrote. "We unshipped our ventilators, forge, and all unnecessary gear round the deck. Covered our quarterdeck and fantail with loose sheets of iron and then coiled hawsers on top of them." That afternoon they went alongside a barge and took on an additional thirty-five bales of hay, which were spread over the tender parts of the boats and saturated with water. A howling wind delayed their departure, but the cry of "All hands" roused the crew of the *Lafayette* at 12:00 a.m. on April 16. "Went on deck and found it clear and starry," Morison wrote. The *Price* came alongside and tied up. Time passed, and there was no signal to start. According to Morison, a tug arrived "and told us that we were not going down tonight as the army transports (which were to accompany us) were not ready. Several remarks were made, not at all complimentary to Gen'l Sherman."[23]

Transports arrived throughout the day, and at about 8:30 p.m. Porter and his staff boarded the flagship *Benton*. Fifteen minutes later Porter ordered the ironclad's captain to hoist the signal to get under way for the run past Vicksburg. With the tug *Ivy* lashed to it, the *Benton* took the lead. Three transports—*Forest Queen, Henry Clay,* and *Silver Wave*—laden only with stores, followed them. The *Tuscumbia* brought up the rear.

At 9:15 p.m. the *Lafayette* got under way. "The steamer Sterling Price [was] lashed on our starboard side for her protection as she was a wooden boat without any armor," clerk Lyons explained. Pacing the *Lafayette*'s hurricane deck, Walke stared into the darkness. He could just make out the *Benton* ahead with a tugboat lashed to its stern.[24]

At 9:50 p.m. the *Benton* stopped its engines and began to drift downstream. Forty minutes passed, and from the *Benton*'s deck Porter could clearly see the lights of Vicksburg. They passed the point, and the sound of enemy drummers beating the long roll came from shore. A crackle of musketry followed.

From the *Lafayette*'s deck, Morison also searched the darkness. "Everything looked quiet and sleepy, but the signal lights flashing now and then told us that they had their (far from sleepy) eyes on us. About 10:45 P.M. we rounded the Point, when—whang—went a gun and the shell came whistling and screaming through the air. It fell short."[25]

At 11:20 p.m. the first shots rang out from the rebel batteries. Elias Smith, an officer on the *Lafayette*, explained that the admiral "chose to lead the van, and of course received the first salute." Smith said the first shot seemed to be "a rifle projectile—say a 20 pounder Parrott—which passed over the 'Lafayette' fore and aft, with a swinging ascent suggesting haste."[26]

As the *Lafayette* and *Price* glided toward the east bank, a sudden crosscurrent threatened to sweep them sideways. The pilot and the helmsmen struggled to keep the unwieldy ironclads on course, but with the heavy coal barge lashed between them, they were helpless as the current caught them and turned them ninety degrees. "We steamed steadily forward the river current was strong and carried us rapidly close under the rebel batteries," Lyons explained. "Our boat steered very awkward on account of our burden on the Starboard side which could steam much faster than we could. And in a short time we found ourselves heading up the river, and exposing the 'Gen'l Sterling Price' to the full rake of the Rebel batteries.[27]

The rebels opened fire on the *Lafayette* with about a dozen guns. "After a while one struck our bow port but did not come through," Morison wrote. "They are getting the range of us. Crash—the 130 pounder rifled Whitworth came a-tearing through our casemate and making the splinters fly in all directions." As the rebel gunners found the range, the ironclad was repeatedly struck by shot and shell. A 100-pounder rifle shot smacked into the port wheelhouse; another hit the lower edge of the iron plate forward of the wheelhouse amidships, landing just a few feet short of the port cylinder.

The *Lafayette* opened on them with its port broadside guns. Elias Smith, who had command of the rifled guns, wrote, "First our forward broadside 9-inch, then the midship, and lastly the after (port) guns gave out an answering shot in the very teeth of the Confederate batteries."[28]

As Morison noted, "This time we were right in the centre of their fire. Crack, crack, and again we were pierced. It now seemed as if the whole shore for miles was lined with guns." From the pilothouse, Walke called for damage reports as shot after shot struck his vessel. Most did little damage, but he could see enemy shot riddling the *Price*'s upper works and starting fires. "Early in the fight the coal barge, which he had in [tow], received a shot and was now filling rapidly, so we cut her and the 'Price' adrift," Morison wrote. The Union crews kept their broadside guns sending shell, shrapnel, and canister into the town, filling the air with smoke. "The smoke from our own and the rebel guns, with the glare of the burning buildings from the opposite shore, made it difficult for the pilots to make out the direction we were going," Smith recalled. They soon backed around and drifted past the enemy guns. "Shells burst all around the pilot-house, and at one time Mr. John Denning, our pilot, was literally baptized with fire. He thought himself killed, but he brushed the fire from his head, and found he was unhurt."[29]

Perhaps blinded by the light of the fires on shore, the *Louisville*'s captain, Lieutenant Commander Elias Owen, let the ironclad make two complete turns, and it collided with the *Price*. Both ships lost their barges. Two 7.5-inch rifle shells exploded in the *Price*'s officers' quarters and set a couple of fires. The impact from the collision stove in one of the *Louisville*'s boats, but surprisingly, it suffered only one man killed and three injured.

Without the cumbersome coal barge, the *Lafayette*'s helmsmen and pilot were able to regain control, and it steamed down alone, "drifting with the tide as [we] were covering the weaker boats. We touched bottom once and remained still," Morison explained. "Then how the devils cheered and yelled, thinking that we were done for. They now opened with musquetry, field pieces, in fact everything that could throw a shot—and for 15 minutes it was truly awful." The *Lafayette* finally got free and dropped slowly out of range, down past Warrenton, having been under fire for one hour and forty minutes.[30]

Expecting more casualties, Sherman had ordered small boats to pick up any survivors if the ironclads or, more likely, the transports were disabled or sunk. Skiffs and yawls prowled the river that smoky night—now weirdly illuminated by fires on shore—searching for men in boats or clinging to rafts or cotton bales. An object caught the attention of one boat crew—a drifting plank. They headed for the plank, pulled alongside, grabbed on to a soaking wet jacket, and pulled a man to safety. "God bless you!" the man said, "I thought I was a goner." He was the pilot of the transport *Henry Clay,* which had sunk. The *Forest Queen* had been hulled by Confederate shot and shell, but the *Silver Wave* had made it downriver without suffering any damage. Indeed, reports coming in to Porter from his captains indicated that most of the ironclads had run the gauntlet with little damage.[31]

Porter's flagship *Benton* dropped anchor at 2:10 a.m. on April 17, a few miles below Warrenton. When the *Lafayette* came to anchor, Morison went on deck and "found that we had been struck twelve times, three shot having penetrated us (for which we may thank our neutral English cousins), they being all rifled Whitworths which came through. I saw several fragments of round shot which broke to pieces on our sides." At midmorning the fleet got under way and steamed down to New Carthage, where Porter conferred briefly with General McClernand.[32]

Within days, Grant turned his attention to Grand Gulf. The rebels were at work fortifying their position and "will move heaven and earth to stop us if we don't go ahead," Porter told the general. He proposed a combined attack and hoped to be in Grand Gulf in four days. Grant wired Sherman the next day, April 21, and told him that a steam fleet would run the Vicksburg batteries that night. But then he had to inform Porter that there would be a delay getting organized. "Signal lights at Young's Point and here at Grant's headquarters signaling each other," Iowa soldier Milo Dibble noted in his diary. "As blockade running is uppermost for the present, it is guessed, without many dissenting vote, that the all important event is to transpire tonight." Dibble's 10th Iowa Volunteer Regiment was to provide volunteers "to go on the boats preparing here at Grant's Hqtrs. that are to run the blockade. If it is allowed Co I will be represented."[33]

The following morning at 9:00 a.m. the fleet started down the river with the *Benton* in the lead and the *Price* and *Lafayette* bringing up the rear. "Plantations became thicker as the river is descended," Morison noted. "About noon came in sight of Grand Gulf." The vessels turned around, went back up five miles, and made fast to the bank. At 1:30 that afternoon Porter and all the captains boarded the *Lafayette* to "hold a council of war which was concluded in about an hour," Lyons noted. The admiral decided to make a reconnaissance with the entire squadron.[34]

Porter then informed McClernand, "I have been reconnoitering to-day. They have built extensive works and have guns in them. If left to themselves, they will make this place impregnable." He expected to attack the rebel batteries at Grand Gulf in the morning and requested that McClernand bring troops down to hold them. "This is a case where a dash will save everything," the admiral wrote. McClernand received the admiral's message that evening and ordered Brigadier General Peter J. Osterhaus to cooperate with the navy in reducing the enemy defenses at Grand Gulf. Osterhaus's division of eight regiments and two batteries embarked on five steamers and was ready to go down the next morning.[35]

The following day, April 23, the *Lafayette* dropped down on a reconnaissance and engaged the enemy's batteries at Grand Gulf with the 100-pounder Parrott, continuing to fire on them until the admiral ordered it to cease. "Last night about one o'clock a tremendous cannonading commenced at Vicksburg and lasted about an hour and half," Dibble wrote.[36]

The *Price* then came down with a report "that five out of six transports came safely down from the Vicksburg batteries last night. The Capt showed me the 'dispatch' with a feeling of exultation," Lyons noted. "These transports are now moving our troops on their way to some strategic point." Having earlier succeeded in getting transports past the enemy batteries, Grant had sent another six transports down from Milliken's Bend past Vicksburg. When their civilian crews balked and refused to go, army volunteers stepped forward. The *Moderator, Anglo-Saxon, J. W. Cheesman, Horizon,* and *Empire City* all made it safely, but the *Tigress* took fifteen shots, one in the stern, and sank. When officials at the War Department and the White House learned that Grant had managed to get stores and boats past Vicksburg, they were both jubilant and relieved.[37]

The next day, April 24, Grant shifted his headquarters to Perkins Plantation and boarded Porter's flagship for a reconnaissance of Grand Gulf. Through their spyglasses, they could count four guns on a promontory sixty feet above the river. Downstream some thousand yards was another fortification, lower than the first. Grant remarked that Porter's vessels could handle them because the bluffs above the river at Grand Gulf were lower than those at Vicksburg, reducing the chance of damage to the vessels from plunging fire.[38]

When they returned to the Perkins Plantation landing, Grant called for his staff, and they began to work up a plan. After McClernand's troops arrived on transports at Hard Times landing, just above Grand Gulf on the west bank, Porter's ironclads would shell rebel batteries on the opposite bank of the Mississippi River. Dubious about a direct army assault on the position, Porter objected to the plan, but Grant remained firm.

On April 27 the *Price* came down with the plan of attack, which was read to the crew at quarters. "The Turtles are to take the lead, then the 'Tuscumbia' and 'Benton' next. Then we were to float down stern first and when we could use our stern guns no longer, we were then to fight them with our broadside and bow guns," Morison noted in his diary.[39]

By April 29 all of McClernand's troops had arrived and encamped at Hard Times landing. Grant instructed the men that, once ashore, they should seize the most commanding points. The stage was now set for the navy to silence the Confederate batteries at Grand Gulf, allowing Grant's troops to assault the last remaining obstacle on the Mississippi before Vicksburg.[40]

16

Grand Gulf

We had a hard fight with these forts and it is with great pleasure that I report that the Navy holds the door to Vicksburg.

—David Dixon Porter

By the time all the troops had come ashore at Hard Times landing, Porter had assembled his seven ironclads to bombard and silence the enemy batteries at Grand Gulf. In orders issued to his commanders on April 27, he noted: "It is reported that there are four positions where guns are placed, in which case it is desirable that all four places should be engaged." Porter assigned the task of engaging the lower or southernmost works to the *Louisville, Carondelet, Mound City,* and *Pittsburg.* They were to steam past the batteries firing their port broadside, bow, and stern guns, then come about and steam back to shell the upper battery. Porter gave the *Benton, Tuscumbia,* and *Lafayette* the mission of engaging the Confederate batteries above the town of Grand Gulf at the mouth of the Big Black River. "The '*Benton*' and '*Tuscumbia*' will attack the upper battery on the bluff, going down slowly, and firing shell with five-second fuse, one gun to be loaded and fired with canister," the admiral explained. "The *Lafayette* will drop down at the same time, stern foremost, until within six hundred yards, firing her rifled guns with percussion shell at the upper battery." The *Tuscumbia* would then round to and keep astern and inside of the *Benton.* Porter gave specific instructions that if the upper battery were silenced, then a guard flag would be hoisted and a long whistle blown for the *Lafayette* to drop down and assist the four smaller steamers at the lower batteries. The admiral told his captains to take every precaution against fire, keeping water buckets and tubs filled all around the spar deck and to have hammocks, bags, and awnings packed around the pitmans. He ordered them to explain the position of the forts to their pilots, officers, and crew. "Coolness in firing is recommended; let not a shot be thrown away," Porter admonished his men. When they had silenced the rebels, the ram *Price* would escort the six transports and a bevy of barges filled with McClernand's 10,000 troops.[1]

At 7:30 a.m. on April 29, 1863, the federal ironclads moved out. The *Lafayette* was stationed over a shoal in the river above the upper batteries, Walke later explained, "a position most dreaded by her pilots during action. In view of the dangers of navigation the original programme was altered so that the 'Pittsburg' took the lead, Acting Lieutenant Hoel (her commander) being an excellent river pilot, possessing great skill and experience in the management of steamers on the Mississippi, and a brave and competent officer."[2]

"At 7 A.M. the admiral made signal for the fleet to get under weigh. We did so," the *Lafayette*'s coxswain Morison explained. They went to quarters and opened the magazines. "About 8 A.M. the first gun was fired by the rebels at us but it fell over and riccocheted a half mile beyond us. Again and again they tried but with the same result. They now depressed their guns as their shots now fell short as they formerly did beyond us." Fortunately, "about this time the rest of the fleet opened on them with their bow guns (and us with our stern ones) which had the effect of diverting their fire from us onto them."[3]

Lieutenant Commander James A. Greer had conned the flagship *Benton* downstream, and at 7:55 a.m. the rebels opened fire. Almost twenty minutes passed, however, before the *Benton* could return fire with its forward battery. Greer then rounded to and kept firing whenever possible. At 9:00 a shell pierced the thin armor on the *Benton*'s starboard quarter and burst in a shell room, setting it on fire. Damage parties quickly extinguished the blaze. The *Lafayette* also opened fire. "Pretty soon we were abreast of them and opened on them with our nine-inch [guns] and howitzers. The whole atmosphere trembled with the concussion of the repeated broadsides from the boats, nor were the rebels idle as they replied to us almost shot for shot from their various batteries."[4]

In his report Walke wrote, "The *Lafayette*, after firing 35 rounds of 100-pounder rifle shell and shot, turned her broadside and 11-inch bow guns upon them, firing with good effect, apparently until about 10 o'clock a.m." Porter then hoisted the guard flag, signaling Walke to move from his position at the upper battery down to the lower batteries. The *Lafayette* quickly rounded to below them by running its ram into the riverbank. It then opened fire with its starboard broadside and kept up a continuous "vigorous and effective" assault.[5]

While the *Lafayette* went to assist the vessels below, the *Tuscumbia* and *Benton* remained to bombard the upper batteries and absorbed heavy fire from the rebel gunners. The flagship suffered multiple hits. One struck the pilothouse, sending the ship drifting 1,500 yards downstream, caught in an eddy, until Greer nosed the flagship into the bank to get it turned around. Hoel brought the *Pittsburg* up to replace the *Benton* and gallantly took on the upper rebel battery, which fiercely returned fire.[6]

At 12:25 Porter went up in the *Benton* to confer with Grant, who had been observing the battle from a tug. Not long after, the rebels ceased firing at the flagship, and Greer took the *Benton* up to Hard Times landing. All the other federal warships followed, except for the *Tuscumbia*. Shell hits had disabled all but one of the *Tuscumbia*'s starboard battery.[7]

Confederate gunners at Grand Gulf severely pummeled the *Pittsburg*, striking the ironclad thirty-five times, the commanding officer reported. Two shots passed through the pilothouse, and one exploded under the port bow, opening a seam and causing the gunboat to leak. Enemy fire killed the captain of the forecastle on the *Pittsburg*, one landsman, three marines, and one contraband, James Haywood.[8]

The *Benton* suffered its share of casualties as well: seven men killed and nineteen wounded, twelve of them soldiers of the 58th Ohio Volunteers and four of them naval officers. The flagship had been struck by enemy shot or shell forty-seven times. One shot penetrated the pilothouse and lodged inside, wounding the pilot and shattering the wheel. A flying splinter from a burst 7-inch shell hit Porter, who was standing on the upper deck, but inflicted only a slight injury.[9]

Lieutenant Byron Wilson noted that during the morning engagement the *Mound City* suffered no injuries and no serious damage to its hull. The *Louisville* received just seven shots and had no injuries to report. Likewise, the *Carondelet* escaped serious damage and, according to Lieutenant McLeod Murphy, had no casualties.[10]

Porter then signaled Walke to cease firing and come up with the *Lafayette*. As it steamed up, it fired into the upper battery on the "Point of Rocks," Walke recalled, "enfilading it from below with her XI-inch bow-guns, as it approached that point." The *Louisville, Carondelet,* and *Mound City* followed, steaming in a circle and pummeling the battery with their guns. The *Pittsburg,* Walke wrote, "remained in her original position under the bank opposite the middle battery." They fired until all but one of the rebel guns fell silent. The *Benton* then signaled the gunboats to follow it up the river. When the *Lafayette* arrived, Walke reported to Porter, but not long afterward the admiral sent his secretary to instruct Walke to return with the *Lafayette* to the upper batteries and silence them.[11]

According to Morison, the rebel fire began to slacken at 11:30, and at 12:30 p.m. he saw "all their batteries silenced except one (the upper) four-gun battery on the first bluff, and they were so high above us we could not hit them as often as we wished." By then, only the *Lafayette* continued to engage the Confederate batteries. "The 'Tuscumbia,' having been partially disabled, had dropped down out of the way. The 'Louisville' also staid below, and the others had gone up and left us to contend with the battery alone. We got a good position in an eddy at a distance of nine hundred yards and then didn't the sand fly, but it was no use as we could not dislodge them." The *Lafayette* then steamed up to join the fleet, making fast to a tree astern of the *Pittsburg.* Morison concluded, "The retreat was beaten, and I left my gun, having been five and a half hours at it, and I may safely say it was the hardest fight I ever was in."[12]

"We were struck by 16 rebel shot and one shell," the *Lafayette*'s clerk wrote. "One shell came through the unprotected part of the paddle-house and buried itself in the pitman. Some of their shot broke against our iron armor and fell off harmless." The captain's barge (davits and all) was shot away, three cutters were shattered, and the smokestacks were riddled. "The mainmast had about 2/3 of its diameter shot away but it still stood." One shot struck and sent a splinter into the face of a sharpshooter, but no one else was injured. Lyons credited Michael O'Malley, captain of the No. 2 11-inch gun, with dismounting a rebel gun, and George Billington, captain of the No. 2 Parrott rifle, with dismounting another.[13]

At 2:15 p.m. Walke piped the *Lafayette*'s crew to dinner. "Not much to eat as the fires had been out all day," Morison noted. At 3:00, observing that the enemy had begun to repair their batteries, Porter ordered the *Lafayette* to run down and lob a few rounds at the upper battery. Walke had the ram fire a few rounds from the bow guns, which silenced the battery; then it began a steady bombardment with the 100-pounder rifled guns until the vessel anchored at 8:00 p.m.[14]

Grant was now faced with a crucial question: had the rebel batteries at

Grand Gulf truly been silenced, and could he safely run his troop-laden transports, waiting on the western shore, past them? Grant concluded that Porter's ships had not dealt with the Confederate guns effectively enough to allow the transports to run past Grand Gulf, so he decided to disembark the troops and march them down the west side of the river. That night, the transports would run past the enemy batteries while Porter's gunboats occupied them with another bombardment. Word spread quickly among the troops. "Some transports are to run the blockade and it is reported that we are to cross over into Miss below it," 10th Iowa Infantry soldier Milo Dibble jotted in his diary.[15]

Clerk Lyons faithfully recorded this evening bombardment: "9 P.M. The flagship 'Benton' and the rest of the Turtles steamed down past us at full speed, opening on the rebel batteries as soon as they got in range." The *Lafayette* weighed anchor and at 9:20 p.m. "We were at 'Action Quarters.' We dropped down firing our rifles deliberately, and in the meantime the 'Genl Sterling Price' and all the Transports came down and passed the rebel batteries keeping close to the Louisiana shore." The transports came down one by one, under cover of the smoke, "and got around the point. It looked fine to see the shells go twirling and twinkling back and forth," Morison wrote. The rebels had returned to the batteries and "were now firing as fresh and as vindictive as ever. We were also giving them 'Parrott' to keep them busy." By the time the *Lafayette* got down to the upper batteries, the rest of Porter's vessels had gone past. Lyons noted, "the enterprising rebels give their whole attention to peppering us. But their balls bounced like hail stones." In his report the ship's carpenter, Clark Underwood, agreed: "While passing the batteries in the same evening, the vessel was struck thirteen times, doing but slight damage."[16]

The *Lafayette* ceased firing at 10:35 and rounded down along the Louisiana shore. At 11:30 the crew turned in. "I felt very glad as I was extremely tired and sore, having fired eighty-five rounds through the day," Morison explained. Lyons also gladly went to bed. "I have reason to be thankful to the Lord for his care over and shielding us from dangers seen and unseen," he wrote in his diary.[17]

The following day the first Union troops to cross the river from the Louisiana shore to Bruinsburg embarked in gunboats and transports. The *Lafayette* took on a couple of infantry regiments and ran ten miles downriver, landed the soldiers, and came back for more. "The soldiers are full of zeal and fire to carry on the war until Rebellion is crushed out," Lyons noted. Soldiers of the 10th Iowa Volunteer Infantry were among the 1,500 troops transported on the *Lafayette*. "We are now supposed to be within 8 miles of Grand Gulf," Dibble noted in his diary. The men marched through a thick cypress swamp following the levy, and at "about 11 o'clock we came out to the Miss again and about five miles below Grand Gulf. Here we saw several gunboats and four or five transports. They have been busy since yesterday morning at 2 o'clock transporting the Inf. and the transports the Cav. Artillery teams." Dibble's regiment was "marched aboard the Ram Lafayette. From the top of the boat we could see Grand Gulf at the mouth of the big black river." The ram started down the river and "landed at Rodney landing in Miss about five miles farther down the river." From there, a good road led directly to Grand Gulf. Before returning for more troops, the *Lafayette* stopped to take on coal, allowing Lyons to see the damage done to the ironclad *Tuscumbia*. He found that its "upper works were badly damaged with rebel shot and shell. The rebels had not spared any part of her."[18]

The *Tuscumbia* had, in fact, been struck eighty-one times and suffered a large number of casualties, five fatal. Four died when a shell struck the outer edge of the shutter of the midship port, entered the turret, and exploded. Among the wounded was the pilot, Joseph McCammant, who remained at his station at the wheel until he fainted from blood loss. The number of wounded kept the *Tuscumbia*'s assistant surgeon Fred E. Potter busy; he reported twenty-four officers and men injured, several with fractures and many others with contusions and face and neck wounds.[19]

That afternoon the *Lafayette* "took another load of soldiers down belonging to Major General McPherson's 17th Army Corps," Morison jotted. On the way back upstream the *Lafayette* stopped alongside the transport *Anglo-Saxon* to take on coal, and "some of the boys had found out some barrels of whiskey on board of her. It was soon circulating pretty freely, guards to the contrary notwithstanding. I, of course, had a moderate allowance, which made me sleep sound."[20]

When Grant's soldiers landed in Mississippi, they began marching eastward to the town of Port Gibson, twenty-five miles south of Vicksburg. More troops followed. President Lincoln and General Halleck wanted Grant and Banks to join forces and advance on Port Hudson and then on Vicksburg, but Grant preferred for his troops to live off the land and not be dependent on river-borne supplies. The *Lafayette* spent May 1 steaming up and down the river carrying troops. "There is a long dark string of Union troops marching down the Louisiana shore. Genrl Sherman is reported as being between Haines Bluff and Vicksburg," Lyons noted.[21]

Suspecting that the rebels were evacuating the batteries at Grand Gulf, Porter ordered the *Lafayette* up on a reconnaissance on May 2. Morison's diary provided details of the day's bombardment: "At 11 A.M. we got under weigh and went up slowly to go within a mile and then we opened on them with our bow guns. Pretty soon a cloud of smoke and the whizzing of a shell convinced us that there was whiskey in that corn. After a few exchanges we left them for a short time." That afternoon, the ram *Switzerland* arrived from the Red River with word that Farragut and Banks had thirty rebel transports and three rebel gunboats penned there. After supper the *Lafayette*'s crew learned that they would assist in capturing them. Walke immediately made preparations, sending one watch to take on coal and another out in boats to take ammunition off the *Tuscumbia*.[22]

Bright and early on May 3, a Sunday, Morison learned that four explosions had taken place at Grand Gulf, "which looked as if the rebels had evacuated, blowing up their magazines behind them." Walke immediately informed the admiral, who ordered Walke to proceed with the *Lafayette* and attack Grand Gulf. As the sun rose, the ram got under way. "By a contraband who deserted them," Lyons explained, "we learned that they were reinforced from Vicksburg by 4500 men and intended to fight Genl Grant and Genl McClernand to-day." The ironclad ran up at full speed, followed by the rest of the fleet. "When within a distance of a mile, we slacked up and fired two eleven-inch shell at the works but no answer was returned," Morison recorded in his journal. "Then we got out three blank charges and ran up alongside, shoved out a gangplank, and then our marines, followed by the first division of sharpshooters, went racing up the bluffs at railroad speed to see who could gain the fortification first." The first man to enter the works was George Dawson, "who waved his cutlass over his head and took possession of the hill in the name of the United States. Then John Beffel hoisted the 'Stars and Stripes' and we saluted it with three rousing cheers." The *Lafayette* then moved up to the four-gun Confederate battery, ran alongside, and tied up to a tree. "There was a strife among all the boats, as to which should plant the first colors on the upper battery which was some distance from the lower one," Lyons wrote. Walke dubbed it a "spirited race" and recalled that the *Lafayette* had the lead until the *Carondelet* blocked the way and gained the honor of raising the flag over the enemy's works. "But just then the admiral in the 'Benton' (the old war-horse!), came up, and all had to give place to the flag." The *Lafayette's* men did plant its flag on the lower battery, and Lyons wrote, "Our men from the 'Lafayette' planted one, the 'Pittsburg's' crew one, the 'Carondelet's' crew another."[23]

Walke and most of the officers went ashore to look at the works. "The battery was very strong, mounting three sixty-eights and one seven-inch rifle. They were all spiked, of course," Morison explained. The industrious coxswain went ashore as well, where he found several sailors foraging, one chasing a chicken with a drawn cutlass, and another hunting an old gander with a pistol. Morison managed to grab a bobtailed chicken and made it back to the boat safely, "but the others were not so fortunate as they met the admiral on the bluff. He abused them for thieving and ended up by ordering them to take the things on board of the 'Benton' where they went to enrich his larder, bless his gallant and magnanimous heart."[24]

"We had a hard fight with these forts," Porter told the navy secretary, "and it is with great pleasure that I report that the Navy holds the door to Vicksburg."[25] Satisfied that matters were well in hand at Grand Gulf, Porter decided to go down to the Red River and take over the blockade from Farragut. He left the *Louisville* at Grand Gulf and took the *Lafayette, Pittsburg,* and *Price;* the ram *Switzerland;* and the tug *Ivy* with him. Jotting down his impressions of the journey, Lyons wrote that after taking on coal, the *Lafayette* went downstream past Bruinsburg. "Here the women turned out in their best bonnet and gown and saluted Capt. Officers and crew as we passed along. Capt. Walke facetiously called our 'contrabands' on deck and made them return the salute by touching their hats to the colored ladies." As the *Lafayette* passed Natchez, crowds lined the bluffs, gazing curiously at the federal ships. When the flotilla reached the mouth of the Red River, Lyons spotted Farragut's flagship, the *Hartford.* Soon officers from the frigate came on board the *Lafayette,* and Farragut received the welcome news that Porter was relieving him of blockade duty. Porter then headed up the Red River with the *Benton, Lafayette, Pittsburg, Price, Switzerland,* and *Ivy.* When they met two of Farragut's vessels, the *Arizona* and *Estrella,* coming downstream, Porter detained them and took them back with him.[26]

"We are now on the Red River literally as the water is the color of iron rust," Morison explained. "Got along very slowly as the river does not exceed 200 feet in width in most places and turns about every fifty yards or so. Sometimes our bow touched one shore and our stern on another." The *Lafayette* consequently fell behind the other federal vessels but managed to take a river pilot on board. "We are now in rebel country," Walke's clerk wrote, "and guerillas fire on us whenever they get a chance. We have sharp shooters stationed on the paddleboxes, to draw a bead on them if they come in sight." Just before sunset, they passed two plantations, "where the people came out and saluted us."[27]

The *Lafayette* arrived at Gordon's Landing at 7:30 p.m. and found a burning raft lighting up the anchorage. "Here the rebs had three heavy guns mounted and a raft of iron chain stretched across the river to stop us," Morison wrote. The *Price* forced the obstructions and shelled a three-gun battery, "but there was no one there to answer her, they having evacuated. They threw two of their guns into the river but did not have time for the third as [we] were too close." When the *Lafayette* tied up to a tree, Lyons expressed great unease about their new location: "We are now far into the rebel country, and it will require great vigilance to prevent the rascals from surprising us and overpowering us by superior numbers. We are in a close place, and have not much advantage over a mass of infantry, and light artillery."[28]

The next evening they arrived at Fort de Russey. Porter found that the rebels had evacuated the fort, removing all but one 64-pounder gun. The *Price* ran against a raft the enemy had put in the river, opening a passage for the other vessels. After lying near the fort for the night, Porter decided it would take too much time to destroy it, so he pushed on to Alexandria, sending the *Arizona* ahead to surprise any steamer in the town. The flotilla weighed anchor and steamed upstream.[29]

"The swamps and the bush were replaced by the well-tilled farm and the springing crop of sugar cane," Morison wrote in his diary. "Habitations became more frequent and from them whites and blacks would rush out to look at us as we slid past." His comment about the local population is telling. "The welcomes were in all cases poor men and vice versa and the darkies cut up great figures when they were not seen by any white folks." At 7:00 p.m. the federal vessels anchored, as reports indicated the rebels had some batteries several miles above. That evening, Morison found "all hands at quarters with orders to sleep at their guns so as to be ready in case we were attacked through the night."[30]

The next morning, once a heavy mist had cleared, the flotilla moved up to the city of Alexandria. "Five contrabands come down to greet us with various gestures that tell us that the 'Rebs' had all 'done gone,'" Lyons wrote.[31]

Porter's General Order called for the *Benton* to anchor directly off the town of Alexandria, with the *Estrella* and *Lafayette* ahead of it, followed by the *Pittsburg, Arizona,* and *Price.* "Guns will be left ready to fire day and night and small arms handy. No boats to visit the shore without permission," Porter told his captains. When the flotilla arrived, it discovered that the *Arizona* had taken possession of the city, and Morison noted, "The Stars and Stripes were now floating from the top of a tree in front of the city (much to Admiral Porter's chagrin)." The citizens of Alexandria, white and black, had turned out on the levee "to look at us but not one gave us a welcome." According to Porter, "There was great rejoicing among the Union men at our arrival, and no indisposition on the part of anyone to meet us in friendly spirit." Morison thought Alexandria a "lively-looking place" with "a couple of churches and some very fine brick buildings." The *Benton* sent soldiers ashore to post sentries at the principal street corners. About 5:30 that evening (May 7), a regiment of Union cavalry rode into town "at a full gallop, cheering our fleet as they hove into sight." The cavalry was the advance of General Banks's army. Banks arrived at about 7:00, earlier than expected; he boarded the *Lafayette* and then "took quarters at the hotel opposite where we are lying."[32]

Porter turned the city of Alexandria and a crowd of noisy Union sympathizers over to Banks. "The water is to[o] low for us to ascend higher up the Red River and return with safety," Porter explained. He intended to return to Grand Gulf in a few days and left Walke and the *Lafayette* at Alexandria, along with the *Switzerland, Arizona,* and *Estrella,* to cooperate with Banks in case he needed navy services. Porter then went down to the mouth of the Red River, attempting to destroy the Fort de Russey works en route. His men could not get at the main fort, located on a hill some 900 yards from the water, but they destroyed three heavy casemates commanding the channel and a small water battery of two guns below it. They also blew up a raft closing the entrance, sawed it in two, "and presented it to the poor of the neighborhood."[33]

On Friday, May 8, Porter sent the *Arizona,* Commander Woodworth in the *Price,* the *Switzerland,* and the *Pittsburg* up the Black River on a reconnaissance, hoping to locate and recapture the *Queen of the West* and the *Webb.* Woodworth found heavy batteries that the rebels refused to surrender, so his boats shelled them, without much effect. He did not have the force to take them, so he returned.[34]

On Saturday the *Benton* went downriver to the Mississippi and up to Vicksburg, leaving the *Lafayette* and *Estrella* on station. "About 4 P.M. our marines and first division of sharp shooters were called away in a hurry as some guerillas had made their appearance on the bank." They soon landed and, after a few minutes' chase, succeeded in capturing two guerrillas. "One of the guerillas said he was captain of a gang amounting to 100." He was "drunk and said more than he would if he was sober. He was armed with a rifle, a pistol, and a bowie knife and was splendidly mounted." At 4:00 p.m. Morison went ashore with a boat to bring off Banks and some of his staff. He described Banks as "a very compact, upright figure with a pleasant face and an eye which beamed with good nature and shrewdness combined, and in fact he looked every inch the soldier and good man." Banks questioned the guerrilla and put him in irons; the other was turned over to the provost marshal.[35]

The *Lafayette* remained in the Red River at Alexandria until Banks returned to Port Hudson. It then joined the *Pittsburg* to blockade the mouth of that river. Walke lamented their location, writing, "This was a long, tedious and sickly position for the crews of these two vessels."[36]

The *Lafayette* weighed anchor early in the morning and headed downstream, passing Gordon's Landing at noon. They discovered that on its way down, the *Benton* had destroyed the batteries and Gordon's house there. "Saw alligators for the first time in my life," Morison wrote. The vessel arrived on the Mississippi River at 9:00 a.m. on May 15, joining the *Hartford, Pittsburg,* and *Sachem* performing blockade duty off the mouth of the river.[37]

Their new station gave the *Lafayette*'s paymaster the opportunity to go ashore and procure supplies, including "some fish, milk, eggs, Irish potatoes, cauliflower, black berries and chickens. Some of the crew also availed themselves of a chance to go swimming in the river." Other than that, there was little to break the monotony of blockade duty. On May 17 the *Estrella* arrived from Vicksburg with news that the rebels had evacuated Warrenton and Grant had taken Jackson, Mississippi. That day, clerk Lyons recorded the arrival of three contrabands who "joined the naval service. The Capt. emptied the ale bottle to one of them. In an hour they were rigged up in 'Navy uniform.'" The dull routine was broken on May 23, when Morison noticed refugees coming down from above, "the rebs having driven them out as they were 'French' and flew the tri-color on their flat boat. Splendid news from Grant but no sign of a mail. Awful lonesome here," he lamented. As the month of May came to a close, the *Lafayette* remained on blockade duty, with little to relieve the monotony. But that was soon to change.[38]

In a turnabout, Banks had decided not to support Grant's move on Vicksburg; instead, he would cooperate with Farragut in taking Port Hudson. He ordered Brigadier General Cuvier Grover to bring his division east through Simmesport, cross the Mississippi River, and place his troops in the rear of Port Hudson. Federal troops coming up from Baton Rouge also engaged the rebels at Plains Store, driving them back. By May 23 Banks had his corps poised to attack Port Hudson. That afternoon, Farragut arrived in the *Monongahela* to join the *Essex, Richmond, Kineo,* and *Genesee,* which had already started lobbing shells at the Confederate batteries. "There are three more gunboats on the way which are expected here today, making in all nine fighting crafts," the *Kineo*'s surgeon A. S. Oberly wrote to his girlfriend Maria Woodford.[39]

After undergoing repairs for damage suffered earlier at Port Hudson, the *Kineo* had taken part in an expedition at Sabine Pass, then returned to New Orleans. On Monday, May 18, it coaled ship and got under way. On the afternoon of May 23 it "steamed up to the fleet and participated in the firing at the Port Hudson batteries," Oberly wrote in his diary. "All the vessels viz Monongahela, Richmond, Genesee, Kineo + Essex engaged at long range. Some of the shots were well directed. Enemy fired but little + without doing any injury. Mortars fired slowly all the time." That evening the *Kineo* returned to its station.[40]

Although the rebel batteries did not inflict any damage, the following day when the *Kineo* steamed up to the flagship with dispatches, it "ran afoul of the Richmond's jib-boom on our return carrying away the fore-yard, mainmast, +c. Mr. Rodgers had his shoulder dislocated." With the assistance of Dr. Fisher, Oberly reduced it. "Accident occurred as the captain states through the error of the pilot's judgement," he noted, once again highlighting the importance of having experienced pilots with knowledge of the river. Oberly also jotted that the army was skirmishing that day and wrote, "Mortars at work during the night + the army firing also." Banks had ordered his artillery, some ninety guns, to join the bombardment. At 5:00 a.m. on May 27 "the fleet moved up + in concert with the mortars fired on the batteries." Banks's assault on Port Hudson had begun. Farragut's ships supported the army's determined efforts to storm the Confederate breastworks, but the bluecoats were repulsed, and at 2:00 the next day Banks asked for a cease-fire to allow his men to gather up the dead and wounded.[41]

The first day of the attack the *Kineo* was ordered to take prisoners and wounded from the *Sallie Robison.* When the gunboat returned from Baton

Rouge, Oberly was asked to go ashore and assist the wounded. "Worked diligently until 7 A.M.," he wrote. "About 150 wounded arrived during the night. Drs. Fisher + Lynd tired out." Oberly's diary entries indicate that the fight for Port Hudson was a costly one. "Wounded coming in rapidly. Gen. Sherman wounded. Friday May 29th at Springfield Landing. Wounded + cotton coming in." Union casualties were reported to be around 2,000 men, including Brigadier General Thomas W. Sherman. At Banks's request, Farragut's fleet remained off Port Hudson to bombard the rebel positions, but Oberly remained on shore tending the casualties. He noted, however, that Dr. Baumgarten had returned to the *Monongahela* and Dr. Murphy to the *Richmond*, "both tired and weary."[42]

The siege of Port Hudson went on. "I will shell them but I do not believe it does much good," Farragut lamented. The range of his mortars and Dahlgren guns did not permit them to reach all the enemy batteries. Banks procured a battery of 9-inch Dahlgrens, but he had no trained gunners to man them. Farragut solved that problem quickly, ordering men from the *Richmond* ashore. On June 1, as the *Kineo* lay anchored off the landing, Oberly wrote, "Took a walk ashore. Lieut Terry of the Richmond with a detachment of marines + sailors were ordered to take charge of the heavy siege guns. About 9 P.M. several soldiers came to the river's bank and serenaded us with beautiful singing." With summer in full swing, the temperatures climbed into the nineties, and Oberly started sleeping on deck, "annoyed by mosquitoes." On June 7 the *Kineo* received twenty-five Confederate prisoners from the *Monongahela*. That evening, the prisoners went to the tug *Anglo American*. "Mississippi River has fallen fifteen or more feet during the last three weeks," Oberly wrote. Four days later, Oberly recorded news from the battlefield: "Gen. Wetzel's forces attempted an assault last night but was repulsed with a loss in killed + wounded of 7 to 800."[43]

Banks's failed assault and the lack of progress against Vicksburg did not bode well for the Union cause. The first four months of 1863 had yielded few if any Union victories in the field. This had encouraged antiwar politicians and fueled protests about emancipation and the enactment of national conscription. Success against Confederate forces at Port Hudson and Vicksburg—thereby securing navigation of the entire Mississippi River and splitting the Confederacy in two—would go a long way toward raising Northern morale and squelching criticism of Lincoln and his administration. But achieving victories at Port Hudson and Vicksburg would take Union forces two more months of fighting.

17

Blockade and Siege

Milliken's Bend and Simmesport

This was the first important engagement of the war in which colored troops were under fire. These were very raw, having all been enlisted since the beginning of the siege, but they behaved well.

—Ulysses S. Grant

While Banks's siege of Port Hudson went into its third week, and Farragut's bombardment of rebel batteries entered its fifth week, to the north, General Grant's federal troops and Admiral Porter's fleet were focused on reducing the rebel stronghold at Vicksburg. "The enemy no doubt have a stronghold at this place, as their batteries are behind high bluffs where we cannot easily dislodge them," surgeon Oberly explained in a letter to his fiancée. "They are said to have 7000 in place and 5000 more close by which can be on hand at short notice. This place is naturally of great interest for them for when once lost the railroad communication will be broken between the east section & west taking the Mississippi River as the dividing line." The federal commanders had resolved to attack Vicksburg, Oberly explained, and in a postscript he wrote, "Enemy determined to fight. Their women & children ordered to leave the place. Attack I believe is to commence tomorrow morning."[1]

From the deck of his flagship *Black Hawk* on the morning of May 19, 1863, Porter listened to the sound of gunfire in the rear of Vicksburg and knew that Grant was approaching the city. Realizing that the rebels on the Yazoo were cut off from joining Confederate forces in the city, Porter quick-

261

ly ordered Breese to take the *De Kalb,* the *Choctaw,* and the tinclads *Linden, Romeo, Petrel,* and *Forest Rose* up the Yazoo to open communication with Grant and Sherman. Within hours, both generals had informed Porter of their success.[2]

At Grant's request, the admiral sent Lieutenant Commander John Walker in a gunboat up the Yazoo to see whether the enemy had evacuated Drum Gould's. He found federal cavalry already in possession of the bluff, prompting Porter to dispatch the gunboats from below Vicksburg to fire on the hill batteries. "At midnight they moved up to the town and opened on it for about an hour," Porter reported, "and continued at intervals during the night to annoy the garrison."[3]

As Grant's men invested Vicksburg, Porter's vessels kept up their bombardment of rebel positions on the river. The admiral also placed six mortars in position, ordering them to fire on Vicksburg day and night. In a very short time, Porter informed Welles, Grant would make a general assault on Vicksburg, and he expected the rebel stronghold to fall. "It is a mere question of a few hours, and then, with the exception of Port Hudson (which will follow Vicksburg), the Mississippi will be open its entire length."[4]

To support Grant's attack on Vicksburg, scheduled for that very day, May 19, Porter ordered Lieutenant Commander Greer to move up toward the city with the *Benton, Tuscumbia,* and *Carondelet* and shell the forts if the rebels opened fire on federal troops. For some reason, the order failed to reach Greer, so late in the evening, Porter told Greer to send the *Tuscumbia* up that night to shell the town. Then he admonished Greer, "The army will likely go in to-morrow, and we must do our share, even if the vessels suffer."[5]

Grant's first assault on Vicksburg's determined Confederate defenders was repulsed, so the next day, Porter beefed up the navy's round-the-clock bombardment with the addition of six mortar boats. On May 21 Grant informed Porter that he intended to renew his attack on Vicksburg at 10:00 the following morning and asked the admiral to send the gunboats below the city to shell the enemy entrenchments for one hour before and half an hour after the assault began. The general also suggested that the mortars annoy the enemy that night. Porter complied, ordering the *Benton, Mound City,* and *Carondelet* to shell the water batteries and anywhere the rebel troops might be resting that night.[6]

Early the next morning, Lieutenant Byron Wilson took the *Mound City* across the river and attacked the hill batteries opposite the canal. An hour later, Porter joined him with the *Benton, Tuscumbia,* and *Carondelet,* and they proceeded to pound the enemy into silence. Leaving the *Tuscumbia* to occupy the hill batteries, Porter then went up to shell the water batteries with the *Benton, Carondelet,* and *Mound City.* Rebel gunners fought back with accurate and incessant fire, but the federal vessels closed the range to 440 yards and kept firing for two hours. "This was the hottest fire the gunboats have ever been under," Porter noted, "but owing to the water batteries being more on a level with them than usual, the gunboats threw in their shell so fast that the aim of the enemy was not very good." Although the gunboats were struck repeatedly by rebel shot and shell, the squadron suffered few casualties.[7]

After Grant's second assault on May 22 failed to take Vicksburg, Sherman's troops occupied positions on the right above the city, McPherson's men were positioned in the center, and McClernand's were on the left, securing the road to Warrenton. With the navy holding the river, the investment of Vicksburg was complete. "My line was more than fifteen miles long," Grant wrote later, "extending from Haynes Bluff to Vicksburg, then south to Warrenton." Having decided that a frontal assault would not succeed, Grant explained, "I now determined upon a regular siege—to 'outcamp' the enemy as it were, and to incur no more losses." Guessing that the rebels could not hold out much longer, he asked Porter for the assistance of every gunboat and mortar available. The vessels complied, conducting attacks on enemy points along the riverfront and lobbing shells into Vicksburg day and night, tormenting the city's defenders.[8]

Having no siege guns on hand, Grant asked Porter to supply him with a battery of large-caliber naval guns. The work of building and entrenching this battery fell to the pioneer troops and to African Americans who ventured within federal lines and were paid for their work. On May 23 Porter informed Grant that Banks was not, in fact, coming up to Vicksburg with his troops, as anticipated. He had landed at Bayou Sara to attack Port Hudson.[9]

Four days after the failed attack on Vicksburg, Grant pleaded with Porter to use his ironclads to support Sherman's men and clear the southern slope. The admiral reluctantly agreed and ordered George Bache to take the *Cincinnati* down "to enfilade some rifle pits which barred the progress of our army." The admiral was under the impression that the Confederates had moved their guns to the land side and the *Cincinnati* would be facing only rifle pits. As a diversion, Porter ordered Woodworth to move his gunboats opposite the canal and try to silence the hill batteries. If he succeeded, then he was to move up and feint as if he were attacking the water batteries. Grant promised that Steele's sharpshooters would occupy the battery while the ironclads went to work. At 8:30 on May 27, 1863, the gunboats, accompanied by the *Carondelet, Mound City,* and *Benton,* steamed up and engaged the hill batteries for over an hour, but they were unable to silence the rebel gunners. The *Carondelet* worked its bow guns and starboard battery, but the *Mound City,* lying behind the *Benton,* could not get into a good firing position.[10]

The *Cincinnati* had recently arrived from the Carondelet shipyards, where it had undergone extensive repairs following its service in the Yazoo. "We had protected our stern with bales of hay, also piled them around the Pilothouse," Daniel Kemp recalled, "although it was protected by iron plating. Our sides were partially protected, but only on the sides next to our boilers, so we hung chains over the starboard and port bows." However, he pointed out, "we were poorly protected as we had to fight head on, going down stream, and it was impossible to keep her so, because every time our big guns went off, our boat swung around and exposed our poorly protected parts to the enemy."[11]

The *Cincinnati* got under way on the morning of May 27 and steamed down abreast of where the mortars lay, then rounded to. According to Kemp, "At 8:30 a.m. with a full head of steam the gunboat headed for the assigned position" to shell a water battery at the edge of a ravine that separated the two armies. "Just as soon as we got within range of their guns the battle began, and we fought not only a water battery but every battery at Vicksburg was pouring shot and shell into our doomed gunboat, and they had the range so perfect that almost every shot struck us, and came through, and did alot of damage." According to Bache, "We were especially annoyed by plunging shot from the hills, an 8-inch rifle and a 10-inch smoothbore doing us much damage. The shot went entirely through our protection— hay, wood and iron." One ball entered the *Cincinnati*'s magazine, flooding it. Another carried the starboard tiller away. "Another shot struck the Pilothouse and, striking a bolt, drove it through the casemate into our Pilot's back, killing him," Kemp recalled. Bache told Kemp and another sailor to carry the wounded pilot down to the gun deck. "He was not dead when we lifted him, but was suffering intensely, and praying to us most piteously, 'Shoot me, for God's sake, shoot me.' We laid him down on the deck and his sufferings were soon over. I hope I may never see another such death."[12]

Instead of stationing himself on the spar deck to give directions, Bache had "safely tucked himself away in the pilot house," Kemp explained. "One of our quartermasters, who was also in the Pilothouse when our Pilot was killed, had his breast badly torn by the splinters that flew around, but Captain Bache was not even scratched." Fearing the *Cincinnati* would sink, Bache ran the gunboat upstream as close to the right-hand shore as the ironclad's damaged steering apparatus would permit. He nudged the damaged vessel toward the bank and put out a plank for the wounded to get ashore. "Many of our boys were hurt by splinters," Kemp recalled, but "I was very fortunate, as I was only struck by a small block of wood that came flying my way, which hit me on the right shin. It did not break my leg, but it hurt like mischief." They got a hawser and fastened the *Cincinnati* to a tree, but "unfortunately," Bache wrote, "the men ashore at the hawser left it without making it fast, the enemy still firing." The gunboat began to drift. Believing the water to be deep, Bache called out for the men to swim to shore. "The men were jumping into the water when a shell came flying over, struck into the mud, exploded and sent the mud high into the air, coming down onto the heads of the men in the water." Kemp opined, "I think many of our men were drowned at this time. Leopold Snyder, a Buffalo boy and friend of mine, I never saw again, so I think he was drowned at that time." The veteran gunboat sank in three fathoms of water, but Bache assured Porter, "The vessel went down with her colors raised to the mast, or rather the stump of one, all three having been shot away. Our fire, until the magazine was drowned, was good, and I am satisfied did damage."[13]

When the hospital flag was raised, "they got down the second cutter and put the dead and wounded into it and took them up to the Flagship," Kemp recalled. Because he was one of the dinghy's crew, he went in the cutter and helped it up to the flagship. "We left a wreck of what, an hour before, was one of the finest gunboats on the river." Every night a boat crew would go down to check on the wreck, and on the sixth night they discovered that the rebels had "set fire to what was left of the Cincinnati, burned it to the water's edge, and carried away our flag which we had left fastened to the stump of our forward mast. This was certainly a bold undertaking."[14]

The majority of the *Cincinnati*'s officers and men went to the gunboat *Lexington,* but Kemp and several other sailors went to the *Choctaw,* a 260-foot side-wheel steamer converted in 1862 to an ironclad ram. Commissioned in March 1863 and armed with a 100-pounder rifle, three 9-inch smoothbores, and two 30-pounder rifles, the *Choctaw* was a formidable addition to Porter's squadron. During the diversionary attack on Haynes' Bluff in late April, the ram suffered fifty-three hits but continued to serve in the Yazoo until being sent down to Milliken's Bend on June 6, in response to reports that Confederate troops were threatening federal camps there and at Young's Point.[15]

The army kept a quantity of stores at Milliken's Bend, guarded by two black regiments and men of the 29th Iowa Regiment. Anticipating that they might need naval support, Porter ordered the *Choctaw* and *Lexington* up to the bend. At 3:15 the next morning, an army officer hailed the *Choctaw* and told the gunboat's commanding officer, Lieutenant Commander Frank Ramsay, that their pickets had been attacked by enemy troops. When the rebels attacked the post in the predawn hours, the black soldiers "met the onset manfully," Porter noted, and "a company of the Iowa regiment stood at their post until they were slaughtered to a man, killing an equal number of rebels." The overpowered Union soldiers retreated behind the bank near the water's edge. Twenty minutes later, observing sharp firing close to the federal camp, Ramsay ordered the *Choctaw* to open fire with its 100-pounder rifle and 9-inch gun. "It was impossible for me to see the enemy on account of the high banks, and I could learn their position only by hailing our troops," Ramsay reported. At 8:30 a.m., however, he observed the rebels retreating into the woods. Half an hour later the *Lexington* came up and threw twenty-four rounds into the woods. "Had not a gunboat been present the enemy would have captured everything," Ramsay noted.[16]

Although part of the rebel force had retreated, the firing continued until around noon. When the gunboats arrived, they opened fire with shell, grape, and canister. The enemy, Porter wrote, "fled in wild confusion, not knowing the gunboats were there or expecting such a reception." In their haste, the rebels left eighty of their dead behind. Ramsay sent Ensign Ezra Beaman with boats to bring twenty wounded officers and men to the gunboat, where the *Choctaw*'s acting assistant surgeon Eugene P. Robbins did his best to care for them. One of the officers, Captain Thomas Blondin, died, but the others were sent to army transports to be taken to hospitals. Of the 1,148 men in the defending force, 492 were killed, wounded, or missing—a staggering casualty rate of 43 percent.[17]

"The moment I heard of it, I went up in the *Black Hawk*," Porter told Grant, "and saw quite an ugly sight. The dead negroes lined the ditch inside of the parapet, or levee, and were mostly shot on the top of the head. In front of them, close to the levee, lay an equal number of rebels, stinking in the sun. . . . They were miserable looking wretches."[18]

Writing after the war, Grant noted, "This was the first important engagement of the war in which colored troops were under fire. These were very raw, having all been enlisted since the beginning of the siege, but they behaved well."[19]

While most of the Mississippi Squadron was supporting the siege of Vicksburg, the ram *Lafayette* was down at the mouth of the Red River, with orders to cooperate with General Banks. With the concurrence of Commodore Palmer, Walke had remained there until May 24. Refugees from Alexandria had informed Walke that the rebels had reoccupied the place and were bringing their gunboats down. "The river is falling very fast," Walke reported to Porter, "and if it continues to fall at this rate I shall be obliged in a few days to drop down below the bar, or near the mouth of this [Red] river." He also told Porter that he had received a dozen good contrabands but could not accommodate any more, "so I shall have to send any others that may come on board to General Banks, unless you will have them otherwise disposed of. They state that General Taylor has about 2,000 troops at Alexandria." In conclusion, Walke informed the admiral that he needed another coal barge and was short of provisions, particularly bread, and small stores.[20]

The next day, writing from the *Black Hawk,* Porter told Walke, "Do not get uneasy. I will see that you get everything in time." Porter was hauling coal overland and assured Walke that he would send him a large load in a day or two. "We are fighting hard here, but Vicksburg is bound to fall. Keep at Black River as long as you can; the *Pittsburg* will join you."[21]

About noon on May 24 the *Pittsburg* came from Bayou Sara, bringing the news that Vicksburg and Port Hudson could hold out only a few days longer. "I wish they were taken as I want to get home, not having heard from there in Six weeks," a worried Morison wrote in his diary. Numerous transports went down the river that day carrying troops, contrabands, and siege artillery. "They all cheered as they passed and we returned the compliment." Two more contrabands boarded the *Lafayette* and promptly joined the navy. By now, the weather had turned very warm, and Lyons noted that more of the crew had taken ill. The clerk also recorded another incident: "William A. Lowe put into the 'Brig' for sticking a needle into a soldier's shoulder." During the night, more refugees sought sanctuary on the ironclad. "One Frenchman, two other white men, (all refugees), three contrabands (men) and two mulatto girls come on board and still remain."[22]

The following day, a Sunday, the *Lafayette* held religious services and muster as usual. Afterward Morison penned his news: "I received my discharge and pay, which amounted to [amount left blank]. Shook hands with almost everyone on board. All said they were sorry to lose me for a shipmate. I shook hands with the captain. He wished me good fortune and said that he would be very glad to have me under his command again, especially in war time." Morison boarded the *Price* at 1:30 p.m., and "in fifteen minutes more, a bend in the river had the 'Lafayette' from my view forever (I hope)," Morison wrote. He was replaced as coxswain by Thomas Tempest, "a very unpopular choice," Lyons explained.[23]

The *Price* brought word from Commodore Palmer that he expected "Port Hudson will fall some day. General Banks is very anxious about the enemy's massing at Simmesport." Palmer had learned that the rebel Kirby Smith was marching down with a large force to a point opposite Port Hudson, "where we have a force of 400 men, who are in great consternation." Palmer asked Walke to send the *Switzerland* down "to see if there is any truth in this report. I do not credit it."[24]

Before ordering Lieutenant Colonel J. A. Ellet and the *Switzerland* down to Simmesport, Walke attempted a look-see of his own. The prospect of action against the enemy buoyed the crew's spirits—at least those who were healthy enough to man their stations. On June 3 the ironclad weighed anchor and started down the river. The *Switzerland* went ahead, and the *Pittsburg* followed the *Lafayette*. They steamed about ten miles but found the navigation too difficult, so returned. Then, Lyons explained, Walke sent the *Switzerland* down the Atchafayala Bayou to reconnoiter. "A short distance from the Red River they fell in with a Rebel Battery of Flying Artillery and engaged with them. The 'Switzerland' had her exhaust pipe cut off and three men wounded, one of them mortally. About noon she returned and made her report."[25]

Next, Walke sent the ram down to Palmer with a request for "a few troops to capture the enemy's artillery after I had driven them away from their guns at Simmesport." However, "she returned this morning without obtaining any assistance from the army or promise of any."[26] Not to be denied, Walke ordered Ellet to take the *Switzerland* to Bayou Sara, report to Banks, and ask for troops "to clear out the rebel nest." When Ellet returned on June 4 and reported that the general had declined to send any of his troops, Walke decided to take matters into his own hands and teach the rebels a lesson. He transferred the *Lafayette*'s sick to the *Switzerland* and went to Simmesport with the *Pittsburg*. There, the two gunboats shelled the rebels away from their breastworks and fired into their camp and into houses they had occupied as quarters. An officer on the ironclad wrote, "'Lafayette' approached the rebel fort unseen and fired two 11 inch shell 'close to if not into their works.'" Walke had stationed sharpshooters in towers on the *Lafayette*'s wheelhouse, and they "poured a raking, plunging fire down into their forts, causing the whole party to pick up and skedaddle in the greatest possible haste," leaving personal luggage, official papers, and such behind. The two vessels then returned to their former anchorage, and on June 5 the *Lafayette* went downstream to the mouth of the Red River.[27]

Morison had left the *Lafayette* by the time of the Simmesport incident, but life went on for his former shipmates and for the numerous contrabands who had taken refuge on the ironclad. Clerk Lyons recorded one particular incident: "About this time, a body of colored—I can not say Negro for many of them were almost white, population appeared on the shore signaling for us to take them away. They seemed to be in great consternation about something. There were about 600 in all, both great and small. They all took some luggage with them when they left the shore." The *Lafayette* started up the Red River, but when they got to the entrance, "we kept on up the Mississippi about a mile and made fast to the Louisiana shore. Sent out pickets—then a working party to tear a old house down to get lumber to build a shelter for the 'Contrabands.'" The ship went up to an old anchorage, repaired a coal barge, and moved the contrabands into it. Subsequently, the transport steamers *Laurel Hill* and *Empire Parish* came down, took all the contrabands on board, and went down to Port Hudson.[28]

The commanding officers of Union navy vessels usually welcomed Union refugees, taking them on board and sending many of them north. In some cases, however, captains promptly put them ashore. Lyons recorded on June 3, 1863: "6 P.M. The two so-called refugees were put on shore with the things which they brought and two or three days rations. So much for the American Republic in these waters," he bitterly noted.[29]

African Americans fleeing their masters or avoiding conscription by the Confederates were not the only refugees who found their way to the gunboat. On the afternoon of June 18, "two young ladies came on board from the Louisiana side of the river. They reported that they had been confined in Shreveport for uttering Union sentiments and had just been sent out of the Rebel lines. The Capt. entertained them at his table." At 7:00 the ladies were sent to Colonel Acklin's mansion.[30]

The month of June ushered in the hot, humid Southern summer, as well as hordes of annoying mosquitoes. Wise Mississippi sailors like Lyons took measures to protect themselves from the insects. "I bought some mosquito netting from Henry Williams, the Colored Cook of the Wardroom," he wrote on June 1. Unknown at the time, the pesky mosquitoes also carried illness, and Lyons mentioned the growing number of sick sailors. "Sick list increasing, Dover's Powder keeps them quiet," he wrote on June 8. The next day he noted that there was some discussion of sending the sick men ashore, and the "surgeon was preparing a plea for the station to be relieved on account of his own health and the health of the men." As more men fell ill, Walke set the *Lafayette's* crewmen to scrubbing and cleaning in an attempt to prevent more illness. As more men succumbed, the *Lafayette's* gun deck became a hospital. Lyons complained: "One officer raises an objection to taking the sick on shore. . . .Consequently the poor sufferers are kept on board in this sweat-box." That evening, a cool breeze came up, and Lyons could hear heavy firing from the direction of Port Hudson. The next day he felt feverish and weak. A man on the ship died of heart disease, and at 2:00 the following afternoon the *Lafayette* sent a party on shore to bury the dead. "No service read on board of the ship—Catholic Service read at the grave." Three days later the clerk noted that the carpenter was fitting up a coal barge for a hospital.[31]

The best the *Lafayette's* officers and crew could hope for was a change of station from the Red River to a base farther north, but the gunboat remained on blockade duty for the rest of June. To cope with the monotony, one cool evening in late June the officers were heard singing. The captain had continued his hobby of sketching and doing watercolors and was painting a representation of the "Grand Gulf Fight." Unfortunately, scarce provisions meant the men could not look forward to mealtime as a diversion from the boredom and the sultry weather. "Provisions getting scarcer in the messes," Lyons explained. "Wardroom bread is bad. Got some berries and milk for our mess." As provisions continued to dwindle, the ironclad frequently sent cutters ashore to forage for food. "Obtained honey, fish, potatoes, green beans, etc," the clerk happily wrote. The *Lafayette* also sent cutters out "to trade with the Africans, it being the best market day here, as it is in all the Southern cities and towns on the Sabbath."[32]

By June 14, the sick list had grown to thirty people, including Lyons, who had resorted to taking ipecac and had vomited "with great distress." Later that afternoon they took on more contrabands, and the following day the *Pittsburg* returned with another 182. As Lyons explained, "The 'Pittsburg' went on down the river to intercept some 'Contrabands' which the rebels are driving away to Texas to get them outside of the Union lines. The 'Contrabands' which belong on our boat as enlisted men held a prayer-meeting on the Spar deck last night." Within two days, fourteen more contraband men, women, and children had sought refuge on the *Lafayette.* Their numbers prompted both gunboats to dispatch foraging parties, for "our provisions are now being diminished very rapidly." Lyons lamented, "One cutter from the 'Pittsburg' and one from our boat went out foraging for beef and brought back twelve contrabands instead." Several days later, fifteen or twenty more fugitive slaves arrived, adding to the number already being fed and protected by the gunboats. Most of these contrabands were housed on the coal barge, which had become a village unto itself. "Last night there was a wedding ceremony and dance in one end of the barge, a religious prayer meeting in the middle and a birth in the other end of the barge." Walke set some of the able-bodied male contrabands to work, and his clerk occasionally referred to their duties. For instance, "Mr. Deming (the pilot) started down to Port Hudson in a skiff with two contrabands for propelling power."[33]

On June 20 Walke informed Porter of the situation. "Contrabands are accumulating, about 126 being on board at present. I have sent 220 to Commodore Palmer at Port Hudson." Walke told Porter that he had sent up 420 contrabands since his last report. He also informed the admiral that his vessel needed to be docked as soon as possible, as the keelson timber under the fire bed was burnt. "Our sick are increasing daily," Walke added, and he needed to replenish his coal, medicines, and provisions. The river had fallen so much and so fast that he had been compelled to leave Old River and anchor at its mouth. Although he had sent the *Pittsburg* and boats up several times, he could not "cut off the enemy's intercourse with the Atchafalaya without a light-draft gunboat of some speed."[34]

On June 20 Walke and the gunboat's crew heard the sound of heavy gunfire from the direction of Port Hudson. "Genl Banks has made a charge on Port Hudson but was repulsed," Lyons wrote in his diary the following day. Union troops under Banks had surrounded the rebel bastion at Port Hudson in late May, but the cautious general had not immediately attacked, giving the rebels time to fortify their position and move artillery to the riverfront. After an unsuccessful frontal assault on May 27, Banks laid siege to Port Hudson, supported by the arrival of additional infantry regiments, artillery pieces, and 9-inch Dahlgren smoothbores from the USS *Richmond.* Lyons was probably referring to Banks's second infantry assault on the morning of June 13, an hour-long bombardment followed by an uncoordinated predawn attack. Hampered by fog and poor planning, the second Union assault on Port Hudson was repulsed, with heavy casualties. Almost 1,800 Union men were killed or wounded, including a division commander who was wounded in the main attack and had to have his leg amputated.[35]

18

Final Push to Victory

The fall of Vicksburg ensured the fall of Port Hudson and the opening of the Mississippi River, which I am happy to say can be traversed from its source to its mouth without apparent impediment, the first time during the war.

—David Dixon Porter

Farther up the Mississippi River, Grant's troops continued to besiege the rebel stronghold at Vicksburg, supported by Porter's ironclads and gunboats. "From early June, 1863, Vicksburg was besieged day and night," Lieutenant Colonel George Currie wrote. "Our army was thoroughly and effectively investing the city, the right resting on the river above, thence in a crescent encircling it reaching the Mississippi again, below the city. Our Navy patrolled the river above, the peninsula opposite was in our possession, completely cutting off every avenue of supply and communication to the rebel garrison so hemmed in." Currie observed, "I see some northern newspapers are afraid that Grant will get in a tight place, but if they knew the man or the situation, their fears on that score would vanish." The colonel had confidence in "that quiet, unassuming man who is coolly walking along the line, with that cigar always in his mouth, and seeing everything that has been done or is to be done. . . . In him every soldier of this army has full confidence, and think 'the taking of Vicksburg has settled down to a mere question of time.'"[1]

In addition to time, the lack of food and provisions was a factor. As Sherman wrote to his wife on June 11, "The truth is we must trust to starvation." The siege progressed, but the rebels seemed determined to hold out.[2]

Porter, however, remained optimistic about the eventual fall of Vicksburg. His fleet kept bombarding the city, and he mounted a 10-inch gun on a scow to fire on the upper battery. Daniel Kemp remembered it well: "After we came down the river, we found the scow on which had been mounted a 10-inch Dahlgren gun in readiness for us to take down to some point near Vicksburg." Porter assigned Ramsay, the *Choctaw*'s commanding officer, to manage the three heavy guns placed on scows. "We first went down two or three hundred feet below our mortar boats," Kemp recalled, "which were used in throwing shells into Vicksburg, and remained there two days. Then we thought we would try to get a little closer, under cover of night, nearly opposite the *Cincinnati*'s wreck. There we laid under cover of darkness, within a few hundred yards of Vicksburg, for several days." Protected by the bend of the river, they kept up a constant fire at a battery on the Vicksburg side of the ravine that separated the two armies. "We did good execution, for we struck their breastworks a number of times, and it was said we dismounted one of their guns. Our shells struck among their tents many times, causing great commotion among the occupants." The rebels gave back, too, their pickets firing at Union pickets across the narrow river. They were getting their location, Kemp recalled, and one day sent over a shell "which burst directly over us, and you ought to have seen our officer in charge dive for the bank. The Rebels generally know about where to shoot, and waste no ammunition."[3]

In the meantime, the *Lafayette* continued its monotonous vigil. The boredom was broken only by the arrival of contrabands, which had become an almost daily event by June 1863. On June 22 Lyons noted that they picked up two small contrabands, "one of them being driven to Texas. He was sent back to get provisions and carry a letter. Instead of returning where he was sent he came down opposite the gunboats, tied his saddle to a tree and let the mule go at large. Then making the 'Contraband Signal'—he was brought on board—letter and all." Lyons added, "He is apparently fourteen years old and very cute." The following day ten contrabands arrived, three of them females, and were assigned to the barge. "The women are dressed in their former mistresses cast-off clothing of gay colors." The next day seven more former slaves boarded the gunboat, including three women and three children. Lyons explained that "fiddleing and dancing is the order of exercise on the Barge among the Free Africans of American or European descent." Local whites occasionally attempted to reclaim their runaway slaves. One of them known as "Old Ferris (a rebel) came on board of our Ship after his negroes—Capt. Walke told him that he was a prisoner, and could not go on shore anymore. Afterward, he let him go but kept his negroes."[4]

By June 22, the *Lafayette*'s sick list had grown to forty-two, among them clerk Lyons. "Capt. Walke came on deck from his breakfast and 'disrated' me without giving any reason or making any complaint about anything. I was taken sick, with bilious colic, and completely prostrated." According to Lyons, Walke replaced the clerk with a nonrated "white contraband" named Benjamin Holmes. That afternoon the doctor gave Lyons an emetic.[5]

A week later, Porter received word from General Dennis, commanding the post at Young's Point, that black troops at Goodrich's Landing, Louisiana, had been attacked, and "the rebels were getting the upper hand of them." Two African American regiments, the 1st Arkansas and 10th Louisiana, garrisoned Goodrich's Landing, on the west bank of the Mississippi River, at the time. They guarded a military supply depot and surrounding government-run plantations on which freedmen had been put to work growing cotton and other crops. They had also erected two forts on an old Indian mound. Porter had already dispatched a gunboat, but he quickly sent another and directed Brigadier General Alfred Ellet to proceed there with the Marine Brigade and remain "until everything was quiet."[6]

Ellet went immediately to Goodrich's Landing with his entire command, arriving at 2:00 in the morning. The side-wheel steamer *John Raine* approached the scene first, just as the rebels were setting fire to the government plantations. When Ellet arrived a few hours later, he "could plainly see the evidence of the enemy's operation in burning mansions, cotton gins, and negro quarters as far as the eye could reach." As Ellet later learned, the previous day, Colonel William H. Parson's rebels had attacked two black companies that had retreated into the smaller of the two forts. The rebels surrounded the fort and captured the soldiers "after a spirited resistance and considerable loss to the enemy," Ellet wrote. Sources claim that on June 29, Brigadier General James Tappan's brigade demanded that the black soldiers surrender. The regiment's three white officers agreed to this demand, provided they would be treated as prisoners of war, but the rebels would not guarantee the same treatment for the black soldiers. The rebels then took 116 men prisoner. Rather than seize the larger fort as well, the Confederate marauders plundered and burned cotton gins, plantations, and slave quarters. They also engaged Parson's mounted infantry near Lake Providence the following day.[7]

Assuming that the *Raine* was an ordinary, unarmed transport, the rebels opened fire with fieldpieces, and the *Raine*'s captain ordered his two 12-pounder brass guns to pour shrapnel into the enemy ranks. The rebels fled, and many of the African Americans they had captured broke free as well. The *Raine* then sent a landing party ashore; it gathered up twenty-three stands of small arms and rescued hundreds of captured blacks.

About this time, alerted by the sound of gunfire, Lieutenant John Vincent Johnston brought his wooden gunboat *Romeo* up the river. When he observed rebels setting fire to plantations, he ordered the ship's gunners to shell them. Chased along the riverbank by the gunfire, the rebel marauders set fire to everything as they went along, resulting in almost total destruction of houses and property along the riverfront.

In the predawn hours, Ellet's brigade arrived and disembarked. At daylight, eager to get going, Ellet sent his men off without breakfast to search for the enemy. When they reached the federal outposts, Ellet allowed the hungry infantrymen to rest and munch on blackberries while he sent the cavalry ahead to "push" the retreating rebels. His horsemen overtook the rebels, engaged them, and held them in check until Ellet came up with his main body. Because the rebels had crossed the bayou and burned the bridge behind them, Ellet's men could not pursue them, so they returned to the river. The brigade suffered only three casualties—two black soldiers slightly wounded, and Captain W. H. Wright of Company D mortally wounded. Although the Confederates had nearly twice as many troops, Ellet observed that "they were evidently not inclined to make a standing fight, their main object being to secure the negroes stolen from the plantations along the river, some hundreds of whom they had captured."[8]

During this engagement at Goodrich's Landing, the ram *Lafayette* had remained on station near the mouth of the Red River. But plantations in that vicinity were not immune to rebel raids. "On the 29th of June, the rebels made a raid upon Colonel Acklen's and the neighboring plantation," Walke recalled. "At about three o'clock in the morning, twenty five or thirty of their cavalry rode in haste and captured two of our sick men in a temporary hospital near the bank of the river where the gunboat 'Pittsburg' was anchored." The rebel cavalry also succeeded "in carrying off a negro patient."[9]

More than a week prior to this incident, Walke had informed Porter that the *Lafayette* needed to be "docked as soon as possible." Unless he heard from Porter or could get up the river soon, Walke explained, he would have to send the *Pittsburg* up to Vicksburg and make his way down to New Orleans to dock and repair his vessel. "I am very sorry to hear of your mishap. You can come up here whenever you like," Porter replied on June 29, 1863. The admiral assured Walke that he was trying to get provisions and coal to him and would send the *Switzerland* down with a barge as soon as he could get one filled. Porter urged Walke, "Hold on for a few days til *Switzerland* arrives if you can." He also explained, "We will have Vicksburg on the 5th of July certain, the rebels being determined to hold out until then."[10]

Grant had been pressing the siege of Vicksburg for weeks, and on June 20 he ordered a general bombardment. At 4:00 a.m. all the federal shore batteries, Porter's gunboats, mortars, and armed scows had opened fire on Vicksburg. "There was no response whatever, the batteries were all deserted," the admiral reported to Welles. "The only demonstration made by the rebels from the water front was a brisk fire of heavy guns from the upper batteries on two 12 pounder rifled howitzers that were planted on the Louisiana side by General Ellet's Marine Brigade."[11]

Grant had informed Porter that he expected the Confederates under Joe Johnston to attack within forty-eight hours. He had ordered Sherman to meet the rebels and advised Porter to keep a gunboat at Milliken's Bend in case the enemy attacked there as well. On June 23 Porter ordered his gunboats and the *Switzerland* to move up to the canal if the enemy attempted to cross over and "push in amongst the boats and destroy them and all in them."[12]

Three days later, Porter sent Welles a report: "I was in hopes ere this to have announced the fall of Vicksburg, but the rebels hold out persistently, and will no doubt do so while there is a thing left to eat." The rebels were hoping for relief from Johnston—"a vain hope," in Porter's opinion, "for even if he succeeded in getting the better of General Sherman (one of the best soldiers in our Army), his forces would be so cut up that he could take no advantage of any victory he might gain." Sherman, the admiral explained, had only to fall back on federal entrenchments at Vicksburg. The gunboats and a few men at Young's Point have held the enemy in check, Porter assured Welles, and "although they annoy the transports a little, the gunboats are so vigilant and give them so little rest that they have done no damage worth mentioning." He had landed ten heavy naval guns from the gunboats in the rear of Vicksburg, some manned by sailors, "and they have kept up a heavy fire for days, doing great execution." Deserters had reported that the rebels had just six days of provisions left but would "not yield until that is gone." Porter also updated Welles on operations against Port Hudson, saying that Banks had been repulsed twice "but will likely succeed in his next attempt."[13]

As June drew to a close, federal authorities off Vicksburg expected the rebels to evacuate the city and defensive works any day by boat. On June 29 Shirk had written to Woodworth, informing him that they had recently intercepted a letter from Confederate general A. J. Smith to his wife. "He says everything looks like taking a trip North. All seem to think that Saturday or Sunday will tell of the fall of Vicksburg."[14]

To keep pressure on the rebels, Porter's gunboats and mortars kept up their bombardment on the enemy stronghold. The constant firing had, however, taken a toll on the mortars. "I am as busy as I can be keeping the mortar boats in repair," William A. Minard, serving on the *Black Hawk,* explained in a letter to a friend. Vicksburg "isn't taken yet. I don't know when it will be either. The damn Rebs are in it and may hold it for six weeks to come. It can't be taken by storm. The only way is to just set right down and stare them out." Minard remained optimistic, however. "Vicksburg is played out. We are bound to have it."[15]

Only a few days later, on July 3, 1863, white flags appeared on part of the rebel works, and Major General James Bowen, a Confederate division commander, and Colonel Montgomery, aide-de-camp to General Pemberton, came to Union lines to propose an armistice and arrange terms of surrender. Grant wired Porter: "The enemy have asked armistice to arrange terms of capitulation. Will you please cease firing until notified or hear our batteries open? I shall fire a national salute into the city at daylight if they do not surrender."[16]

Grant refused Pemberton's proposal to arrange terms of surrender through appointed commissioners, telling him, "The effusion of blood you propose stopping by this source can be ended at anytime you may choose, by an unconditional surrender of the garrison." He assured the general that his men would be treated as prisoners of war. Grant told Bowen to inform Pemberton that he would meet with him that day at 3:00, which he did. The two men met on a hillside by a stunted oak tree. "Pemberton and I had served in the same division during a part of the Mexican war. I knew him very well, therefore, and greeted him as an old acquaintance," Grant recalled. However, Grant again refused to accept any terms of surrender other than those he had proposed. Anxious negotiations followed, and the general wired Porter, "I have given the rebels a few hours to consider the proposition of surrendering; all to be paroled here, the officers to take only side arms."[17]

Grant's new terms stated that, upon their acceptance, he would send in one federal division as a guard, and once rolls were made and paroles were signed, the Confederate officers and men would be allowed to march out, the officers taking their sidearms with them. Pemberton accepted these terms, and on July 4, "at the appointed time, the garrison of Vicksburg marched out of their works, and formed line in front, stacked arms, and marched back in good order. Our whole army present witnessed this scene without cheering," Grant wrote. At 5:30 a.m. on July 4, Grant wired Porter that the enemy had accepted his terms and would surrender the city, works, and garrison at 10 a.m. That morning, as promised, Grant rode into Vicksburg with the troops "and went to the river," he stated later, "to exchange congratulations with the navy upon our joint victory."[18]

In his letter of congratulations to Porter, Sherman wrote, "I can appreciate the intense satisfaction you must feel at lying before the very monster that has defied us with such deep and malignant hate and seeing your once disunited fleet again a unit; and, better still, the chain that made an enclosed sea of a link in the great river broken forever."[19]

Fourth of July proved to be a memorable day for Walke and the men of the *Lafayette* as well. "I have received a letter from the admiral for me to proceed to Vicksburg. The ram *Switzerland* will be sent to your assistance in keeping the blockade at Red River, and the *Sachem* will remain with you until she arrives," Walke wrote to William Hoel. The ram must have gotten under way for Vicksburg that same day, for off Grand Gulf, Lieutenant Commander E. K. Owen of the *Louisville* wrote, "The *Lafayette* is in sight, coming up."[20]

When the Vicksburg campaign ended, Admiral Porter summarized the navy's role in the long struggle to open the Mississippi River. "When I took command of this squadron, this river was virtually closed against our steamers from Helena to Vicksburg," Porter wrote. All that he had to do, the admiral told Welles, was to impress upon the officers and men of the squadron the importance of opening communication with New Orleans, and "every one, with few exceptions, have embarked in the enterprise with a zeal that is highly creditable to them, and with a determination that the river should be opened if their aid could effect it." Admitting that opening the Mississippi took longer than originally expected, Porter first praised Captain Pennock, the fleet captain and commandant at Cairo, for keeping the squadron supplied and for managing the Tennessee and Cumberland Squadrons, which had able officers in Lieutenant Commanders Phelps and Fitch. Porter then went on to commend Captain Walke; Commander Woodworth; Lieutenant Commanders Breese, Greer, Shirk, Owen, Wilson, Walker, Bache, Murphy, Selfridge, Prichett, and Ramsay; and Acting Volunteer Lieutenant Hoel for their "active and energetic attention to all his orders and ready cooperation with the army corps commanders." After mentioning specific actions involving the gunboats and the light drafts, Porter also praised the mortar boat commander, gunner Eugene Mack, "who for thirty days stood at his post, the firing continuing night and day," and Ensign Miller, who took charge when Mack fell ill. "We know that nothing conduced more to the end of the siege than the mortar firing, which demoralized the rebels, killed and wounded a number of persons, killed the cattle, destroyed property of all kinds, and set the city on fire." The admiral also lauded the work of Selfridge, who had commanded the naval battery on the right wing of Sherman's corps, firing 1,000 shells into the enemy's works, and he praised Walker, who had relieved him a few days before the surrender. In addition, Porter commended Acting Master Charles B. Dahlgren, who had managed the two 9-inch guns, and Acting Master J. Frank Reed of the *Benton,* who had charge of the four gun batteries at Fort Benton.

Thanking the army for the capture of Vicksburg, Porter wrote, "This has been no small undertaking; the late investment and capture of Vicksburg will be characterized as one of the greatest military achievements ever known." He gave due credit to General Grant for his role in planning and carrying out the operation. "The work was hard, the fighting severe, but the blows struck were constant. In forty-five days after our army was landed, a rebel army of 60,000 men had been captured, killed, and wounded, or scattered to their homes, perfectly demoralized, while our loss has been only about 5,000 killed, wounded, and prisoners, and the temporary loss of one gunboat."

Concluding his report to Welles, Porter summed up the main achievement of the Vicksburg campaign thusly: "The fall of Vicksburg ensured the fall of Port Hudson and the opening of the Mississippi River, which I am happy to say can be traversed from its source to its mouth without apparent impediment, the first time during the war."[21]

Conclusion

The strategy to win the war proposed by Winfield Scott and dubbed the Anaconda Plan called for a Union blockade of the southern coast and for Union forces to seize New Orleans and push down the Mississippi River, capturing enemy strongpoints, turning them into bases, and opening the river. Controlling the Mississippi would not only allow goods from the North to flow freely again to New Orleans but it would also assure a Union victory by cutting the Confederacy in two. Union planners focused on seizing control of the Mississippi River, but they also understood that Southern railroads had limitations when it came to moving men and supplies. Using rivers and waterways offered the Union a more effective means to penetrate the Confederacy with combined forces, seize bases, and ensure communication and transportation.

To implement the strategy outlined in the Anaconda Plan, the Union army had to raise thousands of volunteer troops and outfit, train, and transport them to theaters of war. In the case of the western theater, they had to be marched overland or conveyed by rail and river steamer to staging areas such as Cincinnati or Cairo. To transport men and supplies and to secure control of the Mississippi and other western rivers, the Union navy had to lease, purchase, or construct a flotilla of steam-powered vessels suitable for operations on these narrow, shallow rivers. The navy had to protect the vital areas of these river craft from shot and shell, and it had to arm these newly constructed or acquired vessels with modern ordnance and staff them with officers and men.

Creating a brown-water navy almost from scratch called for innovativeness. The first steamers acquired by the Union navy for western service in 1861—the *A. O. Tyler, Lexington,* and *Conestoga*—were converted from commercial side-wheel steamers. Protected by five-inch timber bulwarks, they were, as one officer remarked, unprotected against "anything more formidable than musketry." However, these ungainly looking timberclads proved their worth at the battle of Belmont and continued to serve the flotilla at Forts Henry and Donelson, during the battle for Shiloh, on the Yazoo River, and in the lower Mississippi.[1]

The timberclads were followed by a class of warship specially designed for service on western rivers. The seven city-class ironclads—the *Cairo, Cincinnati, Carondelet, St. Louis, Mound City, Louisville,* and *Pittsburg*—completed in 1861 extended the navy's capabilities and made a vital contribution to the war in 1862 and well into 1863. The new ironclads' sterling performance in their baptism of fire at Fort Henry had the unfortunate consequence of convincing many that these Pook turtles were invincible, but Fort Donelson's gunners disabused them of that notion. The city-class ironclads were, indeed, vulnerable to enemy fire. In a running fight with CSS *Arkansas,* for example, the *Carondelet* sustained considerable damage, one 8-inch shot striking it in the stern, gutting the captain's cabin, and knocking a twelve-inch oak log into splinters.[2]

Despite being struck repeatedly by enemy shot and shell in engagements with Confederate gunboats, rams, and fortifications, the Pook turtles were remarkably sturdy vessels, and several that were damaged or disabled underwent repairs and returned to service. On the *St. Louis,* casemates greased with tallow deflected enemy shot from Fort Hindman, but the gunboat suffered casualties when shot entered its gun ports, and one that landed on the muzzle of a 10-inch gun caused an explosion. Three other city-class ironclads were eventually lost: an enemy mine sank the *Cairo* in December 1862, a boiler explosion caused by enemy shot claimed the *Mound City,* and, pummeled by enemy fire at Vicksburg, the *Cincinnati* sank.

The next large ironclads constructed by the Union navy for western service—the rams *Lafayette* and *Choctaw*—were better able to withstand enemy shot and shell. Although hit nine times while passing the Vicksburg batteries, the *Lafayette* suffered little damage. The *Choctaw,* converted from a side-wheel river steamer, had one-inch armor over one inch of India rubber, but the rubber proved useless, and the armor and armament were too heavy for the hull. Nonetheless, the ironclad served at Haynes' Bluff on the Yazoo in May 1863, sustaining eighty-one hits, and then went on to participate in the Red River expedition.

The *Chillicothe,* commissioned in September 1862, followed by the *Tuscumbia* and *Indianola,* commissioned in January 1863, were smaller and had an unusual arrangement of machinery consisting of both side wheels and screw propellers; they were armed with 11-inch smoothbores. A Confederate vessel rammed the *Indianola* near Vicksburg in February 1863, running it aground. The *Tuscumbia* proved far sturdier, being hit eighty-one times during the bombardment of Grand Gulf. Rebel gunners at Fort Pemberton on the Yazoo River aimed their fire at the *Chillicothe,* putting a shot through the bow gun port as the gun was being loaded, and both exploded. After repairs, however, the *Chillicothe* returned to the squadron in September 1863.

The most formidable ironclad in the Mississippi Squadron was the *Essex,* formerly the snag boat *New Era.* It was acquired in the fall of 1861 and converted by Eads into a timberclad, then an armored vessel with three inches of iron on the casemates. The *Essex* served in the Cumberland River expedition and at Fort Henry, and it took part in the attacks on CSS *Arkansas.* A lucky shot hit the *Essex* at Fort Henry and caused a boiler explosion, but commanding officer William Porter had the vessel repaired and upgraded, enabling the ironclad to support the bombardment of Port Hudson and the 1864 Red River expedition.

The Mississippi Squadron's flag boats, the *Benton* and *Black Hawk,* were also converted to ironclads from river steamboats. The *Benton,* though formidably armed, was not impervious to shot and shell. Enemy fire roughed the vessel up at Grand Gulf and in the Yazoo, and in July 1862 a shot from an enemy Whitworth rifle went clean through the bow, exploding and injuring several sailors.

The little gunboats dubbed tinclads—the *Marmora, Signal, Rattler,* and *Red Rover*—were not yet in service and thus did not take part in the battles for New Orleans or Memphis or in the engagements with the *Arkansas,* but they made valuable contributions to Union naval operations on the Mississippi, Ohio, Tennessee, Cumberland, Yazoo, and Red Rivers. Designed to patrol shallow, twisting western rivers, they were converted from steamboats by the addition of thin boilerplate iron as armor. The Union produced sixty-three of these tinclads during the war, and they served admirably, fighting rebel sharpshooters, enforcing revenue, and acting as towboats and dispatch vessels.[3]

During the Vietnam War, the US Navy looked back to these unique river craft and designed or converted similar, lightly armed vessels to patrol the Mekong Delta. For example, the 130 PBR Mark 1 patrol boats deployed for Operation Game Warden were modified commercial sports craft ordered in 1963 from American builders; they were armor plated and armed with three .50-caliber machine guns and a 40 mm grenade launcher.[4]

In addition to these navy craft, in 1862 Charles Ellet developed steam-powered rams by purchasing river steamers and reinforcing their hulls and bows with timber. The Army Quartermaster Department converted the *Lioness, Lancaster, Mingo, Queen of the West, Switzerland,* and *Monarch.* Ellet formed a command that was independent of the navy, but his rams took part in the battle of Memphis and passed the gauntlet of fire from the Vicksburg batteries.

To bombard Confederate batteries, especially those positioned on bluffs above the Mississippi River, the Union navy turned to the army's 13-inch seacoast mortars. The Western Gunboat Flotilla ordered flat-bottomed rafts to carry these monstrous mortars and manned them with fifteen-man crews. Lacking their own propulsion, the mortar boats had to be towed into position. Initially, the new mortar boats went into action against Confederate batteries at Island No 10. Foote had great confidence in the effectiveness of the new boats and told his commanders to "let the mortar boats do the work." They could not, however, silence the rebel defenses. In the battle for New Orleans, Porter deployed twenty-one 13-inch mortars placed on mortar schooners. Firing every ten minutes, the mortars pounded Fort Jackson, setting fire to the citadel, but enemy fire managed to damage two of the schooners. When Farragut and Davis met at Vicksburg in July 1862, Porter's mortars were placed along the riverbanks in the hope they might reduce some of the enemy defenses. Sailors like coxswain John Morison of the *Carondelet* continued to have faith in the efficacy of these mortars, but orders from Secretary Welles sent Porter and twelve of the mortar boats back to Hampton Roads.[5]

Porter continued to believe in mortars, and when he assumed command of the Mississippi Squadron he took mortars to the Yazoo in December 1862 to support the army's assault at Chickasaw Bluffs. Mortar boats also participated in the fifty-two-day bombardment of Fort Pillow, and by April 1862, they had fired 531 of these 13-inch shells. Mortars played an important role in the prolonged siege of Vicksburg as well, augmented by naval guns brought ashore to bombard the rebel fortifications at that stronghold.

Although typically used to bombard enemy batteries on bluffs, owing to their arching fire, the Union navy occasionally employed mortars against enemy vessels. The most famous incident involved Mortar Boat No. 16, which had only its mortar to defend itself against a rebel attacker. Mortar schooners also fired on the CSS *Arkansas.*

Union navy mortar boats were plagued by bad fuses, and because long-range, direct fire requires sophisticated fire control, their 13-inch shells had a limited impact on rebel batteries. Although the Union navy continued to employ mortars against enemy fortifications along the Mississippi River, these mortar boats never lived up to the navy's expectations for them.

The Western Gunboat Flotilla, renamed the Mississippi Squadron in September 1862, took part in three engagements with Confederate naval forces and repeatedly dueled with rebel gun batteries and riverfront defenses. In addition, the Confederate navy initiated construction on several ironclads and put together a Confederate River Defense Force of rams and "cotton-clad" gunboats. Yet there were only two confrontations between Union and Confederate forces that could be classed a general fleet action. The first engagement took place off Plum Point above Memphis. In this "sharp but decisive" engagement with the Confederate River Defense Force in May 1862, the federal squadron parried the rebel rams, but the *Cincinnati* and *Mound City* suffered serious damage before the Yankee boats retreated to shallower water and the Confederates withdrew. Then, when Davis's flotilla met Confederate rams above Memphis, it was Ellet's rams *Queen of the West* and *Monarch* that boldly dashed past them to take on the enemy.

Union gunboats, mortars, and rams also bombarded and exchanged gunfire with Confederate forts and gun batteries on numerous occasions. The first was the battle of Belmont, when Walke's timberclads fended off rebel fire. The Western Gunboat Flotilla moved down to Paducah and then to Forts Henry and Donelson on the Tennessee and Cumberland Rivers. Cautiously advancing against Fort Henry's eleven river-facing guns, the four Eads ironclads encountered less than robust return fire from the rebel batteries, as those at water level had been rendered useless by flooding. All the ironclads were hit by rebel shot and shell but sustained no serious damage, and Fort Henry's defenders surrendered before Union troops could make an assault, handing Foote a victory. When most of the enemy troops withdrew to nearby Fort Donelson, that became the flotilla's next objective. There, the ironclads closed Confederate batteries positioned on bluffs above the river, allowing rebel gunners to pour plunging fire down on them. Unable to elevate their guns to return fire, the Pook turtles took a beating.

The flotilla's pummeling at Fort Donelson made Foote cautious about exposing his ironclads to enemy batteries at Island No. 10—until Walke agreed to run the *Carondelet* down past them under cover of darkness. Farragut had less compunction about Confederate river defenses and took his Gulf Squadron past the forts at New Orleans, Vicksburg, Grand Gulf, and Port Hudson. Foote and Porter, Davis's successor, confronted enemy batteries on the Yazoo River, at Fort Hindman at Arkansas Post, and at Vicksburg. The Mississippi Squadron, in fact, became the army's "floating artillery."

In many of these engagements with Confederate gun batteries, Union naval vessels came through relatively unscathed, despite being struck repeatedly. As the war progressed, commanders learned that coiling chains, placing hay or cotton bales on deck and near bulwarks, or greasing casemates with tallow helped protect their vessels from shot and shell. During the attack on Fort Hindman, for example, enemy shot struck the *Cincinnati* at least eight times but simply bounced off the greased casemates.

Chains and tallow could not always protect a vessel's boilers, and pilothouses were vulnerable as well. Union ironclad gunboats and rams were conned from pilothouses sheathed in iron plate, but the pilothouses were often targeted by enemy gunfire, and when shot or shell penetrated them, the splinters could inflict serious damage and casualties. When officers stepped outside these pilothouses, they risked injury, as Roger Stembel learned when a rebel sharpshooter's bullet struck him during the battle of Plum Point.

Whether down on the gun deck or in the pilothouse, the officers and men of the Western Gunboat Flotilla risked death or injury from musketry, enemy shot, splinters, and gun or boiler explosions. The bursting of a rifle gun onboard the *St. Louis* on March 17, 1862, for example, killed two seamen and wounded fifteen. A similar gun explosion killed fourteen men on the *Chillicothe* in the Yazoo River. During the assault on Fort Donelson, a shell hit the *Carondelet,* killing four men and wounding the pilot and twenty-seven other crewmen. At Chickasaw Bluffs, the flagship *Benton* suffered twelve sailors killed, and in the assault on Arkansas Post and Fort Hindman, Porter's flotilla incurred thirty-one killed and wounded in capturing that enemy strongpoint. Even one well-placed enemy shot could inflict devastating damage, as was the case with the *Mound City.*

Confederate gunfire did not discriminate. Foote suffered an injured foot, Stembel was shot by a sharpshooter, Augustus Kilty died from burns suffered in the *Mound City* boiler explosion, A. Boyd Cummings lost a leg, and William Gwin was mortally wounded. The ships and gunboats of Farragut's fleet also sustained casualties during operations on the Mississippi

River. Farragut's squadron, for example, suffered five killed and sixteen wounded, and Davis's Mississippi Squadron had thirteen killed and thirty-four wounded while passing the Vicksburg batteries.

Combined operations in the West during the Civil War required senior army and navy commanders working together to formulate strategy and to allocate troops and resources. Cooperation with the Union army proved essential in the assaults on Confederate strongholds at Vicksburg, Port Hudson, and Grand Gulf. Naval gunboats and mortars shelled these fortifications, attempting to silence the rebel batteries, but in many cases it took federal troops—"boots on the ground"—to assault, occupy, and hold these positions. The Union army's failure to allocate sufficient troops could doom these combined operations to failure, as was the case with the first Vicksburg campaign.

In addition to Confederate gun batteries and naval forces, Union naval units faced opposition from rebel sharpshooters, from irregular Confederate troops or guerrillas, and from a new weapon—the "torpedo," or mine. From almost the beginning of the war in the West, Union naval vessels, army transports, and other river steamers found themselves under fire from local pro-Southern citizens, armed bands, and Confederate guerrillas. Walke's flotilla at Milliken's Bend repeatedly encountered enemy sharpshooters, and sharpshooters harassed Porter's vessels during the Steele's Bayou expedition as well. In fact, guerrillas visited the banks of the Mississippi with impunity, took potshots at passing transports, and seized the *Sallie Wood*. When federal rams or gunboats pinpointed these enemy guerrilla bands or rebel artillery pieces, they did not hesitate to lob a few shells at them, as the *Lancaster* did against one band of rebels. The *Forest Rose* surprised a guerrilla camp on the Yazoo, and in some cases the army landed men to pursue guerrillas. Towns were not spared the federals' wrath either. When rebel guerrillas fired on a dinghy from Farragut's flagship *Hartford* off Baton Rouge, the ship's gunners immediately retaliated by firing into the town. None of these guerrilla attacks on Union naval vessels inflicted serious damage or caused a large number of casualties, but they did force commanders to use caution and in some cases to carry their own sharpshooters on board.

The Confederacy contested Union naval operations on the Mississippi, Cumberland, Tennessee, and Ohio Rivers with both steam-powered rams and gunboats, but also with a new weapon: the "torpedo," or mine. These "infernal machines" proved capable of causing serious damage to federal gunboats, sinking the USS *Cairo* in December 1862. Dragging for floating mines became one of the Yankee flotilla's ongoing missions, consuming time and manpower. Furthermore, mines could render stretches of the river unsafe for federal gunboats, curbing their ability to provide fire support to the army.

The Mississippi River itself proved a challenge to Union naval operations and sometimes seemed to be the "enemy." The Mississippi River rose with winter and spring rains, causing extensive flooding; then it fell with the approach of warm weather. Low water proved hazardous to Farragut's deep-draft wooden vessels. The *Hartford* grounded on its way north, and many others, even lighter-draft gunboats such as the *Winona,* also went briefly aground. Federal vessels also risked damage from snags or sawyers, collisions, and falling trees, and the swift current in these narrow western rivers made positioning the gunboats to bombard enemy positions difficult.

Manning the burgeoning number of ironclads and gunboats of the Western Gunboat Flotilla proved even more challenging than constructing or converting them. Foote repeatedly asked the Navy Department to send him men to fill out the complements of new vessels and to replace men whose terms of enlistment had expired or who had fallen ill. The Union navy competed with the Union army for recruits, and when recruiting efforts failed to produce enough seamen, the navy turned to foreigners, African Americans, and Confederate prisoners of war who were willing to enlist. As a last resort, commanders asked the army to detail soldiers to serve on naval vessels.

When federal gunboats appeared on the Mississippi River and its tributaries, African Americans, most of them slaves belonging to plantations situated on these waterways, often greeted them warmly. Some of them offered to provide food or information about Confederate activity or to act as guides. Soon, increasing numbers of slaves, and even some free blacks, began to seek safety on federal vessels. Naval commanders did not always oblige these fugitives, but they gradually came to value the intelligence they provided about the enemy. They employed these contrabands as crewmen, stevedores, and laborers, and the women worked as cooks, laundresses, and aides in Union hospitals and aboard hospital boats such as the *Red Rover.*

Union navy policy toward African Americans in the West varied over time. In deference to the bias of the Southern people, Foote did not want contrabands shipped on his vessels, and the enlistment of blacks had to wait until April 1862. Porter issued regulations to segregate blacks in his crews;

they were to be "messed by themselves and also [to] be kept in gangs by themselves at work." But segregation on shipboard was not always possible, and Porter finally had to admit that his contraband sailors "do first rate."[6]

In the summer of 1862 the army employed a large force of slaves, along with some troops, to dig a canal across the peninsula opposite Vicksburg. When Davis and General Williams departed, scores of African Americans who had dug the canal were left behind, denied their promised freedom. Sherman, however, welcomed slaves as laborers, putting them to work and housing their families. In the fall of 1862 he ordered that runaway slaves be treated as free, pending a final ruling by the courts. This opened the "floodgates of freedom," and the fugitive population grew sharply as a result.[7]

African Americans seeking sanctuary on Union vessels presented commanding officers with opportunities, but also with the challenge of feeding and protecting them. Many were sent ashore to army commanders, but the navy retained the able-bodied males as first-class boys, coal heavers, and landsmen. By the summer of 1862, many Union warships, rams, and gunboats had African American crewmen. Black sailors fought alongside their white comrades on Union vessels and risked injury and death. One contraband had both his arms and a leg shot off while serving on the ram *Lancaster*. Shot and shell from the *Arkansas* also injured seven black deckhands and coal heavers.

When the Union army recruited African Americans as troops and deployed them in the Mississippi Valley campaigns, Union gunboat commanders were asked to support these black soldiers and defend them against enemy attack. The extent to which African Americans, slave or free, supported the Union war effort in the West has not been extensively studied, but as this narrative of Union naval operations on the Mississippi River has shown, African Americans made substantial contributions to the Union navy's opening of the river.[8]

Union navy vessels operating on these western rivers did incur combat casualties, but more officers and men suffered from various illnesses. Fevers and gastrointestinal illnesses often drastically reduced the number of seamen fit for duty on navy vessels. When the *Carondelet* met the CSS *Arkansas*, for example, half its crew were ill, and Walke could man only one gun division. Foote himself succumbed to an injury and the debilitating effects of the Southern climate. Watson Smith asked to be relieved of command of the Yazoo expedition because of an unspecified illness, possibly suffering a nervous breakdown.

Naval operations on the Mississippi River involved transporting these ill and wounded sailors and soldiers from the battlefields to hospitals in Memphis and Cairo. Numerous cases of fever and other illnesses prompted the Union navy to outfit river steamers as hospital boats, the *Red Rover* being the most famous example. Naval gunboats also carried prisoners north to Union prison camps or escorted vessels carrying flags of truce or conveying prisoners of war for exchange.

Service in the brown-water navy was not glamorous duty. As one historian put it, "the brown water sailors of the riverine war struggled like their army comrades with a hostile, combatant populace, disease, boredom, and death in the shadows from marksmen known as bushwhackers." The almost two-year battle to implement Scott's Anaconda Plan to "open the Mississippi River" might not have succeeded without the brown-water fleet. As Admiral Porter wrote, "The services of the Navy in the West had as much effect in reducing the south to submission as the greater battles fought in the East."[9]

Acknowledgments

The completion and publication of this work would not have been possible without the assistance and encouragement of many individuals. My research was facilitated by the staff and archivists at the National Archives and Library of Congress, Washington, DC; the Honnold–Mudd Library, Claremont, California; the Huntington Library, San Marino, California; my local library in Camarillo, California; the Butler Center for Arkansas Studies, Little Rock, Arkansas; the Cincinnati Historical Society, Cincinnati, Ohio; the Illinois State Historical Library, Springfield, Illinois; and the Princeton University Library, Princeton, New Jersey.

I am indebted as well to Kevin P. Leonard of the Leonard Group Inc. for assistance with my research. At the University Press of Kentucky, acquisitions editor Anne Dean Dotson and assistant acquisitions editor Bailey Johnson were patient and helpful during the publishing process.

My deepest appreciation goes to friends and family who supported me during the lengthy process of researching, writing, rewriting, and editing this study of the Union Navy on the Mississippi River. I thank Sally Monastiere for her hospitality and encouragement during my frequent visits to the Claremont College libraries and John and Nancy Wilson for hosting me during a research trip to Washington, DC. I owe a debt of gratitude to my daughters Brooke and Page for their continuing love and support; my sons-in-law James Marca and Dan Wilson for their technical advice about the mysteries of the personal computer; my grandchildren Grace, Emma, Theo, and Miles for the joy they bring me and for their interest in history; and my husband Fred Tomblin for his patience with my many bouts of frustration and endless questions about the computer. Finally, I cannot fail to mention the years of companionship and devotion bestowed on us by our beloved

Little Kitty and the contribution of our newest family member, Whis-kers—a kitten who never asks questions but walks over the laptop keyboard to add her personal edits.

Notes

Abbreviations

ORA   *The War of the Rebellion: A Compilation of Official Records of the Union and Confederate Armies,* 70 vols. (Washington, DC: Government Printing Office, 1880–1901)

ORN   *Official Records of the Union and Confederate Navies in the War of the Rebellion,* 31 vols., ser. 1 (Washington, DC: Government Printing Office, 1894–1927)

Introduction

1. *St. Louis Daily Missouri Republican,* April 14, 1861; William T. Sherman, *The Memoirs of General W. T. Sherman,* 2 vols. (New York: D. Appleton, 1899), vol. 1, chap. 7.

2. John D. Milligan, *Gunboats down the Mississippi* (Annapolis, MD: Naval Institute Press, 1965), 3–4; James B. Eads, "Recollections of Foote and the Gunboats," *Battles and Leaders* 1 (1956): 338; Edward Bates, *The Diary of Edward Bates, 1859–1866,* ed. Howard K. Beale (Washington, DC: US Government Printing Office, 1933), 183–84.

3. Shelby Foote, *The Civil War 1861 Narrative: Fort Sumter to Perryville* (New York: Vintage Books, 1986), 51.

4. David Donald, *Lincoln* (New York: Simon & Schuster, 1995), 296; James M. McPherson, *Tried by War: Abraham Lincoln as Commander in Chief* (New York: Penguin, 2009), 22, 25.

5. Sherman, *Memoirs,* 1:170; Sherman to John Sherman, May 20, 1861, and Sherman to Ewing, June 3, 1861, in *Home Letters of General Sherman,* ed. Mark A. DeWolfe Howe (1909; reprint, Whitefish, MT: Kessinger Publishing, 2005), 198; Edwin C. Bearss, *Decision in Mississippi* (Jackson: Mississippi Commission on the War between the States, 1962), 1.

6. J. Marcus Wright, *General Scott* (New York: D. Appleton, 1894), 299; Rowena Reed, *Combined Operations in the Civil War* (Annapolis, MD: Naval Institute Press, 1978), 6.

7. Craig L. Symonds, *Lincoln and His Admirals* (New York: Oxford University Press, 2008), 38–40; Myron J. Smith Jr., *The Timberclads in the Civil War*

(Jefferson, NC: McFarland, 2008), 40–41; John Niven, *Gideon Welles: Lincoln's Secretary of the Navy* (New York: Oxford University Press, 1973), 389. Niven does not attribute the earlier blockade proposal to Scott, and Symonds argues that Lincoln's blockade proclamation would not become part of Scott's Anaconda Plan for another two weeks.

8. Foote, *Civil War*, 111; Jeffrey Wert, *Sword of Lincoln* (New York: Simon & Schuster, 2005), 8; Gary D. Joiner, *Mr. Lincoln's Brown Water Navy: The Mississippi Squadron* (New York: Rowman & Littlefield, 2007), 9; Allan Nevins, *The War for the Union,* 4 vols. (New York: Charles Scribner's, 1959–1971), 1:151–54; James M. McPherson, *Battle Cry of Freedom: The Civil War Era* (New York: Oxford University Press, 1988), 333–35; McPherson, *Tried by War,* 34; Ari Hoogenboom, *Gustavus Vasa Fox of the Union Navy* (Baltimore: Johns Hopkins University Press, 2008), 77. Doris Kearns Goodwin, *Team of Rivals: The Political Genius of Abraham Lincoln* (New York: Simon & Schuster, 2006), 351, does not attribute the plan to Scott.

9. W. Scott to Lincoln, May 2, 1861, *ORA,* ser. 1, vol. 51, pt. 1, 339; Scott to McClellan, May 3, 1861, ibid., 369–70.

10. Alex Randall to Abraham Lincoln, May 6, 1861, *ORA,* ser. 3, vol. 1, 167–70.

11. Ulysses S. Grant, *The Personal Memoirs of Ulysses S. Grant* (New York: C. L. Webster, 1885), 52–54; Brooks D. Simpson, *Ulysses S. Grant: Triumph over Adversity, 1822–1865* (Boston: Houghton Mifflin, 2000), 78–79; General Sir James Marshall-Cornwall, *Grant as Military Commander* (New York: Barnes & Noble, 1970), 35. Edwin B. Quiner, *Military History of Wisconsin* (Chicago: Clarke & Co., 1866), 48–49, 64, lists the specific companies of the three regiments.

12. Robert M. Browning Jr., *From Cape Charles to Cape Fear: The North Atlantic Blockading Squadron during the Civil War* (Tuscaloosa: University of Alabama Press, 1993), 1–2. See also McPherson, *Battle Cry of Freedom*, 322–23; McPherson, *Tried by War,* 23.

13. Browning, *From Cape Charles to Cape Fear,* 1–2; Spencer Tucker, *Arming the Fleet* (Annapolis, MD: Naval Institute Press, 2000), chap. 7; Joiner, *Mr. Lincoln's Brown Water Navy,* 9; Barbara Tomblin, "From Sail to Steam" (PhD diss., Rutgers University, 1988); James M. McPherson, *War on the Waters: The Union & Confederate Navies, 1861–1865* (Chapel Hill: University of North Carolina Press, 2012), 25–26; Hoogenboom, *Gustavus Vasa Fox,* 77–78; Craig L. Symonds, *The Civil War at Sea* (New York: Praeger, 2009), chap. 1; Symonds, *Lincoln and His Admirals,* 57.

14. Joiner, *Mr. Lincoln's Brown Water Navy,* 3; J. K. Moorhead to Sec. of War Cameron, May 27, 1861, *ORN,* 22:281–82.

15. Edwin C. Bearss, *Hardluck Ironclad: The Sinking and Salvage of the* Cairo (Baton Rouge: Louisiana State University Press, 1980), 14–15; Joiner, *Mr. Lincoln's Brown Water Navy,* 18; *ORN,* 22:277; Smith, *Timberclads,* 41–43.

16. John Fiske, *The Mississippi Valley in the Civil War* (Boston: Houghton Mifflin, 1900), 10–19.

17. Bearss, *Hardluck Ironclad,* 10–11.

18. Eads to Welles, April 29, 1861, *ORN,* 22:278–79.

19. Bearss, *Hardluck Ironclad,* 11–13; Welles to Rodgers, May 16, 1861, *ORN,* 22:280; Robert Edwin Johnson, *Rear Admiral John Rodgers, 1812–1882* (Annapolis, MD: Naval Institute Press, 1967), 156; Stephen R. Taaffe, *Commanding Lincoln's Navy* (Annapolis, MD: Naval Institute Press, 2009), 64–66; Smith, *Timberclads,* chap. 2.

20. Jay Slagle, *Ironclad Captain: Seth Ledyard Phelps and the U.S. Navy, 1841–1864* (Kent, OH: Kent State University Press, 1996), 113–14; Rodgers to Welles, June 8, 1861, *ORN,* 22:283; Welles to Pook, May 20, 1861, ibid., 281; William Still, *Civil War Ironclads: The U.S. Navy and Industrial Mobilization* (Baltimore: Johns Hopkins University Press, 2002), 52, 60. Still claims that the *Lexington* was converted in Cincinnati at John Litherbury's shipyard, located very near the Marine Railway and Dry Dock Company.

21. Johnson, *Rodgers,* 158–59, 161.

22. Rodgers to Ann, July 6 and 9, 1861, Rodgers family papers, Manuscript Division, Library of Congress; Spencer C. Tucker, *Andrew Hull Foote* (Annapolis, MD: Naval Institute Press, 2000), 116; Rodgers to Welles, September 7, 1861, *ORN,* 22:318–20.

23. Slagle, *Ironclad Captain,* 118–21; Phelps to Rodgers, July 21 and 25, 1861, *ORN,* 22:289–94.

24. Rodgers to Welles, August 9, 1861, *ORN,* 22:297–98; Rodgers to Bishop, August 5, 1861, ibid., 296.

25. James M. Merrill, "Cairo, Illinois: Strategic Civil War River Port," *Journal of Illinois State Historical Society* 76 (Winter 1983): 243, Smith, *Timberclads,* 35–36; Eads to Welles, April 29, 1861, *ORN,* 22:278–79; "Our Army at Cairo," *Harper's Weekly,* June 29, 1861, 410; War of the Rebellion, hosted by Ancestry.com; Gen. McClellan, May 4, 1861, *ORA,* vol. 51, pt. 1, 370.

26. Simpson, *Grant,* 91–92.

27. Phelps to Rodgers, August 16, 1861, *ORN,* 2:299; Stembel to Rodgers, August 16, 1861, *ORN,* 22:299–300.

28. Rodgers to Col. Oglesby, August 18, 1861, *ORN,* 22:300–301; Rodgers to Welles, August 22, 1861, ibid., 302–3; Johnson, *Rodgers,* 164; Slagle, *Ironclad Captain,* 123–24.

29. Bearss, *Hardluck Ironclad,* 13–15, 23–27; Johnson, *Rodgers,* 159–60; Merrill, "Cairo, Illinois," 244.

1. The Western Gunboat Flotilla

1. G. V. Fox to Walke, September 6, 1861, *ORN,* 22:318; Taaffe, *Commanding Lincoln's Navy,* 66–67; Henry Walke, "The Gunboats at Belmont and Fort Henry," *Battles and Leaders* 1 (1956): 359.

2. Smith, *Timberclads,* 15, 84, 146.

3. Obituary of Rear Admiral Henry Walke, *New York Times,* March 9, 1896; Henry Walke, *Naval Scenes and Reminiscences of the Civil War in the United States on Southern and Western Waters during the Years 1861, 1862, and 1863* (New York: F. R. Reed, 1877), 24.

4. James M. Perry, *A Bohemian Brigade: The Civil War Correspondents—Mostly Rough, Sometimes Ready* (New York: John Wiley & Sons, 2000), 67–69; Franc Wilkie, *Pen and Powder* (Boston: Ticknor, 1888), 84–85.

5. Rodgers to Ann, July 9, 1861, Rodgers family papers, Manuscript Division, Library of Congress; Johnson, *Rodgers,* 166–67; Tucker, *Foote,* 116; Rodgers to Welles, September 7, 1861, *ORN,* 22:318–20.

6. Tucker, *Foote,* 116–17; Walke, "Gunboats at Belmont and Fort Henry," 358–60.

7. Walke, "Gunboats at Belmont and Fort Henry," 359; Jack D. Coombe, *Thunder along the Mississippi: The River Battles that Split the Confederacy* (New York: Sarpedon, 1996), 20–21; Slagle, *Ironclad Captain,* 112.

8. Walke, *Naval Scenes,* 24.

9. Milligan, *Gunboats down the Mississippi,* 32–33; Slagle, *Ironclad Captain,* 126; Benton Rain Patterson, *The Mississippi River Campaign, 1861–1863: The Struggle for Control of the Western Waters* (Jefferson, NC: McFarland, 2000), 7–8.

10. Paul H. Silverstone, *Warships of the Civil War* (Annapolis, MD: Naval Institute Press, 1989), 159; Slagle, *Ironclad Captain,* 118–19; Smith, *Timberclads,* 61; Foote to Walke, September 17, 1861, *ORN,* 22:336; Walke to Foote, September 23, 1861, ibid., 349; report of Captain Foote, September 13, 1861, ibid., 318; Foote to Welles, September 12, 1861, ibid., 323; Rodgers to Welles, September 12, 1861, ibid., 332–34; Walke, *Naval Scenes,* 27.

11. Obituary of Walke; Rear Admiral Henry A. Walke, USN, Department of the Navy, Naval Historical Center.

12. John Rodgers to Joshua Bishop, August 5, 1861, *ORN,* 22:296; Rodgers to Bishop, August 19, 1862, and endorsement, ibid., 301–2; Slagle, *Ironclad Captain,* 118–19, 122; Smith, *Timberclads,* 100–101.

13. Simpson, *Grant,* 88–89; Wilkie, *Pen and Powder,* 97–98, 159–60; Bruce Catton, *Grant Moves South* (Boston: Little Brown, 1960), 3, 17, 46; John Brinton, *Personal Memoirs of John H. Brinton* (New York: Neale, 1914), 52; Marshall-Cornwall, *Grant as Military Commander,* 29–33, 37.

14. Simpson, *Grant,* 93–96; Charles B. Flood, *Grant and Sherman* (New York: Harper, 2005), 62–63; Milligan, *Gunboats down the Mississippi,* 32.

15. Walke, *Naval Scenes,* 27; Simpson, *Grant,* 96; Victor Hicken, *Illinois in the Civil War* (Urbana: University of Illinois Press, 1966), 13.

16. Walke, *Naval Scenes,* 27.

17. Roger Nelson Stembel, Rear Admiral, USN, www.arlingtoncemetery.net;

Dictionary of American Fighting Ships, Naval Historical Center; obituary for Rear Admiral Roger Nelson Stembel, *News of Newport,* November 20, 1900, at nytimes .com.

18. Walke, *Naval Scenes,* 28.

19. Foote to Walke, October 5, 1861, *ORN,* 22:359.

20. Walke, *Naval Scenes,* 29; report from Walke to Foote, October 7, 1861, *ORN,* 22:362; Walke to Grant, October 7, 1861, ibid., 363.

21. Walke, *Naval Scenes,* 30.

22. Walke, "Gunboats at Belmont and Fort Henry," 360.

23. Simpson, *Grant,* 97; Walke, "Gunboats at Belmont and Fort Henry," 360; Smith, *Timberclads,* 149–50.

24. Simpson, *Grant,* 97; Patterson, *Mississippi River Campaign,* 30; Grant's report, November 3, 1861, *ORA,* 3:268.

25. Walke, *Naval Scenes,* 33.

26. Reed, *Combined Operations,* 228–29; Simpson, *Grant,* 89; Smith, *Timberclads,* 15, 84, 146.

27. Walke, *Naval Scenes,* 33.

28. Nathaniel C. Hughes Jr., *The Battle of Belmont* (Chapel Hill: University of North Carolina Press, 1991), 19–21.

29. Brinton, *Memoirs,* 68–69, 71.

30. Slagle, *Ironclad Captain,* 115; Rodgers to Welles, June 8, 1861, *ORN,* 22:283.

31. Reed, *Combined Operations,* 72.

32. Abstract log of USS *Lexington, ORN,* 22:780; Hughes, *Battle of Belmont,* 49. The *Lexington's* log lists all the transports except *Rob Roy.* Patterson, *Mississippi River Campaign,* 30, claims that Grant landed 2,500 men.

33. Hicken, *Illinois in the Civil War,* 20–22; Hughes, *Battle of Belmont,* 80; Catton, *Grant Moves South,* 75.

34. Grant to Brig. Gen. Seth Williams, November 17, 1861, *ORN,* 22:404–6; Hughes, *Battle of Belmont,* 81; Grant, *Personal Memoirs,* chap. 20; Catton, *Grant Moves South,* 74–81.

35. Walke to Foote, November 9, 1861, *ORN,* 22:400–402; Walke to Grant, November 8, 1861, ibid., 402–4; Walke, *Naval Scenes,* 45–47.

36. Brinton, *Memoirs,* 72.

37. Hughes, *Battle of Belmont,* 86; Hicken, *Illinois in the Civil War,* 21–24 .

38. Simpson, *Grant,* 99; Gen. McClernand's Report of the Battle of Belmont, *Illinois State Register,* November 22, 1861, NIU Libraries Digitalization Projects; Hughes, *Battle of Belmont,* 89, 109–10, 115.

39. Brinton, *Memoirs,* 73–74.

40. Walke, *Naval Scenes,* 46; Walke to Foote, November 9, 1861, *ORN,* 22:400–402; Tucker, *Foote,* 129–30.

41. Walke, *Naval Scenes,* 36; Walke to Foote, November 9, 1861, *ORN,* 22:401.

42. Walke, *Naval Scenes,* 36–37; Walke to Foote, November 9, 1861, *ORN,* 22:401.

43. Simpson, *Grant,* 100.

44. According to Marshall-Cornwall, *Grant as Military Commander,* 41, the federal soldiers reached the camp at about noon.

45. Catton, *Grant Moves South,* 76; Grant, *Personal Memoirs,* 273–74; Hughes, *Battle of Belmont,* 150–51.

46. Walke, *Naval Scenes,* 38. According to Catton, *Grant Moves South,* 77, Brinton called Grant's attention to two boats loaded with troops leaving Columbus.

47. Walke, *Naval Scenes,* 38–40.

48. Hughes, *Battle of Belmont,* 91–92, 116, 162–63.

49. Simpson, *Grant,* 101.

50. Milligan, *Gunboats down the Mississippi,* 35–36; letter in the *Ohio State Journal,* quoted in Walke, *Naval Scenes,* 4; abstract log of *Lexington,* November 7, 1861, *ORN,* 22:70.

51. Abstract log of *Lexington,* November 7, 1861, *ORN,* 22:780.

52. Foote to Welles, *ORN,* 22:399–400; Perry to Foote, November 7, 1861, ibid., 398; Symonds, *Lincoln and His Admirals,* 110; Coombe, *Thunder along the Mississippi,* 40; McPherson, *War on the Waters,* 73; Foote to Welles, *ORN,* 22:398–400; Walke, *Naval Scenes,* 47; Walke to Foote, November 9, 1861, *ORN,* 22:400–402; Slagle, *Ironclad Captain,* 142; Catton, *Grant Moves South,* 81.

53. Slagle, *Ironclad Captain,* 141–42.

54. Catton, *Grant Moves South,* 80–81; report of Brigadier General Grant, US Army, November 17, 1861, *ORN,* 22:405; Patterson, *Mississippi River Campaign,* 32; Walke, *Naval Scenes,* 45; Milligan, *Gunboats down the Mississippi,* 36; Joiner, *Mr. Lincoln's Brown Water Navy,* 36; Simpson, *Grant,* 102–3; Tucker, *Foote,* 129–31. Joiner, Slagle, Milligan, and Tucker do not discuss Foote's failure to credit the gunboats.

2. The USS *Carondelet* and Fort Henry

1. Slagle, *Ironclad Captain,* 132; abstract log of USS *Tyler, ORN,* 22:772–73; Walke, *Naval Scenes,* 48.

2. Walke to Foote, December 29 and 30, 1861, *ORN,* 22:476. Walke does not discuss the events after Belmont and prior to Fort Henry in his *Naval Scenes.*

3. Walke, *Naval Scenes,* 53; Slagle, *Ironclad Captain,* 146. Walke probably welcomed his new assignment, for as Phelps said of the *Conestoga,* it was "a second rate craft that could not approach batteries when the southern moment takes place."

4. Walke, *Naval Scenes,* 53; Brooks D. Simpson, *America's Civil War* (Wheeling, IL: Harland Davidson, 1996), 49–50; McPherson, *Tried by War,* 61–62.

5. Walke, *Naval Scenes,* 53–54; *New York Times,* Februray 8, 1862. For the construction and design process of the ironclad, see Myron J. Smith Jr., *USS Carondelet: A Civil War Ironclad on Western Waters* (Jefferson, NC: McFarland, 2010).

6. Walke, *Naval Scenes,* 54; *New York Times,* February 8, 1862.

7. *New York Times,* February 8, 1862; Smith, *USS* Carondelet, 37.

8. Smith, *USS* Carondelet, 14–15; Foote to wife, December 17, 1861, in Andrew Hoppin, *Life of Andrew Hull Foote, Rear Admiral, United States Navy* (New York: Harper & Brothers, 1874), 189.

9. Slagle, *Ironclad Captain,* 115–17; Smith, *USS* Carondelet, 34–35; Joiner, *Mr. Lincoln's Brown Water Navy,* 25–26; Hoppin, *Life of Foote,* 165–66.

10. Tucker, *Foote,* 120; Reed, *Combined Operations,* 84. In late December assistant navy secretary Fox requested men. When Halleck asked Grant to provide men for the flotilla, he refused, claiming they would not serve without their officers.

11. Marshall-Cornwall, *Grant as Military Commander,* 52.

12. Ibid., 53–54; Walke, *Naval Scenes,* 51. According to US Navy and Marine Corps records of living officers, the *Carondelet's* acting volunteer officers included masters John Dorety and Charles C. Gray; surgeon John S. McNeely; paymaster George J. W. Nexsen; mater's mates Theodore Gilmore and Edward E. Brennard; chief engineer William H. Faulkner; and engineers Charles H. Caven, Samuel L. Brooks, and Augustus F. Crowell. Carpenter Oliver Donaldson, gunner Richard Adams, and armorer H. H. Rhodes also served as Walke's junior officers; these men had no professional naval training but, like Wade, had some experience on the river. In addition to these officers, the *Caronelet* had two pilots: Willaim Hinton and Daniel Weaver.

13. Smith, *USS* Carondelet, 34–35; Tucker, *Foote,* 138; Coombe, *Thunder along the Mississippi,* 23–24; Bearss, *Hardluck Ironclad,* 33.

14. Slagle, *Ironclad Captain,* 149–50.

15. W. D. Porter to Foote, January 13, 1862, *ORN,* 22:499–500; Slagle, *Ironclad Captain,* 148, 152; Tucker, *Foote,* 132.

16. Catton, *Grant Moves South,* 130–31; Marshall-Cornwall, *Grant as Military Commander,* 54; Grant, *Personal Memoirs,* 1:286; Tucker, *Foote,* 131–32; Simpson, *Grant,* 108–10; Foote to Halleck, January 28, 1862, *ORA,* 7:120. Foote proposed that Fort Henry could be taken with troops and his four ironclad gunboats. "Have we your authority to move for that purpose when ready?" he asked Halleck.

17. Catton, *Grant Moves South,* 129–33; Joiner, *Mr. Lincoln's Brown Water Navy,* 38–39; R. Thomas Campbell, *Confederate Naval Forces on Western Waters* (Jefferson, NC: McFarland, 2005), 30–40; Halleck to Grant, *ORA,* 7:121–22.

18. Slagle, *Ironclad Captain,* 153–54.

19. Lewis Wallace, *Lew Wallace: An Autobiography* (New York: Harper & Brothers, 1906), 35–38.

20. *Chicago Tribune* cited in Catton, *Grant Moves South,* 138; Tucker, *Foote,* 138–39. Smith, *USS* Carondelet, 56, states that most enlisted bluecoats knew the expedition's destination. Grant had 17,000 men. According to Hicken, *Illinois in the Civil War,* 19, by the end of October, Grant had five brigades: McClernand's at Cairo, Colonel Richard Oglesby's and Colonel W. H. L. Wallace's at Bird's Point, Colonel Joseph Plummer's at Cape Giradeau, and Colonel John Cook's at Fort Holt in Kentucky.

21. Catton, *Grant Moves South,* 134–35; Simpson, *Grant,* 110–11.

22. Special Orders No. 1, enclosure, Foote to Welles, February 3, 1862, *ORN,* 22:536. Hoppin, *Life of Foote,* 197–98, includes Orders 1, 2, and 3.

23. Foote to Welles, February 3, 1862, *ORN,* 22:534, 536, enclosure, Special Orders No. 2; Smith, *USS* Carondelet, 56.

24. Simpson, *Grant,* 110–11. Catton, *Grant Moves South,* 139, claims that on the afternoon of February 3, steamers with McClernand's troops reached Fort Henry and began sending men ashore.

25. Catton, *Grant Moves South,* 139; Franc Wilkie, *New York Times,* February 7, 1862.

26. Walke, "Gunboats at Belmont and Fort Henry," 362; *New York Times,* February 7, 1862; Slagle, *Ironclad Captain,* 157; Milligan, *Gunboats down the Mississippi,* 38. Walke states that the *Essex* was hit on February 5. The February 6 edition of the *Philadelphia Inquirer* reported, "One shot struck the gunboat *Essex,* going through a corner of Captain Porter's cabin." David Dixon Porter, *The Naval History of the Civil War* (Mineola, NY: Dover Publications, 1998), 144, states that Grant did not have all his men ashore until 11:00 p.m.

27. Smith, *USS* Carondelet, 59.

28. Walke, *Naval Scenes,* 55.

29. H. Allen Gosnell, *Guns on the Western Waters* (Baton Rouge: Louisiana State University Press, 1949), 46–48, quotes the version of the story told by Eliot Callender, "What a Boy Saw on the Mississippi," in *Military Essays and Recollections: Papers Read before the Commandery of the State of Illinois, Military Order of the Loyal Legion of the United States,* vol. 1 (Chicago: A. C. McClurg, 1891); Slagle, *Ironclad Captain,* 158; Joiner, *Mr. Lincoln's Brown Water Navy,* 40; Tucker, *Foote,* 139.

30. Smith, *USS* Carondelet, 60, explains that without the ironclad's log for this period, it is not possible to know how its crew spent their time, but based on Walke's statement that his gun captains "had their men well drilled," he surmises that numerous drills had been conducted.

31. Walke, "Gunboats at Belmont and Fort Henry," 362; Walke, *Naval Scenes,* 55. Smith, *USS* Carondelet, 62–63, describes the rebel torpedoes (either twelve or

twenty—acounts differ) anchored in the western chute where Panther Island divided Fort Henry from the unfinished Fort Heinman.

32. Tucker, *Foote,* 142. Walke, *Naval Scenes,* 55. Smith, *USS* Carondelet, 61–62, claims Foote rowed to each of his boats (visiting the *Carondelet* first) to inspect the men, give a pep talk, and offer a prayer. Tucker claims Foote did this sometime before the fifth.

33. Catton, *Grant Moves South,* 143; McClernand report, February 10, 1862, *ORA,* 7:129.

34. Walke, "Gunboats at Belmont and Fort Henry," 368.

35. Tucker, *Foote,* 141, quoting Porter, *Naval History,* 145; Walke, "Gunboats at Belmont and Fort Henry," 362; Gosnell, *Guns on Western Waters,* 49–50; Joiner, *Mr. Lincoln's Brown Water Navy,* 37–41; Patterson, *Mississippi River Campaign,* 39.

36. Walke, "Gunboats at Belmont and Fort Henry," 363.

37. A. J. Sypher to *Lancaster Daily Evening Express,* February 14, 1862, Lancaster at War website.

38. Slagle, *Ironclad Captain,* 160–61; Walke, "Gunboats at Belmont and Fort Henry," 363.

39. Patterson, *Mississippi River Campaign,* 40–42; Milligan, *Gunboats down the Mississippi,* 40–43.

40. "Interesting Letter from the Second Master of the 'Essex,' James Laning," in Walke, *Naval Scenes,* 59–65; Coombe, *Thunder along the Mississippi,* 50.

41. Sypher to *Lancaster Daily Evening Express,* February 14, 1862; Walke, "Gunboats at Belmont and Fort Henry," 365; Hoppin, *Life of Foote,* 201; Smith, *USS* Carondelet, 68. One 68-pound shot struck the center part of the pilothouse, indenting the ship's side; shot also perforated the chimneys, and a 32-pound ball came through the starboard side, killing one seaman and wounding many more.

42. Walke, "Gunboats at Belmont and Fort Henry," 365; Hoppin, *Life of Foote,* 201; Smith, *USS* Carondelet, 68. One 68-pound shot struck the center part of the pilothouse, indenting the ship's side; shot also perforated the chimneys, and a 32-pound ball came through the starboard side, killing one seaman and wounding many more.

43. Tucker, *Foote,* 143; Slagle, *Ironclad Captain,* 161.

44. Sypher to *Lancaster Daily Evening Express,* February 14, 1862.

45. Walke, "Gunboats at Belmont and Fort Henry," 366; Walke, *Naval Scenes,* 57.

46. Walke, "Gunboats at Belmont and Fort Henry," 366; Walke, *Naval Scenes,* 58–59.

47. Catton, *Grant Moves South,* 145; Walke, "Gunboats at Belmont and Fort Henry," 367.

48. Walke, *Naval Scenes,* 68; Walke to Foote, February 1862, quoted in ibid., 69.

49. Walke, *Naval Scenes,* 68.

50. Phelps to Foote, February 10, 1862, *ORN*, 22:572–73. Slagle, *Ironclad Captain*, 162–73, has a detailed account of this expedition to Florence.

51. Chas. H. Caven and George J. W. Nexsen to H. Walke, February 8, 1862, *ORN*, 22:544; Slagle, *Ironclad Captain*, 162–67.

52. Coombe, *Thunder along the Mississippi*, 50; Walke, *Naval Scenes*, 70, which includes Secretary Welles's letter of congratulations to Foote and the squadron; G. V. Fox to Foote, February 8, 1862, *ORN*, 22:546; Welles to Foote, February 13, 1862, ibid., 547; Wise to Foote, February 10, 1862, ibid., 549–50. General John McClernand also wrote Foote a congratulatory letter and stated, "I have taken the liberty of giving the late Fort Henry the new and more appropriate name of Fort Foote." Ibid., 544.

53. Sypher to *Lancaster Daily Evening Express*, February 14, 1862.

54. Slagle, *Ironclad Captain*, 175; *New York Times*, February 22, 1862; *Cincinnati Daily Gazette*, February 17, 1862. The Friday, February 7, 1862, edition of the *New York Times* did credit the ironclads, citing Foote's report.

3. Fort Donelson

1. Porter, *Naval History*, 149; Catton, *Grant Moves South*, 147, 149–51; Simpson, *Grant*, 112–13; Patterson, *Mississippi River Campaign*, 54–55; McPherson, *War on the Waters*, 76; *ORA*, 1:325.

2. Catton, *Grant Moves South*, 150–51; Tucker, *Foote*, 151; Milligan, *Gunboats down the Mississippi*, 45; Porter, *Naval History*, 150.

3. Henry Walke, "The Western Flotilla at Fort Donelson, Island Number Ten, Fort Pillow, and Memphis," *Battles and Leaders* 1 (1956): 430; Foote to Welles, February 17, 1862, enclosure, Walke to Foote, February 15, 1862, *ORN*, 22:587–88; Joiner, *Mr. Lincoln's Brown Water Navy*, 44; Catton, *Grant Moves South*, 155–56. The surrender of Fort Donelson is covered in *ORN*, 22:582–86.

4. Simpson, *Grant*, 113; Catton, *Grant Moves South*, 153.

5. Catton, *Grant Moves South*, 153; Simpson, *Grant*, 113–14; Wilkie, *Pen and Powder*, 104–5; Patterson, *Mississippi River Campaign*, 66.

6. Walke, "Western Flotilla," 431; Catton, *Grant Moves South*, 155.

7. Walke, "Western Flotilla," 431–33.

8. Ibid.; Lew Wallace, "The Capture of Fort Donelson," *Battles and Leaders* 1 (1956): 403; Coombe, *Thunder along the Mississippi*, 64.

9. Slagle, *Ironclad Captain*, 177–78; Walke, "Western Flotilla," 433; Tucker, *Foote*, 154.

10. Walke, "Western Flotilla," 433; Catton, *Grant Moves South*, 160–61. Dennis Ringle, *Life in Mr. Lincoln's Navy* (Annapolis, MD: Naval Institute Press, 1998), 130–31, mentions the issuing of coffee and hardtack before a battle.

11. Walke, "Western Flotilla," 433; Tucker, *Foote*, 155.

12. Walke, "Western Flotilla," 433–36; *ORN*, 22:586–87; Milligan, *Gunboats down the Mississippi*, 46–48; Tucker, *Foote*, 156.

13. Walke, "Western Flotilla," 434–35; Walke, *Naval Scenes,* 78; Joiner, *Mr. Lincoln's Brown Water Navy,* 44; Coombe, *Thunder along the Mississippi,* 67–68; Catton, *Grant Moves South,* 161.

14. Foote, *Civil War,* 204–5; Simpson, *Grant,* 114; Joiner, *Mr. Lincoln's Brown Water Navy,* 47.

15. Foote to Welles, February 15, 1862, *ORN,* 22:585–86, and enclosure, Casualties; Slagle, *Ironclad Captain,* 179–80; Tucker, *Foote,* 157. McPherson, *War on the Waters,* 78, argues that Foote realized the Pook turtles' vulnerability to plunging shot, but other historians (including Milligan, *Gunboats down the Mississippi,* 48) claim the damage done by the rebel batteries came as a surprise.

16. Simpson, *Grant,* 116–17.

17. Ibid., 115; Catton, *Grant Moves South,* 163–64; Foote, *Civil War,* 207–9; Foote to Welles, February 15, 1862, *ORN,* 22:586; Porter, *Naval History,* 151.

18. Catton, *Grant Moves South,* 166–67.

19. Cited in ibid., 168; Grant to Foote, February 15, 1862, *ORA,* 7:618.

20. Catton, *Grant Moves South,* 168; Slagle, *Ironclad Captain,* 181–82; Dove to Foote, February 16, 1862, *ORN,* 22:588–89.

21. Catton, *Grant Moves South,* 176; Tucker, *Foote,* 161.

22. Slagle, *Ironclad Captain,* 183; Tucker, *Foote,* 161; Catton, *Grant Moves South,* 175–78; testimony of Maj. Gen. L. Wallace in the case of Commander Dove, US Navy, *ORN,* 22:589; James Weaver to wife, February 19, 1862, James B. Weaver letters, 1860–1864, 10, Iowa Digital Library.

23. Walke, "Western Flotilla," 437.

24. Slagle, *Ironclad Captain,* 185.

25. Ibid., 184–85; *ORN,* 22:584–85; Walke, "Western Flotilla," 436–37; Porter, *Naval History,* 150–52. Tucker, *Foote,* 157, argues that the gunboats were not badly damaged and had done little real damage to the Confederate batteries.

26. Slagle, *Ironclad Captain,* 183; Porter, *Naval History,* 152; Tucker, *Foote,* 161; Catton, *Grant Moves South,* 175–77. Reed, *Combined Operations,* 84–85, argues that Fort Donelson was prematurely surrendered and that the combined operation to capture both forts was not an unqualified success.

4. Island No. 10

1. Porter, *Naval History,* 158; Tucker, *Foote,* 164–65; Catton, *Grant Moves South,* 189–91, 193. Porter attributes Halleck's decision to the conservative policy "that seemed to influence General Halleck on all occasions."

2. Porter, *Naval History,* 152; Gosnell, *Guns on Western Waters,* 70.

3. Reed, *Combined Operations,* 81; Foote to Halleck, December 7, 1861, *ORN,* 22:454–55; Foote to Welles, January 11, 1862, ibid., 492; Craig Swain, "The Unfavorable Mortar Boats," April 16, 2012, Civil War Navy Sesquicenten-

nial blog at the Maritime Naval Museum website; Phelps to Foote, January 21, 1862, *ORN,* 22:512–13.

4. Symmes Browne, February 24, 1862, in *From the Freshwater Navy, 1861–1864: The Letters of Acting Master's Mate Henry R. Browne and Acting Ensign Symmes E. Browne,* ed. John D. Milligan (Annapolis, MD: Naval Institute Press, 1970), xvi, 31–32; Tucker, *Foote,* 164–65, 167.

5. John G. Morison diary, February 24, 1862, 44; Walke, *Naval Scenes,* 94.

6. Tucker, *Foote,* 166; Pennock to Chief of Bureau of Ordnance, February 21, 1862, *ORN,* 22:632; Foote to Welles, February 24, 1862, ibid.; Foote to Chief of Bureau of Ordnance, February 24, 1862, ibid., 636; Wise to Foote, February 24, 1862, ibid.

7. Slagle, *Ironclad Captain,* 194; Smith, *USS* Carondelet, 88–89.

8. George M. Blodgett to aunt, April 14, 1862, George M. Blodgett Letters, Butler Center for Arkansas Studies.

9. Report of Flag Officer Foote, March 1, 1862, *ORN,* 22:650–51; Tucker, *Foote,* 168; Slagle, *Ironclad Captain,* 194–95.

10. Morison diary, March 3, 1862, 45.

11. Ibid., March 4, 1862, 45–46.

12. Ibid.; Slagle, *Ironclad Captain,* 194. Smith, *USS* Carondelet, 88–89, covers the occupation of Columbus very briefly.

13. Tucker, *Foote,* 168–69; Milligan, *Gunboats down the Mississippi,* 20–25, 53; Coombe, *Thunder along the Mississippi,* 92.

14. Fox to Foote, March 1, 1862, *ORN,* 22:648–49; H. A. Wise to Foote, March 1, 1862, ibid., 649–50; Foote to Welles, March 4, 1862, ibid., 652; Foote to Chief of Bureau of Ordnance, March 5, 1862, ibid., 656, 657; Foote telegram, March 7, 1862, ibid., 659; Foote to Lt. H. A. Wise, March 12, 1862, enclosing a telegram to Halleck, ibid., 685.

15. Browne, March 7 and 9, 1862, in Milligan, *Freshwater Navy,* 36; L. Polk to Benjamin, March 2, 1862, *ORN,* 22:654; Polk to Jefferson Davis, March 11, 1862, ibid., 654; Alfred Thayer Mahan, *The Navy in the Civil War,* vol. 3, *The Gulf and Inland Waters* (Honolulu, HI: University Press of the Pacific, 2006), 19.

16. Foote to Wise, enclosing a copy of the telegram to Halleck, March 12, 1862, *ORN,* 22:685; Halleck to Foote, March 12, 1862, ibid., 686; Halleck to Foote, March 13, 1862, ibid., 687. J. Thomas Scharf, *History of the Confederate States Navy from Its Organization to the Surrender of Its Last Vessel* (New York: Rogers & Sherwood, 1887), 244–45, 304–5, has a brief account; see also Larry Daniel and Lynn Bock, *Island No. 10: Struggle of the Mississippi Valley* (Tuscaloosa: University of Alabama Press, 1996).

17. Morison diary, March 12, 1862, 47; Foote to Walke, general order, March 13, 1862, *ORN,* 22:688.

18. Walke, "Western Flotilla," 439; Walke to Foote, March 13, 1862, *ORN,* 22:688.

19. Walke to Foote, March 13, 1862, *ORN,* 22:688; Walke, *Naval Scenes,* 94; Pope to Foote, *ORN,* 22:689–90; Patterson, *Mississippi River Campaign,* 70–71.

20. Morison diary, March 14 and 15, 1862, 47–48; Browne to Fannie, March 19, 1862, in Milligan, *Freshwater Navy,* 40–41.

21. Morison diary, March 15, 1862, 48. For a list of crew on the USS *Carondelet* and soldiers transferred to the gunboat in March 1862, see *ORN,* 22:736–37.

22. Browne to Fannie, March 19, 1862, in Milligan, *Freshwater Navy,* 40–44; Morison diary, March 15, 1862, 48.

23. Ranger, "Our Army Correspondence, 'From the Mississippi Flotilla,'" on board the *Judge Torrence,* March 20, 1862, *Daily Evening Express,* March 27, 1862, at "Into Battle on Mississippi Mortar Boat with 'Ranger,'" Lancaster at War website.

24. Browne, March 19, 1862, in Milligan, *Freshwater Navy,* 42; Morison diary, March 15 and 17, 1862, 48, 50.

25. Morison diary, March 17, 1862, 50; Smith, *USS* Carondelet, 91–92; Browne, March 19, 1862, in Milligan, *Freshwater Navy,* 44. Milligan indicates there were ten mortars; Slagle, *Ironclad Captain,* 199, claims eight.

26. Walke, "Western Flotilla," 439; Foote to Welles, March 22, 1862, enclosure, J. B. Dill to Paulding, list of killed and wounded on gunboat *St. Louis,* March 17, 1862, *ORN,* 22:694.

27. Roger Stembel, *ORN,* 22:691, 777; abstract log of *Lexington,* August 16, 1861, to April 11, 1862, ibid., 777.

28. Foote to Welles, March 17, 1862, *ORN,* 22:693.

29. Morison diary, March 17, 1862, 50; *Harper's Weekly,* April 5, 1862, 219; telegram from Foote to Welles, March 17, 1862, *ORN,* 22:694.

30. Foote to Welles, March 17, 1862, *ORN,* 22:693–94; Tucker, *Foote,* 181–82. As Foote told Welles, "If we attempt to run past six forts with fifty guns, surely not a single gunboat will survive."

31. Morison diary, March 17 and 18, 1862, 50–51; Walke, *Naval Scenes,* 103.

32. Slagle, *Ironclad Captain,* 205.

33. Ranger, "Our Army Correspondence."

34. Morison diary, March 23, 1862, 51–52.

35. Ranger, "Our Army Correspondence"; Slagle, *Ironclad Captain,* 204; Tucker, *Foote,* 182.

36. Tucker, *Foote,* 182; Coombe, *Thunder along the Mississippi,* 88–89; Foote to Welles, March 20, 1862, *ORN,* 22:697–98; Halleck to Pope, March 24, 1862, ibid., 698–99; Pope to Foote, March 2, 1862, ibid., 701.

37. Browne to Fannie, March 31 [30?], 1862, in Milligan, *Freshwater Navy,* 49.

38. Telegram from Halleck to Foote, March 28, 1862, *ORN,* 22:703; Slagle, *Ironclad Captain,* 205; Daniel and Bock, *Island No. 10.*

39. Walke, *Naval Scenes,* 117–18; Walke, "Western Flotilla," 441–42; Smith, *USS* Carondelet, chap. 6; Slagle, *Ironclad Captain;* Tucker, *Foote,* 164–65.

40. Foote to Walke, March 30, 1862, *ORN*, 22:704–5; Walke, *Naval Scenes*, 117–18.

41. Walke, *Naval Scenes*, 117, 152. John Ford, who served on the *Carondelet* during the event, wrote his account in February 1874.

42. Walke, *Naval Scenes*, 124–25; letter from a *New York Times* correspondent, April 5, 1862, cited in ibid., 137; Morison diary, April 4, 1862, 53; Walke, "Western Flotilla," 443–44.

43. Smith, *USS* Carondelet, 94; correspondence of *Chicago Tribune*, April 2, 1862; Walke, *Naval Scenes*, 107, 112.

44. Walke, *Naval Scenes*, 124; letter from a *New York Times* correspondent, ibid., 137.

45. Morison diary, April 4, 1862; Walke, *Naval Scenes*, 124–25, 128–29. As a mariner, Walke undoubtedly knew that moonlight (the moon was not even in its first quarter) would not be a real deterrent to running past the rebel batteries.

46. Walke, *Naval Scenes*, 125, 128–29; Morison diary, April 4, 1862.

47. *New York Times* correspondent Franc B. Wilkie, known as "Galway," quoted in Walke, *Naval Scenes*, 130; Walke, "Western Flotilla," 443; Patterson, *Mississippi River Campaign*, 78– 80. Mahan, *Navy in the Civil War*, 3:21, identified the seaman heaving the coal as Charles Wilson, who was "standing sometimes knee-deep in the water that boiled over the forecastle."

48. Morison diary, April 4, 1862, 53.

49. Ibid.; Wilkie (aka Galway) quoted in Walke, *Naval Scenes*, 127, 134; Smith, *USS* Carondelet, 103; Ford's account in Walke, *Naval Scenes*, 152.

50. Smith, *USS* Carondelet, 104. He is quoting an army officer.

51. Morison diary, April 5, 1862, 53–54.

52. Browne, [April 7, 1862], in Milligan, *Freshwater Navy*, 54–55; Walke, "Western Flotilla," 445; Patterson, *Mississippi River Campaign*, 81.

53. Morison diary, April 5, 1862, 54–55; Smith, *USS* Carondelet, 105. The two bow guns were the 30- and 50-pounder Dahlgrens recently installed.

54. Walke, "Western Flotilla," 442–43.

55. Morison diary, April 7, 1862, 56–57; Walke, *Naval Scenes*, 147–49; Slagle, *Ironclad Captain*, 208; Patterson, *Mississippi River Campaign*, 78, 87–88; Smith, *USS* Carondelet, 108.

56. Smith, *USS* Carondelet, 108–9; log of *Carondelet*, in Walke, *Naval Scenes*, 151.

57. Morison diary, April 8, 1862, 57.

58. Coombe, *Thunder along the Mississippi*, 94; Walke, "Western Flotilla," 445–46; Tucker, *Foote*, 188; Milligan, *Gunboats down the Mississippi*, 58–59.

59. William M. Fowler Jr., *Under Two Flags* (New York: Norton, 1990), 172; note in Milligan, *Freshwater Navy*, 59.

5. Securing New Orleans

1. John Keegan, *The American Civil War* (New York: Alfred A. Knopf, 2009), 86.

2. McPherson, *War on the Waters,* 55–56; Keegan, *American Civil War,* 85–86; Chester G. Hearn, *Admiral David Glasgow Farragut: The Civil War Years* (Annapolis, MD: Naval Institute Press, 1997), 45.

3. McPherson, *War on the Waters,* 55–56; Campbell, *Confederate Naval Forces,* 25–26.

4. Joiner, *Mr. Lincoln's Brown Water Navy,* 78–79; Hearn, *Farragut,* 47–50.

5. Oscar Smith diary, February 13, 1862, National Archives, Washington, DC.

6. Hearn, *Farragut,* 59–60; Smith diary, January 19, 1862.

7. Hearn, *Farragut,* 60.

8. Smith diary, February 28, 1862.

9. George Perkins, March 31, 1862, in *Letters of Captain George Hamilton Perkins, U.S.N.* (Whitefish, MT: Kessinger Publishing, 2010), 79. See also Carroll Storrs Alden, *George Hamilton Perkins, Commodore U.S.N.* (Boston: Houghton Mifflin, 1914), 108.

10. Porter, *Naval History,* 217–18.

11. Smith diary, March 9, 1862; Charles Lee Lewis, *David Glasgow Farragut: Our First Admiral* (Annapolis, MD: Naval Institute Press, 1943), 26.

12. Hearn, *Farragut,* 66–67.

13. Smith diary, April 8 and 9, 1862; Richard S. West Jr., *The Second Admiral: A Life of David Dixon Porter, 1819–1891* (New York: Coward-McCann, 1937), 126–27; Porter to Welles, April 30, 1862, *ORN,* 18:362.

14. Hearn, *Farragut,* 83; Porter to Farragut, April 30, 1862, *ORN,* 18:364–65; Admiral D. D. Porter, "The Opening of the Lower Mississippi," *Battles and Leaders* 2 (1956): 35.

15. Smith diary, April 19, 1862; West, *Second Admiral,* 130, 134.

16. Porter, *Naval History,* 217–18.

17. Francis Asbury Roe diary, *ORN,* 18:767.

18. Lewis, *Farragut,* 47.

19. Roe diary, *ORN,* 18:767.

20. Patterson, *Mississippi River Campaign,* 108–9.

21. Perkins, *Letters,* 110–11.

22. Roe diary, *ORN,* 18:768–69.

23. Ibid.

24. Smith diary, April 24, 1862.

25. John Russell Bartlett, "The Brooklyn at the Passage of the Forts," *Battles and Leaders* 2 (1956): 56.

26. West, *Second Admiral,* 138; Hearn, *Farragut,* 112–13.

27. McPherson, *War on the Waters,* 65; Forts Jackson and St. Philip, enclosure to John C. Palfrey to Lt. Gen. Weitzel, May 16, 1862, *ORA,* 15:428.

6. The Battle of Plum Point Bend

1. Foote to Welles, April 12, 1862, *ORN,* 23:3.

2. Ibid.

3. Morison diary, April 12, 1862, 58.

4. George Yost diary, April 11, 1862, Illinois State Historical Library; Coombe, *Thunder along the Mississippi,* 120; Joiner, *Mr. Lincoln's Brown Water Navy,* 68.

5. Morison diary, April 13, 1862, 59; Bearss, *Hardluck Ironclad,* 49; George M. Blodgett to aunt, April 14, 1862, Blodgett Letters, Butler Center for Arkansas Studies; Coombe, *Thunder along the Mississippi,* 119; Walke, "Western Flotilla," 446.

6. Morison diary, April 13, 1862, 59; Joiner, *Mr. Lincoln's Brown Water Navy,* 63; Tucker, *Foote,* 11; Coombe, *Thunder along the Mississippi,* 120; Bearss, *Hardluck Ironclad,* 51; Campbell, *Confederate Naval Forces,* 83–86. In his *Naval Scenes,* Walke barely mentions this incident.

7. Yost diary, April 13, 1862.

8. Blodgett to aunt, April 14, 1862.

9. Foote to Welles, April 14, 1862, *ORN,* 23:4–5; Bearss, *Hardluck Ironclad,* 51; Tucker, *Foote,* 191.

10. Morison diary, April 14, 1862, 60. Bearss, *Hardluck Ironclad,* 52, says the tugs towed seven scows, not six.

11. Bearss, *Hardluck Ironclad,* 51; Walke, "Western Flotilla," 446; Browne, April 15, 1862, in Milligan, *Freshwater Navy,* 62.

12. Yost diary, April 14, 1862.

13. Walke, "Western Flotilla," 446; Walke, *Naval Scenes,* 245–46; Foote to Welles, April 14, 1862, *ORN,* 23:5.

14. Pope to Foote, April 16, 1862, *ORN,* 23:6; Tucker, *Foote,* 194; Foote to Welles, April 17 and 19, 1862, *ORN,* 23:8–9.

15. Yost diary, April 16, 1862; Bearss, *Hardluck Ironclad,* 53.

16. Bearss, *Hardluck Ironclad,* 53; Yost diary, April 18, 1862.

17. Browne to Fannie, April 20, 1862, in Milligan, *Freshwater Navy,* 64; Morison diary, April 20, 1862, 60. Morison mistakenly wrote Saturday, April 20, but it was actually Sunday.

18. Foote to Welles, April 23, 1862, *ORN,* 23:10.

19. Foote to Welles, April 30, 1862, *ORN,* 23:11–12.

20. Morison diary, April 28 and 29, 1862, 62; Slagle, *Ironclad Captain,* 216; Joiner, *Mr. Lincoln's Brown Water Navy,* 64–65; Walke's report to Pennock, May 3, 1862, *ORN,* 23:81.

21. Yost diary, April 27, 28, 30, and May 1, 1862; Bearss, *Hardluck Ironclad,* 54–55.

22. Maynadier to Foote, May 3, 1862, enclosure, *ORN,* 23:82.

23. Browne to Fannie, April 30, 1862, in Milligan, *Freshwater Navy,* 70.

24. Browne, May 8, 1862, in Milligan, *Freshwater Navy,* 71–72.

25. Morison diary, May 8, 1862, 62; Browne to Fannie, April [May] 8, 1862, in Milligan, *Freshwater Navy,* 72–73.

26. Ibid.; Smith, *USS* Carondelet, 112.

27. Slagle, *Ironclad Captain,* 217.

28. Morison diary, May 9, 1862, 62–63; Slagle, *Ironclad Captain,* 218.

29. Morison diary, May 10, 1862, 63.

30. Walke, "Western Flotilla," 447; Smith, *USS* Carondelet, chap. 7.

31. T. B. Gregory to Capt. Maynadier, May 10, 1862, *ORN,* 23:15–16.

32. Callender, "What a Boy Saw." Callender was appointed an assistant ensign on October 1, 1862, and resigned February 18, 1864.

33. Ibid.; Slagle, *Ironclad Captain,* 221.

34. Callender, "What a Boy Saw"; Gosnell, *Guns on Western Waters,* 87; report of Fleet Captain Pennock, May 13, 1862, *ORN,* 23:20; Davis to Welles, May 11, 1862, ibid., 14. According to Milligan, *Gunboats down the Mississippi,* 66, Stembel later wrote that the wound left him "paralyzed from the waist."

35. Callender, "What a Boy Saw."

36. Morison diary, May 10, 1862, 63. Morison described the engagement in detail.

37. Walke, "Western Flotilla," 447–48; Walke to Davis, May 10, 1862, *ORN,* 23:15.

38. Browne, May 12, 1862, in Milligan, *Freshwater Navy,* 76.

39. Ibid., 77; Bearss, *Hardluck Ironclad,* 62; Phelps to Foote, May 11, 1862, *ORN,* 23:19.

40. Walke, "Western Flotilla," 448; Slagle, *Ironclad Captain,* 223.

41. Walke, "Western Flotilla," 448; Morison diary, May 10, 1862, 63–64.

42. Yost diary, May 10, 1862; Phelps to Foote, May 11, 1862, *ORN,* 23:19; Walke, "Western Flotilla," 449; Phelps to Foote, May 17, 1862, *ORN,* 23:24; J. E. Montgomery to Gen. G. T. Beauregard, May 12, 1862, ibid., 55–56; M. Jeff Thompson to Gen. Beauregard, May 10, 1862, ibid., 54–55.

43. Yost diary, May 10, 1862; Bearss, *Hardluck Ironclad,* 63; Gosnell, *Guns on Western Waters,* 89–91.

44. Morison diary, May 13, 1862; Yost diary, May 13, 1862. In a later, fuller version of his diary reprinted in *Life* magazine in February 1965, Yost's account is slightly more boastful, shaving the time from ten minutes to four.

45. Morison diary, May 14, 1862, 64–65.

46. Ibid.; Yost diary, May 20, 1862.

47. Yost diary, May 21, 1862; Bearss, *Hardluck Ironclad,* 65; Milligan, *Gunboats down the Mississippi,* 68, 70–71.

7. The Battle of Memphis

1. Browne to Fannie, May 25, 1862, in Milligan, *Freshwater Navy,* 83; Warren D. Crandall and Isaac D. Newell, eds., *History of the Ram Fleet and the Mississippi Marine Brigade* (St. Louis: Buschart Brothers, 1907), 42–46; C. H. Davis to Welles, May 16, 1862, *ORN,* 23:23.

2. Yost diary, May 30, 31, and June 1, 1862; Charles Ellet Jr. to E. M. Stanton, May 26, 1862, *ORN,* 23:29–30; Ellet to Davis, May 28, 1862, ibid., 32; C. H. Davis to Welles, May 24, 1862, ibid., 28. Davis said he did not expect the rebel gunboats to renew the attack.

3. Browne to Fannie, May 25, 1862, in Milligan, *Freshwater Navy,* 81.

4. Yost diary, May 27 and 28, 1862.

5. Browne to Fannie, May 25, 1862, in Milligan, *Freshwater Navy,* 82; George Blodgett to aunt, May 31, 1862, Blodgett Letters, Butler Center for Arkansas Studies; Blodgett to Davis, May 23, 1862, *ORN,* 23:28. Blodgett's gunboat, the *Conestoga,* had been sent on detached duty.

6. Yost diary, May 13 and 15, 1862; Phelps to Foote, May 22, 1862, *ORN,* 23:26.

7. Morison diary, June 3, 1862, 66; Ellet to Stanton, June 3, 1862, *ORN,* 23:41–42; Ellet to Davis, June 3, 1862, ibid., 42; Ellet to Hon. E. M. Stanton, June 4, 1862, ibid., 43–44.

8. Yost diary, June 3, 1862; Ellet to Stanton, June 4, 1862, *ORN,* 23:43–44; Col. G. N. Fitch to Maj. Gen. John Pope, June 5, 1862, ibid., 45–46.

9. Morison diary, June 4, 1862, 67; Our Special Correspondent, Fort Pillow, Thursday noon, June 5, 1862, published in *New York Tribune,* June 11, 1862.

10. Morison diary, June 4, 1862, 67.

11. Our Special Correspondent, Fort Pillow, *New York Tribune,* June 11, 1862; Yost diary, June 5, 1862; Crandall and Newell, *History of the Ram Fleet,* 56–60; Gosnell, *Guns on Western Waters,* 94–95; Smith, *USS* Carondelet, 118.

12. Yost diary, June 5, 1862.

13. Morison diary, June 5, 1862, 67; Battle of Memphis, June 6, 1862, *ORN,* 23:118.

14. Morison diary, June 5, 1862, 67; Davis report, June 6, 1862, *ORN,* 23:119. See also pilot John S. Tennyson's report, ibid., 137–38.

15. Morison diary, June 6, 1862, 68; Davis report, June 6, 1862, *ORN,* 23:119; Smith, *USS* Carondelet, 118.

16. Yost diary, June 6, 1862. Joiner, *Mr. Lincoln's Brown Water Navy,* 70, points out that this was a brilliant tactic, learned from the difficulties experienced by the ponderous ironclads in the Mississippi's current at Plum Point.

17. Morison diary, June 6, 1862, 68; Davis report, June 6, 1862, *ORN*, 23:119; Walke report, ibid., 123; Yost diary, June 6, 1862.

18. Davis report, June 6, 1862, *ORN*, 23:119–20; Walke report, June 6, 1862, ibid., 122; Ellet report, June 6, 1862, ibid., 125–26.

19. Crandall and Newell, *History of the Ram Fleet,* 52–56; Joiner, *Mr. Lincoln's Brown Water Navy,* 71; Campbell, *Confederate Naval Forces,* 95. Patterson, *Mississippi River Campaign,* 127, quotes Alfred Ellet, who said it was the *Beauregard* on one side and the *Sumter* on the other. Milligan, *Gunboats down the Mississippi,* 75, claims it was the *Sumter.* Crandall and Newell say it was the *Beauregard.* Captain Hart of the *Beauregard* reported that the *Sumter* struck the *Queen* amidships.

20. Morison diary, June 6, 1862, 68; Walke report, *ORN*, 23:123.

21. Crandall and Newell, *History of the Ram Fleet,* 54–55; Milligan, *Gunboats down the Mississippi,* 75; Walke, "Western Flotilla," 450; Walke report, *ORN*, 23:123.

22. Morison diary, June 6, 1862, 68.

23. Yost diary, June 6, 1862.

24. Report from Davis to Welles, *ORN*, 23:118, 119–21; Milligan, *Gunboats down the Mississippi,* 76. See also Patterson, *Mississippi River Campaign,* chap. 17. In addition, the Yankees captured four rebel rams that were later repaired and joined the Western Flotilla.

25. Morison diary, June 6, 1862, 68–69; Ellet, June 7, 1862, *ORN*, 23:127.

26. Milligan, *Gunboats down the Mississippi,* 76–77.

27. Browne to Fannie, June 8, 1862, in Milligan, *Freshwater Navy,* 88; H. W. Halleck to Davis, June 8, 1862, *ORN*, 23:159; Halleck to Stanton, June 8, 1862, ibid., 161.

28. Davis to Fitch, June 14, 1862, *ORN*, 23:164.

29. Blodgett to aunt, June 15, 1862.

30. Browne to Fannie, June 14, 1862, in Milligan, *Freshwater Navy,* 90–92.

31. Ibid.; Davis to Welles, June 16, 1862, *ORN*, 23:165.

32. Blodgett to aunt, June 15, 1862.

33. Blodgett to aunt, June 24, 1862; Lt. W. McGunnegle to Davis, June 18, 1862, *ORN*, 23:165–67; Preston Bishop to Father, June 21, 1862, mss. 11.52, Butler Center for Arkansas Studies.

34. McGunnegle to Davis, June 18, 1862, *ORN*, 23:165–66.

35. Browne, June 18, 1863, in Milligan, *Freshwater Navy,* 93; Smith, *Timberclads,* 331.

36. Blodgett, June 18, 1863.

37. Browne to Fannie, June 18, 1862, in Milligan, *Freshwater Navy,* 92–93.

38. Blodgett to aunt, June 24, 1862.

39. McGunnegle to Davis, June 18, 1862, *ORN*, 23:167.

40. Preston Bishop to Father, June 21, 1862; Smith, *Timberclads,* 331.

41. Preston Bishop to Father, June 21, 1862; McGunnegle to Davis, June 18, 1862, *ORN,* 23:167.

42. Slagle, *Ironclad Captain,* 247–48. Kilty was severely injured and lost an arm, but he served as an ordnance officer in 1863–1864, commanded the frigate *Roanoke* during the last year of the war, and was promoted to commodore on July 25, 1866.

8. On to Vicksburg!

1. Joiner, *Mr. Lincoln's Brown Water Navy,* 81–82; Lewis, *Farragut,* 78–79; Hearn, *Farragut,* 127–30; Coombe, *Thunder along the Mississippi,* 135; Reed, *Combined Operations,* 195–96.

2. Lewis, *Farragut,* 78–80; Spencer Tucker, ed., *The Civil War Navy Encyclopedia,* 2 vols. (Santa Barbara, CA: ABC-CLIO, 2010), 1:131–32.

3. Anthony O'Neil diary, May 2–7, 1862, Library of Congress; Palmer to Farragut, May 9, 1862, *ORN,* 18:473; Craven to his wife, June 3, 1862, ibid., 528–29.

4. O'Neil diary, May 7, 1862.

5. Ibid.; Barbara B. Tomblin, *Bluejackets & Contrabands: African Americans and the Union Navy* (Lexington: University Press of Kentucky, 2009), 40–41.

6. O'Neil diary, May 9, 1862.

7. Henry Bell diary, May 8, 1862, *ORN,* 18:700.

8. Ibid., 700–701; Campbell, *Confederate Naval Forces,* 87.

9. O'Neil diary, May 7, 1862; Bell diary, May 9, 1862, *ORN,* 18:701.

10. Bell diary, May 9, 1862, *ORN,* 18:699; Lewis, *Farragut,* 80–81; Hearn, *Farragut,* 131.

11. Bell diary, May 11, 1862, *ORN,* 18:701; Farragut to Palmer, May 10, 1862, ibid., 478; Palmer to Farragut, May 13, 1862, ibid., 488.

12. O'Neil diary, May 18, 1862.

13. Lee to authorities at Vicksburg, May 13, 1862, *ORN,* 18:491–93; Jas L. Autrey to Lee, May 18, 1862, ibid., 492; Dudley Taylor Cornish and Virginia Jeans Laas, *Lincoln's Lee: The Life of Samuel Phillips Lee, United States Navy, 1812–1897* (Lawrence: University Press of Kansas, 1986), 103.

14. Lizzie to Lee, May 18, 1862, in *Wartime Washington: The Civil War Letters of Elizabeth Blair Lee,* ed. Virginia Jeans Laas (Chicago: University of Illinois Press, 1991), 148–49; Cornish and Laas, *Lincoln's Lee,* 103.

15. Bell diary, May 12, 14, 15, and 16, 1862, *ORN,* 18:702–3.

16. Smith diary, May 15 and 16, 1862.

17. Bell diary, May 19, 1862, *ORN,* 18: 702–4; Keegan, *American Civil War,* 154; Hearn, *Farragut,* 133; Lewis, *Farragut,* 83.

18. Bell diary, May 19 and 20, 1862, *ORN,* 18: 703–4; instructions of Flag Officer Farragut, US Navy, to Commander Lee, US Navy, regarding operations against Vicksburg, May 22, 1862, *ORN,* 18:508–9; Lewis, *Farragut,* 83.

19. Bell diary, May 23, 1862, *ORN,* 18:704–5; Lewis, *Farragut,* 83; Hearn, *Farragut,* 133.

20. O'Neil diary, May 20, 1862.

21. Bell diary, May 23, 1862, *ORN,* 18:705.

22. Lewis, *Farragut,* 79–85; Winston Groom, *Vicksburg 1863* (New York: Vintage Civil War Library, Vintage Books, 2009), 139; abstract log of *Hartford, ORN,* 18:725.

23. Lewis, *Farragut,* 84, 87; Farragut to Lee, May 22, 1862, *ORN,* 18:508–9; Bell diary, May 25, 1862, ibid., 705.

24. Bell diary, May 25, 1862, *ORN,* 18:705–6. Bell covers more days' events in this entry.

25. Ibid.; Lewis, *Farragut,* 87–88; Hearn, *Farragut,* 134; Keegan, *American Civil War,* 154–55.

26. *Hartford* log, *ORN,* 18:725; Smith diary, May 24, 25, and 26, 1862. O'Neil's diary confirms the departure of these vessels.

27. Smith diary, May 28, 1862; *Hartford* log, *ORN,* 18:725; Bell diary, May 28, 1862, ibid., 706–7.

28. Bell diary, May 28, 1862, *ORN,* 18:706–7; "Late from New Orleans," *Cincinnati Daily Gazette,* June 28, 1862.

29. O'Neil diary, May 28 and 30, 1862; abstract log of *Winona, ORN,* 18:820.

30. Ibid.

31. Ibid.

32. O'Neil diary, June 5, 1862. *Winona's* log does not mention this incident or the capture of the *Ruby.*

33. O'Neil diary, June 7 and 8, 1862; *Wissahickon* log, *ORN,* 18:797. The *Wissahickon's* log provides more detail about the exchange between the gunboats and the rebel batteries.

34. Smith diary, June 7, 1862.

35. Lewis, *Farragut,* 91–93; West, *Second Admiral,* 145–46, 151; Hearn, *Farragut,* 136–37; Groom, *Vicksburg,* 140.

36. Bell diary, June 6, 1862, *ORN,* 18:708; Lewis, *Farragut,* 93.

37. Smith diary, June 8, 1862.

38. O'Neil diary, June 10 and 11, 1862; abstract log of *Winona,* June 10 and 11, 1862, *ORN,* 18:820; abstract log of *Wissahickon,* ibid., 798.

39. O'Neil diary, June 14, 1862. The *Winona's* log does not have entries for June 12, 13, and 14, 1862.

40. Bell diary, June 20, 1862, *ORN,* 18:710; Smith diary, June 20, 1862; West, *Second Admiral,* 153.

41. O'Neil diary, June 20, 1862, 56.

42. Smith diary, June 22, 1862; Bell diary, June 22, 1862, *ORN,* 18:711.

43. Smith diary, June 22, 1862.

44. Ibid., June 24, 1862; Bell diary, June 28, 1862, *ORN*, 18:711.

45. Smith diary, June 25, 1862; Bell diary, June 25, 1862, *ORN*, 18:711; Hearn, *Farragut*, 140–41.

46. Smith diary, June 25, 1862.

47. Bell diary, June 26, 1862, *ORN*, 18:711.

48. West, *Second Admiral*, 136; Bell diary, June 26, 1862, *ORN*, 18:711.

49. Smith diary, June 27, 1862.

50. Bell diary, June 28, 1862, *ORN*, 18:712. See also Lee report, June 28 attack, ibid., 612–13; USS *Richmond* casualties, ibid., 613; *Hartford* report, ibid., 615; Nichols report, ibid., 618; Lewis, *Farragut*, 98; Joiner, *Mississippi River Campaign*, 168–69.

51. Smith diary, June 28, 1862; O'Neil diary, June 28, 1862; Lt. Palmer to Farragut, June 30, 1862, *ORN*, 18:619.

52. Smith diary, June 28, 1862; Bell diary, June 28, 1862, *ORN*, 18:713; O'Neil diary, June 28, 1862; Hearn, *Farragut*, 143–44.

53. Bell diary, June 28, 1862, *ORN*, 18:712–13.

54. Lewis, *Farragut*, 98; Nichols report, June 28, 1862, *ORN*, 18:618; O'Neil diary, June 28, 1862; Bell diary, June 28, 1862, *ORN*, 18:712.

55. Nichols report, June 28, 1862, *ORN*, 18:618; O'Neil diary, June 28, 1862; *Winona* log, *ORN*, 18:821.

56. Smith diary, June 28, 1862.

57. Lewis, *Farragut*, 99; Bell diary, June 28, 1862, *ORN*, 18:713.

58. Palmer to Farragut, June 30, 1862, *ORN*, 18:619; Lewis, *Farragut*, 98–99; Bell diary, June 28, 1862, *ORN*, 18:713. Bell said the captains came on board at 6:20 p.m.

59. De Camp to Farragut, June 29, 1862, *ORN*, 18:623–24; abstract log of *Wissahickon*, *ORN*, 18:798.

60. Crosby to Farragut, June 30, 1862, *ORN*, 18:621. Lieutenant A. P. Cook worked the guns.

61. Lee to Farragut, June 28, 1862, *ORN*, 18:612.

62. Donaldson to Farragut, June 28, 1862, *ORN*, 18:617.

63. Wainwright to Farragut, June 29, 1862, *ORN*, 18:615.

64. Nichols report, June 28, 1862, *ORN*, 18:618.

65. Farragut to Welles, June 28, 1862, *ORN*, 18:588.

66. Woodworth report, June 30, 1862, *ORN*, 18:622.

67. Lewis, *Farragut*, 100–101; Reed, *Combined Operations*, 202; Van Dorn to Davis, June 28, 1862, *ORN*, 18:651; Groom, *Vicksburg*, 152.

68. O'Neil diary, June 29, 1862.

9. CSS *Arkansas*

1. O'Neil diary, July 1, 1862; Smith diary, July 1, 1862.

2. Smith diary, July 6, 1862.

3. Morison diary, July 1, 1862, 71.

4. Slagle, *Ironclad Captain,* 251–52; Bell diary, July 1, 1862, *ORN,* 18:714.

5. Bell diary, July 1, 1862, *ORN,* 18:714.

6. Groom, *Vicksburg,* 147–48; Simpson, *America's Civil War,* 56.

7. Groom, *Vicksburg,* 147–48; Knute Nelson to his parents, July 8, 1863, in *Some Civil War Letters of Knute Nelson,* ed. Millard L. Giekse, www.naha.stolaf .edu/pubs/nas/volume23v0123_2.html.

8. Morison diary, July 3, 1862, 71.

9. Ibid., July 4, 1862; O'Neil diary, July 4, 1862; Smith diary, July 4, 1862. To teetotaler Farragut's credit, the *Hartford* did "splice the main brace" on the evening of July 4.

10. Lewis, *Farragut,* 107.

11. *Cincinnati Daily Gazette,* July 9, 1862; Bell diary, July 13, 1862, *ORN,* 18:716.

12. Correspondent, *Queen of the West* off Napoleon, Arkansas, "From the Lower Mississippi," July 3, 1862, *Cincinnati Daily Gazette,* July 12, 1862.

13. Morison diary, July 13, 1862.

14. Farragut to Welles, July 4, 1862, *ORN,* 18:624; Lewis, *Farragut,* 107.

15. West, *Second Admiral,* 161.

16. O'Neil diary, July 12, 1862; Nichols report, *ORN,* 19:24–25, 26. The abstract log of the *Winona* ends on July 12, 1862.

17. Slagle, *Ironclad Captain,* 259–61; Captain Isaac N. Brown, "The Confederate Gun-boat 'Arkansas,'" *Battles and Leaders* 3 (1956): 572–73.

18. Walke, *Naval Scenes,* 330.

19. Walke to Davis, July 15, 1862, *ORN,* 19:41–42; Walke, *Naval Scenes,* 330; James R. Soley, "Naval Operations in the Vicksburg Campaign," *Battles and Leaders* 3 (1956): 555; Milligan, *Gunboats down the Mississippi,* 82–85; Joiner, *Mr. Lincoln's Brown Water Navy,* 84–87. According to Lewis, *Farragut,* 112, the *Queen of the West,* "armed only with her ram, carried a company of sharpshooters." The ram later carried one 30-pounder cannon and three 12-pounder howitzers.

20. Abstract log of USS *Tyler, ORN,* 19:39–40; Lt. Gwin, July 15 and 16, 1862, ibid., 36–37; Brown, "Confederate Gun-boat 'Arkansas,'" 580. A note in Brown's article has the *Carondelet*'s log for July 15, 1862.

21. Slagle, *Ironclad Captain,* 264; Patterson, *Mississippi River Campaign,* 173.

22. Lt. Gwin, July 15 and 16, 1862, *ORN,* 19:36–37.

23. Morison diary, July 15, 1862, 72.

24. Ibid., 71; Brown, "Confederate Gun-boat 'Arkansas,'" 580; Walke to Davis, July 15, 1862, *ORN,* 19:41–43; Soley, "Naval Operations in Vicksburg Campaign," 555.

25. Slagle, *Ironclad Captain,* 265; Walke, *Naval Scenes,* 304–5.

26. Walke, *Naval Scenes,* 305; Morison diary, July 15, 1862, 72–73; Walke report, July 25, 1862, *ORN,* 19:41–43.

27. Morison diary, July 15, 1862, 72–73; Walke to Davis, July 15, 1862, *ORN*, 19:41; *Carondelet's* log, July 15, 1862.

28. Gosnell, *Guns on Western Waters*, 113–14.

29. Ibid., 114–15.

30. Ibid.

31. O'Neil diary, July 15, 1862.

32. Gosnell, *Guns on Western Waters*, 115–16.

33. Wainwright report, July 16, 1862, *ORN*, 19:20; O'Neil diary, July 15, 1862.

34. Lt. Breese to Davis, July 18, 1862, *ORN*, 19:27–28.

35. Brown, "Confederate Gun-boat 'Arkansas,'" 576.

36. Renshaw report, *ORN*, 19:27–28, 29–30.

37. O'Neil diary, July 15, 1862.

38. J. S. R., on board the ram *Lancaster* No. 3, "From Vicksburg," July 15, 1862, *Cincinnati Daily Gazette*, July 24, 1862, 1. Albert, *Hartford* engineer, to Father, July 17, 1862, in Frank Moore, *The Rebellion Record: A Diary of American Events* (New York: D. Van Nostrand, 1882), 5:555, says the shot that hit the *Lancaster* could have been from a federal vessel.

39. Alden quoted in Crandall and Newel, *History of the Ram Fleet*, 102–3; *Lancaster* log, July 15, 1862, *ORN*, 23:244; J. S. R., "From Vicksburg."

40. O'Neil diary, July 15, 1862.

41. Gosnell, *Guns on Western Waters*, 121.

42. O'Neil diary, July 15, 1862; Phelps to Foote, July 29, 1862, *ORN*, 19:58–59.

43. Lewis, *Farragut*, 113; Hearn, *Farragut*, 157–58; Patterson, *Mississippi River Campaign*, 177; Crandall and Newell, *History of the Ram Fleet*, 113.

44. Gosnell, *Guns on Western Waters*, 121.

45. Lewis, *Farragut*, 118; Crandall and Newell, *History of the Ram Fleet*, 99–103; Winslow report, July 7, 1862, *ORN*, 2:253.

46. Wainwright to Davis, July 16, 1862, *ORN*, 19:20; report of J. M. Foltz, fleet surgeon, ibid., 21; Smith diary, July 15, 1862.

47. Lewis, *Farragut*, 114; Hearn, *Farragut*, 159; Farragut to Welles, July 17, 1862, *ORN*, 19:4; list of wounded, ibid., 5; Wainwright report, ibid., 20 (with the *Hartford's* log); Crandall and Newell, *History of the Ram Fleet*, 99–103; J. S. R., "From Vicksburg."

48. "From Farragut's Fleet," *Cincinnati Daily Gazette*, July 24, 1862.

49. Morison diary, July 21 and 22, 1862, 73–74; Smith diary, July 18, 1862.

50. Morison diary, July 21 and 22, 1862.

51. Bell diary, July 16, 1862, *ORN*, 19:713; Hearn, *Farragut*, 159.

52. Farragut to Davis, July 16, 1862, *ORN*, 23:236.

53. Lewis, *Farragut*, 116; Farragut to Davis, July 17, 1862, *ORN*, 19:10–11; Davis to Farragut, July 17, 1862, *ORN*, 23:237.

54. Crandell and Newell, *History of the Ram Fleet*, 104; Lewis, *Farragut*, 116–17; Milligan, *Gunboats down the Mississippi*, 86–87.

55. Dungannon, "Latest from Vicksburg," July 23, 1862, *Cincinnati Daily Gazette,* August 2, 1862, 1; Lewis, *Farragut,* 118.

56. W. D. Porter to Welles, August 1, 1862, *ORN,* 19:60–61.

57. Dungannon, "Latest from Vicksburg." According to Crandall and Newell, *History of the Ram Fleet,* 104–5, the names of the volunteers were preserved, but the authors do not list them. The *Gazette* listed the volunteers as "James M. Hunter, 53rd Illinois Vols and four sharpshooters; Alexander Ford, B. F. Ray, Roley S. McKay, pilots; Jacob Lauber, John McCullough, John P. Skelton, Granvile Roberts, engineers; Thompson Woods, blacksmith; James Kerr, greaser; Peter Brown, Martin Tremp, mates; Geo. Lee, Alexander Cook, Thornton Stewart, Geo. Ball, James Johnson, Geo. Williams, Timothy Harvey, John Wilson, firemen; Wm H. Nixon, John Montague, Joseph Taylor, (refugee), deck hands."

58. Brown, "Confederate Gun-boat 'Arkansas,'" 577–78, states that some officers and all but twenty-eight of the crew were in hospitals ashore. Walke's report is in *ORN,* 19:43.

59. Gosnell, *Guns on Western Waters,* 128–29.

60. Ibid.; Brown, "Confederate Gun-boat 'Arkansas,'" 578.

61. Dungannon, "Latest from Vicksburg"; Porter to Davis, July 22, 1862, *ORN,* 19:50; Brown, "Confederate Gun-boat 'Arkansas,'" 577–78; Porter report on *Essex,* August 1, 1862, *ORN,* 19:60. There seems to be no report from the *Cincinnati* on this action.

62. O'Neil diary, July 22, 1862.

63. Gosnell, *Guns on Western Waters,* 130.

64. Lewis, *Farragut,* 118–20.

65. Phelps to Foote, July 29, 1862, *ORN,* 19:56–58.

66. Lewis, *Farragut,* 121; Bell diary, July 23, 1862, *ORN,* 19:715. In his journal, Bell noted that he had told Farragut "he should not stake the command of the river upon an attack from the ram under the batteries at Vicksburg."

67. Smith diary, July 24, 1862; Lewis, *Farragut,* 121; Hearn, *Farragut,* 162; Bell diary, July 21, 1862, *ORN,* 19:716 .

68. Gideon Welles, *Diary of Gideon Welles* (New York: Houghton Mifflin, 1911), 1:72 (August 10, 1862); Lewis, *Farragut,* 123.

69. Charles H. Davis Jr., *Life of Charles Henry Davis, Rear Admiral, 1807–1877* (Boston: Houghton Mifflin, 1899), 268–69, 270–71; *Cincinnati Daily Gazette,* August 2, 1862, 1.

70. Ellet to Stanton, July 25, 1862, in Crandall and Newell, *History of the Ram Fleet,* 118.

10. The Mississippi Squadron

1. Walke to Davis, July 30, 1862, *ORN,* 23:272–73; Morison diary, July 23, 1862, 74.

2. Morison diary, July 23, 1862, 74.

3. Walke to Davis, July 30, 1862, *ORN,* 23:272–73.

4. Morison diary, July 25, 1862, 75.

5. Dungannon, *Cincinnati Daily Gazette,* August 2, 1862, 1; Crandall and Newell, *History of the Ram Fleet,* 114; Mahan, *Navy in the Civil War,* 54. Dungannon had taken passage up the Mississippi River on the *Queen of the West.*

6. Dungannon, *Cincinnati Daily Gazette,* August 2, 1862.

7. Morison diary, July 28, 1862, 75; Phelps to Foote, July 29, 1862, *ORN,* 19:58.

8. Coombe, *Thunder along the Mississippi,* 162; Brown, "Confederate Gun-boat 'Arkansas,'" 572.

9. Gift quoted in Gosnell, *Guns on Western Waters,* 132.

10. Patterson, *Mississippi River Campaign,* 189–90; Gosnell, *Guns on Western Waters,* 134.

11. "The USS *Essex,* CSS *Arkansas,* and the 4th Master D. P. Rosenmiller," Lancaster at War website.

12. Gosnell, *Guns on Western Waters,* 133–35; Brown, "Confederate Gun-boat 'Arkansas,'" 579; Patterson, *Mississippi River Campaign,* 190; Joiner, *Mr. Lincoln's Brown Water Navy,* 87; Coombe, *Thunder along the Mississippi,* 162; Milligan, *Gunboats down the Mississippi,* 90.

13. Slagle, *Ironclad Captain,* 283, 285–86, 287–88; McPherson, *War on the Waters,* 94–95.

14. Ringle, *Life in Mr. Lincoln's Navy,* 70–71; Joiner, *Mr. Lincoln's Brown Water Navy,* 90.

15. West, *Second Admiral,* 169–72; Slagle, *Ironclad Captain,* 299–300, 303.

16. West, *Second Admiral,* xii–xiii.

17. Ibid., 173, 176–77; Chester G. Hearn, *Admiral David Dixon Porter: The Civil War Years* (Annapolis, MD: Naval Institute Press, 1996), 144; Slagle, *Ironclad Captain,* 310.

18. Porter, *Naval History,* chap. 24, 283.

19. West, *Second Admiral,* 176–78.

20. Porter to Welles, October 18 and 26, 1862, *ORN,* 23:422, 449–50; Porter to Foote, November 6, 1862, ibid., 466; West, *Second Admiral,* 179; Myron J. Smith Jr., *Tinclads in the Civil War: Union Light-Draught Gunboat Operations on Western Waters, 1862–1865* (Jefferson, NC: McFarland, 2009), introduction, 51–53. In Secretary Welles's endorsement of Porter's request for boats, scows, and gunboats, he wrote, "We must give the Mississippi Squadron vigorous support."

21. Yost diary, September 12, 1862; Bearss, *Hardluck Ironclad,* 80–81.

22. Crandall and Newell, *History of the Ram Fleet,* 137–38.

23. Morison diary, October 19, 20, 21, 22, and 23, 1862, 79–81; Yost diary, October 23 and 13, 1862. The *Carondelet* log, *ORN,* 23:688, confirms that it arrived at Helena on October 23, 1862, but it has no further entries until October 29.

24. Daniel Kemp, "Civil War Reminiscences" (aboard the USS *Cincinnati,* 1862–1863), www.civilwarhome.com.

25. Morison diary, November 2, 3, and 9, 1862; Walke to Porter, November 8, 1862, *ORN,* 23:472–73.

26. McPherson, *Tried by War,* 150, 166; Reed, *Combined Operations,* 231–33.

27. Wallace, *Lew Wallace,* 603–5. West, *Second Admiral,* 181, says this meeting occurred about December 1, 1862.

28. West, *Second Admiral,* 181–82.

29. Porter to Walke, November 21, 1862, *ORN,* 23:495; Walke to Porter, November 25, 1862, ibid., 507.

30. Morison diary, November 24, 1862; James W. Shirk to Porter, November 27, 1862, *ORN,* 23:508–9.

31. Morison diary, November 24, 25, and 27, 1862, 84–85.

32. Ibid., November 29, 1862, 85; Walke to Porter, November 29, 1862, *ORN,* 23:516–17. *Carondelet*'s abstract log has no entries from October 30 to November 28.

33. Walke to Porter, November 29, 1862, *ORN,* 23:516–17; *Carondelet*'s abstract log, November 29, 1862, ibid., 688; Getty to Porter, November 29, 1862, ibid., 515–16.

34. Special order of Captain Walke, US Navy, to commanders of vessels in the vicinity of Yazoo River, December 1, 1862, *ORN,* 23:523.

35. Walke to Porter, December 1, 1862, *ORN,* 23:521–23.

11. The First Vicksburg Campaign

1. Ellet to Porter, December 4, 1862, *ORN,* 23:532, also cited in Crandall and Newell, *History of the Ram Fleet,* 142. The *Horner* was laid up for repairs. Major John W. Lawrence commanded the *Switzerland,* Lieutenant E. W. Bartlett the *Monarch,* Lieutenant W. F. Warren the *Lancaster,* First Master Thomas O'Reilly the *Lioness,* First Master Robert Dazell the *Horner,* and First Master S. Cadman the *Fulton.*

2. J. W. Lawrence to Col. Ellet, December 5, 1862, in Crandall and Newell, *History of the Ram Fleet,* 140–41.

3. Walke to Porter, December 8, 1862, *ORN,* 23:540; West, *Second Admiral,* 181–82.

4. Porter to Welles, December 12, 1862, *ORN,* 23:542–43.

5. Sherman to Porter, December 8, 1862, *ORN,* 23:539.

6. Porter to Sherman, December 11, 1862, *ORN,* 23:540–41; Porter to Fox, December 5, 1862, ibid., 535. Porter had anticipated that Walke would need rams on the Yazoo.

7. Morison diary, December 9, 1862, 87.

8. Yost diary, December 8, 1862.

9. Morison diary, December 8, 1862, 87; Yost diary, December 8, 1862; Bearss, *Hardluck Ironclad,* 94; "Action Aboard the 'Cairo,'" *Life,* February 12, 1965.

10. Porter to Welles, December 12, 1862, *ORN,* 23:543–44; Aaron S. Oberly to Maria Woodford, November 2, 1862, Aaron Shimer Oberly Letters, Auburn University Digital Library.

11. Yost diary, December 9 and 10, 1862.

12. Walke to Porter, December 13, 1862, *ORN,* 23:546; Bearss, *Hardluck Ironclad,* 95; Patterson, *Mississippi River Campaign,* 195.

13. Walke to Porter, December 13, 1862, *ORN,* 23:546; Morison diary, December 12, 1862, 87.

14. Walke to Porter, December 13, 1862, *ORN,* 23:546–47; Bearss, *Hardluck Ironclad,* 97–98.

15. Bearss, *Hardluck Ironclad,* 98; Walke to Porter, December 13, 1862, *ORN,* 23:546–47.

16. Fentress to Walke, December 13, 1862, *ORN,* 23:546; Bearss, *Hardluck Ironclad,* 98; Coombe, *Thunder along the Mississippi,* 179.

17. Fentress to Walke, December 13, 1862, *ORN,* 23:547; Getty to Pennock, December 19, 1862, ibid., 53.

18. Selfridge to Walke, December 13, 1862, *ORN,* 23:548–50.

19. Fentress to Walke, December 13, 1862, *ORN,* 23:547–48. The Fentress papers are in the Naval Historical Foundation collection at the Library of Congress. His letters and "Memoirs and Naval Life" are at the Alexander Library, Rutgers University, New Brunswick, NJ.

20. Selfridge to Walke, December 13, 1862, *ORN,* 23:548–50; Bearss, *Hardluck Ironclad,* 99, quoting Yost's later, fuller description of the mine hit. The February 12, 1965, issue of *Life* magazine featured the *Cairo* in an article titled "Resurrection of an Ironclad" and offered quotes from the later version of Yost's diary used by Bearss in *Hardluck Ironclad.*

21. Selfridge to Walke, December 13, 1862, *ORN,* 23:548–50; Bearss, *Hardluck Ironclad,* 100; John C. Wideman, *The Sinking of the USS* Cairo (Jackson: University Press of Mississippi, 1993). See also David Riggs, "Sailors of the USS *Cairo:* Anatomy of a Gunboat Crew," *Civil War History* 28, no. 3 (September 1982).

22. Bearss, *Hardluck Ironclad,* 100; Hoel to Walke, December 13, 1862, *ORN,* 23: 550–51; Selfridge to Walke, December 13, 1862, ibid., 550.

23. Yost diary cited in Bearss, *Hardluck Ironclad,* 100. In his later version of the *Cairo*'s demise, Yost added, "The 'Logbook,' the Signal book (which however was bound with leaden covers), and the ship's official papers were all lost." Secretary Welles learned of the incident by telegram on December 18.

24. Hoel to Walke, December 13, 1862, *ORN,* 23:550–51; Ellet report, ibid.,

554–55; Getty to Pennock, December 19, 1862, ibid., 553; Getty to Walke, December 13, 1862, ibid., 552–53; Yost diary cited in Bearss, *Hardluck Ironclad,* 100.

25. Walke to Selfridge, December 13, 1862, *ORN,* 23:556.

26. Porter to Walke, December 13, 1862, *ORN,* 23:556.

27. West, *Second Admiral,* 182–83; Coombe, *Thunder along the Mississippi,* 182; Joiner, *Mr. Lincoln's Brown Water Navy,* 101.

28. David Dixon Porter, *Incidents and Anecdotes of the Civil War* (New York: Sherman, 1886), 126–27; West, *Second Admiral,* 184–85.

29. Coombe, *Thunder along the Mississippi,* 189; Joiner, *Mr. Lincoln's Brown Water Navy,* 101–2.

30. Morison diary, December 17, 18, 19, and 20, 1862, 88.

31. Ibid.

32. "Memorandum E. Paul Reichhelm, Sergeant Major, Third Infantry, Missouri Volunteers, U.S.A. 1862," 4, Thomas Ewing Family Papers, Library of Congress; hereafter cited as Reichhelm diary.

33. West, *Second Admiral,* 186–87.

34. Reichhelm diary, 2.

35. Morison diary, December 20, 1862, 88.

36. Porter to Walke, December 20, 1862, *ORN,* 23:566.

37. Porter to Gwin, December 19 and 20, 1862, *ORN,* 23:567.

38. Walke to Walker, December 22, 1862, *ORN,* 23:569.

39. Walke to Porter, December 24, 1862, *ORN,* 23:569–70, enclosing Walker report, December 23, 1862, *ORN,* 23:570–71; Morison diary, December 23, 1862, 89.

40. Morison diary, December 24, 1862, 89. Morison referred to the tug *Laurel* by its former name, *Erebus.*

41. Perry, *Bohemian Brigade,* 138.

42. Reichhelm diary, 3.

43. Morison diary, December 25, 1862, 89.

44. West, *Second Admiral,* 189.

45. Sherman, *Memoirs,* 289; Patterson, *Mississippi River Campaign,* 197; Joiner, *Mr. Lincoln's Brown Water Navy,* 98.

46. Porter order, December 25, 1862, *ORN,* 23:565, 562.

47. Morison diary, December 26, 1862, 89.

48. Milligan, *Freshwater Navy,* 126; Morison diary, December 26, 1862, 89.

49. Reichhelm diary, 4.

50. Sherman to Porter, December 27, 1862, *ORN,* 23:579; Milligan, *Gunboats down the Mississippi,* 108–9; Patterson, *Mississippi River Campaign,* 196–97.

51. Reichhelm diary, 4–5.

52. William L. Shea and Terence Winshel, *Vicksburg Is the Key: The Struggle for the Mississippi River* (Lincoln, NE: Bison Books, 2005), 52–53.

53. Porter to Gwin, December 27, 1862, *ORN,* 23:571; Porter to Walker, December 27, 1862, ibid., 561.

54. Porter to Bache, December 27, 1862, *ORN,* 23:572.

55. Porter to Welles, December 27, 1862, *ORN,* 23:573; Joiner, *Mr. Lincoln's Brown Water Navy,* 102–3.

56. Porter to Welles, December 27, 1862, *ORN,* 23:572–73.

57. Lord to Porter, December 28, 1862, *ORN,* 23:576; Porter to Pennock, December 27, 1862, ibid., 574.

58. Porter report, *ORN,* 23:572–73; Porter to Brown, December 27, 1862, ibid., 578.

59. Reichhelm diary, 6, 7.

60. Ibid., 9–10.

61. Morison diary, December 28, 1862, 90.

62. Porter to Foote, January 3, 1863, *ORN,* 23:603–4.

63. Diary of Corporal William Warner Reid, 16th Ohio Volunteer Infantry, 1861–1864, transcribed by Robert Fisher, www.mkwe.com/home.htm. For a detailed account of the battle, see Edwin C. Bearss, *The Vicksburg Campaign,* 3 vols. (Dayton, OH: Morningside, 1991).

64. Morison diary, December 29, 1862, 90; Porter to Welles, January 3, 1863, *ORN,* 23:604–5.

65. Sherman, *Memoirs,* 1:320; West, *Second Admiral,* 190–92; Perry, *Bohemian Brigade,* 139–40; Porter, *Incidents and Anecdotes,* 128–29.

66. Porter, *Incidents and Anecdotes,* 128–29.

67. Reichhelm diary, 161–67.

68. Sherman to Porter, January 3, 1863, *ORN,* 23:606–7; Milligan, *Gunboats down the Mississippi,* 110–11.

69. Walke to Porter, December 29, 1862, *ORN,* 23:586–87; Smith, *USS Carondelet,* 144–45; Porter to Walke, December 30, 1862, *ORN,* 23:588–89; Morison diary, December 31, 1862, 90. West, *Second Admiral,* does not mention this conversation; nor does Porter in his *Incidents and Anecdotes.*

70. Sherman, *Memoirs,* 1:321; Reed, *Combined Operations,* 239–40; Perry, *Bohemian Brigade,* 139–40.

71. Morison diary, December 31, 1862, 90; Stephen R. Wise, *Lifeline of the Confederacy: Blockade Running during the Civil War* (Columbia: University of South Carolina Press, 1988), 72.

12. Arkansas Post and Fort Hindman

1. Morison diary, January 1, 1863, 91; Milligan, *Gunboats down the Mississippi,* 111.

2. Morison diary, January 1, 1863, 91–92; Porter to Ellet, January 4, 1863, *ORN,* 24:98; Porter to Smith, January 4, 1863, ibid., 99.

3. Smith, *USS* Carondelet, 143–44; Morison diary, January 4 and 6, 1863, 91–92.

4. Smith, *USS* Carondelet, 144; Morison diary, January 4 and 6, 1863, 91–92.

5. Journal of Thomas Lyons, kept on board of the US steam gunboat *Carondelet,* January 8, 1863, Manuscript Division, Library of Congress; hereafter cited as Lyons diary.

6. Ibid.; Morison diary, January 10, 1863.

7. Lyons diary, January 10, 1863; Gary Joiner, ed., *Little to Eat and Thin Mud to Drink: Letters, Diaries, and Memoirs from the Red River Campaigns, 1863–1864* (Knoxville: University of Tennessee Press, 2007), 222.

8. Lyons diary, January 11 and 16, 1863.

9. Morison diary, January 12, 1863, 93–94; Lyons diary, January 12, 1863; Smith, *USS* Carondelet, 145.

10. Lyons diary, January 13, 1863.

11. Ibid., January 14, 1863: "stormy thru out the day. Grew colder and *Cricket* came down and brought mail"; Morison diary, January 16, 1863, 94.

12. Lyons diary, January 17 and 18, 1863.

13. West, *Second Admiral,* 195. See also Philip M. Thienel, *Seven Story Mountain: The Union Campaign at Vicksburg* (Jefferson, NC: McFarland, 1998), 24–25.

14. Reid diary, January 2, 1863.

15. Morison diary, January 2, 1863, 91.

16. Porter to McClernand, January 7, 1863, enclosure, *ORN,* 24:100–101.

17. Patterson, *Mississippi River Campaign,* 202–3; West, *Second Admiral,* 195; Sherman to Porter, January 3, 1863, *ORN,* 23:605–6.

18. West, *Second Admiral,* 196; Patterson, *Mississippi River Campaign,* 203. The Vicksburg expedition was organized into two corps, with Sherman in command of one.

19. Diary of Frederic Davis, in Mark K. Christ, "'Them Dam'd Gunboats': A Union Sailor's Letters from the Arkansas Post Expedition," *Arkansas Historical Quarterly* 66, no. 4 (Winter 2007): 452–67.

20. Porter General Order, January 7, 1863, *ORN,* 24:100. For army records, see *ORA,* vol. 17, pt. 3, 537.

21. Kemp, "Civil War Reminiscences."

22. Porter to McClernand, January 8, 1863, *ORN,* 24:102.

23. Kemp, "Civil War Reminiscences."

24. West, *Second Admiral,* 198; detailed report of Acting Rear Admiral Porter, US Navy, January 11, 1863, *ORN,* 24:107–8.

25. Porter to Ellet, January 4, 1863, *ORN,* 24:98; Porter to Smith, January 4, 1863, ibid., 99; Christ, "'Them Dam'd Gunboats,'" 452–67. See also Edwin C.

Bearss, "The Battle of Arkansas Post," *Arkansas Historical Quarterly* 18 (Autumn 1959): 237–39.

26. Porter report, January 11, 1863, *ORN*, 24:107–8.

27. Kemp, "Civil War Reminiscences."

28. Porter report, January 11, 1863, *ORN*, 24:107, 108; Owen report, January 11, 1863, ibid., 111–13.

29. Campbell, *Confederate Naval Forces*, 178.

30. Milligan, *Gunboats down the Mississippi*, 116.

31. Christ, "'Them Dam'd Gunboats.'" The *De Kalb* had seventeen casualties; see report of assistant surgeon John Wise, *ORN*, 24:110.

32. Kemp, "Civil War Reminiscences."

33. Geo. M. Bache to Porter, January 12, 1863, *ORN*, 24:115; Porter to Welles, January 12, 1863, ibid., 116. Porter noted that tallow was also applied to the light drafts and tinclads.

34. Porter to Welles, January 13, 1863, *ORN*, 24:119; abstract log of *Louisville*, ibid., 697; Kemp, "Civil War Reminiscences."

35. Col. Ellet to Brig. Gen. Alfred Ellet, January 12, 1863, in Crandall and Newell, *History of the Ram Fleet*, 150.

36. Sherman, *Memoirs*, 327–29.

37. Christ, "'Them Dam'd Gunboats.'"

38. Porter to Pennock, January 11, 1863, *ORN*, 24:114–15; Porter to Welles, January 13, 1863, ibid., 118–19; report of Colonel Ellet, commanding the US Ram Fleet, January 13, 1863, ibid., 120.

39. Sherman, *Memoirs*, 300–303; Francis V. Greene, *The Mississippi* (New York: Appleton, 1897), 88–89, 90; Groom, *Vicksburg*, 227–29.

40. Kemp, "Civil War Reminiscences."

41. Porter to Flanner, January 11, 1863, *ORN*, 24:111; Greene, *The Mississippi*, 88–89; West, *Second Admiral*, 200.

42. Porter to Walker, January 12, 1863, *ORN*, 24:153; Porter to Welles, January 16, 1863, ibid., 154; Walker to Porter, January 14, 1863, ibid., 155; Kemp, "Civil War Reminiscences."

43. Porter to Gen. Gorman, January 19, 1863, *ORN*, 24:160; Porter to Walker, January 19, 1863, ibid., 158; Porter to Welles, January 26, 1863, ibid., 159.

44. Master George Brown, commanding *Forest Rose*, to Porter, January 20, 1863, *ORN*, 24:158; Yost diary, January 28, 1863.

13. The Steele's Bayou Expedition

1. Henry Walke to Commodore Charles Davis, September 4, 1863, *ORN*, 19:43.

2. Walke, *Naval Scenes*, 347.

3. Morison diary, January 18, 1863, 94–95.

4. Lyons diary, January 18, 1863, 3–4; Morison diary, January 18, 1863, 94–95.

5. Morison diary, January 20, 1863, 95; Lyons diary, January 20, 1863.

6. Morison diary, January 20, 1863, 95–96.

7. Walke, *Naval Scenes,* 347, 358–59.

8. Lyons diary, January 28, 1863; Morison diary, February 27, 1863, 98.

9. Morison diary, March 2, 1863, 99; Walke to Porter, March 3, 1863, *ORN,* 24:452; Smith, *USS Carondelet,* 144–45.

10. Morison diary, March 2 and 3, 1863, 99; Kemp, "Civil War Reminiscences."

11. Morison diary, March 4 and 5, 1863, 99.

12. Ibid., March 9, 1863, 99–100; Walke, *Naval Scenes,* 351.

13. Walke, *Naval Scenes,* 351.

14. Joiner, *Mr. Lincoln's Brown Water Navy,* 127; Porter's report on Steele's Bayou expedition, March 26, 1863, *ORN,* 24:475–76.

15. Nimian Pinckney to Mary, March 21, 1863, box 1, folder 1858–1863, General Correspondence, Nimian Pinckney Letters, Manuscript Division, Library of Congress.

16. Porter, *Incidents and Anecdotes,* cited in Gosnell, *Guns on Western Waters,* 147.

17. Porter to Welles, March 26, 1863, *ORN,* 24:474.

18. Gosnell, *Guns on Western Waters,* 148; Grant to Halleck, March 17, 1863, *ORN,* 24:484–86.

19. *Carondelet* log, *ORN,* 24:687; Porter to Welles, March 26, 1863, ibid., 474; Milligan, *Gunboats down the Mississippi,* 137; West, *Second Admiral,* 207.

20. Gosnell, *Guns on Western Waters,* 149, 152; *Carondelet* log, *ORN,* 24:687. According to the gunboat's log, the *Carondelet* went up Steele's Bayou preceded by the tug *Thistle.*

21. Newspaper extract from the USS *Cincinnati* journal, *ORN,* 24:492–93. The journal may have been kept by assistant paymaster John R. Carmody.

22. *Carondelet* log, March 16, 1863, *ORN,* 24:687–88; Porter, Joint Expedition to Steele's Bayou, *ORN,* 24:474–75; Gosnell, *Guns on Western Waters,* 150–51.

23. Porter to Grant, March 16, 1863, *ORN,* 24:480–81; Grant to Sherman, March 16, 1863, ibid., 481.

24. Sherman to Coleman, March 16, 1863, *ORN,* 24:482–83. David Crockett Coleman commanded the 8th Missouri Volunteer Infantry.

25. Gosnell, *Guns on Western Waters,* 152.

26. Porter on Yazoo River to Pennock, March 4, 1863, *ORN,* 24:455; Steven J. Ramold, *Slaves Sailors Citizens: African Americans in the Union Navy* (De Kalb: Northern Illinois University Press, 2002), 98–99; Michael J. Bennett, *Union Jacks: Yankee*

Sailors in the Civil War (Chapel Hill: University of North Carolina Press, 2004), 47; Mark Grimsley, *The Hard Hand of War* (Cambridge: Cambridge University Press, 1994), 41; extract from *Cincinnati* journal, March 16 and 17, 1863, *ORN*, 24:493.

27. Kemp, "Civil War Reminiscences"; Porter to Welles, March 26, 1863, *ORN*, 24:475; Gosnell, *Guns on Western Waters,* 153, quoting from Porter's *Incidents and Anecdotes,* 150–51.

28. Gosnell, *Guns on Western Waters,* 153. I found no report from Bache on this operation, although Porter in *Incidents and Anecdotes* claims Bache was on the *Cincinnati* at this time; Milligan, *Gunboats down the Mississippi,* seems to agree.

29. Gosnell, *Guns on Western Waters,* 157–60; Porter, *Incidents and Anecdotes,* 155–56; Smith, *USS* Carondelet, 156.

30. *Carondelet* log, March 18, 1863, *ORN,* 24:688.

31. Kemp, "Civil War Reminiscences"; *Cincinnati* log, March 18, 1863, *ORN,* 24:494.

32. Smith, *USS* Carondelet, 158–59; Kemp, "Civil War Reminiscences," Friday, March 20, 1863; Gosnell, *Guns on Western Waters,* 160.

33. *Carondelet* log, March 2, 1863, *ORN,* 24:687–93; Kemp, "Civil War Reminiscences," 1.

34. *Louisville* log, *ORN,* 24:697–98; *Carondelet* log, March 21, 1863, ibid., 688; extract from *Cincinnati* journal, ibid., 492. The later log says Smith arrived with 800 men.

35. Col. Giles A. Smith to Capt. C. MacDonald, Adj. Gen., March 28, 1863, *ORA,* vol. 24, pt. 1, 438–40.

36. Kemp, "Civil War Reminiscences"; Gosnell, *Guns on Western Waters,* 173; Smith, *USS* Carondelet, 159.

37. Gosnell, *Guns on Western Waters,* 164.

38. *Carondelet* log, March 25, 1863, *ORN,* 24:688; Porter, *Incidents and Anecdotes,* 169, 172; extract from *Cincinnati* journal, March 21, 1863, *ORN,* 24:496.

39. Extract from *Cincinnati* journal, March 21, 1863, *ORN,* 24:496.

40. *Carondelet* log, *ORN,* 24:688–89; extract from *Cincinnati* journal, March 21, 1863, ibid., 496.

41. Detailed report of Acting Rear Admiral Porter, US Navy, March 26, 1863, *ORN,* 24:47–89.

14. The Yazoo Pass Expedition of 1863

1. West, *Second Admiral,* 213–15; Milligan, *Gunboats down the Mississippi,* 123–25; Joiner, *Mr. Lincoln's Brown Water Navy,* 109–10.

2. Joiner, *Mr. Lincoln's Brown Water Navy,* 115–16; Milligan, *Gunboats down the Mississippi,* 126–27; Crandall and Newell, *History of the Ram Fleet,* 179.

3. Crandall and Newell, *History of the Ram Fleet,* 184; Milligan, *Gunboats down the Mississippi,* 127–28; Robert Collins Suhr, "USS *Indianola:* Union Iron-

clad in the American Civil War," *American Civil War,* July 1993, historynet.com, June 12, 2006.

4. Crandall and Newell, *History of the Ram Fleet,* 184; Joiner, *Mr. Lincoln's Brown Water Navy,* 116–77; Milligan, *Gunboats down the Mississippi,* 129–30.

5. Myron J. Smith Jr., *The Fight for the Yazoo, August 1862–July 1864: Swamps, Forts and Fleets on Vicksburg's Northern Flank* (Jefferson, NC: McFarland, 2012), chap. 7. Yost diary, February 1 and 3, 1863, states that Grant's engineers discharged a mine to breach a levee at Moon Lake.

6. Yost diary, February 4, 5, and 6, 1863. See Richard J. West Jr., "Gunboats in the Swamps: The Yazoo Pass Expedition," *Civil War History* 9, no. 2 (June 1963): 157–66.

7. Porter to Smith (extract), February 16, 1863, *ORN,* 24:243–44.

8. Milligan, *Gunboats down the Mississippi,* 131, says there were thirteen; Smith, *Fight for the Yazoo,* 177, states that the *Signal* was not expected to arrive from Memphis until that evening. Order of Maj. Gen. Prentiss to Brig. Gen. Ross, February 21, 1863, *ORN,* 24:259; Porter to Smith (extract), February 16, 1863, enclosure report of Lt. Cdr. Smith, commanding expedition to Yazoo, November 2, 1863, ibid., 243–44. Ross took command of the 13th Division, XIII Corps, just before the Yazoo expedition.

9. Yost diary, February 27, 1863; Smith to Porter, February 18, 1863, *ORN,* 24:257; Smith to Johnston, February 18 and 24, 1863, ibid., 422, 433.

10. Yost diary, February 26 and 27, 1863; "The Yazoo Pass Expedition: Moon Lake the Rendezvous of the Expedition," *New York Times,* February 22, 1863; Smith to Porter, February 26 and March 2, 1863, *ORN,* 24:259–60, 261.

11. Yost diary, February 28, 1863; *Detroit Free Press,* February 28 and March 1, 1863.

12. Yost diary, March 1, 1863; Smith, *Fight for the Yazoo,* 183. The *Emma* carried men of the 29th Iowa.

13. Smith report, March 3, 1863, *ORN,* 24:262–63.

14. *New York Herald,* March 10, 1863.

15. Yost diary, March 9 and 10, 1863.

16. From "Our Expeditionary Correspondence," March 10, 1863, *New York Herald,* March 25, 1863; Yost diary, March 10, 1863.

17. Smith to Porter, March 11, 1863, *ORN,* 24:268; abstract log of the *Chillicothe,* ibid., 693–94. The *Herald* reporter mistakenly claimed that although struck four times, "the *Chillicothe* returned from the reconnaissance without having sustained the slightest injury."

18. *New York Herald,* March 25, 1863; acting assistant surgeon W. C. Foster, list of killed and wounded, *ORN,* 24:269; Jas. Foster report, *ORN,* 24:272–73.

19. *New York Herald,* March 25, 1863; Brig. Gen. Ross report to Maj. Gen. Prentiss, March 13, 1863, *ORN,* 24:279.

20. Smith to Porter, March 13, 1863, *ORN,* 24:247, 268; Ross report, ibid., 279; *New York Herald,* March 12 and 13, 1863.

21. Smith to Porter, March 13, 1863, enclosure, Walker to Porter, April 13, 1863, *ORN,* 24:475; "Daily Chronicles of the American Civil War, the Yazoo Pass Expedition," *New York Herald,* March 13, 1863. This was the last of his articles.

22. Walker to Porter, April 13, 1863, *ORN,* 24:475.

23. Jas. Foster report, *ORN,* 24:275–76.

24. Smith, March 13, 1863, *ORN,* 24:247; Milligan, *Gunboats down the Mississippi,* 134.

25. Foster to Smith, March 14, 1863, *ORN,* 24:276–77; Smith, March 16, 1863, ibid., 277–78. According to Foster, the enemy was firing 68-pound shot.

26. Porter to Welles, April 13, 1863, *ORN,* 24:282. Smith took a leave of absence and returned home to Trenton, New Jersey. He returned and served in the Red River campaign, fell ill again, and died on December 19, 1864.

27. Yost diary, March 18, 1863; Fentress to Porter, March 22, 1863, *ORN,* 24:286; Smith, *Fight for the Yazoo,* 224.

28. Foster to Porter, April 13, 1863, *ORN,* 24:283–84; Quimby to Foster, March 21, 1863, ibid., 285.

29. Foster to Porter, April 13, 1863, *ORN,* 24:282–84; Quimby to McPherson, March 25, 1863, ibid., 289–90.

30. Foster to Porter, April 13, 1863, *ORN,* 24:282–84. Porter was with the Steele's Bayou expedition, so Walke was in command. The admiral did not return until March 25.

31. Porter to Welles, April 13, 1863, *ORN,* 24:482, enclosure, Foster to Porter, April 13, 1863, ibid., 282; Quimby to McPherson, March 25, 1863, ibid., 289.

15. Port Hudson

1. Lewis, *Farragut,* 168–69; Hearn, *Farragut,* 189–91. Milligan, *Gunboats down the Mississippi,* 143, does not describe in detail the passing of the rebel defenses at Port Hudson.

2. Lewis, *Farragut,* 169; Gosnell, *Guns on Western Waters,* 204–5; Farragut to Welles, March 16, 1863, *ORN,* 19:665; Thomas Scott Bacon, "The Fight at Port Hudson," *Independent,* March 14, 1901, quoted in Gosnell, *Guns on Western Waters,* 208–9.

3. Farragut to Welles, March 16, 1863, *ORN,* 19:665; Gosnell, *Guns on Western Waters,* 204–5.

4. Aaron Shimer Oberly diary, March 14, 1863, Auburn University Digital Library; detailed report of Rear Admiral Farragut, US Navy, March 16, 1863, *ORN,* 19:666.

5. Farragut report, *ORN,* 19:668–69.

6. Oberly diary, March 14, 1865.

7. Hearn, *Farragut,* 195–96.

8. Bacon, "Fight at Port Hudson," quoted in Gosnell, *Guns on Western Waters,* 208–9.

9. Oberly diary, March 14, 1863.

10. Lewis, *Farragut,* 173–74; Hearn, *Farragut,* 197–98, 194 (including a sketch of the line of federal ships); Farragut report, *ORN,* 19:665–66; Palmer to Farragut, March 16, 1863, *ORN,* 19:671.

11. Bacon, "Fight at Port Hudson," quoted in Gosnell, *Guns on Western Waters,* 208–9; Farragut report, *ORN,* 19:666.

12. Surgeon's report, *ORN,* 19:676; Alden to Welles, March 23, 1863, ibid., 677. Alden addressed the gunboat crew and recounted Cummings's exact words after he was wounded. Alden report, March 15, 1863, ibid., 672; W. H. Macomb, report to Alden, March 17, 1863, ibid., 678–79.

13. Dewey quoted in Gosnell, *Guns on Western Waters,* 212; George Dewey, *Autobiography of George Dewey, Admiral of the Navy* (New York: Scribner's Sons, 1913), 88–93.

14. Dewey, *Autobiography,* 88–93; report of Captain Smith, March 17, 1863, *ORN,* 19:680–81; Gosnell, *Guns on Western Waters,* 214–15, 218.

15. Oberly diary, March 14, 1863; Crandall and Newell, *History of the Ram Fleet,* 192–93; Milligan, *Gunboats down the Mississippi,* 144.

16. Lyons diary, March 25, 1863, 19–20; Morison diary, March 25, 1863, 102–5.

17. Lyons diary, March 25, 1863, 20; Morison diary, March 25, 1863, 102–3. In *Naval Scenes,* Walke recounts this episode only briefly. Lyons said there were "two half frightened men," not three.

18. West, *Second Admiral,* 218–19.

19. Morison diary, April 10, 1863, 103, 104, 105.

20. Grant to Porter and Porter to Grant, March 29, 1863, *ORA,* vol. 24, pt. 3, 151–52; Catton, *Grant Moves South,* 408; Grant to Farragut, March 23, 1863, *ORA,* vol. 24, pt. 3, 125–26, 131; Milligan, *Gunboats down the Mississippi,* 143.

21. Porter, *Naval History,* 308.

22. Porter General Order, April 10, 1863, in Walke, *Naval Scenes,* 352.

23. Morison diary, April 14 and 16, 1863, 105.

24. Lyons diary, April 16, 1863.

25. Morison diary, April 16, 1863, 106.

26. Walke, *Naval Scenes,* 353–55; Walke to Porter, April 17, 1863, *ORN,* 24:557; carpenters' report, ibid., 558. Walke refers to an anonymous officer, E. S., who was presumably Elias Smith. A Rhode Island native who had been an attaché at the *New York Times* before the war, Smith's letters were printed in that newspaper.

27. Lyons diary, April 16, 1863.

28. Morison diary, April 16, 1863, 107; Walke, *Naval Scenes,* 355.

29. Morison diary, April 16, 1863, 106–7; Walke, *Naval Scenes,* 355; Selim E. Woodworth to Porter, April 17, 1863, *ORN,* 24:559.

30. Morison diary, April 16, 1863, 107; Walke, *Naval Scenes,* 356–57.

31. West, *Second Admiral,* 222–23; Lt. Byron Wilson to Porter, April 17, 1863, *ORN,* 24:559.

32. Morison diary, April 17, 1863, 107–8.

33. Porter to Grant, April 20, 1863, *ORN,* 24:600–601; Grant to Sherman, April 21, 1863, ibid., 601; Grant to Porter, April 21, 1863, ibid., 602; Milo Dibble diary, April 22, 1863. On August 23, 1861, Dibble, from Fairview, Iowa, had joined the 10th Iowa Volunteer Infantry. He was later promoted to hospital steward.

34. Morison diary, April 22, 1863, 108–9; Lyons diary, April 22, 1863, 27; Porter, April 22, 1863, *ORN,* 24:605.

35. McClernand to Osterhaus, enclosure, Porter to McClernand, April 22, 1863, *ORN,* 24:603; McClernand to Grant, April 23, 1863, ibid., 604. General Osterhaus commanded the 12th Missouri Volunteer Infantry.

36. Lyons, April 23, 1863, 27; Walke, *Naval Scenes,* 366; Dibble diary, April 23, 1863. Dibble wrote on April 21 that his colonel had notified the men that anyone who volunteered to run the blockade would be arrested and treated as a deserter. Fifty of the men were detailed to work on the boats at the landing, however, and one fellow fell off and drowned.

37. Flood, *Grant and Sherman,* 158–59; Patterson, *Mississippi River Campaign,* 225–26; Lyons diary, April 23, 1863, 27.

38. Milligan, *Gunboats down the Mississippi,* 152. Porter said on April 24 that he was awaiting Grant's arrival that night. West, *Second Admiral,* says nothing about this or preparations for the assault.

39. Morison diary, April 27, 1863, 110.

40. Grant, *Personal Memoirs,* 111; Simpson, *Grant,* 188–89.

16. Grand Gulf

1. Porter to Walke, April 27, 1863, cited in Walke, *Naval Scenes,* 373; West, *Second Admiral,* 223–24.

2. Walke, *Naval Scenes,* 374; Milligan, *Gunboats down the Mississippi,* 153–54; Joiner, *Mr. Lincoln's Brown Water Navy,* 134.

3. Morison diary, April 29, 1863, 110.

4. Ibid.; Greer report, *ORN,* 24:613.

5. Walke report, *ORN,* 24:622–23; Walke, *Naval Scenes,* 375.

6. Hoel to Porter, April 30, 1863, *ORN,* 24:615–16.

7. Shirk to Porter, April 30, 1863, *ORN,* 24:620–21.

8. Hoel to Porter, April 30, 1863, *ORN,* 24:616–17.

9. Greer report, *ORN,* 24:613; report of Newton L. Bates, surgeon, ibid., 615; West, *Second Admiral,* 224. The pilot, Beverly S. Williams, suffered a severe wound to his foot.

10. Murphy to Porter, May 2, 1863, *ORN,* 24:625.

11. Walke, *Naval Scenes,* 376–77; Morison diary, April 29, 1863, 111.

12. Morison diary, April 29, 1863, 111.

13. Lyons diary, April 29, 1863, 29.

14. Morison diary, April 29, 1863, 111; Walke, *Naval Scenes,* 380.

15. Catton, *Grant Moves South,* 424; Milligan, *Gunboats down the Mississippi,* 156–57; West, *Second Admiral,* 224; Dibble diary, April 29, 1863.

16. Lyons diary, April 29, 1863, 29; Morison diary, April 29, 1863, 112; Walke to Porter, May 2, 1863, in Walke, *Naval Scenes,* 380; carpenter Clark M. Underwood, April 29, 1863, quoted in Walke, *Naval Scenes,* 381.

17. Morison diary, April 30, 1863, 112; Lyons diary, April 29, 1863, 29.

18. Lyons diary, April 30, 1863, 30; Dibble diary, April 20, 1863.

19. Shirk report, *ORN,* 24:620–21; Potter report, ibid., 621. Walke, *Naval Scenes,* has an account by the engineer.

20. Morison diary, April 30, 1863, 112.

21. Lyons diary, April 30, 1863, 30; Morison diary, April 30 and May 1, 1863, 112–13.

22. Lyons diary, May 2, 1863, 31; Morison diary, May 2, 1863, 113; Walke, *Naval Scenes,* 377.

23. Morison diary, May 3, 1863, 113–14; Lyons diary, May 3, 1863, 31.

24. Lyons diary, May 3, 1863, 31. Lyons confirms Morison's story: "The Admiral—D. D. Porter—who reached there after the rest took the chickens and geese from every one for himself—causing much ill feeling."

25. Walke, *Naval Scenes,* 379; Porter to Welles, cited in ibid., 383.

26. West, *Second Admiral,* 227–28; Lyons diary, May 3, 1863, 31–32; Porter report, May 7, 1863, *ORN,* 24:645.

27. Morison diary, May 5, 1863, 115–16; Lyons diary, May 5, 1863, 32.

28. Morison diary, May 5 and 6, 1863, 115–16; Red River operations, May 4–17, 1863, *ORN,* 24:645–52; Lyons diary, May 5, 1863, 32.

29. Porter report, May 7, 1863, *ORN,* 24:645.

30. Morison diary, May 6, 1863, 116. Lyons also wrote that all hands were at their quarters, ready to fire at a moment's notice.

31. Lyons diary, May 6, 1863, 33.

32. Porter, order of anchoring before the town of Alexandria, May 7, 1863, William Hoel Papers, Cincinnati Historical Society; Lyons diary, May 9, 1863, 34; Morison diary, May 7, 1863, 117.

33. Porter report, May 13, 1863, *ORN,* 24:646–47. West, *Second Admiral,* 228, says Porter set contrabands to work leveling the embankments of Fort de Russey.

34. Lyons diary, May 8, 1863, 34; Porter report, May 13, 1863, *ORN*, 24:646–47.

35. Lyons diary, May 9 and 12, 1863, 34; Morison diary, May 9, 1863, 118.

36. Walke, *Naval Scenes,* 396.

37. Morison diary, May 13 and 15, 1863, 118–19.

38. Lyons diary, May 17, 20, and 22, 1863, 36; Morison diary, May 22 and 23, 1863, 119–20. Lyons also noted that he "saw several alligators."

39. A. S. Oberly to Maria, May 23, 1863, Oberly Letters and Diary; Hearn, *Farragut,* 212; Lewis, *Farragut,* 199.

40. Oberly diary, May 18–19 and 23, 1863.

41. Ibid., May 25 and 26–27, 1863. Hearn, *Farragut,* blames Banks's repulse on the general's poor tactics and the competence of his opponent, General Gardner.

42. Oberly diary, May 27–29, 30–31, and June 1–2, 1863.

43. Hearn, *Farragut,* 213; Farragut to Banks, May 28, 1863, *ORN,* 20:216–17; Oberly diary, June 1, 7, and 8–9, 1863. June 13, 1863, is the final entry in Oberly's surviving diary.

17. Blockade and Siege

1. Oberly to Maria, May 21 and 22, 1863, Oberly Letters.

2. West, *Second Admiral,* 231–32; Milligan, *Gunboats down the Mississippi,* 162–63.

3. Porter report, May 20, 1863, *ORN,* 25:5–6.

4. Ibid.; Milligan, *Gunboats down the Mississippi,* 162–63; Oberly to Maria, May 21 and 22, 1863.

5. Porter to Greer, May 19, 1863, *ORN,* 25:18; Greer to Porter, May 19, 1863, ibid., 19–20. If the *Tuscumbia* could not do so, Greer was to go up with the *Benton* and *Carondelet.* "By shifting your 40-pounder to the bow, you can easily throw shell into the town. The object is to throw shell about the courthouse, if possible," Porter wrote from the *Black Hawk* at Haynes' Bluff. In answer to the admiral's inquiry, Greer reported that he had gone up to Vicksburg, but a rebel gun had opened fire on them; if they went back, he explained, they would be caught in a cross fire from three enemy batteries. Porter accepted this explanation, but in a postscript to his May 19 letter he told Greer to carry out his order and give the town a good shelling.

6. Grant to Porter, May 21, 1863, *ORN,* 25:21; Porter to Brig. Gen. Arthur, May 23, 1863, ibid., 22; Milligan, *Gunboats down the Mississippi,* 163–64.

7. Porter to Welles, May 23, 1863, *ORN,* 25:22. The *Mound City* was struck once and had six men wounded; the *Benton* was hit thirteen times.

8. Ulysses S. Grant, "The Vicksburg Campaign," *Battles and Leaders* 3 (1956): 518.

9. Porter to Grant, May 23, 1863, *ORN,* 25:32; Grant to Porter, May 24, 1863, 1:00 p.m., and Porter to Grant, May 24, 1863, ibid., 33.

10. Porter to Woodworth, May 26, 1863, *ORN,* 25:34; Woodworth to Porter, May 27, 1863, ibid., 34–35; Greer report on *Benton,* ibid., 35; Wilson report on *Mound City,* ibid., 36.

11. Kemp, "Civil War Reminiscences." "We came off the ways on the 13th and left Carondelet on the 18th," crewman Daniel Kemp recalled. "A new turret of half inch iron had been built on the wheel house, and two 12 inch howitzers are to be put into it when we reach Cairo. This for our protection against guerillas, and would be a wonderful help if we got into a place like Sunflower Bayou again." Silverstone, *Warships of the Civil War,* 151, does not mention the addition of 12-inch howitzers.

12. Kemp, "Civil War Reminiscences"; Bache to Porter, May 27, 1863, in Walke, *Naval Scenes,* 406.

13. Bache to Porter, May 27, 1863, in Walke, *Naval Scenes,* 406. Three of the dead were from the 58th Ohio Infantry Regiment. See W. Craig Gaines, *Encyclopedia of Civil War Shipwrecks* (Baton Rouge: Louisiana State University Press, 2008), 92.

14. Kemp, "Civil War Reminiscences."

15. Silverstone, *Warships of the Civil War,* 157. The *Choctaw* was relieved by the *Lexington* on June 10, 1863. For the *Choctaw's* part in the Yazoo operations, see *ORN,* 25:5–13, 278.

16. Porter to Welles, June 9, 1863, *ORN,* 25:162; Ramsay to Porter, June 10, 1863, ibid., 163. Porter told Welles he had given the order on June 7, but Ramsay reported that he proceeded to Milliken's Bend on June 6.

17. Porter to Welles, June 9, 1863, *ORN,* 25:162; Ramsay to Porter, June 10, 1863, ibid., 163. Linda Barnickel, *Milliken's Bend* (Baton Rouge: Louisiana State University Press, 2013), 95, 99, 101; Earnest McBride, "The Battle of Milliken's Bend: The Central Role of Black Troops in the Siege of Vicksburg," *Jackson Advocate* (2000), www.jacksonadvocateonline.com.

18. Porter to Grant, June 7, 1863, *ORN,* 25:164–65.

19. Grant, "Vicksburg Campaign," 524–25.

20. Walke to Porter, May 25, 1863, *ORN,* 25:137.

21. Porter to Walke, May 26, 1863, *ORN,* 25:137.

22. Morison diary, May 24, 29, and 31, 1863, 120; Lyons diary, May 24, 25, and 26, 1863, 37–38.

23. Morison diary, May 31, 1863, 120; Lyons diary, June 1, 1863, 39.

24. Palmer to Walke, May 30, 1863, *ORN,* 25:154.

25. Lyons diary, June 3, 1863, 39.

26. Walke to Porter, May 30, 1863, *ORN,* 25:154–55. Palmer later informed Walke that he did not receive the request from Ellet and, in fact, had seen neither the *Switzerland* nor its commander on that occasion.

27. Lyons diary, June 4 and 5, 1863, 40–41. Walke, *Naval Scenes,* 398–99,

tried to correct what he dubbed an inaccurate Confederate version of this incident.

28. Lyons diary, June 7, 1863, 41.

29. Ibid., June 3, 1863, 39.

30. Ibid., June 18, 1863, 44.

31. Ibid., June 1, 8, and 9, 1863, 39, 41–42.

32. Ibid., June 6, 1863, 41.

33. Ibid., June 5, 7, 8, and 17, 1863, 40, 41, 43.

34. Walke to Porter, June 20, 1863, *ORN,* 25:190.

35. Lyons diary, June 21, 1863, 44.

18. Final Push to Victory

1. "From the 23rd Wisconsin, Its Part in the Campaign against Vicksburg," *State Journal,* June 8, 1863.

2. Howe, *Home Letters of Sherman,* 266–67.

3. Kemp, "Civil War Reminiscences." In his report commending the officers under his command, Porter referred to the scows during operations against Vicksburg on July 13, 1862; see *ORN,* 25:278. Groom, *Vicksburg,* does not mention Kemp.

4. Lyons diary, June 1 and 22, 1863, 39, 44.

5. Ibid., June 25, 1863, 45. This is the last entry in Lyons's diary.

6. Porter to Welles, July 2, 1863, *ORN,* 25:212–14. General Lorenzo Thomas had begun a program in March 1863 to lease abandoned and confiscated plantations where contrabands could provide service and become self-sufficient.

7. Ellet report, July 8, 1863, *ORN,* 25:214–16; McPherson, *War on the Waters,* 167.

8. Chester G. Hearn, *Ellet's Marine Brigade* (Baton Rouge: Louisiana State University Press, 2000), 174; Crandall and Newell, *History of the Ram Fleet,* 309–11; Ellet report, *ORN,* 25:214–16.

9. Walke, *Naval Scenes,* 414–15.

10. Walke to Porter, June 20, 1863, *ORN,* 25:190; Porter to Walke, June 29, 1863, ibid., 210. The *Lafayette* appears on Porter's list of vessels to be at Vicksburg.

11. Porter to Welles, June 20, 1863, *ORN,* 25:83.

12. Grant to Porter, June 22, 1863, *ORN,* 25:90; Porter special order, June 23, 1863, ibid., 91.

13. Porter to Welles, June 26, 1863, *ORN,* 25:95–96.

14. Shirk to Woodworth, June 29, 1863, *ORN,* 25:98–99.

15. A. A. Hoehling, *Vicksburg: 47 Days of Siege* (Englewood Cliffs, NJ: Prentice-Hall, 1969), 247.

16. Ibid., 246–47, 264–65; Grant to Porter, July 3, 1863, *ORN,* 25:102.

17. Grant to Porter, July 3, 1863, *ORN,* 25:102; telegram from Grant to Porter, July 3, 1863, ibid.; Hoehling, *Vicksburg,* 266–67.

18. Grant to Porter, July 4, 1863, *ORN,* 25:103; Grant, "Vicksburg Campaign," 530–35.

19. Sherman to Porter, July 4, 1863, *ORN,* 25:105–6.

20. Walke to Hoel, July 4, 1863, *ORN,* 25:226; Owen to Porter, July 4, 1863, ibid., 101.

21. Porter to Welles, July 13, 1863, *ORN,* 25:277–79. Selfridge's battery report is in *ORN,* 25:107–8. Milligan, *Gunboats down the Mississippi,* 176, termed Porter's report, on the whole, moderate in claim.

Conclusion

1. Silverstone, *Warships of the Civil War;* Slagle, *Ironclad Captain,* 118–19; Smith, *Timberclads,* 61; Foote to Walke, September 17, 1861, *ORN,* 22:336; Walke to Foote, September 23, 1861, ibid., 349. The *Tyler* boasted six 64-pounder guns and one siege 32-pounder stern gun. It was the slowest of the three ships and, at 420 tons, the heaviest. See *ORN,* 22:318, 323, 332–34; Walke, *Naval Scenes,* 27.

2. Walke, *Naval Scenes,* 305; Morison diary, July 15, 1862, 72–73; Walke report, July 25, 1862, *ORN,* 19:41–43.

3. Smith, *Tinclads.*

4. Coombe, *Thunder along the Mississippi,* 227; Lt. Col. Victor Croizat, USMC, *Vietnam River Warfare, 1945–1975* (Cambridge, MA: Blandford Press, 1986), 119. Coombe argues that they used Eads-designed river craft as examples.

5. Halleck to Foote, March 12, 1862, *ORN,* 22:686; telegram from Halleck to Foote, March 13, 1862, ibid., 687.

6. Bennett, *Union Jacks,* 166–67, 169.

7. Ira Berlin, ed., *Freedom: A Documentary History of Emancipation, 1861–1867,* vol. 1, *The Mississippi Valley* (Cambridge: Cambridge University Press, 1985), 55–56.

8. Tomblin, *Bluejackets & Contrabands,* 284, n. 30.

9. Smith, *Timberclads,* 1–2; Joiner, *Mr. Lincoln's Brown Water Navy,* 175.

Selected Bibliography

Manuscripts

Auburn University Digital Library, Civil War Letters Collection
Aaron Shimer Oberly Diary and Letters (1861–1865)
Butler Center for Arkansas Studies, Little Rock, Arkansas
Preston Bishop Letters
George M. Blodgett Letters
Mahlon Hockett Letters
Cincinnati Historical Society, Cincinnati, Ohio
William Hoel Papers
Huntington Library, San Marino, California
Papers of David Glasgow Farragut
Papers of David Dixon Porter
Papers of Gideon Welles
Illinois State Historical Library, Springfield, Illinois
George Yost Diary
Library of Congress, Manuscript Division, Washington, DC
Thomas Ewing Papers
Corporal John G. Jones Letters
Thomas Lyons Journal
Anthony O'Neil Diary
Nimian Pinckney Letters
Sergeant Major Edward Paul Reichhelm Diary
Harrie Webster Letters
National Archives, Washington, DC
Oscar Smith Diary
Online
Daniel Kemp, "Civil War Reminiscences," www.civilwarhome.com

Civil War diary of John G. Morison, 1861–1865, dmn.nygov/historic/reg/hist/
. . . 30thInf._Diary_Morison.htm

Some Civil War Letters of Knute Nelson, ed. Millard L. Gieske, www.naha
.stolaf.edu/pubs/nas/volume23v0123_2.html

Diary of Peter J. Perrine, 16th Ohio Volunteer Infantry, 1861–1864, www
.mkwe.com/home.htm

Diary of Corporal William Warner Reid, 16th Ohio Volunteer Infantry, 1861–
1864, transcribed by Robert Fisher, www.mkwe.com/home.htm

Account of the USS *Essex* by D. P. Rosenmiller, *Inquirer,* August 26, 1862,
www.lancasteratwar.com

Aquilia Standifird's Civil War journal, www.crolyar.com/aquiliastadnifird
.htm

A. J. Sypher of the *St. Louis,* "From the Mississippi Flotilla," April 17, 1862,
www.lancasteratwar.com

Princeton University Library, Princeton, New Jersey
Samuel Philips Lee Letters

Private Collection
Milo Dibble Diary in possession of Marilyn Gregory, Camarillo, California

Books and Articles

Barnickel, Linda. *Milliken's Bend.* Baton Rouge: Louisiana State University Press,
2013.

Bates, Edward. *The Diary of Edward Bates, 1859–1866.* Edited by Howard K.
Beale. Washington DC: US Government Printing Office, 1933.

Bearss, Edwin C. "The Battle of Arkansas Post." *Arkansas Historical Quarterly* 18
(Autumn 1959): 237–39.

———. *Decision in Mississippi.* Jackson: Mississippi Commission on the War between the States, 1962.

———. *Hardluck Ironclad: The Sinking and Salvage of the* Cairo. Baton Rouge:
Louisiana State University Press, 1980.

———. *The Vicksburg Campaign.* 3 vols. Dayton, OH: Morningside, 1991.

Bennett, Michael J. *Union Jacks: Yankee Sailors in the Civil War.* Chapel Hill: University of North Carolina Press, 2004.

Berlin, Ira, ed. *Freedom: A Documentary History of Emancipation, 1861–1867.* Vol.
1, *The Mississippi Valley.* Cambridge: Cambridge University Press, 1985.

Bock, Larry Daniel, and Lynn Block. *Island No. 10: Struggle of the Mississippi Valley.* Tuscaloosa: University of Alabama Press, 1996.

Bradford, James. *Captains of the Old Steam Navy.* Annapolis, MD: US Naval Institute Press, 1986.

Brinton, John. *Personal Memoirs of John H. Brinton.* New York: Neale, 1914.

Brown, Captain Isaac N. "The Confederate Gun-boat 'Arkansas.'" *Battles and Leaders* 3 (1956): 572–80.

Browning, Robert M., Jr. *From Cape Charles to Cape Fear: The North Atlantic Blockading Squadron during the Civil War*. Tuscaloosa: University of Alabama Press, 1993.

Callender, Eliot. "What a Boy Saw on the Mississippi." In *Military Essays and Recollections: Papers Read before the Commandery of the State of Illinois, Military Order of the Loyal Legion of the United States*. 2 vols. Chicago: A. C. McClurg, 1891.

Campbell, R. Thomas. *Confederate Naval Forces on Western Waters*. Jefferson, NC: McFarland, 2005.

Canney, Donald L. *Lincoln's Navy*. Annapolis, MD: Naval Institute Press, 1998.

Catton, Bruce. *Grant Moves South*. Boston: Little Brown, 1960.

Christ, Mark K. "'Them Dam'd Gunboats': A Union Sailor's Letters from the Arkansas Post Expedition." *Arkansas Historical Quarterly* 66, no. 4 (Winter 2007): 452–67.

Coombe, Jack D. *Thunder along the Mississippi: The River Battles that Split the Confederacy*. New York: Sarpedon, 1996.

Cornish, Dudley Taylor, and Virginia Jeans Laas. *Lincoln's Lee: The Life of Samuel Phillips Lee, United States Navy, 1812–1897*. Lawrence: University Press of Kansas, 1986.

Crandall, Warren D., and Isaac D. Newell, eds. *History of the Ram Fleet and the Mississippi Marine Brigade*. St. Louis: Buschart Brothers, 1907.

Croizat, Lt. Col. Victor, USMC. *Vietnam River Warfare, 1945–1975*. Cambridge, MA: Blandford Press, 1986.

Davis, Charles H., Jr. *Life of Charles Henry Davis, Rear Admiral, 1807–1877*. Boston: Houghton Mifflin, 1899.

Dewey, George. *Autobiography of George Dewey, Admiral of the Navy*. New York: Scribner's Sons, 1913.

Donald, David. *Lincoln*. New York: Simon & Schuster, 1995.

Eads, James B. "Recollections of Foote and the Gun-boats." *Battles and Leaders* 1 (1956): 338–43.

Ellet, Alfred. "Ellet and His Steam-Rams at Memphis." *Battles and Leaders* 1 (1956): 453–59.

Farragut, Loyall. *Life of David Glasgow Farragut*. New York: D. Appleton, 1879.

Fiske, John. *The Mississippi Valley in the Civil War*. Boston: Houghton Mifflin, 1900.

Flood, Charles B. *Grant and Sherman*. New York: Harper, 2005.

Foote, Shelby. *The Civil War 1861 Narrative: Fort Sumter to Perryville*. New York: Vintage Books, 1986.

Fowler, William M., Jr. *Under Two Flags*. New York: Norton, 1990.

Fremont, John C. "In Command in Missouri." *Battles and Leaders* 1 (1956): 278–88.

Gift, George W. "Story of the Arkansas." *Southern Historical Society Papers* 12 (January–April 1884).

Goodwin, Doris Kearns. *Team of Rivals: The Political Genius of Abraham Lincoln.* New York: Simon & Schuster, 2006.

Gosnell, H. Allen. *Guns on the Western Waters.* Baton Rouge: Louisiana State University Press, 1949.

Grant, Ulysses S. *The Personal Memoirs of Ulysses S. Grant.* New York: C. L. Webster, 1885.

———. "The Vicksburg Campaign." *Battles and Leaders* 3 (1956).

Groom, Winston. *Vicksburg 1863.* New York: Vintage Civil War Library, Vintage Books, 2009.

Hearn, Chester G. *Admiral David Dixon Porter: The Civil War Years.* Annapolis, MD: Naval Institute Press, 1996.

———. *Admiral David Glasgow Farragut: The Civil War Years.* Annapolis, MD: Naval Institute Press, 1997.

———. *The Capture of New Orleans 1862.* Baton Rouge: Louisiana State University Press, 1996.

———. *Ellet's Marine Brigade.* Baton Rouge: Louisiana State University Press, 2000.

Hicken, Victor. *Illinois in the Civil War.* Urbana: University of Illinois Press, 1966.

Hoehling, A. A. *Vicksburg: 47 Days of Siege.* Englewood Cliffs, NJ: Prentice-Hall, 1969.

Hoogenboom, Ari. *Gustavus Vasa Fox of the Union Navy.* Baltimore: Johns Hopkins University Press, 2008.

Hoppin, Andrew. *Life of Andrew Hull Foote, Rear Admiral, United States Navy.* New York: Harper & Brothers, 1874.

Howe, Mark A. DeWolfe, ed. *Home Letters of General Sherman.* New York: Charles Scribner's, 1909. Reprint, Whitefish, MT: Kessinger Publishing, 2005.

Huffstot, Robert D. "The Carondelet." *Civil War Times Illustrated* 6 (1967).

Hughes, Nathaniel C., Jr. *The Battle of Belmont.* Chapel Hill: University of North Carolina Press, 1991.

Johnson, Robert Edwin. *Rear Admiral John Rodgers, 1812–1882.* Annapolis, MD: Naval Institute Press, 1967.

Joiner, Gary D. *Mr. Lincoln's Brown Water Navy: The Mississippi Squadron.* New York: Rowman & Littlefield, 2007.

———, ed. *Little to Eat and Thin Mud to Drink: Letters, Diaries, and Memoirs from the Red River Campaigns, 1863–1864.* Knoxville: University of Tennessee Press, 2007.

Jones, Virgil C. *The Civil War at Sea.* 3 vols. New York: Holt, Rinehart & Winston, 1960–1962.

Keegan, John. *The American Civil War*. New York: Alfred A. Knopf, 2009.

Laas, Virginia Jeans, ed. *Wartime Washington: The Civil War Letters of Elizabeth Blair Lee*. Chicago: University of Illinois Press, 1991.

Lewis, Charles Lee. *David Glasgow Farragut: Our First Admiral*. Annapolis, MD: Naval Institute Press, 1943.

Mahan, Alfred Thayer. *The Navy in the Civil War*. Vol. 3, *The Gulf and Inland Waters*. Honolulu, HI: University Press of the Pacific, 2006.

Marshall-Cornwall, General Sir James. *Grant as Military Commander*. New York: Barnes & Noble, 1970.

McBride, Earnest. "The Battle of Milliken's Bend: The Central Role of Black Troops in the Siege of Vicksburg." *Jackson Advocate* (2000). www .jacksonadvocateonline.com.

McBride, Robert. *Civil War Ironclads*. Philadelphia: Chilton Books, 1962.

McPherson, James M. *Battle Cry of Freedom: The Civil War Era*. New York: Oxford University Press, 1988.

———. *Tried by War: Abraham Lincoln as Commander in Chief*. New York: Penguin, 2009.

———. *War on the Waters: The Union & Confederate Navies, 1861–1865*. Chapel Hill: University of North Carolina Press, 2012.

Melton, Maurice. *The Confederate Ironclads*. New York: Chilton Books, 1962.

Merrill, James M. "Cairo, Illinois: Strategic Civil War River Port." *Journal of Illinois State Historical Society* 76 (Winter 1983): 242–56.

Milligan, John D. *Gunboats down the Mississippi*. Annapolis, MD: Naval Institute Press, 1965.

———, ed. *From the Freshwater Navy, 1861–1864. The Letters of Acting Master's Mate Henry R. Browne and Acting Ensign Symmes E. Browne*. Annapolis, MD: Naval Institute Press, 1970.

Moore, Frank. *The Rebellion Record: A Diary of American Events*. New York: D. Van Nostrand, 1882.

Moran, Daniel. "Battle of Belmont." Military History Online. www .militaryhistoryonline.com.

Nevins, Allan. *The War for the Union*. 4 vols. New York: Charles Scribner's, 1959–1971.

Niven, John. *Gideon Welles: Lincoln's Secretary of the Navy*. New York: Oxford University Press, 1973.

"Our Army at Cairo." *Harper's Weekly*, June 29, 1861, 410. www.sonofthesouth .net.

Patterson, Benton Rain. *The Mississippi River Campaign, 1861–1863: The Struggle for Control of the Western Waters*. Jefferson, NC: McFarland, 2000.

Perkins, George Hamilton. *Letters of Captain George Hamilton Perkins, U.S.N.* Whitefish, MT: Kessinger Publishing, 2010.

Perry, James M. *A Bohemian Brigade: The Civil War Correspondents—Mostly Rough, Sometimes Ready.* New York: John Wiley & Sons, 2000.

Porter, David Dixon. *Incidents and Anecdotes of the Civil War.* New York: Sherman, 1886.

———. *The Naval History of the Civil War.* Mineola, NY: Dover Publications, 1998.

Pratt, Fletcher. *Civil War on Western Waters.* New York: Holt, 1956.

Quiner, Edwin B. *Military History of Wisconsin.* Chicago: Clarke & Co., 1866.

Ramold, Steven J. *Slaves Sailors Citizens: African Americans in the Union Navy.* De Kalb: Northern Illinois University Press, 2002.

Read, C. W. "Reminiscences of the Confederate States Navy." *Southern Historical Society Papers* 1 (May 1876): 331–62.

Reed, Rowena. *Combined Operations in the Civil War.* Annapolis, MD: Naval Institute Press, 1978.

Ringle, Dennis J. *Life in Mr. Lincoln's Navy.* Annapolis, MD: Naval Institute Press, 1998.

Scharf, J. Thomas. *History of the Confederate States Navy from Its Organization to the Surrender of Its Last Vessel.* New York: Rogers & Sherwood, 1887.

Shea, William L., and Terence Winshel. *Vicksburg Is the Key: The Struggle for the Mississippi River.* Lincoln, NE: Bison Books, 2005.

Sherman, William T. *The Memoirs of General W. T. Sherman.* 2 vols. New York: D. Appleton, 1899.

Silverstone, Paul H. *Warships of the Civil War.* Annapolis, MD: Naval Institute Press, 1989.

Simpson, Brooks D. *America's Civil War.* Wheeling, IL: Harland Davidson, 1996.

———. *Ulysses S. Grant: Triumph over Adversity, 1822–1865.* Boston: Houghton Mifflin, 2000.

Slagle, Jay. *Ironclad Captain: Seth Ledyard Phelps and the U.S. Navy, 1841–1864.* Kent, OH: Kent State University Press, 1996.

Smith, Myron J., Jr. *CSS* Arkansas. Jefferson, NC: McFarland, 2011.

———. *The Fight for the Yazoo, August 1862–July 1864: Swamps, Forts and Fleets on Vicksburg's Northern Flank.* Jefferson, NC: McFarland, 2012.

———. *The Timberclads in the Civil War.* Jefferson, NC: McFarland, 2008.

———. *Tinclads in the Civil War: Union Light-Draught Gunboat Operations on Western Waters, 1862–1865.* Jefferson, NC: McFarland, 2009.

———. *USS* Carondelet: *A Civil War Ironclad on Western Waters.* Jefferson, NC: McFarland, 2010.

Snead, Col. Thomas L. "The First Year of the War in Missouri." *Battles and Leaders* 1 (1956): 262–77.

Soley, James R. "Naval Operations in the Vicksburg Campaign." *Battles and Leaders* 3 (1956): 555–70.

Still, William. *Civil War Ironclads: The U.S. Navy and Industrial Mobilization.* Baltimore: Johns Hopkins University Press, 2002.

Suhr, Robert Collins. "USS *Indianola:* Union Ironclad in the American Civil War." *American Civil War,* July 1993. Published online at historynet.com, June 12, 2006.

Sutherland, Daniel E. *A Savage Conflict: The Decisive Role of Guerrillas in the American Civil War.* Chapel Hill: University of North Carolina Press, 2009.

Symonds, Craig L. *The Civil War at Sea.* New York: Praeger, 2009.

———. *Lincoln and His Admirals.* New York: Oxford University Press, 2008.

Taaffe, Stephen R. *Commanding Lincoln's Navy.* Annapolis, MD: Naval Institute Press, 2009.

Thienel, Philip M. *Seven Story Mountain: The Union Campaign at Vicksburg.* Jefferson, NC: McFarland, 1998.

Tomblin, Barbara B. *Bluejackets & Contrabands: African Americans and the Union Navy.* Lexington: University Press of Kentucky, 2009.

———. "From Sail to Steam." PhD diss., Rutgers University, 1988.

True, Rowland S. "Life Aboard a Gunboat." *Civil War Times Illustrated,* February 1871, 36–43.

Tucker, Spencer C. *Andrew Hull Foote.* Annapolis, MD: Naval Institute Press, 2000.

———. *Blue & Gray and Navies: The Civil War Afloat.* Annapolis, MD: Naval Institute Press, 2006.

———, ed. *The Civil War Navy Encyclopedia.* 2 vols. Santa Barbara, CA: ABC-CLIO, 2010.

Walke, Henry. "The Gunboats at Belmont and Fort Henry." *Battles and Leaders* 1 (1956): 358–67.

———. *Naval Scenes and Reminiscences of the Civil War in the United States on Southern and Western Waters during the Years 1861, 1862, and 1863.* New York: F. R. Reed, 1877.

———. "The Western Flotilla at Fort Donelson, Island Number Ten, Fort Pillow, and Memphis." *Battles and Leaders* 1 (1956).

Wallace, Lewis. *Lew Wallace: An Autobiography.* New York: Harper & Brothers, 1906.

Welles, Gideon. *Diary of Gideon Welles.* New York: Houghton Mifflin, 1911.

Wert, Jeffrey. *Sword of Lincoln.* New York: Simon & Schuster, 2005.

West, Richard S., Jr. "Gunboats in the Swamps: The Yazoo Pass Expedition." *Civil War History* 9, no. 2 (June 1963): 157–66.

———. *The Second Admiral: A Life of David Dixon Porter, 1819–1891.* New York: Coward-McCann, 1937.

Wilkie, Franc. *Pen and Powder.* Boston: Ticknor, 1888.

Winters, John D. *The Civil War in Louisiana.* Baton Rouge: Louisiana State University Press, 1963.

Wise, Stephen R. *Lifeline of the Confederacy: Blockade Running during the Civil War.* Columbia: University of South Carolina Press, 1988.
Wright, J. Marcus. *General Scott.* New York: D. Appleton, 1894.

Index